June 4–6, 2015
Newport Beach, CA, USA

I0041873

acm

**Association for
Computing Machinery**

Advancing Computing as a Science & Profession

SIGMIS-CPR'15

Proceedings of the 2015 ACM SIGMIS Conference on
Computers and People Research

Sponsored by:
ACM SIGMIS

In cooperation with:
NSF

Supported by:
*The George Washington University, Trident University,
Claremont Graduate University,
California State University, San Bernadino, and Cal Poly Pomona*

Association for
Computing Machinery

Advancing Computing as a Science & Profession

The Association for Computing Machinery
2 Penn Plaza, Suite 701
New York, New York 10121-0701

Notice to Past Authors of ACM-Published Articles
ACM intends to create a complete electronic archive of all articles and/or other material previously published by ACM. If you have written a work that has been previously published by ACM in any journal or conference proceedings prior to 1978, or any SIG Newsletter at any time, and you do NOT want this work to appear in the ACM Digital Library, please inform permissions@acm.org, stating the title of the work, the author(s), and where and when published.

ISBN: 978-1-4503-3557-7 (Digital)

ISBN: 978-1-4503-3868-4 (Print)

Additional copies may be ordered prepaid from:

ACM Order Department
PO Box 30777
New York, NY 10087-0777, USA

Phone: 1-800-342-6626 (USA and Canada)
+1-212-626-0500 (Global)
Fax: +1-212-944-1318
E-mail: acmhelp@acm.org
Hours of Operation: 8:30 am – 4:30 pm ET

Printed in the USA

Chairs' Welcome

It is our great pleasure to welcome you to the *2015 ACM SIGMIS Computers and People Research Conference – CPR '15*. CPR has long been the premier forum for the presentation of research and experiential reports on themes related to developing and managing the information technology (IT) workforce. This year's conference extends that tradition with the theme: Cyber Security Workforce in the Global Context. CPR provides both researchers and practitioners with a unique opportunity to share their perspectives with others interested in the various aspects of building the IT workforce globally.

The call for papers attracted forty-seven submissions from global researchers. Submissions from Australia, Austria, Canada, France, Germany, India, Iran (Islamic Republic of), New Zealand, Pakistan, Singapore, United Arab Emirates, and the United States covered a variety of topics including; gaming and competitions related to information security, digital inequality, cyber security skills, teamwork, surveillance, and security judgment. The program includes five panels on cybersecurity workforce development, an industry panel, one focus group and a poster session. The doctoral consortium welcomes six Ph.D. students and we thank the generosity of the doctoral consortium mentors who will work to advance their research. In addition to the paper sessions, we also encourage participants to attend our keynote speech and invited presentations. These valuable and insightful talks can and will guide us to a better understanding of the future. We are pleased to highlight our keynote address:

- *Key Traits of Successful Cyber Security Practitioners,* Mark G. Graff of Tellagraff, LLC (most recently the CISO of NASDAQ and the 2014 Internet Security Executive of the Year for the Northeast United States)

Putting together *CPR '15* was a team effort. We first thank the authors for providing the content of the program. We are grateful to the members of the conference committee for their hard work in all aspects of the conference: Local Arrangements and Publicity Co-Chair: Conrad Shayo, Cal State San Bernardino, USA; Treasurer Susan Yager, Southern Illinois University Edwardsville, USA; Publicity Co-Chairs Americas Region: Joon Park, Syracuse University, USA; European Region: Andreas Eckhardt, Goethe University Frankfurt, Germany; Austral-Asia-Pacific Region: Rajendra Bandi, Indian Institute of Management Bangalore, India; Doctoral Consortium Co-Chairs Lorne Olfman, Claremont Graduate University, USA; Damien Joseph, Nanyang Technological University, Singapore. We thank the reviewers who provided valuable feedback to authors and the program committee. Finally, we would like to thank our university sponsors who have generously provided support for this meeting and our primary sponsor, ACM SIGMIS, for its continued support of these successful meetings.

We hope that you will find this program interesting and thought provoking, and that the conference will provide you with a valuable opportunity to share ideas with other researchers and practitioners from institutions around the world.

Diana L. Burley
CPR '15 Conference Co-Chair
The George Washington University, USA

Indira R. Guzman
CPR '15 Conference Co-Chair
Trident University International, USA

Daniel P. Manson
CPR '15 Program Co-Chair
California State Polytechnic University, Pomona, USA

Leigh Ellen Potter
CPR '15 Program Co-Chair Griffith University, Australia

Table of Contents

Doctoral Consortium

Session Chairs: Lorne Olfman *(Claremont Graduate University)* and Damien Joseph *(Nanyang Technological University)*

Focus Group

Session Chair: Diana Burley *(George Washington University)*

Panel: Education and Industry Panel

Session Chair: Indira Guzman *(Trident University)*

Panel: Industry Panel

Session Chair: Daniel Manson *(California State Polytechnic University)*

Keynote Address

Session Chair: Diana Burley *(George Washington University)*

Session 5: Posters
Session Chair: Daniel Manson *(California State Polytechnic University)*

Session 6: Occupational Stress
Session Chair: Sven Laumer *(Otto-Friedrich-University Bamberg)*

Panel: Future IT Professionals
Session Chair: Leigh Ellen Potter *(Griffith University)*

Session 7: Security Judgement
Session Chair: Indira Guzman *(Trident University)*

Session 8: Theoretical Issues
Session Chair: Nishtha Kesswani *(Central University of Rajasthan)*

CPR 2015 Conference Organization

Conference Chairs: Diana Burley, The George Washington University, USA
Indira R. Guzman, Trident University International, USA

Program Chairs: Daniel P. Manson, California State Polytechnic University, USA
Leigh Ellen Potter, Griffith University, Australia

Doctoral Consortium Chair: Lorne Olfman, Claremont Graduate University, USA
Damien Joseph, Nanyang Technological University, Singapore

Doctoral Consortium Mentors: Tonia San Nicholas-Rocca, San Jose State, USA
Harminder Singh, Auckland University of Technology, New Zealand
Indira R. Guzman, Trident University International, USA

Treasurer & Registration Chair: Susan Yager, Southern Illinois University Edwardsville

Local Arrangements Chairs: Conrad Shayo, California State University, San Bernardino, USA
Lai-Tee Cheok, Singapore Management University

Publicity Committee: Conrad Shayo, California State University, San Bernardino, USA
Joon Park, Syracuse University, USA
Andreas Eckhardt, Goethe University Frankfurt, Germany
Rajendra Bandi, Indian Institute of Management Bangalore, India

Conference Chairs: Diana Burley, The George Washington University, USA
Indira R. Guzman, Trident University International, USA

Program Chairs: Daniel P. Manson, California State Polytechnic University, USA
Leigh Ellen Potter, Griffith University, Australia

Doctoral Consortium Chair: Lorne Olfman, Claremont Graduate University, USA
Damien Joseph, Nanyang Technological University, Singapore

Additional reviewers:

Monica Adya
Vangel Ajanovski
Rajendra Bandi
Diana Burley
Lewis Carter
Darlinton Carvalho
Tom Ferratt
Damien Joseph
Jessica Korte
Rajeswari Ks
Sven Laumer
Diane Lending
Kathy Mason
Susan Myers
Benyawarath Nithithanatchinnapat
Christina Outlay
Shari Plantz-Masters
James Pomykalski

Norah Power
Jeria Quesenberry
Malu Roldan
Ashay Saxena
Conrad Shayo
Jun Shen
Ashraf Shirani
John Stager
Jose Teixeira
M. Rita Thissen
James Tollerson
Karthikeyan Umapathy
Gianluigi Viscusi
Liisa von Hellens
Alexander von Stetten
Manuel Wiesche
Susan Yager

ACM SIGMIS CPR 2015 Sponsor & Supporters

Sponsor:

In cooperation with:

Supporters:

Crowdsourcing IT Work: A Three-Fold Perspective from the Workers, Buyers, and Platform Providers

Joseph Taylor
Washington State University
425 Todd Hall
Pullman, WA, 99164
509-595-5560
Joseph.d.taylor@email.wsu.edu

ABSTRACT

This paper will present a proposal for research in the area of crowdsourcing. The proposal will highlight the need for research in the area of crowdsourcing as a mechanism to enhance and expand the technology workforce. It does so by examining the technology crowdsourcing phenomenon from three perspectives: the worker (or labor supply), the buyer of technology services (or labor demand) and the marketplaces that facilitates the buyer-seller transaction. It will explore how workforce development and enterprise readiness theories can be applied in explaining how crowdsourcing can be applied to technology tasks. This dissertation will be structured in a three study format. Study one will explore the technology crowdsourcing phenomenon from a "crowdworker" perspective. This study will examine technology crowdwork from a career anchors perspective, and will highlight the potential role of crowdsourcing in expanding the technology workforce to additional sources of worker capacity. This study will establish the theories that describe the motivations and outcomes achieved by workers in crowdsourcing project engagements, and utilize Schein's Career Anchors (Schein 1990) to examine the motivations of workers technology enabled collaborative work environments. Study two will focus on the perceptions and readiness for crowdsourcing labor on the part of buyers of IT services. The research will collect survey data regarding enterprise readiness, and will examine the current state of enterprise readiness to adopt new development techniques. Study three will utilize a design science perspective to examine the ability of crowdsourcing marketplace platforms to meet the needs of IT service buyers and IT service workers as identified in Study's one and two.

Categories and Subject Descriptors

System Architectures, Employment, Computer-supported collaborative work

General Terms

Standardization, Theory, Human Factors.

Keywords

Crowdsourcing; IT Services; Career Anchors; Enterprise Readiness.

SIGMIS-CPR'15, June 4–6, 2015, Newport Beach, CA, USA.
ACM 978-1-4503-3557-7/15/06.
http://dx.doi.org/10.1145/2751957.2755504

1. INTRODUCTION

As demands for technology services continue to escalate companies are increasingly challenged to meet staffing needs. Decreasing numbers of students studying technology related fields, coupled with poor career retention, compounded by pending retirements in the existing technology workforce create a confluence of forces that will continue to create headwinds for IT organizations to meet staffing requirements over the next ten years (Bosworth et al. 2013).

In the face of these headwinds crowdsourcing is an emerging technique for attracting workers. Crowdsourcing has been defined in a variety of ways. Common themes among crowdsourcing definitions include utilizing labor from outside the traditional boundaries of the firm to complete a task (Kaganer et al. 2013). In some instances the contributions of the nontraditional workers are uncompensated, such as contributors to the website Wikipedia, and at other times the contributions of the nontraditional workers are compensated, such as through Amazon's Mechanical Turk (Doan et al. 2011). Crowdsourcing may provide many opportunities to engage a broad spectrum of workers on complex tasks, and thereby dramatically changing the way that workers are attracted, retained and developed. While crowdsourcing has been seen as a means by which software development capacity can be managed (Kim et al. 2012), successful use of crowdsourcing in the delivery of software development may require organizations to think differently about technology sourcing enablement. In order to support emerging business models in crowdsourcing, technology is becoming increasingly critical (Majchrzak and Malhotra 2013). The advances in collaborative technologies have enabled dramatic change not just in business processes, but also in the underlying business models that firms leverage to bring value to their stakeholders.

This paper proposes a research agenda that seeks to take a multifaceted approach to examining the role of crowdsourcing in expanding the technology workforce. In order for a vibrant marketplace to exist three elements must be in place, buyers, sellers and a market to facilitate transactions. This research will examine the technology crowdsourcing phenomenon from each of these three perspectives. Study 1 will examine the crowdsourcing phenomenon from the perspective of the technology worker, or the seller of IT services. The research will examine the interests and motivations for technology workers who participate in crowdsourcing platforms. The first study will use Career Anchors theory (Schein 1990) to characterize and classify worker motivations and seek to address the following question from technology crowdworkers' perspective, Why do technology workers participate in IT crowdsourcing communities, particularly in work environments where traditional employment options are available? This research seeks to address the role of crowdsourcing as a component of career management by technology workers.

Technology crowdsourcing is enabled by advances in standardized technology infrastructure and architecture. Crowdsourcing is dependent upon a shared understanding of standards and interface expectations within the crowdworker community. Technology standardization driven by industry trends such as cloud computing and mobile devices facilitates the creation of common development environments, making collaboration between loosely knit crowdworkers possible (Doan et al. 2011). Increasing levels of technology standardization have been found to facilitate the use of third parties in software development. Industries with higher levels of standards adoption have been found to have a greater propensity to engage 3rd party contractors in software development (Sahaym et al. 2007). Architecture governance programs, such as service oriented architecture have been found to assist in the development of enterprise capabilities across business units (Boh and Yellin 2007). It is posited that the same architectural standards that facilitate distributed intra-firm development, can be used to support crowdsourcing engagements Building on this thesis, Study 2 will explore the awareness, perceived preparation, usage intentions and usage levels of IT crowdsourcing services by IT services buyers. Specifically, Study 2 will examine the following research question: What determines enterprise readiness to use technology crowdsourcing services?

While the motivations of crowdworkers and the usage intentions of IT services buyers are important elements to the growth and stability of the crowdsourcing marketplace, crowdsourcing platforms are a critical linchpin that facilitates the interactions between IT services buyers and services sellers. Study three will use a design science perspective to retrospectively evaluate current crowdsourcing platform designs to assess the viability of these platforms to support the interests of both services buyers and sellers examined in Studies 1 and 2. Specifically, Study 3 will address the following questions: How effective are existing technology crowdsourcing platforms at delivering value to the technology workers and the technology buyers who use them?

2. Research Methodology and Scope
2.1 Scope and limitations
This research will focus on microsourcing activities that occur in online sources environments as described in the *Handbook of IT Outsourcing* (Oshri et al. 2011). Further this research will be constrained by compensation based marketplace platforms, where workers contribute specific technical artifacts for defined compensation.

2.2 Research Methodology
This research will use mixed methods of analysis techniques, and multiple levels of analysis to examine the phenomenon of IT services crowdsourcing. Study 1 will examine the Career Anchors of technology crowdworkers at the individual level by using Revealed Casual Mapping methodology (Nelson et al. 2000) to better understand the causes and effects of crowdwork participation by workers. Study 2 will conduct quantitative analyses at the firm level to evaluate the enterprise readiness (Basole 2005) of firms to adopt crowdsourcing delivery

services. Study 3 will examine crowdsourcing platforms for IT services management at the platform level. This research will use a Design Science perspective (Gregor and Hevner 2013) to evaluate the extent to which the socio-technical environment developed by the platform meets the needs of the buyers and sellers who participate in the platform.

3. REFERENCES

[1] Basole, R.C. 2005. "Mobilizing the Enterprise: A Conceptual Model of Transformational Value and Enterprise Readiness," *26th ASEM National Conference Proceedings*, pp. 364-371.

[2] Boh, W.F., and Yellin, D. 2007. "Using Enterprise Architecture Standards in Managing Information Technology," *Journal of Management Information Systems* (23:3), pp. 163-207.

[3] Bosworth, D., Lyonette, C., Wilson, R., Bayliss, M., and Fathers, S. 2013. "The Supply of and Demand for High-Level Stem Skills,").

[4] Doan, A., Ramakrishnan, R., and Halevy, A.Y. 2011. "Crowdsourcing Systems on the World-Wide Web," *Communications of the ACM* (54:4), pp. 86-96.

[5] Gregor, S., and Hevner, A.R. 2013. "Positioning and Presenting Design Science Research for Maximum Impact," *MIS Quarterly* (37:2), pp. 337-356.

[6] Kaganer, E., Carmel, E., Hirschheim, R., and Olsen, T. 2013. "Managing the Human Cloud," *MITSloan Management Review* (54:2), pp. 23-32.

[7] Kim, J.Y., Altinkemer, K., and Bisi, A. 2012. "Yield Management of Workforce for It Service Providers," *Decision Support Systems* (53:1), pp. 23-33.

[8] Majchrzak, A., and Malhotra, A. 2013. "Towards an Information Systems Perspective and Research Agenda on Crowdsourcing for Innovation," *The Journal of Strategic Information Systems* (22:4), pp. 257-268.

[9] Nelson, K.M., Nadkarni, S., Narayanan, V., and Ghods, M. 2000. "Understanding Software Operations Support Expertise: A Revealed Causal Mapping Approach," *MIS Quarterly*), pp. 475-507.

[10] Oshri, I., Kotlarsky, J., and Willcocks, L.P. 2011. *The Handbook of Global Outsourcing and Offshoring.* Palgrave Macmillan.

[11] Sahaym, A., Steensma, H.K., and Schilling, M.A. 2007. "The Influence of Information Technology on the Use of Loosely Coupled Organizational Forms: An Industry-Level Analysis," *Organization science* (18:5), pp. 865-880.

[12] Schein, E.H. 1990. *Career Anchors: Discovering Your Real Values.* University Associates San Diego.

The Impact of Positive Informal Behaviors on the Effectiveness of Information Systems Departments

Hadi Karimikia
Department of
Business Information Systems
Auckland University of Technology
Tel: 0064-022-3914452
hkarimik@aut.ac.nz

Dr Harminder Singh
Department of
Business Information Systems
Auckland University of Technology
Tel: 0064-9 921-9999 ext. 5029
hsingh@aut.ac.nz

Dr Karin Olesen
Department of
Business Information Systems
Auckland University of Technology
Tel: 0064-9 921-9999 ext. 5327
kolesen@aut.ac.nz

ABSTRACT
Good relationships between information systems (IS) and business employees build shared understanding and cross-domain knowledge, and enhance the level of business-IS alignment in an organization. Most researchers have focused on improving the quality and frequency of communication, and less work has been done on the informal activities IS staff carry out to aid their non-IS colleagues. This limited attention on the behaviors of IS employees restricts our understanding of how positive interaction between IS and non-IS employees can be encouraged and how it affects the effectiveness of an IS department. Drawing on the concept of organizational citizenship behavior (OCB), we derive a set of IS-specific OCBs by reviewing the literature and relate them to characteristics of IS departments and IS employees. Our research questions are: a) When are IS professionals more likely to engage in IS-specific OCBs? b) What is the impact of IS-specific OCBs on the effectiveness of the IS department?

Categories and Subject Descriptors:
J.4 [Professional topics]: Computer Applications

General Terms
Human Factors

Keywords
IS Departments; Organizational Citizenship Behavior; IS Department Effectiveness

1. INTRODUCTION
Information systems (IS) researchers have long argued for the importance of better linkages between IS and business employees to build shared understanding and cross-domain knowledge, so as to ultimately enhance the level of business-IS alignment in an organization. However, in examining the social aspects of these relationships, most research has focused on improving the quality and frequency of communications and little work has discussed

SIGMIS-CPR'15, June 4–6, 2015, Newport Beach, CA, USA.
ACM 978-1-4503-3557-7/15/06.
http://dx.doi.org/10.1145/2751957.2755505

the specific *informal activities* IS staff carry out to aid their non-IS colleagues [6]. This gap means that there is little attention on what IS employees are actually doing, which prevents researchers from understanding how such positive behaviors can be encouraged and how they influence the effectiveness of the IS department. Drawing on the concept of organizational citizenship behavior (OCB), we derive a set of IS-specific OCBs by reviewing the IS literature and relating the IS-specific OCBs to characteristics within IS departments, such as the quality of relationships between IS professionals, between IS managers and their members, and the nature of the IS jobs.

2. LITERATURE REVIEW
The quality of social liaisons and communications between IS professionals and their peers in business units encourages IS-specific positive behaviors to occur, such as providing technical advice or voluntary handholding between IS and business units. Examples of such behaviors include IS professionals sharing software or data in a non-mandatory context, and in the process enhancing their reputation as team-players [2]. Another example could be when IS professionals answer queries in an easy-to-escape context (e.g., on the local intranet), with no regard for who posted the queries or who might read their replies [3].

Such behaviors can be classified into these categories: i) IS helping behaviors [6], ii) voluntary sharing of IT-related knowledge [2], iii) voluntary assumption of responsibilities (leading, scheduling, and attending meetings) [4], and iv) provision of informal training. Helping behaviors have been found to reduce the intent of IT professionals to leave their organization, improve software design productivity, and enhance software development success.

IS staff share knowledge or provide IT-related assistance to satisfy their peers in various business functions. The wider diffusion of IS within and between organizations means that the satisfaction of business users can be enhanced by improving communication from the IS department, providing business units with information on the quality of IS services, information, and systems. Therefore, the quality of the IS department's outputs is reflected in the IS department effectiveness, which leads to user and organizational satisfaction.

3. CONCEPTUAL DEVELOPMENT
This study draws on the concept of OCB from the management literature with the aim of developing its arguments. A review of the antecedents of OCB identifies the quality of relationships

between leaders and their members, and the quality of relationships between members within teams, as the most important determinants of employees' levels of engagement in OCB. Therefore, the quality of relationships within IS departments will be studied as a positive indicator of OCB, which is externally felt by IS professionals.

3.1 What May Encourage the Occurrence of such Positive Behaviors?

Theoretically, the determinants of OCB are the quality of exchange activities between leaders and their members, which is called leader-member exchange (LMX); and between team members, which is called team-member exchange (TMX). The type of within-team interactions (LMX and TMX) which take place depends on the personality traits of members, such as conscientiousness, extraversion, proactivity, and/or positive affectivity [1], and on the individual traits of leaders, such as transformational leadership style [5, 8].

In the IS context, IS professionals need to share hard skills (e.g., IT expertise) and soft skills (e.g., interpersonal skills) with their IS peers to enhance the distribution of IT expertise, collaboration, and satisfaction of a diverse set of stakeholders. The quality of relationships between IS professionals influence IS department outcomes, such as IS project success. In addition, relationships between IS leaders and their members influence IS project success. For example, CIOs discuss leadership training, mentoring, social skills and effective interpersonal communication, IS requirements and non-IS issues (e.g., flexibility in IS professionals' contracts) with their staff to improve the efficiency and effectiveness of the IS department.

3.2 What May Restrict the Occurrence of such Positive Behaviors?

The high level of exhaustion can be attributed to well-known features of the IS profession, such as a large workload, a relatively high incidence of work-life conflict, a lack of autonomy and management recognition, role ambiguity, role conflict, and operating with limited resources. A lack of resources, work overload, limited autonomy and lack of recognition by management are known to affect the performance of IS professionals [7].

Figure 1 depicts the research model that will be tested in this study. By integrating prior research on the determinants and consequences of OCB, along with the literature on IS professionals, this study argues that the incidence of IS-specific OCB is affected by: a) the level of work exhaustion perceived by IS professionals (internally felt), and b) the quality of relationships within the IS department (externally felt), along with the attributes of IS leaders and IS professionals. Consequently, the frequency and extent of IS-specific OCB influences the effectiveness of the IS department.

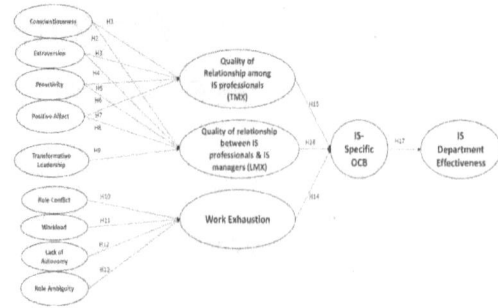

Figure 1. Research Model

4. METHODOLOGY

A survey will be used to gather data from IS and business professionals, who will be matched within their organization. IS professionals will be asked about their personalities, leadership styles, job characteristics, and IS-specific OCB, while business professionals will be asked to rate the quality of their IS department with regards to the quality of their service, information provided, and systems. Large and medium-sized New Zealand organizations in the financial industry will be targeted, as they have frequent and intensive interaction between their IS and non-IS staff, unlike small firms.

5. REFERENCES

[1] Barry, B., & Stewart, G. L. (1997). Composition, Process, and Performance in Self-Managed Groups: The Role of Personality. *Journal of Applied Psychology, 82*(1), 62-78. doi:10.1037/0021-9010.82.1.62

[2] Constant, D., Kiesler, S., & Sproull, L. (1994). What's Mine Is Ours, or Is It? A Study of Attitudes about Information Sharing. *Information Systems Research, 5*(4), 400-421. doi:10.1287/isre.5.4.400

[3] Constant, D., Sproull, L., & Kiesler, S. (1996). The Kindness of Strangers: The Usefulness of Electronic Weak Ties for Technical Advice. *Organization Science, 7*(2), 119-135. doi:10.1287/orsc.7.2.119

[4] Curtis, B., Krasner, H., & Iscoe, N. (1988). A field study of the software design process for large systems. *Communications of the ACM, 31*(11), 1268-1287. doi:10.1145/50087.50089

[5] Graen, G. B., & Uhl-Bien, M. (1995). Relationship-based approach to leadership: Development of leader-member exchange (LMX) theory of leadership over 25 years: Applying a multi-level multi-domain perspective. *The leadership quarterly, 6*(2), 219-247. doi:10.1016/1048-9843(95)90036-5

[6] Jasperson, J., Carter, P. E., & Zmud, R. W. (2005). A Comprehensive Conceptualization of Post-Adoptive Behaviors Associated with Information Technology Enabled Work Systems. *MIS Quarterly, 29*(3), 525-557.

[7] Moore, J. E., & Love, M. S. (2005). IT professionals as organizational citizens. *Communications of the ACM, 48*(6), 88-93. doi:10.1145/1064830.1064832

[8] Seers, A. (1989). Team-member exchange quality: A new construct for role-making research. *Organizational behavior and human decision processes, 43*(1), 118-135. doi:10.1016/0749-5978(89)90060-5

Complexity Reduction in Information Security Risk Assessment

Glourise Haya
Center for Information Systems and
Technology
Claremont Graduate University
Claremont, CA USA

glourise.haya@cgu.edu

ABSTRACT
Results of research done by Dlamini et al. [5] clearly show information security was once focused around technical issues. However, over time, that approach transitioned to a more strategic governance model where legal and regulatory compliance, risk management, and digital forensics disciplines became the significant contributors in the domain. This focus has resulted in a proliferation of information security risk assessment models, which on the whole, have not necessarily helped to reduce risks or appropriately respond to security events. This research seeks to develop a new information security risk assessment model through the aggregation of existing models.

Categories and Subject Descriptors
H.1.1 [**Models and Principles**]: Systems and information theory – value of information; C.4 [**Computer Systems Organization**]: Performance of systems – *measurement techniques; Reliability, availability, and serviceability; modelling techniques;* K.6.5 [**Security and Protection**]: Authentication, Invasive software (e.g., viruses, worms, Trojan horses), Physical security, Unauthorized access (e.g., hacking, phreaking).

General Terms
Management, Security, Standardization, Risk

Keywords
Information Security; Risk Assessment; Risk Management

1. INTRODUCTION
Advances in technology and lower costs for storage have allowed organizations to capture and save more information than could have been imagined decades ago. Cyber-criminals have begun to see the value of this information and use it for various motives. Organizations have a fiduciary responsibility to protect information and its associated infrastructure components used to store and transmit it [8] as key assets [2]. "Risk assessments are the first step in determining how to safeguard enterprise assets and reduce the probability that those assets will be compromised [1, p. 344]."

Saleh and Alfantookh [7] reported there were over 200 Information Systems (IS) risk assessment models. This number has been steadily increasing over the years. Reviewing all of these models to find the ideal one for an organization is a daunting task even for a consulting firm. To-date, there has been no aggregation of these models. The complexity, required time commitment, and sheer number of models to be reviewed makes it next to impossible for small and medium-sized organizations to select one that best fits their needs, size, or industry.

"[A]dvancements in the field of technology require more sophisticated decision-making approaches when it comes to security-technology investments as well as data- and digital-asset protection" [3, p. 25]. These advancements put pressure on the domain of information security risk management to ensure risk models are able to address the newest threats and vulnerabilities.

News reports signify the possibility of churches and faith-based non-profit groups becoming the next generation of targets for cyber-criminals. Individual churches may have congregations that range from less than 100 to over 40,000 members. Non-profit faith-based groups may service from hundreds to thousands of people. Regardless of their size, their information security needs are the same or very similar. The skills of decision makers in these groups will vary greatly. Additionally, people move in and out of roles within these organizations frequently as many are volunteers. This scenario calls for a holistic, yet simple and easy to use information security risk assessment model that would span the breath of these institutions. This research seeks to develop a risk management model for churches and non-profit faith-based groups.

2. RELATED WORK
Information security risk assessment models fall within a three-tier classification system: Tier 1) Paper-based or automated model; Tier 2) Qualitative, Quantitative, or Mixed methodology; and Tier 3) Research Goal: Models that compare existing frameworks; Models that add functionality to existing frameworks; or New frameworks. Comparison models have been created specifically to help organizations make a selection between a handful of existing models. Models that add on to existing models seek to enrich the functionality or fill a gap. New models are created when researchers feel none of the existing models meet their needs. As previously stated, there has been no research focused on consolidating existing models in order to reduce complexity.

SIGMIS-CPR '15, June 04-06, 2015, Newport Beach, CA, USA
ACM 978-1-4503-3557-7/15/06.
http://dx.doi.org/10.1145/2751957.2755506

3. RESEARCH QUESTIONS

As stated above, this research seeks to propose a risk assessment model for churches and faith-based groups. This research will answer the following questions:

1. Are there existing risk assessment models that will meet the needs of small and medium sized organizations such as churches and faith-based groups?
2. Can the similarities and differences of existing models be identified, categorized, and combined to make a single holistic model (simplification)? If so, could the design of such a model make it easy to add new research models in the future?
3. Would the structure of the design make it possible to construct an automated, interactive interface that would at a minimum provide a visual comparative display of easy to understand selectable functionality?
4. Could this new model be used by all churches and faith-based groups regardless of size and technical sophistication to protect their assets?

4. METHODOLOGY

A design research approach will be used. Steps in the process include: 1) Perform a literature search to identify potential journal articles for review. 2) Perform an ethnographic content analysis (ECA) [4] to: eliminate articles that will not be included in the study; make an in-depth analysis of the framework in each article to identify taxonomies used, functionality and special features; compare each framework to all other frameworks in the study to identify similarities and differences; and categorize taxonomies, functionalities, special features, etc. 3) Design and develop a database to capture the outputs from Step 2 above. 4) Develop a web-based application using the database that will serve as the end-user interface. 5) Perform a proof of concept with the help of churches and faith-based groups. 6) Document and report results of study.

5. CONTRIBUTION TO EXISTING KNOWLEDGE

From a human perspective, this research addresses the information security needs of small and medium sized organizations such as churches and non-profit faith-based groups. Drucker [6] described three assumptions organizations need to maintain in order to remain relevant. One of the assumptions, mission, is related to how an organization sees itself contributing to the economy and society at large. Churches and faith-based groups exist to contribute to society at large. Undertaking this research project establishes a partnership with these groups and ultimately would contribute to society at large for myself as well as for researchers that will build on it in the future. It provides a feeling of having done something important that goes beyond just the research itself. To-date, there has been no research calling for the simplification and aggregation of information security risk

management models. Advantages of simplification include, but are not limited to:

- Bringing the research community together to focus on the improvement of a single model;
- Providing more visibility for academic research in the domain;
- Paving the way to ensure better and more effective information security solutions due to a concentrated focus;
- Providing a visual and interactive interface that will be easy for practitioners in organizations of any size in any industry to use;
- Reducing the number of new information security risk assessment frameworks due to the ability to incorporate new functionality in one model.

6. ACKNOWLEDGMENTS

I wish to thank Dr. Lorne Olfman and Dr. Tamir Bechor for their support and advice.

7. REFERENCES

[1] Atyam, S. Effectiveness of security control risk assessments for enterprises: Assess on the business perspective of security risks. *Information Security Journal: A Global Perspective*, 19, (2010), 343-350. DOI: 10.1080/19393555.2010.514892.

[2] Behnia, A., Rashid, R., and Chaudhry, J. A survey of information security risk analysis methods. *Smart Computing Review*, 2(1), (2012), 79-94

[3] Bojanc, R. & Jerman-Blažič, B. A quantitative model for information-security risk management. *Engineering Management Journal*, 25(2), (2013), 25-37.

[4] Bryman, A. Social Research Methods (4th Ed.) Oxford University Press, Inc., New York, NY, 2012.

[5] Dlamini, M., Eloff, J, and Eloff, M. Information Security: The moving target. *Computers and Security, 28*, (2009), 189-198. doi: 10.1016/j.cose.2008.11.007

[6] Drucker, P. & Maciariello, J. The Theory of Business. In Management (pp. 83-96). Harper Collins, New York, NY. 2008.

[7] Saleh, M. and Alfantookh, A. New comprehensive framework for enterprise information security risk management. Applied Computing and Informatics, 9(2), (2011), 107-118.

[8] von Solms, R. and Niekerk, J. From information security to cyber security. *Computers & Security*, 38, (2013), 97-103.

Personal Information Sharing with Major User Concerns in the Online B2C Market: A Social Contract Theory Perspective

John R. Magrane, Jr.
Trident University International
5757 Plaza Drive, Suite 100
Cypress, CA 90630
john.magrane@my.trident.edu

ABSTRACT

The cyber world has seen growth in the online business over the past two decades and e-commerce continues to expand. Moreover it has brought ease and comfort in the lives of the people and now there is no distinction of states and regions. Mainstream people can buy anything from anywhere in the world through web-platforms such as Amazon.com, thus enhancing e-commerce. However, the major concern that arises is the security apprehension. This research paper studies the willingness of the online shopper to disclose personal information. The study will use a conceptual model to examine customers' online activities and how variables such as user trust, knowledge sharing behavior, and loyalty intentions influence users' privacy concerns, and further moderated by one's perceived environmental security in the B2C Internet market. Social Contract Theory (SCT) will be used to analyze the issue in the behavioral perspective, based on the human obligations towards one another and on the state as the supreme authority that establishes the principles that maintain the balance of a society.

Categories and Subject Descriptors

K.4 Computers and Society, K.6 Management of Computing and Information Systems, K.7 The Computing Profession

General Terms

Management, Security, Human Factors, Theory, Legal Aspects

Keywords

Trust, knowledge sharing behavior; loyalty; privacy concerns; environmental security; personal information

1. INTRODUCTION

The aim of this research is to investigate and evaluate users' concerns about sharing their information in the online B2C market. With rising cases of information theft as well as online scams in the B2C online market there is a need to investigate the reasons why users are reluctant to share information. It is critical to evaluate the concerns that users have in order to determine the necessary steps that should be taken by online stores to ensure that these issues are addressed. Technology used in online shopping has advanced to a state where collection, enhancement and aggregation of information are instantaneous. This proliferation of customer information focused technology brings with it a host of issues surrounding customer privacy and the desire not to disclose personal information. Social Contract Theory (SCT) will be used to understand how government, businesses and individuals need to interact within a social contract structure to foster a functional B2C market. With this IT societal environment in mind, the study will use a conceptual model, referred to as a social contract structure, to examine customers' online activities and how variables such as user trust, knowledge sharing behavior, and loyalty intentions influence users' privacy concerns, and further moderated by one's perceived environmental security in the B2C internet market. SCT will be used to analyze the issue in the behavioral perspective based on moral and/or political obligations, and the State as the supreme authority that establishes the principles that maintain the balance of a society.

2. LITERATURE REVIEW

The Social Contract premise extends an increased outlook on the requirement related to social order, which is a set of linked social structures, institutions and practices which conserve, maintain and enforce ways of relating and behaving (Leon-Guerrero, 2014). Although, many believe that Hobbes (1651) was amongst the initiators of the Social Contract, Socrates gave the concept with his words and practices long before. As citizens, we enter into an implied agreement, or "Social Contract", that benefits us by offering security and other comforts, and in fulfillment we, in return, give our allegiance, taxes, as well as service; and we agree to respect its laws and if necessary accept its punishment. Hobbes' theory is based on people mutually agreeing to create a State in which the State has only enough power to provide protection of their well being, e.g., the protection from cyber threats to the online shopper. However, in Hobbes' SCT, once the power is given to the State, the people then give up any right to that same power. The human condition of partial altruism in contrast to Hobbes' SCT thus creates a schism between the State and its citizens. The writings of others such as Locke (1690), Rousseau (1762), and Donaldson (1982) are also studied.

Given that a Web site is both an IT and the channel through which consumers interact with an e-vendor, technology-based and trust-based antecedents should work together to influence the decision to participate in e-commerce (Gefen et al. 2003). It is important for managers to understand how to boost-customer' trust in their firms' handling of personal information (Malhotra et al. 2004).

3. RESEARCH PLAN

This research studies the willingness of the online shopper to disclose personal information.

SIGMIS-CPR '15, June 4-6, 2015, Newport Beach, CA, USA.
ACM 978-1-4503-3557-7/15/06.
http://dx.doi.org/10.1145/2751957.2755507

3.1 Theoretical Foundation

Social Contract Theory is relevant because online shopping is made possible by using Information Technology (IT). IT may be viewed as a subsystem within our societal environment. This view considers IT to be value-neutral. In other words value-free (neither good nor bad in itself), and what matters is not IT in itself, but rather the way in which we choose to use it. This is the world in which we now live, and through which we live (Skovira, 2005). In a world that increasingly depends upon the use of technological artifacts to apply knowledge, and accomplish tasks, also provides a new context of living. This paradigm shift changes the notion of the Social Contract and the emerging foundation of the information society. Another view of IT is that it contributes in major ways to how we live and understand the world. While this may be only one aspect of our experiences, it does place society in the framework of an IT driven society. A society in which government, corporate, and personal behaviors share in the responsibilities and obligations of doing business. Usually these actions are given in legal contracts that enforce these responsibilities and obligations, and are dependent upon morals framed by the Social Contract (Skovira, 2005). It was in this spirit that Winston Churchill declared that "we shape our buildings and afterwards our buildings shape us" (Chandler, 2014).

3.2 Methodology

A cross-sectional survey would be conducted. The study will use a conceptual model (see below) to examine customers' online activities and how variables such as user trust, knowledge sharing behavior, and loyalty intentions influence users' privacy concerns, and further moderated by one's perceived environmental security in the B2C Internet market. In addition, the demographic questions will be carefully chosen in order to understand the target audience.

3.3 The Conceptual Model

The model shows willingness to disclose personal information as the dependent variable and is the main focus of the study. The other variables introduced in the conceptual framework are the user privacy concerns as a mediating variable and perceived environmental security as a moderating variable. The independent variables are user trust, knowledge sharing behavior, and loyalty intentions towards online shopping. These variables are linked to the user privacy concerns variable because it is the users' privacy concerns that affect their willingness to disclosing personal information. The variables introduced are also supported by various criterion and control variables.

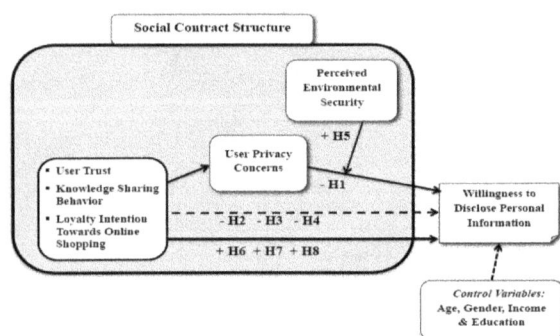

Figure 1. Social Contract Structure Model

Based on the above model, the following research questions will be addressed:

1. Do user privacy concerns predict willingness to disclose personal information?

2. Do user privacy concerns mediate the relationship between user trust and willingness to disclose personal information?

3. Do user privacy concerns mediate the relationship between knowledge sharing behavior and willingness to disclose personal information?

4. Do user privacy concerns mediate the relationship between loyalty intentions towards online shopping and willingness to disclose personal information?

5. Is the relationship between user privacy concerns and willingness to disclose personal information moderated by perceived environmental security?

6. Does user trust predict willingness to disclose personal information?

7. Does knowledge-sharing behavior predict willingness to disclose personal information?

8. Does loyalty intention towards online shopping predict willingness to disclose personal information?

4. ANTICIPATED RESULTS

Online business is ever growing and evolving but the problem of user reluctance remains, thus the importance to find solutions to privacy concerns. By finding such solutions, several objectives will be achieved at the conclusion of this study. (1) Review the existing literature in the domain of online information sharing and studying the problems that users and customers are confronting. (2) Generate fresh knowledge related to the topic and state the issues of online information sharing from a different perspective. (3) Create a useful resource for the following stakeholders:

1. Business professionals, clerics, salesman, etc.- will help illustrate how privacy concerns arise, factors contributing towards reluctance in sharing information and means to resolve the issue.
2. Government - within the context of SCT, will help to formulate policies and procedures to alleviate the issue.
3. Academics and researchers - discover insights about the topic.
4. Organization managers – help to formulating internal business processes in line with the research findings.

5. REFERENCES

[1] Chandler, D. (2014). Technological or Media Determinism, Technology as Neutral or Non-neutral.

[2] Donaldson, T. (1982). *Corporations and Morality.* NJ: Prentice Hall: Englewood Cliffs.

[3] Gefen, D., Karahanna, E., & Straub, D.W. (2003). Trust and TAM in online shopping: An integrated model. *MIS Quarterly,* (27(1), 51-90.

[4] Hobbes, T. (1651). *Leviathan. Or The Matter, Forme, & Power of a Common-Wealth Ecclesiastical and Civill.* Andrew Crooke, London: reprinted by Oxford University Press, Oxford, 1965.

[5] Leon-Guerrero, A. (2014). Just the Facts101. Exploration in Classical Sociological Theory: Seeing the Social World, 2nd edition. E-Study Guide.

[6] Locke, J. (1690). *Second Treatise of Civil Government.*

[7] Malhotra, N., Kim, S., & Agarwal, J. (2004). Internet users' information privacy concerns, The construct, the scale and the casual model. *Information Systems Research.* 15(4), 336-355.

[8] Rousseau, J. J. (1762). Discours sur l'origine et les fondements de L'in´egalit´e parmi les hommes. Paris, 1971: reprinted by Editions Sociales.

[9] Skovira, R.J. (2005). The Social Contract Revised

Youth, Information Quality, and Fitness Information within Social Media: A Brief Look at a Dissertation in Progress

Kayla M. Booth
The Pennsylvania State University
330B IST Building
University Park, PA 16802 USA
1.814.865.8952
kmb5445@ist.psu.edu

ABSTRACT
This paper summarizes a dissertation in progress that explores youth and information quality. The qualitative, interview-driven study employs an Intersectionality approach and is guided by Gasser et al.'s [3] youth-oriented information quality framework. This research is situated within a larger context of IS research examining the ways in which multiple identity characteristics intersect and relate to the ways individuals interact with ICTs.

Categories and Subject Descriptors
K.4.0 [**Computers and Society**]

Keywords
Youth; ICT; Information Quality; Intersectionality; Social Media; Health Information

1. INTRODUCTION
The evolution of an information-driven society and development of Web 2.0 has enabled individuals to generate and access content in ways historically impossible. While trained scholars, journalists, editors, and publishing companies once controlled the content, authorship, perspectives, and styles that were distributed to the masses, now any Internet user with access and a specific skill set can publish self-generated content. Responding to this evolution, scholars have raised questions surrounding how users make decisions about the quality of this content. While numerous research veins have emerged, one significant exploration has been surrounding how youth make these assessments. Some research has taken an adult-normative approach. This approach defines how quality or credibility *should* be measured from an adult perspective; subsequently, researchers determine whether or not young people's behaviors match the established criteria.

This study seeks to employ a youth-oriented perspective that explores what behaviors young people are already engaging in and what they perceive to be important. These questions are particularly relevant when it comes to high-stakes information such as health information, which some studies suggest influences the health-related decisions users make offline. This paper will briefly outline the background and methodology of a dissertation in progress that seeks to explore how young people make decisions about health information online.

2. BACKGROUND
While a critical part of life for millions in the US, the Internet provides a uniquely important space for young people. Many youth turn to the Internet for information about topics that are difficult to talk about and of a sensitive nature [2][5]. Many of these topics are health-related, which may be particularly difficult subjects since many young people have not developed an individual relationship with medical professionals or other experts [2][5]. While health information encompasses many topics and subtopics, the research summarized in this paper is interested in "fitness" information, specifically information surrounding nutrition and exercise. According to a 2010 study conducted by The Pew Research Center's Internet & American Life Project 31% of teens have looked online for "health, dieting, or physical fitness information" [4]. This prevalence is of particular interest given the increasing number of social networking sites dedicated to these topics, sometimes promoting problematic or dangerous messages [1].

3. METHODOLOGY
This research employs qualitative, semi-structured interviews to explore how young people assess this information, specifically that with which they interact via social media platforms.

These interviews are shaped by Gasser et al.'s [3] youth-oriented conceptual framework. This approach is unique in that it seeks to understand more than just the assessment of a piece of information; rather, it encourages the examination of the entire process including search, evaluation, and content creation.

Extant literature suggests users' demographics may play a role in how these processes unfold [3]. Recent IS research [6] suggests that exploring these demographics as they interact with one another, rather than as separate entities, may provide a more nuanced understanding of how these characteristics relate to individuals' interactions with ICTs. This study is situated within this movement by applying an Intersectionality approach. In addition to the information quality framework, interview questions are guided by an exploration of how gender, race, socio-economic status, and sexuality intersect with one another. By examining these intersections, this study aims to explore how these identity characteristics relate to the ways in which youth search for, evaluate, and create information.

4. REFERENCES
[1] Custers, K. (2015). The urgent matter of online pro-eating disorder content and children: Clinical practice. European Journal of Pediatrics, 174(4), 429. doi:10.1007/s00431-015-2487-7

[2] Eysenbach, Gunther. (2008.) Credibility of Health Information and Digital Media: New Perspectives and Implications for Youth. *Digital Media, Youth, and Credibility*. Edited by Miriam J. Metzger and Andrew J. Flanagin. The John D. and Catherine T. MacArthur Foundation Series on Digital Media and Learning. Cambridge, MA: The MIT Press, 2008. 123–154. doi: 10.1162/dmal.9780262562324.123

[3] Gasser, U., Cortesi, S., Malik, M., and Lee, A. (2012). "Youth and Digital Media: From Credibility to Information Quality." Berkman Center Research Publication No. 2012-1.

[4] Lenhart, A., Purcell, K., Smith, A., Zickuhr, K. (2010). Social Media & Mobile Internet Use Among Teens and Young Adults. Pew Research Center: Internet, Science & Tech.

http://www.pewinternet.org/files/oldmedia//Files/Reports/2010/PIP_Social_Media_and_Young_Adults_Report_Final_with_toplines.pdf

[5] Ridout, V. (2001). "Generation Rx.com: How Young People Use the Internet for Health Information." Henry Kaiser Family Foundation: Menlo Park, CA. http://kff.org/health-costs/report/generation-rx-com-how-young-people-use/

[6] Trauth, E. M., Cain, C., Joshi, K. D., Kvasny, L., & Booth, K. (2012). The Future of Gender and IT Research: Embracing Intersectionality. In *Proceedings of the ACM SIGMIS Computers and People Research Conference.*

Conceptualizing a Business Process Knowledge Construct

Jose O Angeles
Trident University International
5757 Plaza Drive, Suite 100
Cypress, CA 90630
(305) 794-3331
jose.angeles@my.trident.edu

ABSTRACT

This paper provides a glimpse of an ongoing dissertation effort evolving a new theory that enhances existing explanations and predictions related to information systems (IS) use. The new theory defends the existence of a construct labeled *Perceived Business Process Knowledge* (PBPK). The author hopes to: 1) define PBPK and 2) identify its relationship to attitudes associated with use of IS in organizational environments. The endeavor also encompasses developing an associated measure. This paper offers a short discussion of challenges faced in the PBPK theory and construct development effort, as well as, future goals that may help others.

Categories and Subject Descriptors

H.1.1 [Systems and Information Theory]: General Systems Theory – *Construct Validation, Measure Development*

General Terms

Measurement, Theory

Keywords

Business Processes; Knowledge; Technology Acceptance Model

1. INTRODUCTION

Ives et al., [3] described IS theories as those related to IS use, development, and operations existing within internal and external organizational contexts. Gregor [4] pointed out, that even halfway through the turn of this century, academics continued to call for unique IS theory and also prescribed that IS theories should be developed to help: a) analyze, b) explain, c) predict, d) explain and predict, or e) enable design and action. As of 2012, the editor of MIS Quarterly [6] was still addressing dilemmas in IS related theories.

The Theories Used in IS Wiki [7] currently catalogs 88 theories associated with IS research. Upon close inspection, one notices that a number of these theories are not uniquely within the IS realm, but are used by researchers in combination with other theories as lenses to explain or predict IS related phenomena.

As noted earlier, scholars have identified challenges in IS theory creation and identified concerns with few new theories emerging.

SIGMIS-CPR '15, June 04-06, 2015, Newport Beach, CA, USA
ACM 978-1-4503-3557-7/15/06.
http://dx.doi.org/10.1145/2751957.2755509

The originator of the PBPK theory chose a path not taken by many in satisfying dissertation requirements; the defense of a new theory and associated construct combined with the development of a practical measure to test its existence. Given the limited number of unique IS theories, there are limited bodies of work that serve as examples of the effort required to develop a new theory. The level of effort undertaken, coupled with many starts and stops, resulted in a study now going on its seventh year since inception. Had there been more information or better discussion on how to develop a new theory, the process might have been short circuited.

The following identifies challenges faced in defense of PBPK. The conclusion continues the discussion related to new theory development. For a summary and current status of the theory refer to *Perceived Business Process Knowledge, the Construct, Its Dimensions, and the Measurement* [1].

2. THEORY DEVELOPMENT CHALLANGES

New theory development, sometimes requires exhaustive research. In the case of PBPK, the first step in defending the theory was articulating a "so-what" factor. Table 1 below proposes that prior Technology Acceptance models [3] may produce flawed results if an organizatonal member has a weak grasp on business processes.

Table 1-PBPK versus Perceived Usefulness Contingency Table

	Low Perceived Usefulness (PU)	High Perceived Usefulness (PU)
Low BPK	PU result could be a false indicator of IS benefit. Member may not understand how IS fits with work tasks (i.e. member is less or misinformed). IS might be inadvertently removed when it may be of benefit.	PU result could be a false indicator of IS benefit. Mmember may not understand how IS fits with work tasks (i.e. member is less or misinformed). IS might not be considered for modification/removal when it might be of little benefit.
High BPK	Opinion of individual valid. IS rightfully removed or modified.	Opinion of individual valid. IS rightfully remains or enhanced.

Defending a new theory and especially one that involves developing a construct to support it, may be require rationalization from many perspectives. In the case of PBPK, the final literature review supported a focal construct comprised of 5 formative sub-dimensions (see fig. 1).

Defense of this theory is multiplied by six because not only must the focal construct be justified, but also the 5 sub-dimensions.

The next step was to rationalize the focal construct. Given this phenomena has never been addressed in literature, 8 bodies of knowledge were identified to defend its existence (see fig 2.)

For the sub-dimensions, 7 bodies of knowledge were used to defend their existence (see fig 3).

The effort undertaken, from the concept framing and literature review perspectives,

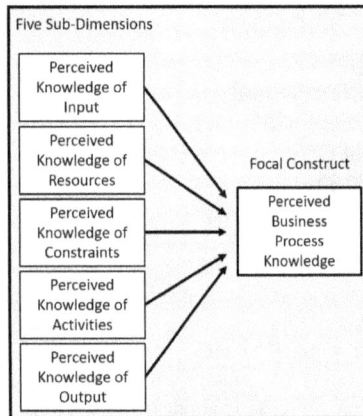

Figure 1. PBPK Construct and Sub-dimensions

was significantly greater than what one may find in many research papers. Discussions with the dissertation committee justified the rigor. In the paraphrased words of one member…*"defending relationships for known constructs is relatively straight forward. Defending the existence of something new, needs to addressed from as many angles as possible to calm the skeptics"*.

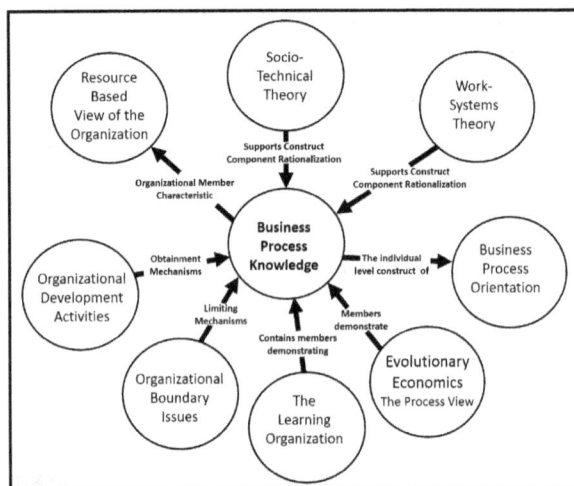

Figure 2. Theoretical Perspectives Supporting the Focal Construct

3. Conclusion

The work to date on the reference construct is the outcome of 7 years of literature review, modeling, remodeling, rationalization, and re-rationalization based on the genesis of an idea (an *ah-ha* moment). The focal construct took many shapes and sizes as did the sub-dimensions until the current model was formed.

Throughout the trials and tribulations, advisors would periodically question the starts and stops, and re-direction. One advisor had a straightforward question; *"why do you want to create and justify this construct?"* This came with the underlying note that, this is not what most individuals set their eyes on their first research effort.

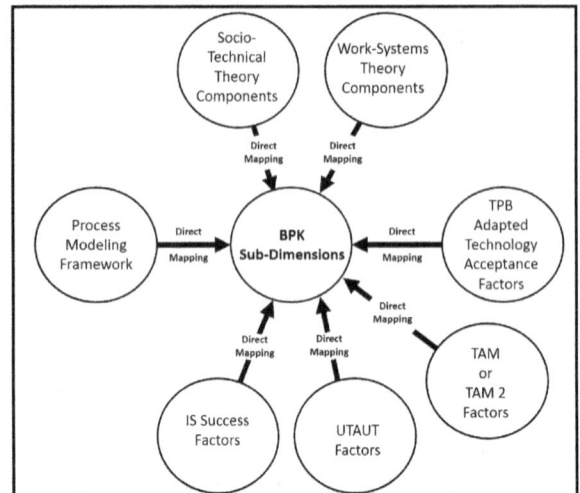

Figure 3. Theoretical and Practitioner Perspectives Supporting the Sub-Dimensions

The response was along the lines of… *"why not, why would someone spend years whether 2 or 6, defending something that was not worthwhile"*. What if the time and audience to collaborate on this might not be available again?

As noted in the beginning of this paper, well known scholars are still asking questions on the shortfalls and limitations of IS theory. A pending query this researcher seeks to answer in preparation for teaching and aiding future researchers is:

> Do methods or bodies of knowledge exist or can new ones be created, to prepare future doctoral candidates or existing scholars in developing new theories?

If this can be accomplished, maybe we can address some of the problems originally posed by Gregor [4] and Straub [7].

4. REFERENCES

[1] Angeles, J., Guzman, I., Barto, T. P, and Hansen, S. 2015. Perceived Business Process Knowledge, The Construct, Its Dimensions, and the Measurement. *Proceedings from the iConference 2015* (Newport Beach, California, March 24-27, 2015). https://www.ideals.illinois.edu/handle/2142/73735

[2] Davis, F. D. 1989. Perceived usefulness, perceived ease of use, and user acceptance of information technology. *MIS Quarterly*, 13,3 (Sep. 1989), 319-339.

[3] Ives B., Hamilton S., Davis, G. 1980. A framework for research in computer-based management information systems; *Management Science*, 26,9 (Sep. 1980), 910-934.

[4] Gregor, S. 2006. The nature of theory in information systems. *MIS Quarterly*, 30, 3 (Sep. 2006), 611-642.

[5] MacKenzie, S. B., Podsakoff, P. M., and Podsakoff, N. P. 2011. Construct measurement and validation procedures in MIS and behavioral research: integrating new and existing techniques. *MIS Quarterly*, 35,2 (Jun. 2011), 293-334.

[6] Straub, D. 2012, Does MIS have native theories, *MIS Quarterly*, 36,2 (Jun. 2012), iii-xii.

[7] Theories Used in IS Research Wiki (n.d.). Retrieved April 7, 2015 from http://is.theorizeit.org

Focus Group – Developing a Resilient, Agile Cybersecurity Educational System (RACES)

Diana Burley
George Washington University
dburley@gwu.edu

Barbara Endicott-Popovsky
University of Washington
endicott@uw.edu

Categories and Subject Descriptors
K.3.2 Computer and Information Science Education
General Terms: Security, Education.

Keywords: IT workforce, accreditation, cybersecurity.

1. INTRODUCTION AND MOTIVATION

As President Obama highlighted in his 2015 State of the Union message, and again through recent executive orders, building a highly capable cybersecurity workforce remains a top US national priority (Obama, 2015). Yet despite significant efforts to increase the size and quality of the workforce, a recent survey of IT managers revealed that 86% of them still believe that the US faces a shortage in skilled cybersecurity professionals (ISACA, 2015). Although the exact nature of the workforce demand (and how to meet it) is actively debated (Burley et al., 2014, Libicki et al., 2014, Reece & Stahl, 2015), frequent reports of major data breaches – see, for example, the recent story on health insurer Anthem (Krebs, 2015) – underscore the critical importance of building the global cybersecurity workforce.

To meet this critical workforce need, the US federal government sponsors several major initiatives that are advancing the development of cybersecurity educational programs. While these initiatives serve as major drivers of cybersecurity workforce development, they have not been sufficient to address the growing demand for cybersecurity professionals. One reason – they are limited by their reliance on a higher educational system that is organized in structured silos and does not easily incorporate innovation. However, in a cybersecurity environment that requires solutions across disciplines, what is needed is a dynamic and integrated approach to learning.

To address this need for a new educational structure, the authors are proposing to establish an interdisciplinary network of investigators to develop the framework of a resilient, agile cybersecurity education system (RACES). The RACES network will engage researchers with expertise in computer science, information assurance/cybersecurity, learning science, organizational learning and change, and cybersecurity workforce

SIGMIS-CPR'15, June 4–6, 2015, Newport Beach, CA, USA.
ACM 978-1-4503-3557-7/15/06.
http://dx.doi.org/10.1145/2751957.2756530

development to develop a framework that dynamically integrates theory, processes, and methodologies from state-of-the-art cybersecurity research and learning science with cybersecurity educational practice.

The collaborative network of academicians, scientific researchers, industry and government stakeholders will develop a structure for researchers to integrate interdisciplinary perspectives and translate findings from basic research on learning and change in educational systems to benefit cybersecurity education and further inform the application of fundamental theories of learning in a dynamic and volatile environment.

The RACES network will work toward achieving the following goals:

- To establish robust processes for translating cybersecurity research to educational practice;

- To integrate existing workforce frameworks (e.g. National Initiative for Cybersecurity Education Workforce Framework), scientific approaches (e.g. Asymmetric Resilient Cybersecurity) with educational practice and policy; and

- To apply learning science (at both the individual and collective levels) to the development of cybersecurity educational structures.

In this focus group session, the organizers will engage on the RACES framework. Participants will discuss strategies for addressing the educational needs of this increasingly critical group of professionals. The focus group will include a range of academicians, scientific researchers, industry, and government stakeholders. Organizing questions to be posed to focus group participants will address each of the goals listed above and are highlighted below.

2. OVERVIEW OF DISCUSSIONS

Following the brief network overview, the organizing questions for the focus group will address each of the stated goals:

How to establish robust processes for translating cybersecurity research to educational practice

- Operationalizing resilience in the context of developing a cybersecurity educational framework. Identifying processes and structures for linking cybersecurity researchers with educators and for translating cybersecurity research to educational practice.

How to integrate existing workforce frameworks (e.g. National Initiative for Cybersecurity Education Workforce Framework), scientific approaches (e.g. Asymmetric Resilient Cybersecurity) with educational practice and policy

- Facilitating the integration of scientific research approaches (e.g. research on asymmetric resilient cybersecurity systems) with educational practice. Leveraging knowledge from the technology transfer environment (e.g. Maughn, Balenstrom, Tudor, 2013) to support the transition research into education practice?

How to apply learning science to the development of cybersecurity educational structures.

- Utilizing theories and research in organizational learning and change in higher education (e.g. Boyce, 2003) in this development process. Is a strategy such as long-term strategic incrementalism (Evans & Henrichsen, 2008) valuable to consider or is a focus on systemic change (Watson & Watson, 2013) more applicable? The role of different collaborative structures (e.g. educational consortia – Burley et al., 2012) in transforming institutions of higher education into learning organizations?

3. BIOGRAPHICAL INFORMATION

Diana Burley is Professor in the Graduate School of Education and Human Development at The George Washington University. In addition to her work in cybersecurity education and workforce development, Dr. Burley has also published extensively on public sector IT use, knowledge management and information sharing. She has significant experience with leading and fostering collaborative research networks. For instance, she is the co-PI and research director for the National CyberWatch Center (NCC) through which she sponsors, promotes, and conducts joint research projects on cybersecurity education. The NCC is an Advanced Technological Education (ATE) NSF-funded center structured to lead collaborative efforts to develop the cybersecurity workforce. Other synergistic activities include service as an elected member of the Institute for Information Infrastructure Protection (I3P) executive committee, a collaborative network of leading cybersecurity research institutions; and PI of the NSF-funded SFS pilot doctoral program *HOLISTiC: Human and Organizational Learning- Integrated Studies in Cybersecurity*. This program is supporting 5 doctoral students who are conducting research in areas related to the proposed RACES network.

Barbara Endicott-Popovsky is Professor in University of Washington Institute of Technology. Dr. Endicott-Popovsky is Executive Director of the Center for Information Assurance and Cybersecurity at the University of Washington, designated by NSA/DHS as a Center of Academic Excellence in Information Assurance Education and Research, Director of the Master of Cybersecurity and Leadership program, Academic Director for the Masters in Infrastructure Planning and Management in the Urban Planning Department of the School of Built Environments, holds a faculty appointment with the Institute of Technology in Tacoma, and was named Department Fellow at Aberyswyth University Wales (2012). Her academic career follows a 20-year career in industry marked by executive and consulting positions in IT architecture and project management during which she managed large-scale collaborations.

4. REFERENCES OF INTEREST

[1] Asymmetric resilient cybersecurity. (2014). Retrieved from: http://cybersecurity.pnnl.gov/arc.stm

[2] Boyce, M. (2003). Organizational learning is essential to achieving and sustaining change in higher education. *Innovative Higher Education, 28*(2), 119-136.

[3] Burley, D., Eisenberg, J., and Goodman, S. February 2014. Would cyber security professionalization help address the cyber security crisis? *Communications of the ACM, 57(2), 24-25.*Retrieved from: http://cacm.acm.org/magazines/2014/2/171681-would-cybersecurity-professionalization-help-address-the-cybersecurity-crisis/abstract

[4] Burley, D., Gnam, C., Newman, R., Straker, H., & Babies, T. (2012). Leveraging higher education consortia for institutional advancement. *International Journal of Educational Management, 26*(3), 274-283.

[5] Evans, N., & Henrichsen, L. (2008). Long-term strategic incrementalism: An approach and a model for bringing about change in higher education. *Innovative Higher Education, 33*(2), 111-124.

[6] ISACA. (2015). *2015 global cybersecurity status report.* (Report). Washington D.C.: Retrieved from http://www.isaca.org/cyber/Documents/2015-Global-Cybersecurity-Status-Report-Data-Sheet_mkt_Eng_0115.pdf

[7] Krebs, B. (02/04/15). Data breach at health insurer anthem could impact millions. Krebs on Security. Retrieved from: http://krebsonsecurity.com/2015/02/data-breach-at-health-insurer-anthem-could-impact-millions/

[8] Libicki, M., Senty, D., and Pollak, J. (2014). Hackers Wanted: An examination of the cybersecurity labor market. RAND: Santa Monica, CA. Retrieved from: http://www.rand.org/content/dam/rand/pubs/research_reports/RR400/RR430/RAND_RR430.pdf

[9] Maughan, D., Balenson, D., Lindqvist, U., & Tudor, Z. (2013). Crossing the" Valley of Death": Transitioning Cybersecurity Research into Practice. *Security & Privacy, IEEE, 11*(2), 14-23.

[10] National initiative for cybersecurity education (NICE). (2015). Retrieved from http://csrc.nist.gov/nice/

[11] Obama, B. Remarks by the president in state of the union address | january 20, 2015. (2015). Retrieved from https://www.whitehouse.gov/the-press-office/2015/01/20/remarks-president-state-union-address-january-20-2015

[12] Reece, R., & Stahl, B. (2015). The professionalisation of information security: Perspectives of UK practitioners. *Computers & Security, 48*, 182-195.

[13] Watson, W. R., & Watson, S. L. (2013). Exploding the ivory tower: Systemic change for higher education. *TechTrends, 57*(5), 42-46.

Panel – Cybersecurity Workforce Development

Indira R. Guzman
Trident University
Indira.guzman@trident.edu

Thomas Hilton
University of Wisconsin-Eau Claire
hiltonts@uwec.edu

Michelle Kaarst-Brown
Syracuse University
Mlbrow03@syr.edu

Jason James
VP Risk Evantix
jason.james@regentsandpark.com

Ashraf Shirani
San Jose State University
ashraf.shirani@sjsu.edu

Shuyuan Mary Ho
Florida State University
smho@fsu.edu

Diane Lending
James Madison University
lendindc@jmu.edu

Categories and Subject Descriptors

K.7.1 **The Computing Profession**: Occupations

General Terms: Human Factors.

Keywords: Cybersecurity Workforce, Information Security Professionals, Panel, Accreditation, Professional Certificates.

1. INTRODUCTION AND MOTIVATION

According to the National Association of State Chief Information Officers (NASCIO) in the United States the number one strategic management priority in 2014 is security. It is therefore imperative for managers to have qualified IT security professionals in order to effectively secure the network infrastructure, protect information, diagnose and manage attacks remediating damage or losses and preparing for disaster recovery to prevent future security attacks.

A single cyber security breach can cost a company hundreds of thousands of dollars. This increase in losses indicates that IT professionals have increased responsibilities in IT security within organizations

In this panel, we will discuss the range of factors that influence the development the cybersecurity workforce, the role that different stakeholders play to ensure IT security professionals are well qualified and have the necessary skills that they should have in order to perform an effective job of securing the network infrastructure of an organization. In addition, we will share different strategies for addressing development needs of this increasingly needed cybersecurity workforce.

Our panel will share both practitioner and academic perspectives on some issues based on research and practical experiences, commenting on curricular challenges and opportunities related to development of cybersecurity workforce during different phases of their careers:

A. The organizational view: Why traditional Cybersecurity training and development is not enough?
B. The academic view: How to keep security programs attractive and relevant?
C. What is the role of professional certifications?
D. What other Stakeholders influence cybersecurity workforce development?

2. OVERVIEW OF PRESENTATIONS

Indira Guzman will moderate the discussion.

Tom Hilton will discuss professional development opportunities available to computing professionals from his perspective as a practicing professional, an academic, and as ICCP director of certification. He will address professional development challenges and opportunities specific to the cybersecurity field and how professional certifications can be used to address them. He will draw upon his ten years as IS department chair and more recent experience developing and teaching the cybersecurity course in his IS program.

Diane Lending will discuss the new ABET requirement for Information Systems programs to include information security and how a program might meet that requirement. She will also discuss James Madison University's innovative Information Security MBA where in addition to the information security electives, each of the core courses addresses issues of information security as it relates to a specific discipline. She will discuss student outcomes and successes of the MBA.

Ashraf Shirani will review selected model curricula and discuss his findings on balancing depth and breadth in cybersecurity education, especially in the contexts of the ISO/IEC Common Criteria international standard and National Cybersecurity Workforce Framework. He will present the argument for and possible ways to incorporate more breadth in cybersecurity education including global and cross-cultural knowledge. A synthesis of the findings will also be presented as an overlay of the information technology education model (ITEM), which he proposed in a recent article.

Jason James will discuss Continuous Professional Education (CPE) and the need for mature security professionals to leverage organizations providing CPE in all forms of Security Risk and Controls. How the role of a security professional is changing at such a rate that today's security expert is yesterday's security historian without some form of educational outlet. How CPE

SIGMIS-CPR'15, June 4–6, 2015, Newport Beach, CA, USA.
ACM 978-1-4503-3557-7/15/06.
http://dx.doi.org/10.1145/2751957.2756529

providers leverage educators, security bleeding edge software providers and work experience from all areas of security, risk and controls practitioners to stay the tide of change. He will also discuss certification and its benefits to the student stating out in a career and the hardened professional deep in the weeds with little time to stick their head up to breath.

Shuyuan Mary Ho will discuss why traditional cybersecurity training and education is inefficient, and illustrate new ways to improve cybersecurity training and curriculum development. Shuyuan will introduce the use of virtual laboratories for implementing hands-on technical defensive and vulnerability identification exercises. Shuyuan will illustrate how to introduce competition to the classroom by annexing extra curricula activities with regional competition activities. For example, creation of a Cybersecurity Club on campus that draws students from multidisciplinary backgrounds (e.g., computer science, information science, criminology, law, business information systems, education, etc.) to solve complex cybersecurity problems. This Club bridges the gap from industry to academia by bringing important industry thought leaders to meet with students.

Michelle Kaarst-Brown will speak to the broader organizational view, specifically why Enterprise Risk Management knowledge and skills are valued in the cybersecurity environment, both within and outside IT security departments. In late 2001, Michelle worked with a group of faculty at her school to develop the Information Security and Assurance concentration, and later the Certificate of Advanced Study (CAS) in Information Security Management. In addition to technical security courses, the program includes courses on behavioral security and broader Enterprise-wide Risk Management (ERM). This ERM course, developed by Michelle, focuses on the broader risk management process and the role that the IT workforce serves in business continuity. The ERM knowledge/skill set has proven to be highly desirable among employers, even those not in the IT security area. Michelle will share why the course is integral to cybersecurity initiatives and continues to attract students from management, computer science, and communications programs at other schools.

3. BIBLIOGRAPHIES

Indira Guzman has been a professor in Information Systems for over twenty years including courses such as Information Security Auditing and Compliance. She is currently the Director of the Ph.D. Program in the College of Business Administration at Trident University. Her research work focuses mostly on human resources in IT, specifically the occupational culture of IT professionals and the role Information Security Professionals in particular. In her previous role as director of Computer Science and Information Technology programs, she developed Information Security curriculum and served as member of the Computer Science Assessment Examination Council for the Institute for the Certification of Computing Professionals (ICCP) developing an exit exam for computer science programs based on CS2013. Dr. Guzman has published in academic journals such as *The DATA BASE for Advances in Information Systems, Information Technology and People, Human Resource Management, and Women's Studies*.

Tom Hilton is a professor of Information Systems in the College of Business at the University of Wisconsin—Eau Claire. Dr. Hilton also serves as director of certification for the Institute for Certification of Computer Professionals (ICCP). His areas of expertise include security, database management, and IS

professional development. Before beginning his academic career, Dr. Hilton worked as a system designer for Accenture Management & Technology Services and for the Link Flight Simulation division of Singer Aerospace and Marine Systems. Dr. Hilton has given presentations and published refereed research papers on various topics in information systems. His preferred research emphasis is the ethics of information use, and he has published and presented throughout the world on this topic.

Diane Lending is the Capital One Information Security Scholar and a Professor of CIS at James Madison University in Virginia. Her research interests are in information systems education, the adoption of information technology, and assessment. Her doctorate is in Management Information Systems from the University of Minnesota. Dr. Lending has written papers published in several journals including the Journal of Information Systems Education; the Journal of Computer Information Systems; Computers, Informatics, Nursing; and Data Base. Prior to joining academia, she was a programmer, systems analyst, and manager of systems development projects..

Ashraf Shirani is a professor of information systems in the Lucas College and Graduate School of Business at San Jose State University where he teaches database, data warehousing, and business intelligence courses at the graduate and undergraduate levels. Dr. Shirani has published in a number of information systems journals including Information & Management, Decision Support Systems, Journal of Computer Information Systems, Issues in Information Systems, Journal of Systems and Software, and DATA BASE, among others. His recent published research in information systems education focuses on identifying data warehousing and business intelligence competencies, and IS curriculum and skills development in developing countries.

Jason James is a security professional with over 25 years in the IT industry. He worked with IBM across Europe and the US during Y2K, with firms like Marsh McLennan and Jefferson Wells on security and compliance for the fortune 100. He runs two compliance companies and co-founder a software companies in the GRC (Governance, Risk & Compliance) space and advices billion dollar organizations and government agencies on date privacy and security. He is the president of ISACA OC and on the board of governors of the IIA OC providing continuous professional education to over 1200 members in the areas of security, controls and risk management.

Shuyuan Mary Ho is Assistant Professor at Florida State University School of Information. Her research focuses on trusted human-computer interactions, specifically addressing issues of cyber insider threats and automated detection of online deception. Shuyuan founded the iSensor Lab in 2010. iSensor Lab is primarily dedicated to socio-technical research related to human factors (e.g., behavioral threat) in cyberspace. Shuyuan received research grants from National Science Foundation (NSF EAGER #1347113 and NSF I-CORPS #1505195), Florida Center for Cybersecurity, and FSU Creativity and Research Council. Shuyuan currently owns an intellectual property (File 15-167 patent pending). Shuyuan's research has been published in ACM, IEEE, Springer, and Journal of the American Society for Information Science and Technology (JASIS&T).

Michelle Kaarst-Brown is an Associate Professor and former Director of the Professional Doctorate Program in Information Management at the School of Information Studies, Syracuse University. Much of her recent research has been in partnership with practitioners in government, industry, and education. Drawing upon prior management and consulting experience, her research studies how social, cultural, knowledge and generational factors influence IT governance and the IT workforce. Dr. Kaarst-Brown has published in a number of top academic and business journals including *MIS Quarterly, Information Technology and People, the Journal of Strategic Information Systems, CIO Canada, and MISQ Executive.*

4. REFERENCES OF INTEREST

[1] Bureau of Labor Statistics (2015). *Occupational Outlook Handbook: Information Security Analysts.* http://www.bls.gov/ooh/computer-and-information-technology/information-security-analysts.htm (accessed April 2015).

[2] Tobey, D. H., Pusey, P., & Burley, D. L. (2014). Engaging learners in cybersecurity careers: lessons from the launch of the national cyber league. *ACM Inroads*, 5(1), 53-56.

[3] Klaper, D., & Hovy, E. (2014, June). A taxonomy and a knowledge portal for cybersecurity. In *Proceedings of the 15th Annual International Conference on Digital Government Research* (pp. 79-85). ACM.

[4] Guzman, I. R., Stam, K. R., Hans, S., & Angolano, C. (2009). Human Factors in Security: The Role of Information Security Professionals within Organizations. In D. K. J. Knapp (Ed.), *Cyber-Security and Global Information Assurance: Threat Analysis and Response Solutions*: IGI Global.

Industry Cybersecurity Workforce Development

Jonathan Chow
Live Nation Entertainment
jonathan.y.chow@gmail.com

Eric Crutchlow
FireEye, Inc.
eric.crutchlow@FireEye.com

Justin Cain
California Governor's Office of
Emergency Services
Justin.Cain@CalOES.ca.gov

Categories and Subject Descriptors

K.7.1 **The Computing Profession**: Occupations

General Terms: Human Factors.

Keywords: IT Workforce, accreditation, computer majors.

1. INTRODUCTION AND MOTIVATION

The Information Systems Audit and Control Association (ISACA) 2015 Global Cybersecurity Status Report recently surveyed more than 3,400 ISACA members in 129 countries. The survey found that 86% of respondents see a global cybersecurity skills gap and 92% of those planning to hire more cybersecurity professionals this year say they expect to have difficulty finding a skilled candidate. An April 1, 2015 article in Tech Target quoted James Arlen, director of risk and advisory services at Leviathan Security Group, who stated, "There are currently over a billion dollars worth of unfilled positions globally."

In this panel, cybersecurity industry leaders will discuss the range of factors that influence the shortage of cybersecurity professionals, and what changes are needed to address industry cybersecurity needs.

Our practitioner panel will provide perspectives on the cybersecurity workforce shortage based on personal experience, and share ways that the academic community can improve the pipeline of cybersecurity graduates with skills needed now and in the foreseeable future.

2. OVERVIEW OF PANELISTS

Jonathan Chow, SVP, Chief Information Security Officer at Live Nation Entertainment

Highly competent, innovative, respected, and recognized Information Technology expert offering over 20 years in securing, architecting, and managing Information Technology systems and infrastructure in an enterprise environment. Demonstrated track record of surpassing expectations despite limited resources. Outstanding communicator, capable of operating in different corporate cultures and exceptionally adept at translating complex technical concepts into understandable language. Astute business leader skilled in aligning Information Technology with business management and managing budgets. Comfortable when placed into triage situations.

Eric Crutchlow, Senior Systems Engineer at FireEye, Inc.

Worked as programmer, analyst, product manager at several software companies. Worked on the other side as applications manager and director of IT. Developed order management, accounting and manfacturing systems. Design and programmed major modules of the SD&G Project Accounting software now sold by Microsoft. Data Base design in Microsoft SQL, Oracle, and MySQL. Currently program and install a web content management system with addon modules for press release, eblasts, meeting scheduler, and membership portal.

With over 20 years experience in business software, I have refined my skills in the area of information management, software development, employee management, Internet, accounting, and manufacturing. Have strong leadership, communication, and organizational skills. Proven ability to implement technology-based solutions for business problems.

Justin Cain, CISSP - Coordinator for the California Cybersecurity Task Force

Justin is the public facing representative for the California Cybersecurity Task Force, a statewide partnership comprised of key stakeholders, subject matter experts, and cybersecurity professionals from California's public sector, private industry, academia, and law enforcement who are all working to advance and strengthen California's cybersecurity.

REFERENCES OF INTEREST

[1] ISACA CSX Cybersecurity Nexus 2015 Global Cybersecurity Status Report, http://www.isaca.org/pages/cybersecurity-global-status-report.aspx

[2] Earls, Alan R. "Information security jobs unfilled as labor pains grow." TechTarget Search Security, April 1, 2015. http://searchsecurity.techtarget.com/feature/Information-security-jobs-unfilled-as-labor-pains-grow

SIGMIS-CPR'15, June 4–6, 2015, Newport Beach, CA, USA.
ACM 978-1-4503-3557-7/15/06.
http://dx.doi.org/10.1145/2751957.2756528

Key Traits of Successful
Cyber Security Practitioners

Key Traits of Successful
Cyber Security Practitioners

Key Traits of Successful
Cyber Security Practitioners

Key Traits of Successful
Cyber Security Practitioners

Mark G. Graff
Tellagraff, LLC
mark@tellagraff.com

Key Traits of Successful
Cyber Security Practitioners

Mark G. Graff
Tellagraff, LLC
mark@tellagraff.com

Key Traits of Successful
Cyber Security Practitioners

Mark G. Graff
Tellagraff, LLC
mark@tellagraff.com

ABSTRACT

The author's view, formed over a decades-long career as a cyber security practitioner, is that successful professionals in the field have historically tended to share certain personality traits. Beyond the knack for problem solving and tolerance for late nights and vending machine food common in Information Technology (IT) circles, elements of integrity and character are, for example, often key to achievement in this career niche.

The author describes several such traits, illustrating with informal case histories their operation and impact – both positive and negative. Implications for education, training and staffing in this field are also discussed.

Categories and Subject Descriptors

K.6.1 [Project and People Management]: Staffing, Training.

General Terms

Human Factors, Management, Security.

Keywords

Cyber security; profession; personality; management; training; staffing.

BIO

A cyber security practitioner and thought leader for over 25 years, Mark Graff is the Founder and CEO at Tellagraff, LLC.

Graff is a seasoned Chief Information Security Officer, having filled that role for NASDAQ for three years and Lawrence Livermore National Laboratory for nine. He was named Internet Security Executive of the Year for the Northeast United States in 2014.

Permission to make digital or hard copies of part or all of this work for personal or classroom use is granted without fee provided that copies are not made or distributed for profit or commercial advantage, and that copies bear this notice and the full citation on the first page. Copyrights for third-party components of this work must be honored. For all other uses, contact the owner/author(s). Copyright is held by the author/owner(s).

SIGMIS-CPR'15, June 4–6, 2015, Newport Beach, CA, USA.
ACM 978-1-4503-3557-7/15/06.
http://dx.doi.org/10.1145/2751957.2751983

Graff has lectured on risk analysis, the future of cyber security and privacy, and other topics before the American Academy for the Advancement of Science, the Federal Communications Commission, the Pentagon, the National Nuclear Security Administration, and many other U.S. national security facilities and "think tanks." He has appeared as an expert witness on cyber security before both Congress and the Presidential Commission on Infrastructure Survivability, and served as an expert witness on electronic voting machine software for the state of California. In the Nineties he served two terms as chairman of the international Forum of Incident Response and Security Teams (FIRST), the world's preeminent body of incident response (CSIRT) practitioners.

Graff's latest book, "Enterprise Security Software: a Confluence of Disciplines" explains how to work with software developers and security practitioners to produce integrated security solutions for business. His 2003 work, "Secure Coding: Principles and Practices", has been used at dozens of universities around the world to teach how to design and build secure software-based systems.

Graff holds a B.S. in Computer Science from the University of Southern Mississippi. His base of operations is New York City.

Video Games as a Training Tool to Prepare the Next Generation of Cyber Warriors

Christopher Herr
Software Engineering Institute
4500 Fifth Avenue
Pittsburgh, PA 15213
cherr@sei.cmu.edu

Dennis Allen
Software Engineering Institute
4500 Fifth Avenue
Pittsburgh, PA 15213
dallen@sei.cmu.edu

ABSTRACT

There is a global shortage of more than 1 million skilled cybersecurity professionals needed to address current cybersecurity challenges [5]. Criminal organizations, nation-state adversaries, hacktivists, and numerous other threat actors continuously target business, government, and even critical infrastructure networks. Estimated losses from cyber crime and cyber espionage amount to hundreds of billions annually [4]. The need to build, maintain, and defend computing resources is greater than ever before.

A novel approach to closing the cybersecurity workforce gap is to develop cutting-edge cybersecurity video games that (1) grab the attention of young adults, (2) build a solid foundation of information security knowledge and skills, (3) inform players of potential career paths, and (4) establish a passion that drives them through higher education and professional growth. Although some video games and other games do exist, no viable options are available that target high-school-age students and young adults that supply both a quality gaming experience and foster the gain of key cybersecurity knowledge and skills. Given the Department of Defense's success with simulations and gaming technology, its sponsorship of a cybersecurity video game could prove extremely valuable in addressing the current and future needs for our next generation cyber warriors.

Categories and Subject Descriptors

I.6.8 [Simulation and Modeling]: Gaming
K.4.4 [Computers and Society]: Security
K.6.1 [Management of Computing and Information Systems]: Training

General Terms

Human Factors; Management; Security

Keywords

Video games; Video gaming;
Cybersecurity games; Cybersecurity education
Cybersecurity game based learning

SIGMIS-CPR'15, June 4–6, 2015, Newport Beach, CA, USA.
Copyright is held by the owner/author(s). Publication rights licensed to ACM.
ACM 978-1-4503-3557-7/15/06...$15.00..
DOI: http://dx.doi.org/10.1145/2751957.2751958

1. The Cybersecurity Workforce Shortage

Several U.S. organizations, including the Department of Defense (DoD), the Department of Homeland Security (DHS), Government Accountability Office (GAO), and the Bureau of Labor Statistics have identified a substantial need for cybersecurity professionals. Leading information technology and security organizations have also researched and validated this critical need. The most common statistics cited relate to the number of currently filled positions, percentage of vacancies, and estimated growth:

- Cisco Systems, Inc. estimates a shortage of over 1 million global cybersecurity professionals in 2014 [5].

- Employment of information security analysts is projected to grow much faster than other occupations at a rate of 37% from 2012 to 2022 [3].

- In the (ISC)² 2013 Global Information Security Workforce Study [8]:
  - 53% of the 12,000 respondents believe there is a cybersecurity workforce shortage.
  - 61% of the U.S. government respondents believe their agency has too few workers to handle their current information security threats.

- U.S. Cyber Command is expected to grow beyond 6,000 employees in 2016 compared to an estimate of 1,800 by the end of 2014 [2].

- The GAO reported a 22% vacancy rate in cybersecurity positions for DHS's National Protection and Programs Directorate (NPPD) citing lower pay compared to industry, difficulty in obtaining security clearances, and lack of clearly defined roles and responsibilities [24].

1.1 Greater Cybersecurity Education Is Needed for Primary/Secondary Students

In June 2014, RAND Corporation released a comprehensive analysis of the cybersecurity labor market. Among other factors, they identified the role education plays in preparing the cybersecurity workforce. An important observation was that 78% of college students decided to study Science, Technology, Engineering, and Math (STEM) in high school or earlier [12]. Unfortunately, the efforts of the National Initiative for Cybersecurity Education (NICE) to integrate cybersecurity into STEM curricula have not gained enough traction at the high school level. An October 2013 study by U.S. government defense contractor Raytheon found that 82% of millennials said, "no high school teacher or guidance counselor ever mentioned to them the idea of a career in cybersecurity," and only 24% were interested in a career as a cybersecurity professional [19].

Although federal programs such as STEM and NICE have been initiated to help address this shortage, the thousands of qualified individuals required are simply not available. More solutions are needed to establish the fundamental knowledge in computing technologies and information security concepts and to spark the desire for cybersecurity careers.

2. Video Games as a Ubiquitous Learning Tool

Traditional cybersecurity training occurs in the classroom, through reading, watching hands-on demonstrations and videos, or practicing at home. However, cybersecurity training also lends itself well to a game-based environment—an environment where players must react to incoming realistic cyber attacks in real time, and make decisions based on their current skills, knowledge, or experience. While traditional learning can take place in several forms, it is only with the game or simulation that cybersecurity professionals can truly put their skills to the test and prepare themselves for events in the real world, without risking real-world assets.

2.1 How Video Games Can Be Effective Learning Tools

Several studies have focused on the effectiveness of game-based learning and shown that playing video games can improve motor skills, spatial reasoning, and decision-making abilities as well as reduce stress. In the 1990's, a group known as the Lightspan Partnership created several PlayStation video games geared towards imparting actual curriculum-based knowledge to elementary-age children. As a result of the study, Lightspan found that children who played a few hours of the games per week outside of class had a 25% increase in vocabulary and language skills and a 50% increase in math skills over students who had only classroom instruction [18]. The results from this study demonstrate the benefit of gaming beyond entertainment value.

Outside of games specifically aimed at education, gamers who play fast-paced action games have been shown to have faster average reaction times when compared to non-gamers, and research also found that this increase in reaction speed had a negligible loss of accuracy [6]. Studies also found that subjects playing 50 hours of the fast-paced role-playing games "Call of Duty 2'' and "Unreal Tournament'' made accurate decisions when exposed to fast-moving visual stimuli--up to 25% faster than subjects who played slower moving strategy-based games [23]. These studies have also shown that video game types, such as first person shooters, have even improved cognitive skills and spatial navigation. The latter has been previously linked to long-term success in STEM careers [13].

Gaming is also often seen as a way to relieve stress and exercise the mind's more emotional side. A January 2014 study published by the American Psychological Association evaluates the cognitive, emotional, social, motivational, and mental benefits of video games. Research found that players learn valuable cooperative skills by playing cooperative and challenging games with others [10]. Granic and others also hypothesize that game playing can invoke moods and emotions that are not only beneficial to our own mental and emotional state but also make us generally more mentally healthy [10].

These studies indicate that gaming can be used as a tool to train your brain and can be used to teach basic quantitative and qualitative skills such as math and language. Furthermore, games can also serve to enhance proper cooperative behaviors and relieve stress. These qualities are necessary for any game that is aimed at effectively teaching future cyber warriors.

2.2 Video Games Reach a Large and Diverse Audience

The makeup of the gamer population has evolved to a more heterogeneous constituency, strengthening the need for a cybersecurity game that reaches a large and diverse audience. One common misconception is that only teenaged and early twenties males are the ones playing video games. There are over 175 million gamers in the United States alone, and recent trends have proven that not only are there far more female gamers than previously thought, but that the average age of gamers is rapidly increasing [14]. The generation who grew up with the Atari or the first Nintendo Entertainment System are now in their 30's or 40's, and the average age of gamers today is still around 35 years old, not the adolescent age one might expect [14]. Forty percent of gamers are women and one out of every four gamers is over the age of 50 [14]. In other words, there is no single target audience or demographic when it comes to gaming.

Perhaps the most valuable trend previously mentioned pertains to the female gamer. Women accounted for almost 47% of the total U.S. labor force in 2012 and just over 45% in the European Union. However, only 11% of the 306,000 global information security workforce that year was composed of women [9]. With almost half of today's gamers being female, it is feasible that cutting-edge video games will not only help cultivate interest and inject talent into the cybersecurity pipeline early, but they may actually do so by reaching a female demographic that is greatly underrepresented within the industry.

2.3 The Prevalence of Video Gaming

Video games are a very lucrative industry, with games being played often and everywhere. While software and hardware sales have fluctuated over the years, gaming is still an $80-billion-a-year industry-- a 30% increase over the last few years [16]. The method by which we play has changed as well. Mobile gaming grew to a $5.6-billion-a-year industry in 2010 and was estimated at over $25 billion in 2014 [17, 21]. Industry leading game researcher and designer Jane McGonigal states that the average gamer may play up to 20 hours a week [14]. Gamers are playing online at staggering amounts as well. Activision claims that gamers spend a combined estimate of 1900 years per day playing some version of their Call of Duty franchise games online [1, 7].

3. Video Game Use by the Department of Defense

In order to understand how game-based learning can be applied to cybersecurity training, it is important to understand how game-based learning and simulations have evolved over the years and how they have been used successfully in the past. One of the largest entities in need of trained cybersecurity professionals is the government and, more specifically, the Department of Defense. The military is no stranger to simulation and game-based training, as we will discuss in the following section. In fact, the military is directly responsible for the invention of the modern-day video games and still sponsors much of the research and enhancements in simulation and game-based training today.

3.1 Video Games Facilitate Scenario-Based Training

Live fire training takes time to coordinate and a lot of resources to accomplish, while virtual or game-based training allows for fast and easy repetition and improvement of cognitive processes. Lieutenant Colonel Michael Newell is quoted as saying,

"...gaming provides an ability to actually put yourself in the scenario, go through it and see it. Back up, change the scenario, go through it a different way. Back up, do it again. There are an infinite number of scenarios I can run through, because it's not about *doing* it per se, it's about having *thought* through it."
"When you actually get the dirt time, I can throw anything at you I want to, because you've seen it already" [15, p.69]

Several military trainers and leaders feel that virtual and game-based training would be a cost effective way to put soldiers' skills to the test and improve thought processes on the battlefield, before ever putting soldiers in a live fire scenario. The wrong time to learn how to shoot, move, and communicate is on the battlefield where real bullets are flying and lives are at stake. If soldiers can learn small team tactics through virtualized training, then the same methodology could be applied to cybersecurity. A video game provides a cybersecurity professional a virtual environment in which to learn skills, practice techniques, and gain confidence, instead of waiting until critical systems and sensitive data are on the line.

3.2 Video Game Origins in the DoD

The origins of militaristic gaming can be traced back to 1962 when the Pentagon funded MIT to develop the game *Spacewar!*. The game consisted of two ships, dots on an oscilloscope screen that could maneuver and fire missiles at each other, both with limited fuel and time. While visually lackluster, this first attempt paved the way for gaming and battle simulation. With the invention of the Atari in the mid 1970's, combat based games began to emerge. *Battlezone* was one of the first games to offer a three-dimensional world and first-person perspective as a tank gunner. Soon afterwards, the Army hired Atari to help modify the game for use as a training implement for the then-new Bradley vehicle, which eventually went on to become known as the Bradley Trainer [15].

The advancements made through games such as the Bradley trainer and *Spacewar!* gained enough notice and attention that the DoD decided to create its own simulation network, known as SIMNET. Many simulators to date were geared towards piloting vehicles. Jack Thorpe, an Air Force captain in 1982, envisioned a network where hundreds or thousands of simulators could be connected to train collectively. While individuals may have been able to pilot a jet or drive a tank in a simulator, groups had never been able to simulate training together. In many cases, the first time pilots flew as a group was in live training exercise or in combat, where the costs of failure could also costs lives [15]. By the early 1990's, SIMNET was online and used in preparation for the invasion of Iraq during the first Gulf War, using the Army's Close Combat Tactical Trainer (CCTT). Because of the success of tank missions during the Gulf War, actual engagement data was collected to be used in future simulations. The Army continues to use varying modifications and versions of the CCTT to this day for mounted and dismounted combat training.

3.3 Marine Doom: A Tool for Practicing Team Tactics and Procedures

With a budget hovering around 4% of the total DoD budget, the annual General Officers Symposium issued a mandate to the Marine Corps Modeling and Simulation Office in 1993, to find war games that might be suitable for training and teaching critical decision-making skills [15, 20]. Marine Lieutenant Scott Barnett and Sergeant Dan Snyder began the effort of combing through the existing war video game library for candidates. The only game that allowed for shareware and actually encouraged user modification was Doom. As a result, Marine Doom was produced in 1995 for the $49 cost of the game, $25,000 in development costs, and six months of effort [15]. A new "skin" put players in forest and urban settings with three other teammates, all working towards a collective mission objective. The team used realistic U.S. military weapons, such as the M-16 rifle and M-249 squad automatic weapon, and a team leader would lead the team through its objectives, drilling on small team tactics and procedures. The game was so popular with the Marines on base that they were literally coming in at night and waiting outside in the hall to get a chance to play [15].

Marine Doom was well received by players, and the numerous reasons for which Marine Doom was developed carried forward into the future of game-based training. The generation entering military service in the 1990's had been living with increased exposure to technology, video games, and computers. The use of game-based training is just one way to keep newer recruits interested and engaged, as well as a method to capitalize on their increased knowledge of technology. Using game-based training can also help reduce costs. While DARPA's SIMNET costs upwards of $140 million over ten years, Marine Doom was produced in a fraction of the time at less than one thousandth of the cost [15].

3.4 America's Army: A Viable Game-Based Training Tool

America's Army is a multiplayer, tactical shooter game where the player acts as a soldier in the U.S. Army. The U.S. Army released the game in 2002 as a recruiting tool, which quickly gained popularity and acclaim for its realism [15]. Although the game was primarily a recruitment tool, it also provided potential soldiers with some knowledge and a virtual experience of what a soldier learns in basic training. The initial development cost of the game was slated at around $7.6 million and the average cost to recruit a soldier was around $15,000 at the time of its release. Colonel Wardynski states that if the Army could bring in 300 to 400 new recruits because of America's Army, then the cost would be worthwhile [11]. Not only did the game serve as a recruitment vehicle, but it also gave new recruits knowledge prior to arriving at Basic Combat Training, or BCT. It was Colonel Wardynski's hope that exposure to the information available in America's Army would reduce the number of washouts, due to a lack of information prior to signing up, and help more recruits complete basic training and move ahead to their individual skill training and their parent units [11]. The game enables new recruits to get a virtual feel for what training is like and provides incoming recruits with insight on what to expect.

America's Army has since gone through a few makeovers, with various versions coming out over the years. As a testament to the game's realism and playability, America's Army has won several awards and accolades. Congress lauded America's Army as one of the most effective contact mechanisms in the recruiting arsenal, and a study by MIT found that 30 percent of Americans age 16-24 had a more positive view of the Army as a result of the game [22]. America's Army boasts more than 11 million registered users over the years and is one of the most downloaded war games of all time.

The Army created an accidental training tool in America's Army by teaching recruits details about weapons, rank structure, military terms, and basic tactics and procedures. America's Army paved the way for a new generation of virtual combat training simulators that evolved in the wake of America's Army and the Iraq and Afghanistan wars. The Virtual Combat Convey Trainer and numerous firearms training simulators grew in response for a need to train troops for war. Simulated training has even expanded to other applications such as field medic training, with Engineering and Computer Simulations' vMedic trainer, which places trainees in an America's-Army-type environment, but with realistic and time-sensitive combat life-saving objectives.

4. Attributes for Effective Cybersecurity Games

Taking the lessons of previous combat games and simulators, we can apply them to the field of cybersecurity to provide game-based training that incorporates realistic scenarios with live fire events that require players to react in real time. Based on experience of the games and simulations used by the DoD, we have identified the following qualities and characteristics that game-based training should incorporate:

- Game/scenarios need to be as realistic as possible, but also must keep the player's interest.

- Games must reinforce key concepts and skills through repetition and learning from past mistakes.

- Games must be complex enough to keep the player engaged, but at the same time be easy enough to understand so the player does not give up.

- Goals and learning objectives should be clear, even if the way to reach said goal is not 100% explicit. These goals also must be worthwhile in the eyes of the player. A good game might include goals defined by the developers but also leave several smaller goals left up to players to determine, based on what they know they need to accomplish in the long term [18].

Additionally, Prensky describes five levels of learning in video games [18], which should be incorporated into cybersecurity game-based training. While these levels were derived from game-based learning for children, they can still be applied to young adults and cybersecurity training.

The following examples demonstrate how a cybersecurity game can embody these five levels of learning.

How: At a high level, players placed in a cybersecurity situation may learn how to successfully defend a network or system. At a lower level, they may also learn skills such as how to create a security policy, monitor for a certain type of activity, or configure a device.

Table 1: The Five Levels of Gaming

How	How to play the game; what are the controls and abilities; how can those abilities be used to achieve goals and objectives
What	The rules of the game; what you can and cannot do as well as what the consequences of certain actions are for negative actions
Why	Why certain actions should be performed in a certain way to succeed
Where	The world, culture and environment of the game; your role may dictate what you can and can't do as well as your abilities (e.g., are you a wizard in a medieval castle or a Samurai warrior in Japan?)
Whether	The decision-making process of the player; decisions create outcomes that may have moral or ethical consequences

What: Players should be given a list of rules to follow. The best games have rules that are based in reality and cannot be broken without consequences. In a military game, these might be called rules of engagement. In a cybersecurity training situation, these rules might limit the systems available to the player or may dictate what the player can and cannot change due to other requirements. For example, players may be allowed to write a firewall rule to block or defend against some type of malicious activity, but they cannot simply disconnect the network to prevent all traffic from flowing.

Why: Players learn why they need to make decisions based on trial and error and real-world experience. There may be several different ways to prevent a virus from reaching a system, but trial and error in the game will teach the players which methods are the most effective and the least time consuming. For example, writing one type of firewall rule may accidentally block a legitimate service. Therefore, the player must adjust and then come up with a more efficient way to solve the problem.

Where: The where of the game is very applicable in the cybersecurity setting. Players may have to request information from other virtual locations to complete their objectives. Also, knowing whether the player is working on a government or Fortune 500 company network may impact the decisions made to achieve their objectives. The role each player has on that organization's team can also dictate his or her actions. Whether the player is the team lead, analyst, or technician may require different types of access and/or limit the actions that they can perform.

Whether: The *Where* of the player also ties into how players make decisions. In any case, players would typically want to confirm or report their findings and actions to some authority figure before enacting a plan of attack. If a Fortune 500 company website is under attack, and your mitigation strategy is to simply power it off, you might have thousands of angry customers who can no longer access important information or services causing loss of revenue. A player's feeling of stress, joy, or even remorse over a decision can also be used to help prepare them for future real-world experiences. Furthermore, assessing consequences and interacting with other players in leadership roles should be a part of any effective cybersecurity training exercise.

Table 2: Recommendations for a New Cybersecurity Video Game

Achievements	Challenging (Continued)
Accomplishments must be tied to key cybersecurity learning objectives.	Real Life: Incorporate actual cybersecurity issues that can be addressed and experience that can be translated to real-world use. For example, use Open Web Application Security Project (OWASP) Top 10 issues to create challenges and/or achievements (e.g., attack/defend SQL injection, cross-site scripting) use a social networking attack/defend challenge that takes advantage of trust relationships.
Certifications: Obtaining badges for basic understanding of certain operating systems or even for achieving key learning objectives from industry certifications, such as A+, Network+, or Security+.	Other current attacks, such as those on well-known retailers, can be incorporated into challenges to highlight the importance of good defense-in-depth controls.
Career Growth: Obtaining badges for system administration, network administration, writing your first script, or even configuring a firewall. For example, these could help career progression from a Systems Administrator to a Network Admin and then to a Security Admin.	Boss Fight: Provide an escalation of adversaries. For example, a system administrator may face a less sophisticated adversary conducting a phishing attack, but later be targeted by a more advanced persistent threat that requires collaboration with other individuals and teams within the game to detect, respond, and mitigate the attack.

Achievements	Collaboration
Item acquisition: The requirement that a gamer achieve certain items before performing a certain task is a great motivator. One sample scenario would require the gamer to obtain an SSL certificate before securely configuring and enabling his or her web server. The understanding of this dependency and its impact on the security posture of a solution can be taught along the way. Similarly, players must acquire items along the way to configure firewalls, intrusion detection systems, routers, and so on.	Teamwork and cooperative play is an integral part in many of today's most popular video games. It supports peer-to-peer learning and fosters comradery and a sense of responsibility.
	Players must be able to post questions and expect responses from other players, team/ guild members, and professional moderators.
Leaderboard: Inclusion of a leaderboard allows individuals to see who has accomplished certain missions, achieved specific goals, and gained expert knowledge in an area. Building a safe communication mechanism into the game also provides a way to share this knowledge in a peer-to-peer teaching and learning model.	Real-time chat and other communications are essential to the peer-to-peer learning process and the social aspect of the game.
	Both virtual and real-person interactions are important. There must be a place or individual that a gamer can turn to for help on-demand that always available.

Character Customization and Growth	Educational
Gamers need to identify with the characters within the game. The ability to customize their starting attributes and improve their skills, toolsets, and other items along the way helps build a relationship with their character, other players, and with the game itself.	To address the critical need to develop future cybersecurity professionals, it is imperative that a video game address key knowledge, skills, and abilities in numerous disciplines.
Avatar: The ability to choose and configure gender, race, style, and other characteristics of gamers helps them feel as if they are indeed part of the game.	The most important rationale for offering a video game is to prepare our next-generation cybersecurity professionals. Teaching the fundamental concepts and providing the opportunity to obtain advanced knowledge is critical to a game's success.
Sidekick: Consider including mascot or partner characters who provide hints/help or increase specific attributes. This idea is based on the concept that not all characters within the game space are actual people. There could and should be teachers or helpers throughout the game to guide learning and gameplay. These characters could be acquired, lost, or even traded throughout the gaming experience to help with certain missions.	Gameplay must support the ability to obtain knowledge or assistance from a subject matter expert: a lecture, demonstration, or directions from a guru or game master.
Cyber Characteristics: Integrate cybersecurity concepts into character selection. For example, the game could start with characters or attributes from white-, black-, or grey-hat security professionals:	The video game should provide easy access to a glossary and other reference material for those looking for direct and specific details on topics.

Character Customization and Growth	Fun & Relevant
White Hat: help desk, system administrator, network administrator, forensic analyst, malware analyst, incident handling specialist	To increase the appeal and "fun" aspects of the video game, it should leverage pop culture, to connect with and engage its audience. It should also replicate relevant real-world processes for obtaining tools and equipment.
Grey Hat: bug bounty hunter, penetration tester, security assessment professional	Movie quotes, tools, and situations from popular fictional movies (e.g., Hackers, The Net, Sneakers, The Matrix, War Games) could increase appeal and help connect with the game's audience.
Black Hat: script kiddie, bot master, malware developer, military adversary	Incorporate popular internet memes or historical events into background events or storylines.

Challenging	Fun & Relevant
Gamers need to participate in difficult, but achievable missions. To support learning objectives, tie these to relevant cybersecurity activities.	Include stores for shopping-- for mascots, gear, and tools to help with missions (e.g., a virtual computer store or marketplace that sells systems, tools, or applications.)

(continued)

Making decisions that will solve the problem, but also have the least impact on critical services, is always paramount for any cybersecurity professional.

4.1 Recommendations for an Effective Cybersecurity Game

A cybersecurity video game must be fun, engaging, and entertaining. It must attract young adults and keep their attention. They have to be excited for the challenges ahead and in their quest to resolve them. In doing so, they will obtain a better understanding and appreciation for cybersecurity. Those who do not go on to become cybersecurity professionals will have a better understanding of threats, mitigations, and impact on the mission or business. Those who pursue formal education, certification, and careers will have a solid foundation of knowledge and skills.

Below are several additional ideas and recommendations that could be incorporated into a new cybersecurity video game:

5. What is Next?

We have shown how there is a desperate need for more cybersecurity professionals in our country and the world in general. As expressed previously, there is a need for more than 1 million positions worldwide and billions of dollars in revenue, infrastructure, and intellectual property at stake. Every year young adults are choosing career paths, and the cybersecurity field needs a way to draw the masses. A cybersecurity-based video game has the potential to make a difference in their choice. Video games have proven to improve cognitive skills, such as reaction time, and the skills taught in the game itself. Games are also valuable teaching tools because they can immerse the player in a realistic environment that is both challenging and rewarding. Additionally, games can provide a virtual proving ground for cybersecurity professionals—cybersecurity is a field where you do not want to experience an attack for the first time on live infrastructure where data and money are on the line. The DoD, U.S. Government, and businesses have much to lose. Our national security, technological secrets, and infrastructure must be protected at all times. The DoD and military has used game-based training and simulation-based training for years. The military was the pioneer in game-based training for aviation and vehicles. Now those games and simulators are being turned to other lifesaving skills such as firearms training, convey operations, and medical response.

The DoD should invest in game-based, cybersecurity training that can be used to prepare our next-generation cyber warriors and information security professionals. We have seen from other examples what a good game requires to be successful. While traditional methods may have positive results, a cybersecurity video game could greatly enhance the effectiveness of the DoD's cybersecurity recruiting and training needs. A game very similar to America's Army could teach cyber warriors valuable skills before they step foot on the production floor. It could give individuals an opportunity to take chances, to test, fail, and retest on their technical skills. Additionally, it could validate individuals' self-assurance that they chose the correct field and can make an impact. With the proper funding and development of a highly realistic and effective cybersecurity game, the DoD has an opportunity to make a large impact on the country and our national security. Training related games could also be produced to encompass numerous other disciplines within the IT field, such

as networking, digital forensics, or programming. In this way, training-based video games could become one of our best tools for improving information security awareness and building the next generation of cyber warriors.

6. REFERENCES

[1] Activision & Blizzard. (2014). First Quarter 2014 Results [PDF Document]. Retrieved from http://investor.activision.com/events.cfm.

[2] Baldor, Lolita C. & Jelinek, Pauline (March 2014). "Pentagon to triple cyber staff to thwart attacks". Associated Press. Retrieved from http://news.yahoo.com/pentagon-triple-cyber-staff-thwart-attacks-194534255--politics.html.

[3] Bureau of Labor Statistics. (Jan 8, 2014).Occupational Outlook Handbook: Information Security Analysts. Retrieved from http://www.bls.gov/ooh/computer-and-information-technology/information-security-analysts.htm.

[4] Center for Strategic and International Studies. (2013).The Economic Impact of Cybercrime and Cyber Espionage. [PDF Document] Retrieved from http://csis.org/files/publication/60396rpt_cybercrime-cost_0713_ph4_0.pdf.

[5] CISCO. (2014). CISCO 2014 Annual Security Report. [PDF Document] Retrieved from http://www.cisco.com/web/offer/gist_ty2_asset/Cisco_2014_ASR.pdf.

[6] Dye, M. W., Green, C. S., & Bavelier, D. (2009). Increasing speed of processing with action video games. Current Directions in Psychological Science, 18(6), 321-326.

[7] Dyer, M. (2013, Nov 4). People Play 1900 Years of Call of Duty Multiplayer Every Day. Retrieved from http://www.ign.com/articles/2013/11/04/people-play-1900-years-of-call-of-duty-multiplayer-every-day.

[8] Frost and Sullivan. (2013). The 2013 (ISC)^2 Global Information Security Workforce Study. [PDF Document] Retrieved from https://www.isc2cares.org/uploadedFiles/wwwisc2caresorg/Content/2013-ISC2-Global-Information-Security-Workforce-Study.pdf.

[9] Frost and Sullivan. (2013). Agents of Change: Women in the Information Security Profession, The (ISC)2 Global Information Security Workforce Subreport. [PDF Document] Retrieved from https://www.isc2cares.org/uploadedFiles/wwwisc2caresorg/Content/Women-in-the-Information-Security-Profession-GISWS-Subreport.pdf.

[10] Granic, I., Lobel, A., & Engels, R. C. (2013). The benefits of playing video games.

[11] Kennedy, B. (2002, July 11). "Uncle Sam Wants You (To Play This Game)." New York Times. http://www.nytimes.com/2002/07/11/technology/uncle-sam-wants-you-to-play-this-game.html.

[12] Libicki, M., Senry, D., & Julia, P. (2014). Hackers Wanted: an examination of the cybersecurity labor market. RAND.

[13] Lubinski, W., Bendow, C.P, & Steiger, J. H. (2010). Accomplishment in science, technology, engineering, and

mathematics (STEM) and its relation to STEM educational dose: A 25-year longitudinal study. Journal of Educational Psychology. 102, 860-871. Doi: 10.1037/a0019454.

[14] McGonigal, J. (2011). Reality is Broken: Why Games Make Us Better and How They Can Change the World. London: Penguin.

[15] Mead, C. (2011). War Play: Video Games and the Future of Armed Conflict. New York: Houghton Mifflin Harcourt.

[16] Merel, T. (2011, July 6). The Big V: The great games market split. Retrieved from http://venturebeat.com/2011/07/06/the-big-v-the-great-games-market-split/.

[17] Pearson, D. (2014). Report: Mobile gaming to become gaming's biggest market by 2015. Retrieved from http://www.gamesindustry.biz/articles/2014-10-22-report-mobile-to-become-gamings-biggest-market-by-2015.

[18] Prensky, M. (2006). "Don't Bother Me Mom – I'm Learning." Sat. Paul: Paragon House.

[19] Raytheon. (2013). Preparing Millennials to Lead in Cyberspace. [PDF Document] Retrieved from http://www.raytheon.com/capabilities/rtnwcm/groups/gallery/documents/digitalasset/rtn_158203.pdf.

[20] Riddell, R. (1994, April). Doom Goes to War. Wired 5.4 Retrieved from http://archive.wired.com/wired/archive/5.04/ff_doom_pr.html.

[21] Rosenberg, D. (2010, May 26). Mobile-gaming revenue to hit $11.4 billion in 2014. Retrieved from http://www.cnet.com/news/mobile-gaming-revenue-to-hit-11-4-billion-in-2014/.

[22] Singer, P. (2009, Nov 17). Video Games Veterans and the New American Politics. Washington Examiner. Retrieved from http://washingtonexaminer.com/video-game-veterans-and-the-new-american-politics/article/20385.

[23] Turman, L. (Sep 27, 2010). "Action video games speed up decision-making process." Washington Post. Retrieved from http://washingtonpost.com/wp-dyn/content/article/2010/09/27/AR2010092705244.html.

[24] United States Government Accountability Office. (Sep 2013). DHS Recruiting and Hiring: DHS is Generally Filling Mission-Critical Positions, but Could Better Track Costs of Coordinated Recruiting Efforts. [PDF Document]. Retrieved from http://www.gao.gov/assets/660/657902.pdf.

A Vignette-based Method for Improving Cybersecurity Talent Management through Cyber Defense Competition Design

David H Tobey, PhD
Holy Cross College
5415 State Road 933 North
Notre Dame, IN 46556-0308
dtobey@hccenter.org

ABSTRACT

The preliminary findings are reported from a four-year study of cybersecurity competency assessment and development achieved through the design of cyber defense competitions. The first year of the study focused on identifying the abilities that should indicate aptitude to perform well in the areas of operational security testing and advanced threat response. A recently developed method for Job Performance Modeling (JPM) is applied which uses vignettes – critical incident stories – to guide the elicitation of a holistic description of mission-critical roles grounded in the latest tactics, techniques and protocols defining the current state-of-the-art, or ground truth, in cyber defense. Implications are drawn for design of scoring engines and achievement of game balance in cyber defense competitions as a talent management system.

Categories and Subject Descriptors

I.6.5 [**Simulation and Modeling**]: Model development—*modeling methodologies*
K.6.1 [**Management of computing and information systems**]: Systems analysis and design—*systems analysis and design, staffing*

General Terms

Human factors; Management.

Keywords

Competency model; Job Performance Model; Critical incident; Vignette; Cyber Defense Competition; Aptitude; KSA; Game balance; Talent management

1. INTRODUCTION

The search for cybersecurity technical talent has moved from a competition to a full blown crisis. Organizations struggle to find, develop, and retain desperately needed talent. Information

SIGMIS-CPR '15, June 04 - 06, 2015, Newport Beach, CA, USA
Copyright is held by the owner/author(s). Publication rights licensed to ACM.
ACM 978-1-4503-3557-7/15/06...$15.00
http://dx.doi.org/10.1145/2751957.2751963

security executives may be criticized for their ineffectiveness at attracting skilled resources to address the growing threats. However, the absence of clear definition or valid indicators of potential performance means cybersecurity talent management programs must rely almost exclusively on professional certifications that are designed to assess possession of domain knowledge, not the skill or ability to perform under pressure. In an attempt to fill the knowledge-skill gap with competent recruits, the already overtaxed cybersecurity staff must spend considerable time designing and overseeing "gauntlets" through which prospective new talent must pass to demonstrate their ability to meet current and projected job demands. This "expert eyes" approach is costly, error-prone, and can only succeed in organizations that have previously been successful in attracting top level talent, creating a *Matthew Effect*: those rich with talent can recruit the best, while those in greatest need are incapable of improving their ability to accurately assess vulnerability or respond to an attack.

Tools, beyond professional certifications, are beginning to emerge to assist in identifying talent for cybersecurity jobs. One category of tools is the use of cyber competitions (challenges) or games. At their core, cybersecurity competitions, like other serious games, are expected to be an engaging learning environment [1], [2], [3], [4]. They are expected to attract the best and brightest by aligning instructional technology with what motivates the incoming generation of workers, and how they think and learn [5]. But are the competencies required defined well enough so that competitions can achieve their purpose?

Recognizing that this question had not been addressed by prior research, the Department of Homeland Security (DHS) Science & Technology (S&T) sponsored a four-year program to develop a new approach to job analysis and competency modeling that could assist the developers of competitions and talent acquisition programs. This paper reports the early findings from this study. In the first year, we sought to answer two research questions: 1) How can we identify the factors and relationships which indicate development of foundational knowledge and differentiating skill and ability, to both validate and increase reliability of competition scoring models? 2) How can we incorporate constantly changing, real world scenarios, the "ground truth" that enables a holistic approach to talent management [6]?

Thus, the purpose of this initial study is to demonstrate how to apply a Job Performance Model (JPM; [7]) to identify cybersecurity competence and by improving cyber defense competition design. The JPM approach can be described in four steps:

1) Establish vignettes (or scenarios) that define situated expertise in job roles;
2) Detail the goals and objective metrics that determine successful performance;
3) Identify responsibilities by job role necessary to achieve the objectives;
4) **Detail the tasks, methods, and tools along with how competence may differ by level of expertise or by the difficulty of achieving that level of expertise.**

2. DEFINING MISSION CRITICAL ROLES

Cybersecurity is a contest of competence. Vulnerabilities are limitless because they emanate from constantly expanding human intellect, imagination, and ingenuity. The mission of the cyber defender is therefore continually shifting; best practice heuristics have a near zero half-life as every day brings new attack vectors, exploitation techniques, or exfiltration targets. According to research on judgment and decision-making, work in such novel, highly variant, or rare problem settings defines a competency-based domain [8, p. 1]: "Such tasks require decisions to be made and actions taken in the face of ambiguous and/or incomplete information. Time pressure is frequently great, and the penalties for failure are often severe."

The research shows that competence-based professions have difficulty identifying and defining optimal performance [7, 8]. Learning curves are steep in competence-based professions. Thus, what is optimal performance differs greatly between beginners, or those merely proficient in methods and tools, and the skilled competent or expert performers. Mastery must be evaluated across the full multidimensionality of competence [7], combining: depth of understanding comprising knowledge; consistency of skills honed through practice; and the generative capacity of abilities by which knowledge and skill are adapted to effectively respond to increased volatility, uncertainty, complexity, and ambiguity that typify competence-based domains [9], [10]. While expertise may be apparent in hindsight, performance models that seek to predict or accredit competency must distinguish between fundamental tasks that define base levels of competence and the differentiating tasks in which both the methods used and outcomes achieved differ across stages of the learning curve [11]. In sum, optimal performance in competence-based professions must be defined and measured differently; what is appropriate to assess differs by stage of expertise development and whether the competency dimension being measured is knowledge, skill, or ability.

In the competence-based domain of cybersecurity the definition of mission-critical roles is highly situated [14] — grounded in scenarios whose "truth" is continually constructed as the interplay between attacker and defender play out in a contest of adaptive expertise [6]. Each scenario involves different goals, objective metrics of performance, responsibilities, tasks, methods, tools, and, of course, varying knowledge, skill, and abilities. Measurement of optimal performance is difficult to achieve in this domain because indicators are needed at a level of detail not typically found in competency models [12]. Additionally, interrelationships among multiple competencies or across multiple job roles must be defined which are not typically identified in job task analysis [13].

According to Brown, Collins and Duguid [15], situated expertise becomes embedded through the interaction of declarative and procedural knowledge during skilled application. Individuals proficient in understanding of the domain must undergo "cognitive apprenticeship" by which the procedures they have learned become generalized and adaptive as a result of varied practice, collaboration, and reflection. Competence forms through repeated application of knowledge and skill. Novices, beginners and the proficient use reasoning based on procedures and rules, but these permit resolution of only well-defined (textbook) problems. The competent practitioner has developed skills through repetitive application enabling them to reason by causal models that demonstrate the situational awareness necessary to address ill-defined (unknown) problems. The expert and the master differ in the degree of ability developed to adapt these causal models and habituated skills. They reason through stories or, more accurately, vignettes that demonstrate finely tuned, situated expertise which is able to address the emergent (unknowable) problem or dilemma that cannot be adequately addressed by those with less expertise.

In summary, mission-critical roles in cybersecurity must be defined at increasing depth of detail to align with the conceptualization and action repertoires of masters, experts, competent practitioners, proficient students, beginners, and novices. These decreasing orders of competency align with representation of situated expertise as vignettes (master level), goals and objectives (expert level), responsibilities (competent level), tasks (proficient level), tool procedures (beginner level), and domain knowledge (novice level) as the basis for performance. Optimal performance at each level differs. Accordingly, assessments or evaluations of performance should consider both the stage of expertise development and the fundamental or differentiating nature of the task. Finally, the development of mission-critical competence in cybersecurity requires the opportunity to fully engage in a contest of competence by which expertise is grounded in the volatility, uncertainty, complexity, and ambiguity that typifies the real-world environment of this competence-based domain.

3. DEVELOPING MISSION-CRITICAL COMPETENCE THROUGH COMPETITION

Cybersecurity competitions are serious games — they are contests of competence that seek to edify and engage, more than to simply entertain [16], [17]. Beyond their educational mission, cybersecurity competitions are developed to assist in recruiting and selecting the next generation workforce. These are high stakes contests for identifying those able to perform under the pressure of real world, job-relevant performance conditions. Though the best provide many forms of feedback, outperforming an adversary provides the ultimate indicator of a player's competence.

Recent studies suggest that for competitions to be effective there must be alignment between game design and the developmental stage of a participant's expertise. The design of games that present challenges adjusted to the learning state and competence level of the player is called *game balance* [18]. Studies applying game balance techniques are finding that they motivate students to achieve mastery in the discipline while at the same time increasing their persistence to learn. These studies show, as Phillips [19] stated: "A good teacher challenges her students, understands their struggles, and provides needed encouragement. A [good] game provides the same level of interaction, but with the added benefit of embedded assessments a student's progress is continually tracked..." The continual guidance towards higher and higher learning goals is called scaffolding. Adapting challenges based on the current competence level of the participant helps to develop critical thinkers that become engaged in and committed to a discipline, and increase motivation to learn. Thus, scaffolding is the difference between a serious game that merely increases awareness or understanding and one that fosters deep learning [20].

However, the opposite effect – the disengagement of the participant – may result if a competition is too challenging. Wouters et al [21] conducted a meta-analysis of the cognitive and motivational effects of serious games. They found students developing foundational competence through drill and practice saw no benefit from participating in a serious game. Further, the study showed that competitions that occur in a single, continuous session were actually less effective than traditional instruction.

A recent study of the National Cyber League (NCL) inaugural competition season [22] offers a potential explanation for the failure of competitions to match or improve upon traditional classroom instruction. During the multi-event NCL season, the students who participated across multiple sessions showed a significant increase in all measures of engagement: dedication, absorption, and vigor towards participating in cybersecurity activities. However, there was a notable decline in engagement for those with little experience in the field – those who had participated in less than two events. These participants frequently dropped out of the competition before the season was over. The conclusion drawn from the data suggests that improved game balance is needed in cybersecurity competitions if they are to accomplish the objective of expanding and enhancing the cybersecurity workforce.

4. CAPTURING THE GROUND TRUTH OF ASSURANCE

The cybersecurity mission is to ensure the security, accuracy, and timely transfer of information [23]. The primary goal is to provide assurance that a computer-based system is reasonably protected by reducing exploitable vulnerabilities and insecure behaviors while maintaining an ability to detect and respond to security incidents and intrusion. This mission is therefore similar to that of other engineering professions, which assess and assure safety. Recently, best practices in safety assurance have been adopted by cybersecurity researchers seeking to develop an evidence-based approach to improve information assurance [24], [25]. In this section, we will briefly describe the relevance and importance of safety assurance case modeling as a method for better identifying the level of cybersecurity competence and achieving game balance in competitions so critical to engaging talented students who have the aptitude necessary to become experts in the field.

The safety assurance case method was originally developed by Kelly and colleagues [26], [27], [28], [29] to document, validate, and evolve safety assessments based on lessons learned from implementation of new technologies. A similar method is used to guide development of competency assessments in large-scale credentialing programs, such as those operated by the Educational Testing Service [30]. Across several studies, Kelly and colleagues showed that this scenario-based method facilitated common understanding of system vulnerabilities and faults across all stakeholders, e.g., system designers, safety professionals, industry regulators, and certifying authorities. Importantly, their studies also showed that scenarios facilitate rapid adaptation of system designs and remedial actions necessary to reduce the number and negative impact of safety incidents.

Accordingly, the safety assurance case method may address a critical issue facing the cybersecurity profession: the dynamic nature of threats and attack patterns require that mission-critical roles and task assignments are continually updated based on evidence gathered from the latest tactics, techniques and procedures used in cybersecurity incidents. To infuse this *ground truth* into workforce planning requires that cybersecurity workforce programs be well integrated and constantly adapted [6]. However, maintaining alignment and currency among the various workforce development programs and tools, such as training, simulations and certifications, is a constant challenge. For example, a recent study of cybersecurity workforce programs in the energy sector found several important job responsibility areas were either missing entirely or varied widely in emphasis in competency frameworks, course designs, and certification programs [31].

Goodenough, Lipson and Weinstock [25] suggest how the safety assurance case method might be applied in developing an evidence-based practice for information assurance. Their adaptation of the Goal-Structuring Notation Method for safety assurance [28] provides a step-by-step process that may be used to model cybersecurity scenarios. The first step in the assurance case method is the definition of a case that captures one or more critical vulnerabilities, system failures, recovery actions and consequences. Each case is further elaborated by creating a structured story – or *vignette* – that enumerates: primary and subsidiary goals; objective measures of expected outcomes or operation; challenges to these goals and objectives introduced by one or more exemplar incidents; and the process steps, strategies (or job responsibilities), and tasks necessary to recognize and effectively respond to return the system to an acceptable operating state. Finally, tools are identified which will provide the evidence necessary to indicate whether a vulnerability has been detected or an intrusion has been thwarted.

As discussed above, cybersecurity work is characterized by decision-making that must be made under high levels of uncertainty, ambiguity, and time pressure where optimal performance is difficult to decipher. Gompert's [32] study of similar jobs in military contexts showed that performance in these contexts is highly situational, where decisions must be made "on the fly" [33]. Success therefore depends on effective sensemaking [34]. What differentiates the competent from the "merely knowledgeable" is the speed and accuracy of incident pattern recognition and classification into known scenarios. This finding is consistent with studies of chess masters which show that recall of game scenarios, especially during the first few moves, are highly predictive of the level of skill [35].

Similarly, cybersecurity skill requires much more than rote memorization. Expert cybersecurity professionals, like their counterparts in military counterintelligence or chess mastery, must possess sufficient situational awareness [36] to adapt the response to meet the unique requirements of the situation. Studies of situational awareness show that simulation systems, such as those used in cyber competitions, can be effective training and assessment mechanisms *if, and only if,* the scenarios used are realistic and grounded in detailed case definitions [37]. These studies also show that fostering learning and the engagement necessary to create the active learning environment needed to develop adaptive expertise requires that the scenarios focus on tasks, tools, and methods that differentiate the performance of novices and beginners from those who are competent or expert cybersecurity professionals [38].

In the current study, we applied and extended the assurance case process to demonstrate how it may be used to identify the situations and conditions that determine the development or demonstration of competence in mission-critical cybersecurity roles. In the next section we will define key terms and provide an overview of how traditional job analysis or competency modeling may be altered by integrating the assurance case method and its core concept of the vignette. Then we will briefly review the process used to implement a vignette-based method for improving talent management program design through identifying the competency factors that can determine the effectiveness of a cybersecurity competition design. The remainder of the paper will discuss the preliminary findings from this study and the implications for the design of cybersecurity competitions as an effective indicator and enabler of skill development.

5. DEFINITION AND APPLICATION OF KEY TERMS

5.1 Job Performance Modeling: Step 1 – Defining Context

Defining the context of job performance is essential because of the situated nature of expertise in cybersecurity. The term *critical incident* is often used to describe a situation in which expertise is exhibited within a competence-based domain [39], [40], [41]. Incident, as the word is used here, is not simply an event requiring a response. Instead, it represents a defining moment when differences in skill level are notable in clearly identifiable outcomes of action. This may be an actual or a potential event, and includes not only sense-and-respond situations, but also proactive or sustaining events critical to achievement of goals and objectives. Hence, the word incident here is more broadly defined. We therefore use the definition of incident proposed by John Flanagan, the inventor of the critical incident technique for task analysis:

> any observable human activity that is sufficiently complete in itself to permit inferences and predictions to be made about the person performing the act. To be critical, an incident must occur in a situation where the purpose or intent of the act seems fairly clear to the observer and where its consequences are sufficiently definite to leave little doubt concerning its effects. [42, p. 327]

However the incident itself does not tell the whole story. In many cases, experts use an incident label to quickly convey a complex and diverse set of conditions and events in a simple, terse manner, especially when conversing with peers [43]. Consequently, we prefer the term *vignette* because it signifies the need to extract the whole story, including several scenarios or differing perspectives of a critical incident [44], [45]. These stories are frequently used by experts to convert tacit into explicit knowledge for communicating an event to less experienced people [46], [47].

The term *vignette* describes the collection of: a critical incident title or description; when the incident occurs (frequency and/or action sequence); what happens during the incident (problem or situation); who is involved (entities or roles); and where the incident might happen, now or in the future (systems or setting). Further definition of a vignette might include why it is important (severity or priority of response) and how the critical incident is addressed (method, tools, or abilities that may be needed). A collection of vignettes and the associated job context forms the basis for developing a Job Performance Model [7], [11] that may

facilitate comparison with other jobs or to identify when an individual is performing the job as classified.

In summary, rather diving into producing lists of example tasks or knowledge, skill and ability (KSA) statements – the typical outcomes of a job analysis or competency modeling effort – the job performance modeling process begins with the elicitation of context that situates the expertise to be elaborated in future stages of the process. This critical first stage involves a six step process. The outcome of the context elicitation is a vignette that emerges from asking subject matter experts to brainstorm answers to what, *when, who, where, why,* and *how* questions about a critical incident.

5.2 Job Performance Modeling: Step 2 – Defining Job Performance

After context is defined, the next stage of a JPM process involves definition of the job mission: a set of goals that establish the objectives to be met by the execution of job responsibilities that involve one or more tasks requiring knowledge, skill and abilities to demonstrate competence. We define a *goal* as a statement that expresses an action that must be successfully completed to accomplish the job mission, or to facilitate the accomplishment of another goal. The goal *objective* is defined as the measurable outcome that establishes the criteria by which the degree of success or effectiveness may be assessed. *Job responsibilities* are defined as outcome states that may be monitored or assessed to determine if an objective has been accomplished.

Accordingly, in a JPM process responsibility statements are elicited by asking subject matter experts to produce statements using passive verbs, such as "ensure", "follow", or "obtain" which are often not considered by traditional job modeling techniques that guides much instructional and certification design. Furthermore, despite the cliché "If more than one person is responsible for something, no one is," responsibilities are often assigned to a team while the execution of a specific task is assigned to an individual. By eliciting responsibilities first, the JPM process helps to define role overlaps, information sharing requirements, and indicators of team performance, and will help to prompt subject matter experts for a detailed list of process steps and tasks necessary to achieve the responsibility outcome.

A *task* is defined as "what a person is required to do, in terms of actions and/or cognitive processes, to achieve a system goal" [48, p. 185]. This definition implies that task statements must be written specifically to highlight the action verb that indicates the execution of the task. It is often the case, though not a requirement of task analysis, that the action verbs used to describe goals and tasks align with Bloom's taxonomy of action verbs [49], [50].

5.3 Job Performance Modeling: Step 3 – Defining Competence

This definition of a task also helps to clarify the definitions for elements of competency: knowledge, skill and ability. These three components of competence are treated as independent dimensions which may be used to understand an individual's or team's level of competence within a three-dimensional space [7], [11].

Knowledge is defined as the understanding of a concept, strategy, or procedure. Knowledge is measured by the depth of understanding, from shallow to deep. Knowledge is therefore independent of task performance. Knowledge is identifiable by the capacity to encode, recall, or associate information, independent of context. For example, organizational knowledge is required to "Understand what is important to the organization and what is mission critical."

Skill is defined as the reliable application of knowledge in the accomplishment of a task to achieve desired outcomes. Skill is measured by the degree of reliability, from inconsistent to consistent, in performance of a task. Skill is always task-specific and context-specific. Skill is identifiable by statements of accomplishment, such as "Establish plan for secure storage and transmission of customer data."

Ability is defined as a mental or physical capacity to transfer or transform knowledge and skills for application to new domains. Ability is measured by the extent of knowledge and skill transfer, from narrow to broad, typically assessed through the use of physical or intelligence tests. Abilities are task-independent. Abilities include many forms of mental or physical manipulation [51], e.g., dexterity, memorizing, deducing, recognizing patterns, and planning.

Traditional job modeling sometimes includes an "Other" category to identify motivation, personality traits, or other factors that may be associated with job performance. These are excluded from a job performance modeling process as they are believed to moderate the effectiveness of knowledge, skill and ability, rather than being a direct determinant of performance. Simply put, no matter how motivated someone is, if they completely lack knowledge, skill or ability, then action is impossible. However, possessing even the smallest amount of knowledge, skill or ability will enable some action, the effort expended towards which may be determined by motivation and other state or trait factors.

Mission critical roles are functional job roles that bring the necessary know-how, competencies, and practices to accomplish the mission of an organization. In a recent interview conducted by Control Engineering Magazine [52], these job roles were defined as being in the "Red Zone", to distinguish them from other cybersecurity job roles that are important but are less direct in impacting the security of deployed systems. Consequently, we define Mission Critical Roles as work to be performed by the cyber functional role that is critical to the defense of an organization or agency's information systems. These roles may be further classified by function or job. A *Functional Job Role* is a category or classification of job roles based on their sharing a significant number of common goals (i.e., functions). A *Job Role* is a category or classification of job titles based on their sharing a significant number of common responsibilities or job duties.

In summary, the job performance modeling process distinctly separates the contribution of three measurable dimensions of competence (i.e., knowledge, skill, and ability) to the production of actions that determine job success. The job performance model is a progressively hierarchical model that emerges from a sequence of subject matter expert brainstorming sessions. At the most detailed level, competence is indicated by the extent to which knowledge, skill and ability are involved in task execution. But, because task performance often involves tacit expertise, subject matter experts must be prompted to facilitate their recall of the complete list of tasks to be performed. The JPM process therefore begins by eliciting the desired outcomes that define the responsibilities of a person or team necessary to meet an objective that measures the degree of goal accomplishment. In the next section, we will review the job performance modeling method applied during this process.

6. METHOD

A series of virtual focus group sessions were conducted with a group of 54 subject matter experts who are members of the National Board of Information Security Examiner's (NBISE) Operational Security Testing (OST) and Advanced Threat Response (ATR) job performance panels (SME panels). NBISE job performance panels are composed by bringing together experts from industry stakeholders, government agencies, research institutions, service companies, and security product vendors. These subject matter experts (SMEs) collaborate to define competency models and develop a standards-based library of validated assessment, curriculum, and simulation-based learning components. The 23-member ATR panel is focused on advanced cyber security threats such as advanced persistent threats and other highly-sophisticated threats. The 31-member OST panel is focused on penetration testing, red teaming, and attacker emulation testing. The functional job roles they evaluated were selected from recommendations put forward to the Secretary of DHS by the Homeland Security Advisory Committee (HSAC; [53]).

6.1 Definition of Mission-Critical Roles

Both SME panels engaged in a discussion and a voting process to select the roles to develop scenario-driven job competency models. The initial project was scoped for two functional roles. However, it is important to note that the brainstormed scenarios that were selected applied to multiple cybersecurity functional roles and can in many cases be used in future projects to help identify the responsibilities and competencies of non-selected or listed cyber roles. The ATR panel identified three jobs as aligned with their panel focus and membership; these jobs are "Security monitoring and event analysis", "Incident responder in-depth", and "Threat analyst/Counter-intelligence analyst." The OST panel identified two jobs as aligned with their panel focus and membership; these jobs are "network and system penetration testing" and "application penetration testing."

6.2 Vignette Identification and Elaboration

With the two focal roles identified, the panel members brainstormed a list of vignettes. In addition to providing a terse description of the critical incident, the panel added exemplars of the scenarios. For example, the vignette "Adversaries are collecting open source intelligence on your organization to be used for targeting and attack" was further defined into a set of scenarios, including "Honeypots could be triggered based on web-scraping" and "Utilizing social networking sites to collect information about the company and employees." As this was a demonstration project, only one master vignette for each subpanel was selected for further analysis. These two master vignettes were: "Discovery of large amounts of sensitive data posted to internet with no clear signs of intrusion" (ATR subpanel); and "Conduct of a comprehensive Red Team penetration test against a sensitive national laboratory conducting advanced research with national security implications" (OST subpanel).

Each of the two master vignettes was further elaborated through a series of six focus group sessions. First, the description of each critical incident was expanded by applying antenarrative dynamic analysis [54] to answer five questions about each incident: *what, when, why, where,* and *how.* Second, the SME panel brainstormed a list of process steps for responding to the critical incident. Third, the goals associated with each master vignette were elicited. Fourth, the SME panel brainstormed a list of job responsibilities for each goal. Fifth, a list of knowledge requirements, tools, and tasks where abilities may be applied were elicited for each master process step. Finally, the tasks for each process step were sorted by the SME panel to determine the relative priority of abilities for job performance, both at the overall vignette level and for each process step.

7. FINDINGS

The ATR and OST panels each elicited job performance model components of the related DHS mission critical job role. Each panel identified a vignette to guide this elicitation and identified goals, responsibilities, master process steps, process steps, knowledge requirements, tools, and abilities associated with their selected job roles. The ATR panel selected the "discovery of large amounts of sensitive data posted to the Internet with no clear signs of intrusion". The OST panel selected the "Red Team assessment of a high security network."

With the vignette identified and described, the panel's brainstormed a list of process steps of an organization or team responding to the critical incident described in the vignette. The ATR panel identified 57 process steps that were sorted into 9 master process steps and the OST panel identified 67 process steps that were sorted into 7 master process steps.

Following the development of the process steps, the panels developed response goals and job responsibilities for the critical job role in addressing the critical event. The ATR panel elicited six response goals and 30 responsibilities for a Security Monitoring & Event Analyst in response to the discovery of large amounts of sensitive data posted to the Internet with no clear signs of intrusion. The OST panel identified four response goals and 18 responsibilities for a Network & System Penetration Tester in support of a Red Team assessment of a high security network. Table 1 lists the goals for each job role.

Table 1: Response goals for each job role

Job Role	Goals
Security Monitoring & Event Analyst (*ATR*)	Communicate incident to appropriate internal groups such as security management, IT management, HR, and Legal
	Conduct an initial triage of the incident
	Directly support the incident response process (e.g. assist in validating containment for hosts or network segments were effective)
	Follow, identify, update whether there is process documentation that covers this scenario
	Gather potential indicators or artifacts of compromise from end user workstations
	Maintain situational awareness throughout the incident for the organization
Network & System Penetration Tester (*OST*)	Develop and execute penetration and testing strategy
	Differentiate between vulnerabilities that are meaningful to the assessment and those that are not
	Manage the administration and logistics of the assessment
	Understand, demonstrate, and educate the client on the real world impact of threats to vulnerabilities in a given environment

Informed by the process steps, goals, and job responsibilities, the panels collaborated to identify the abilities required of, or greatly beneficial to, an individual in each job role in carrying out the job responsibilities in each of the process steps identified for the respective vignettes. A specific ability was deemed important to a process step if 55% or more of the participants associated the ability with that process step. Table 2 and 3 show the five most involved abilities for both the ATR job role and OST job role in their respective vignettes.

Table 2: Ability requirements for ATR vignette

Abilities	# of steps	% of steps
Summarizing (*representing the whole in a condensed statement*)	15	26.3%
Organizing a message (*sequencing elements for the best impact*)	13	22.8%
Contextualizing (*connecting related parts to the environment*)	11	19.3%
Recognizing patterns (*perceiving consistent repetitive occurrences*)	11	19.3%
Deducing (*arriving at conclusions from general principles*)	10	17.5%

Table 3: Ability requirements for OST vignette

Abilities	# of steps	% of steps
Selecting tools (*finding methods to facilitate solution*)	31	45.6%
Contextualizing (*connecting related parts to the environment*)	30	44.1%
Deducing (*arriving at conclusions from general principles*)	25	36.8%
Reusing solutions (*adapting existing methods/results*)	25	36.8%
Planning (*deciding how to use resources to achieve goals*)	19	27.9%

8. DISCUSSION

A primary purpose of the current study was to demonstrate a process for eliciting a detailed definition of mission-critical roles and the abilities required in order to establish an improved framework for evaluating and benchmarking performance through cybersecurity competitions. Kiili [18] proposed an experiential game model in which game balance is achieved through a "cyclical model of ideation, experience, and challenge" which engages the participant by using scaffolding to maintain activity at the edge of the participant's "zone of proximal development" [55].

According to Kiili's experiential game model, cybersecurity competition challenges should be evaluated for their degree of alignment with vignettes that describe a vulnerability pattern or critical incident appropriate for the expertise stage of the participant. The recent development of "semantic templates" [24] for establishing standardized definition of vignettes helps to facilitate mapping of game design to cybersecurity job performance models [7], [10], [11]. Once competition challenges have been mapped to a job performance model vignette, the weighting determined for each competency factor in terms of the degree to which the task is fundamental or differentiating may be used to establish a standardized evaluation framework that can guide accreditation or validation of a competition scoring model. Validated competition scoring models are required for comparing or aggregating scores across multiple competitions.

The first step in this score accreditation is to assess the degree to which a competition design covers the various goals associated with the selected vignette. Second, each challenge should be evaluated in terms of the distribution of responsibilities to the team members. By evaluating responsibility distribution, the evaluation framework enables role-specific analysis while still supporting an overall team assessment. Third, the tasks, methods, and tools used by a competition should be assessed using the weights provided in a cybersecurity job performance model to determine difficulty levels of the gameplay based on the degree to which they indicate fundamental or differentiating competencies. Fourth, the levels of volatility, uncertainty, complexity, and ambiguity (VUCA) manipulated by the game to alter the cognitive load on the participant may provide further guidance on how scoring models compare against other competitions. Fifth, game balance may be assessed using VUCA levels as cognitive load has been found to be the critical determinant of whether a game is adequately, but not excessively, challenging the participant [18], [56].

Finally, additional validation analyses may be performed that are not currently possible because cybersecurity competitions lack a standardized scoring model. First, the reliability of the scoring system could be analyzed. Second, as was suggested by the study of the National Cyber League [22], competitions as an educational and career development program could be evaluated in terms of the level of engagement they create among the participants. Comparison of engagement by the depth of learning which demonstrates proficiency, skill level, and/or ability scores as well as demographic variables would be especially important to assess game balance and the value of the competition for facilitating expansion and diversifying the workforce.

In summary, the integration of mission-critical role definitions with experiential game theory enables substantial improvement in cybersecurity competition program evaluation models and techniques. The purpose of this study was to demonstrate how to develop the components of a job performance model that may be used to support workforce development and/or to assess cybersecurity competitions to support aggregation and comparison of participant performance. The steps in this modeling effort are to: 1) establish vignettes that define situated expertise in mission-critical roles; 2) detail the goals and objective metrics that determine successful performance; 3) identify the responsibilities by job role necessary to achieve the objectives; 4) detail the tasks, methods, and tools along with how competence may differ in level of fundamental or differentiating indicators of expertise levels or the level of VUCA that indicates the difficulty of achieving that level of expertise. Once such a validated model for scoring performance has been established, competition programs may be evaluated on outcome measures such as generalizability of scores, participant engagement, and support for growth and diversification of the workforce.

9. REFERENCES

[1] Anderson, L.W., Krathwohl, D.R., and Bloom, B.S. *A taxonomy for learning, teaching, and assessing: A revision of Bloom's taxonomy of educational objectives.* Longman, New York, 2001.

[2] Assante, M.J. and Tobey, D.H. Enhancing the cybersecurity workforce. *IEEE IT Professional 13*, (2011), 12–15.

[3] Benner, P.E. *From novice to expert: Excellence and power in clinical nursing practice.* Addison-Wesley, Menlo Park, CA, 1984.

[4] Bloom, B.S. *Taxonomy of educational objectives: The classification of educational goals.* Longmans, Green, New York, 1956.

[5] Boje, D.M. The storytelling organization: A study of story performance in an office-supply firm. *Administrative Science Quarterly 36*, (1991), 106–126.

[6] Boje, D.M. Stories of the storytelling organization: A postmodern analysis of Disney as Tamara-land. *Academy of Management Journal 38*, (1995), 997–1035.

[7] Boje, D.M. *Narrative Methods for Organizational and Communication Research.* Sage Publications, London, 2001.

[8] Boyatzis, R.E. *The competent manager: A model for effective performance.* Wiley, New York, 1982.

[9] Brown, Collins, and Duguid. Situated cognition and the culture of learning. *Educational Researcher 18*, (1989), 32–42.

[10] Campion, M.A., Fink, A.A., Ruggenberg, B.J., Carr, L., Phillips, G.M., and Odman, R.B. Doing competencies well: Best practices in competency modeling. *Personnel Psychology 64*, (2011), 225–262.

[11] Charness, N. Expertise in chess: The balance between knowledge and search. In K.A. Ericsson and J. Smith, eds., *Toward a general theory of expertise: Prospects and Limits.* Cambridge University Press, Cambridge, 1991, 39–63.

[12] Chin, C. and Brown, D.E. Learning in science: A comparison of deep and surface approaches. *Journal of Research in Science Teaching 37*, 2 (2000), 109–138.

[13] Le Deist, F.D. and Winterton, J. What is competence? *Human Resource Development International 8*, (2005), 27–46.

[14] Endsley, M.R. Toward a theory of situation awareness in dynamic systems. *Human Factors: The Journal of the Human Factors and Ergonomics Society 37*, (1995), 32–64.

[15] Flanagan, J.C. The critical incident technique. *Psychological Bulletin 51*, (1954), 327–358.

[16] Franke, V. Decision-making under uncertainty: Using case studies for teaching strategy in complex environments. *Journal of Military and Strategic Studies 13*, 2 (2011), 1–21.

[17] Gandhi, R.A., Siy, H., and Wu, Y. Studying software vulnerabilities. *Crosstalk: The Journal of Defense Software Engineering*, (2010), 16–20.

[18] Garris, R., Ahlers, R., and Driskell, J.E. Games, motivation, and learning: A research and practice model. *Simulation & gaming 33*, 4 (2002), 441–467.

[19] Gompert, D.C. *Heads We Win–the Cognitive Side of Counterinsurgency (COIN): RAND Counterinsurgency Study–Paper 1.* RAND Corporation, Santa Monica, CA, 2007.

[20] Goodenough, J., Lipson, H., and Weinstock, C. Arguing Security - Creating Security Assurance Cases. *Build Security In*, 2012.

[21] Guilford, J.P. The structure of intellect. *Psychological Bulletin; Psychological Bulletin 53*, 4 (1956), 267.

[22] Hoffman, L.J., Rosenberg, T., Dodge, R., and Ragsdale, D. Exploring a national cybersecurity exercise for universities. *IEEE Security & Privacy 3*, 5 (2005), 27–33.

[23] Johansen, R. *Get there early: Sensing the future to compete in the present.* Berrett-Koehler Publishers, San Francisco, Calif., 2007.

[24] Kelly, T.P. and McDermid, J.A. Safety case construction and reuse using patterns. *Proceedings of 16th International Conference on Computer Safety, Reliability and Security (SAFECOMP'97)*, Springer (1997), 55–69.

[25] Kelly, T.P. and McDermid, J.A. A systematic approach to safety case maintenance. *Reliability Engineering & System Safety 71*, 3 (2001), 271–284.

[26] Kelly, T.P. and Weaver, R.A. The goal structuring notation– a safety argument notation. *Proceedings of the dependable systems and networks 2004 workshop on assurance cases*, (2004).

[27] Kiili, K. Digital game-based learning: Towards an experiential gaming model. *The Internet and Higher Education 8*, 1 (2005), 13–24.

[28] Klein. *Sources of Power: How people make decisions.* MIT Press, 1998.

[29] Lave, J. and Wenger, E. *Situated learning: Legitimate peripheral participation.* Cambridge University Press, Cambridge, England, 1991.

[30] De Long, D.W. *Lost knowledge: Confronting the threat of an aging workforce.* Oxford University Press, Oxford, 2004.

[31] Mislevy, R.J., Steinberg, L.S., and Almond, R.G. On the structure of educational assessments. *Measurement 1*, (2003), 3–62.

[32] O'Neil, L.R., Assante, M.J., and Tobey, D.H. *Snart Grid Cybersecurity: Job Performance Model Report.* National Technical Information Service, Alexandria, VA, 2012.

[33] O'Neil, L.R., Assante, M.J., Tobey, D.H., et al. *Developing secure power systems professional competence: Alignment and gaps in workforce development programs.* National Technical Information Service, Alexandria, VA, 2013.

[34] Phillips, V. Learning grammar with a joystick and math with a mouse. *Huffington Post*, 2013.

[35] Prensky, M. *Digital game-based learning.* McGraw-Hill, New York, 2001.

[36] Schepens, W.J. and James, J.R. Architecture of a cyber defense competition. *Systems, Man and Cybernetics, 2003. IEEE International Conference on*, (2003), 4300–4305.

[37] Schepens, W.J., Ragsdale, D.J., Surdu, J.R., and Schafer, J. The Cyber Defense Exercise: An evaluation of the effectiveness of information assurance education. *The Journal of Information Security 1*, 2 (2002).

[38] Schraagen, J.M. Task analysis. In *The Cambridge handbook of expertise and expert performance.* Cambridge University Press, Cambridge, UK, 2006, 185–201.

[39] Seddigh, N., Pieda, P., Matrawy, A., Nandy, B., Lambadaris, I., and Hatfield, A. Current trends and advances in information assurance metrics. *Proceedings of the Second Annual Conference on Privacy, Security and Trust*, (2004), 197–205.

[40] Smith, K., Shanteau, J., and Johnson, P.E., eds. *Psychological investigations of competence in decision making.* Cambridge University Press, Cambridge, UK, 2004.

[41] Tobey, D.H. Narrative's Arrow: Story sequences and organizational trajectories in founding stories. *Standing Conference on Management and Organizational Inquiry*, (2007).

[42] Tobey, D.H. *A competency model of advanced threat response. ATR Working Group Report NBISE-ATR-11-02.* National Board of Information Security Examiners, Idaho Falls, ID, 2011.

[43] Tobey, D.H., Gandhi, R.A., Reiter-Palmon, R., Yankelevich, M., and Pabst, K. ADAPTS: An evidence-based cyberlearning network for accelerating proficiency. 2013.

[44] Tobey, D.H., Pusey, P., and Burley, D. Engaging learners in cybersecurity careers: Lessons from the launch of the National Cyber League. *ACM InRoads 5*, 1 (2014), 53–56.

[45] Tobey, D.H., Reiter-Palmon, R., and Callens, A. *Predictive Performance Modeling: An innovative approach to defining critical competencies that distinguish levels of performance. OST Working Group Report.* National Board of Information Security Examiners, Idaho Falls, ID, 2012.

[46] Tyler, J.A. and Boje, D.M. Sorting the relationship of tacit knowledge to story and narrative knowing. In *Handbook of Research on Knowledge-Intensive Organizations.* Information Science Reference, 2008.

[47] Vogel, J.J., Vogel, D.S., Cannon-Bowers, J., Bowers, C.A., Muse, K., and Wright, M. Computer gaming and interactive simulations for learning: A meta-analysis. *Journal of Educational Computing Research 34*, 3 (2006), 229–243.

[48] Vygotsky, L.S. *Thought and language.* MIT Press, Cambridge, MA, 1966.

[49] Weaver, R.A., McDermid, J.A., and Kelly, T.P. Software safety arguments: towards a systematic categorisation of evidence. *Proceedings of the 20th International System Safety Conference (ISSC 2002)*, (2002).

[50] Weick, K.E., Sutcliffe, K.M., and Obstfeld, D. Organizing and the process of sensemaking. *Organization Science 16*, 4 (2005), 409–421.

[51] Welander, P. Cyber Security Advice From The Field: An Interview With Control Engineering, Michael Assante And Tim Conway Offer Security Suggestions For Plant Operators. *Control Engineering*, 2013.

[52] White, G.B. and Williams, D. The collegiate cyber defense competition. *Proceedings of the 9th Colloquium for Information Systems Security Education*, (2005).

[53] Wouters, P., van Nimwegen, C., van Oostendorp, H., and van der Spek, E.D. A meta-analysis of the cognitive and motivational effects of serious games. *Journal of Educational Psychology*, (in press).

[54] Wouters, P., van der Spek, E.D., and van Oostendorp, H. Current practices in serious game research: A review from a learning outcomes perspective. In T. Connolly, M. Stansfield and L. Boyle, eds., *Games-based learning advancements for multi-sensory human computer interfaces techniques and effective practices*. Information Science Reference, Hershey, PA, 2009, 232–250.

[55] Zbylut, M.L. and Ward, J.N. Developing interpersonal abilties with interactive vignettes. 2004.

[56] *Homeland Security Advisory Council CyberSkills Task Force Report.* U.S. Departrment of Homeland Security, Washington, D.C., 2012

Understanding Career Choice of African American Men Majoring in Information Technology

Kadeem Fuller
University of Alabama
Tuscaloosa, Alabama, USA
kadeem_fuller@yahoo.com

Lynette Kvasny
Pennsylvania State University
329C IST Building
University Park, PA 16802
1.814.865.6458
lkvasny@ist.psu.edu

Eileen M. Trauth
Pennsylvania State University
330C IST Building
University Park, PA 16802
1.814.865.6457
etrauth@ist.psu.edu

KD Joshi
Washington State University
Todd 437J
Pullman, WA 99164
1.509.335.5722
joshi@wsu.edu

ABSTRACT

A diverse workforce is essential for developing the nation's technological innovation, economic vitality, and global competitiveness. Yet, the under-representation of women, Latinos and African Americans has persisted in the field. In this study, we focus on African American male undergraduates majoring in information technology (IT). Despite the bleak numbers of African American males in IT there are still those who persist and graduate from a university and enter the workforce. To gain insights into those who do persist, we used a digital inequality framework to inform a qualitative study of undergraduates at two Historically Black Colleges and Universities (HBCUs). We conducted interviews with 20 African American males to uncover factors that contribute to their choice to pursue an IT major. The findings reveal that the five constructs from this framework (technical apparatus, digital skill, social support, autonomy of use, and purpose of use) in addition to two new constructs (work ethic and IT career exposure) help to explain how and why African American males choose IT majors. The study contributes to the limited literature on African American men's academic success, and helps to clarify some of the mixed and contradictory findings about their career choices that exist in the current literature.

Categories and Subject Descriptors

K. Computing Milieu, K.4.2 Social Issues, K.7 The Computing Profession, K.7.1 Occupations

General Terms

Management

Keywords

African American males, career choice, diversity, digital inequality, ethnicity, race, IT workforce

1. INTRODUCTION

Research on under represented groups in the IT profession has been a mainstay of the SIGMIS CPR community since the early 2000s. Indeed, the theme of the 2003 conference was diversity in the IT profession and had a separate track of papers [1]. But while under represented groups encompasses several different demographic groups, the vast majority of this research has dealt only with the under representation of women. Since 2000, 50 papers on the topic of under represented groups have appeared in the conference proceedings. But only ten of these papers have considered the topic of race or ethnicity [2, 3, 4, 5, 6, 7, 8, 9, 10, 11]. Trauth's [12] review of papers on the topic gender and IS that were published in IS journals between 1992 and 2012 shows a similar pattern: only two out of 132 journal articles addressed the topic of race or ethnicity [13, 14]. An additional paper was published in 2013 [15]. Within the already small corpus of research on race and ethnicity, is the even smaller body of research on the topic of African American men. To date, there have been only three papers presented at a SIGMIS conference that have dealt with the topic of under represented groups in the IT profession by focusing on African American men [3, 5, 11]. This points to a clear gap in the IS literature.

This gap in the research stands in stark contrast to current data from Silicon Valley about the current lack of diversity. In 2014, leading IT companies including Apple, Yahoo, Google, Facebook, LinkedIn, Twitter and eBay publicly disclosed workforce diversity statistics compiled as part of the report that major US employers must file with the Equal Employment Opportunity Commission. Collectively, these reports show an IT workforce that is predominantly white and male [16]. For instance, half of Yahoo's workforce of 12,000 is white, 39% Asian, 4% Latino, and 2% African American. Only 37% are women. This pattern holds across the IT sector [16]. The under-representation of women, Latinos, and African Americans is troubling because a diverse IT workforce is essential for developing the nation's technological innovation, economic vitality, and global competitiveness.

Despite the bleak statistics, there are still those few African American men who choose to pursue baccalaureate degrees and enter the IT profession. To understand the factors that shape their career choice, researchers must shift from the question of "why so few?" and focus on how and why the few succeeded. According to Harper [17] the relentless emphasis on the failures of African American men has helped to shape America's low expectations for them. Consequently, of those African American males who do succeed academically, we only know that they managed to avoid failure. The significance of our research is that we study African American males' who defy the odds and pursue IT careers. We conducted interviews with 20 IT majors at two HBCUs to uncover how their perspectives about and interest in IT careers are constructed within their cultural realities and experiences. Prior research has found that African American males' career development and choices unfold differently than for African American women and other ethnic male cohorts [6, 17, 18, 19]. Our analysis is guided by a digital inequality framework, which posits that an individual's access to equipment, skills, social support, purpose of use, and autonomy of use will shape their relationship with technology. However, our analysis also considers emergent factors that help to explain African American men's IT career choice.

2. LITERATURE REVIEW

Overall, African Americans represent only 7% of the entire IT industry but make up 13.1% of the US population [20]. Aggregate numbers from the US Department of Labor [21] show that African Americans experience poorer labor market outcomes than other races both prior to the 2008 recession and during the recovery. In 2014, for instance, the unemployment rate for whites was 5.4% but 11.5% for African American Americans [22]. Even amongst college graduates, in 2013, 12.4% of African American college graduates between the ages of 22 and 27 were unemployed, while the unemployment rate was 5.6% for all college graduates in the same age range [23]. Furthermore, over half (55.9%) of the African American college graduates were underemployed, that is, working in an occupation that typically does not require a four-year college degree [23].

These trends in underemployment and unemployment hold across Science, Technology, Engineering, and Math (STEM) occupations. For the years 2010 to 2012, for example, the average unemployment rate was 10% and the underemployment rate was 32% among African American recent graduates with degrees in engineering. For African American technology graduates, the average unemployment rate was slightly better at 7% but the underemployment rate was 49% [23] reinforcing concerns that racial discrimination presents a barrier for African American IT workers. However, while African Americans face the highest levels of unemployment and underemployment, they are more resilient and seek jobs for longer than whites do [22].

There are also unique gender disparities in workforce participation. African Americans are the only racial or ethnic group for whom women (53.8%) represent a larger share of the employed than do men [21]. These figures demonstrate how African American men face different and greater challenges in the labor market. Expanding the range of African American males' career options within an increasingly technology-oriented workforce may help to alleviate the high levels of unemployment and underemployment experienced by this group.

The longstanding under representation of African American males in the IT sector makes it difficult to attract younger men to the profession. Young African American males need to be able to look at the IT profession and see individuals in the field that look like them in order to truly believe that they can make it in the field [5].

2.1 Digital Inequality

While IT can aid in the empowerment of under represented groups, it can also perpetuate inequality [24, 25, 26]. The term digital divide was first coined and researched extensively from the mid 1990s through the mid 2000s as the Internet diffused into mainstream America. DiMaggio and Hargittai [27], Kvasny and Keil [28], and others reported that the technological "haves" and "have nots" aligned along the historical fault lines of gender, race and class. Technological "haves" usually consisted of men, whites and Asians, and higher income households, while technological "have nots" were usually women, African Americans and Latinos, and low income households.

Concerns about the digital divide receded as the majority of Americans gained Internet access. Research shifted from the digital divide, with its focus on computer and Internet access, to digital inequality with its focus on the effectiveness of IT access and use [27]. Digital inequality represents "a redefined understanding of the digital divide that emphasizes a spectrum of inequality across segments of the population depending on differences among several dimensions of technology access and uses" [27]. For Kvasny [26] digital inequality reflects not only disparities in the structure of access to and use of ICT; it also reflects the ways in which longstanding social inequities shape beliefs and expectations about ICT and its impacts on life chances. Digital inequality grants people from historically privileged races and economic backgrounds a higher level of technological empowerment to use their Internet access to advance their education, their participation in the job market, their social standing, and other life chances [5].

DiMaggio and Hargittai [27] frame digital inequality along five dimensions: technical apparatus or equipment, digital skill, social support, purposes for which technology is employed, and the autonomy of use.

2.1.1 Technical Apparatus

Technical apparatus is "the availability of suitable equipment including computers of adequate speed and equipped with adequate software for a given activity" [27]. In the case of African Americans overall, there is a persistent gap in Internet use (87% of whites and 80% of African Americans), and home broadband adoption (74% of whites and 62% of African Americans). However, when looking specifically at young, college- educated, and higher-income African Americans, these sub-groups are just as likely as their white counterparts to use the Internet and to have broadband service at home [29]. Disparities also disappear when it comes to mobile platforms with African Americans and whites equally likely to own smartphones and a cell phone of some kind [29].

2.1.2 Digital Skill
Digital skill is the ability to use technology efficiently and effectively [27]. There are three layers of skills that ensure that technology is being used in an efficient and effective manner. The first is *instructional skill*, which is the ability to operate hardware and software on a basic level. The next is *structural skill*, which is the ability to operate new formats in which information is being communicated. These are additional skills brought about by new technologies, and include competencies like creating video content or maintaining a LinkedIn profile. The third is *strategic skill*. This is the ability to scan the environment to find, evaluate and use information as a basis for decision-making [30]. While this is not a new skill, the ability to effectively use technological innovations like online search engines and digital libraries is of paramount importance in an information intensive society. These three layers of skills determine an individual's Internet competence [27].

2.1.3 Social Support
Social support from more experienced users is an important mechanism for gaining competence in IT use. As users reach the limits of their own skills, there are three types of social support from which they can draw from – *formal support* from professionals like teachers and tech support staff, *technical assistance* from family and friends, and *emotional support* from family and friends [27]. Family and friends play a vital role in a user's involvement on the Internet. A study concluded that people who have home computers were more likely to stop accessing the Internet without the support of a family member or neighbor to call on for supportive assistance [31]. Social support elevates the user's motivation and digital skills, and also introduces the user to new information sources which facilitates learning.

2.1.4 Purpose of Use
The purpose motivating IT use is shaped by income, education and other factors. For instance, in a study of young adults and creative activity online, Hargittai and Walejko [33] found that content creation is related to socioeconomic status, with those from higher income households more likely to create content. Purpose for using IT is also shaped by the type of activities where instrumental use is valued higher than entertainment and consumption uses. A major factor that contributes to whether an activity is seen as purposeful or not is how much educational value the user can gain from that activity. Thus using the Internet to find job opportunities or complete homework assignments is viewed more positively than downloading music or playing video games [32]. Researchers report that those with higher educational attainment and socioeconomic status tend to engage in more purpose filled activities online [24].

2.1.5 Autonomy of Use
Autonomy of use is the freedom to use technology wherever, whenever, and for whatever reason a person chooses. Autonomy is often dictated by the site from which a user gains access to the technology. For example, every American citizen has access to a public library's free Internet but factors such as hours of operation, Internet filters, and time limits constrain the freedom

users have while on the computers. Internet access from work and school is also constrained by policy restrictions on appropriate use of computing resources, and usage is often monitored for compliance with these policies. Home and mobile access to personally owned computing resources may provide the highest level of autonomy.

3. METHODOLOGY
This research is part of a larger National Science Foundation study involving African American males from four HBCUs. While HBCUs represent a small percentage of universities across the country, they account for a significant portion of African Americans graduating with a bachelor's degree in STEM fields [34]. Owens and colleagues [35] report that in the period from 2001- 2009, about 1.1 million African Americans were awarded bachelor's degrees with HBCUs accounting for 21% of those graduates. HBCUs accounted for 39% of the 110,580 bachelor's degrees awarded to African Americans in a STEM field, and 25% of the 41,287 bachelor's degrees awarded to African Americans in computer science.

The study used semi-structured interviews and a biographical questionnaire to uncover factors that contribute to African American males' choice to pursue an IT major. While 100 men will participate in the overall NSF study, this paper reports on the preliminary analysis of 20 interviews from two HBCUs. The interviews examined individual attributes like interests and family background, significant experiences, and critical incidents in their educational pathway, as well as structural barriers and advantages that they experienced due to their race and gender. Analysis was informed by the five constructs from the digital inequality framework to uncover how these African American males made the jump from a group that is woefully under represented in technology to future professionals in that same field. The digital inequality constructs allow us to see how these men achieved success across these five dimensions. The coding scheme is included in Table 1.

Table 1. Content Codes

Content Code	Definition
Technical Apparatus	Interest in and access to computing equipment
Social Support	Technical and emotional support from friends and family Technical support from professionals
Digital Skill	Instrumental – the operational manipulation of hardware and software Structural – skills required by new IT capabilities Strategic – proactively seeking information regarding skills and careers; developing and applying marketable IT skills
Purpose of Use	Rationale for using IT for instrumental or entertainment purposes
Autonomy of Use	Freedom to use the technology in any way desirable

Table 2. Factors with Frequency Counts

	Equipment	Autonotomy	Skill			Purpose	Social Support		IT Exposure	Work Ethic
			Instrumental	Structural	Strategic		IT Professionals	Friends and Family		
1	2	1	2			1	1	3	3	2
2			1			1	1	2	1	2
3	1						3		2	2
4	6	1	2	2	1	2		1	2	4
5	3						2	4	3	
6	3		3	3	2	3	2	6	5	4
7	2	2	1	2		1	6	2	6	1
8	3	1	2	1		3		3	4	4
9	3					2		3	5	
10	1						1	1		
11	1					1	2	1	1	
12	2		1			1	2	4	2	1
13	9		4	1		4		8	3	2
14	2		1					1	2	1
15	3			1	1	1	2	2	3	5
16	3		2	1	1	1		1	2	2
17	3					1	1	3	2	1
18	1		1					2	2	1
19	1		1			1		4	1	3
20	5		3	2				5	4	4
	54	**5**	**24**	**13**	**5**	**23**	**23**	**56**	**53**	**39**

4. FINDINGS

The analysis reveals that all five of the dimensions discussed in the digital inequality framework hold explanatory power, but two additional factors (IT exposure and work ethic) were discussed extensively during the interviews. Table 2 lists the 20 interviewees. For each interview, we list the number of times each factor was mentioned in each interview. The frequency counts for factor are listed in the final row. The seven factors were placed into one of three tiers based on their frequency count. The factors that were mentioned 30+ times were categorized into tier one (blue), tier two consisted of the factors that were mentioned less than 30 times but above fifteen times (red), and tier three was comprised of factors mentioned less than fifteen times (green).

4.1 Tier One

Tier one was reserved for the constructs mentioned the most by the interviewees. The constructs are: technical apparatus (equipment), friends and family social support, IT exposure, and work ethic.

4.1.1 Technical Apparatus

I think that's when my interest with computers started because after that I started taking apart computers and putting them back together, all that type of stuff, so just trying to figure out how things worked. I think that's how my interest started.

-Eric, Howard University

Equipment was mentioned 54 times and was discussed most often as building up and/ or breaking down hardware such as computers, televisions, and game systems. These men often served as the computer troubleshooter for their friends and families. The interviewees derived pleasure from looking inside of these machines and tinkering to discover how they function. However, these same individuals who expressed a high aptitude for disassembling and reassembling complex machines failed to relate this skill to entering the IT profession. The majority saw their interest in technological apparatus as a hobby or just something fun to do.

4.1.2 Social Support: Families and Family

Some of it (the decision to attend college) came from family. Some of it was enforced by family and they were pushing me to go to college. They actually told me if you're not going [to college] I don't know what you're going to do but you got to get out of here; you have got to find something that you are going to do. I knew I didn't want to go to trade school or work at McDonalds or anything like that so I said, "Hey the next option is going to college." That's what I did.

-Charles, Howard University

Friends and family social support was the highest occurring construct discussed in the interviews being mentioned fifty-six times. The interviewees spoke mainly about how their friends and families encouraged them to attend college. The majority of these young African American men were told from a young age by their parents, grandparents, aunts and uncles that they were expected to attend college. All but one of the interviewees mentioned friends and family social support as a factor that compelled them to attend college. However, fewer than five talked about the influence that friends and family social support had on their decision to pursue an IT major. Those select few men had friends or family members who were in the IT field or knew about the profession enough to advise the interviewee to look into that major. Sean from Southern University recalls, *"Yeah, he [my father] definitely drove me toward the IT part of it. He definitely had the most influence, and then my dad was real, he was, 'if you do cybersecurity, you're going to make a lot of money,' and then my dad's friend, he does something along those lines, and he was definitely pushing. They were pushing me hard. My dad still told me the other week, he said, 'well, you still need to go try to get your certification so you can do cybersecurity.'"*

4.1.3 IT Exposure
I find that crazy. I heard the terms IT and IS (information systems) when I was in high school, but I didn't know what any of it was until I got to college. It's almost like you tell a kid about it when they are five, they will know about it by the time they are fifteen. I was told about it when I was fourteen, and I am learning when I am twenty.

-Christian, Howard University

IT Exposure is an emergent factor that arose from the interview data, and refers to the point in time in which the interviewees discover the many career options IT has to offer. This factor was mentioned fifty-three times. Interviewees generally did not discover that IT was a viable career option until they were enrolled in college. Consequently, IT can be viewed as a discovery major. Initially the men misconstrued the IT profession as sitting alone in front of a computer screen programming. It was not until they arrived to college and took an IT introductory course that these males were informed that careers in IT were quite diverse. Another misperception about IT was the fear that the major would be too difficult. As Shawn from Southern University states, *"I was scared of computer science. I just knew it was hard, a lot of math."* Through exposure to the breadth of technical and nontechnical skills imparted to IT majors, awareness and confidence increased.

4.1.4 Work Ethic
Well I would say I'm definitely a person that I just don't give up very easily. I usually want to find the solution to something that's definitely holding me back or something that I could definitely work on.

-Matthew, Howard University

Work ethic is the second construct that emerged solely from the data, and it was mentioned thirty-nine times within seventeen interviews. Work ethic explains the desire to labor hard to succeed in the IT workforce. Each interviewee described at least one of the following sub- categories as the source of their work ethic:

- A refusal to fail in college
- A desire to go back to their hometown and inspire others □
- Expectation from others (family, mentors, friends) to accomplish great things
- Realization that African American males are poorly represented in IT field

4.2 Tier Two
Tier two was reserved for the constructs that were apparent in the interviews but were mentioned to a considerably lesser degree than the tier one constructs. The constructs in tier two are: instructional skills, purpose, and IT professional social support.

4.2.1 Digital Skills – Instrumental
Any computer science class almost, like I said, will be natural [for me]. The first time programming, when you explained. When you store something here, and then you add a plus there, divide... Okay that does make sense. All the computer stuff came almost... it was just easy for me to understand. I don't know how, but it just made a lot of sense.

-Sean, Southern University

Instructional skills were mentioned twenty-four times in thirteen interviews. The interviewees described this skill as the ability to master IT by learning the inner workings of the hardware and software. Most commonly, them men discussed the difficulty of learning how to program. Only a select few individuals mentioned it as being something as easily mastered as Shawn considered it to be. The majority had to spend many hours studying programming in order to grasp it. As Matthew from Howard University laments, *"Well, I feel like whenever I'd be working on the computer and stuff like that, always looking to maybe...like programming languages or also... I mean, I didn't know anything about them."* Most confided in their interviews that programming continues to be challenging.

4.2.2 Purpose of Use
You're going to have to want to learn. You're going to have to want to learn because if you're not interested in computers or not interested in how they work or not interested in what, what's the word I'm looking for, what would draw you to want to play with a computer, you're not going to really want to do it, because it's a lot of stuff that people don't realize. Like most people, they use the computer and they use the Internet, they use Microsoft Word, but there are so many more things that a computer can do, so if you're not interested in the extra stuff that a computer can do, like how it works, then you're not going to want to do computers.

□-Eric, Howard University

The interviewees discussed purpose as the way in which they interacted with technology. Purpose was mentioned twenty-three times amongst fourteen interviewees. Many of the young men spoke about how videogames had an impact on how they perceived the purpose of technology. As they reflected upon their childhood, they realized that it was their want of knowing how these videogames operated that set the beginning stages of an interest in technology. As these men grew older, their interest progressed from videogames to encompass computers. All of these young men see the importance of computers and know the potential of these machines. They are quite aware that computers are more than just a way to access the Internet, send emails, and even use Microsoft Word, as Eric stated. These interviewees know that, when computers are used properly, they have the power to change lives. These African American males know that it only takes one technological innovation to revolutionize how people perceive technology.

The second purpose of technology was a means to better their socioeconomic prospects of their family and themselves. These young men all look up to the most influential and richest men in IT, and see their chances of achieving similar levels of success as attainable if they are creative and hard working. Bill Gates, Steve Jobs, and Michael Dell are all names of influential IT figures that were mentioned by the interviewees. Race was not perceived as a significant barrier.

4.2.3 Social Support: IT Professional

People in my life pushing me to technology? I would have to say one of my professors. He's a man that, he speaks passionately about technology. He always talks about his background in computer science, how things have changed from his time to now. He always talks about different type of coding. He's really passionate about it and that makes me want to dive deeper in technology.

-Victor, Howard University

Social support in the form of IT professionals was mentioned twenty-three times by eleven interviewees. The interviewees primarily characterized IT professionals as educators in their high schools, after school and summer enrichment programs, and universities who also served as informal mentors. They spoke highly of these IT professionals and many interviewees revealed that professors had a direct impact on them selecting an IT major. The majority of these young men did not begin their collegiate career as IT majors. Rather switched to this major after a professor saw their potential to be successful in IT and persuaded them to pursue the major.

4.3 Tier Three

Tier three was reserved for the factors that were mentioned least during the interviews. This does not mean that the tier three constructs are no longer relevant in the study of digital inequality but rather that they were just not prevalent in this study. The constructs found in this tier are: autonomy, structural skills, and strategic skills.

4.3.1 Autonomy of Use

It's like an artist almost. It's freelance. It's not a really strict schedule. You're coding all day. You're making really creative stuff for other people. I learned in these internship roles, it wasn't really creative. I didn't really like it. I was at a desk all day. I didn't have any type of creative freedom, so things kind of turned full turn for me and I'm still in technology.

-Aaron, Howard University

Autonomy was only mentioned five times in four interviews. The limited responses for autonomy in this study suggests that men did not see autonomy, or freedom to use technology as they see fit, as a hindrance in their journey into IT. The five remarks made by the interviewees about autonomy spoke exclusively on the desire to use their creativity in an entrepreneurial IT career. They explained that a major advantage of choosing an IT profession is the freedom to select their own hours and not work a traditional 9-5 work day. They planned to use IT as an avenue to work for themselves and not for a company. Thus autonomy may serve to inspire entrepreneurship.

4.3.2 Digital Skills: Structural

Yeah, we had computer labs I various parts of the building we will go there, and just go on the Internet, and like just go look up information.

-Richard, Southern University

The interviewees described structural skills as the ability to use the Internet to look up information, and this factor was mentioned thirteen times in eight interviews. The practical use of structural skills was primarily searching the Internet to find information on how to troubleshoot computer issues or supplement coursework. In this regard, the interviewees used structural skills as a supportive ability that enhanced their knowledge of computers.

4.3.3 Digital Skills: Strategic

Information systems, I found out a little more information about that and that seemed more like something that I would want to do because management was too broad for me. With information systems, since that has to do with programming and stuff, I have a lot of ideas for programs like for mobile apps to websites and computer apps that I would like to get stated on to create.

-Jose, Howard University

The individuals in the study defined strategic skills as those needed to successfully research potential careers in IT and make an informed decision. This skill was mentioned five times in four interviews. The strategic skills are primarily focused on technical skills, not managerial or interpersonal skills, needed to be successful in the IT profession.

5. DISCUSSION

There are three significant discussion points that emerge from the findings. First is the discovery that, although the majority of these African American men discovered at a very young age that they had a high aptitude and interest in technology by playing video games, disassembling technological equipment, or troubleshooting technological equipment, it never registered to them that they could pursue a career in IT. This disconnect often occurred because their high school didn't offer IT classes to provide foundational technical skills, the men were counseled to pursue more culturally familiar interests like sports and business, they lacked knowledge about IT careers and had no one in their social networks to inform them about IT careers. This constellation of factors led men to not turn IT from a hobby into a viable career. It was oftentimes the development of the relationship with an IT professional who provided the information and social support to help the men to rediscover their interest in technology and encourage them to major in IT. It is also interesting to note that friends and family strongly encouraged the men to attend college, but these significant influencers did not steer the men to major in IT. Thus there exists an opportunity to educate parents about IT careers, which may in turn increase the number of African American men entering the IT major.

The second point concerns the evolution of the construct of autonomy from the original definition of the freedom to use technology into a career-oriented view of technology as unleashing creativity. This construct may also be the key to unlocking entrepreneurship for African American males in IT.

The final discussion point is the salience of two emergent constructs, IT exposure and work ethic, to the African American males experience with IT. Early exposure helps African American men to develop an interest and aptitude in IT. However, this interest has to be continuously fed by ongoing engagement with IT professionals who can provide opportunities for advanced skills development and career exploration. A strong work ethic is key to the successful career pathways of all African American men, and directly opposes stereotypical notions of African American men as lazy, academically untalented, and unmotivated. When we have high expectations for African American men and give them the information resource and social supports that they need to succeed, they can and will join the IT profession in greater numbers.

6. ACKNOWLEDGMENTS
This work was supported by a grant from the National Science Foundation (1232344). Any opinions, findings, and conclusions or recommendations expressed in this paper are those of the authors and do not necessarily reflect the views of the National Science Foundation.

.

7. REFERENCES
[1] Trauth, E.M. (Ed.) 2003. Freedom in Philadelphia: Leveraging Differences and Diversity in the IT Workforce. *Proceedings of the 2003 ACM SIGMIS Computer Personnel Research Conference* (SIGMIS-CPR '03), ACM, New York, NY USA.

[2] Sien, V.Y., Mui, G.Y., Tee, E.Y.J., and Singh, D. 2014. Perceptions of Malaysian Female School Children Towards Higher Education in Information Technology, *Proceedings of the 2014 ACM Conference on Computers and People Research* (SIGMIS-CPR '14), 97-104.

[3] Cain, C. and Trauth, E. 2012. Black Males in IT Higher Education in The USA: The Digital Divide in the Academic Pipeline Re-visited, *Proceedings of the Americas Conference on Information Systems* (AMCIS 2012). Paper 7. Retrieved June 17, 2014 from http://aisel.aisnet.org/amcis2012/proceedings/SocialIssues/7

[4] Windeler, J.B. and Riemenschneider, C. 2013. Organizational Commitment of IT Workers: Leader Support and Differences Across Gender and Race. *Proceedings of 2013 ACM SIGMIS Computers and People Research Conference* (SIGMIS-CPR '13), 3-14.

[5] Cain, C. and Trauth, E.M. 2013. Stereotype Threat: The Case of African American Males in the IT Profession. *Proceedings of the ACM SIGMIS Computers and People Research Conference* (SIGMIS-CPR '13), 57-62.

[6] Trauth, E.M., Cain, C., Joshi, K.D., Kvasny, L., and Booth, K. 2012. Embracing Intersectionality in Gender and IT Career Choice Research, *Proceedings of the 2012 ACM SIGMIS Computers and People Research Conference* (SIGMIS-CPR '12), 199-212.

[7] Kvasny, L. 2003. Triple Jeopardy: Race, Gender and Class Politics of Women in Technology. *Proceedings of the 2003 SIGMIS Conference on Computer Personnel Research: Freedom in Philadelphia - Leveraging Differences and Diversity in the IT Workforce*, (SIGMIS-CPR '03), 112-116.

[8] Ortiz, J.A., Tapia, A., and Maldonaldo, E. 2006. "Recruiting Diverse, High-skilled IT Employees through Existing Virtual Social Networks". *Proceedings of the 2006 ACM SIGMIS Computer Personnel Research Conference.* (SIGMIS-CPR '06), 4-11.

[9] Payton, F.C. and White, S. 2003. Views from the Field on Mentoring and Roles of Effective Networks for Minority IT Doctoral Students. *Proceedings of the 2003 SIGMIS Conference on Computer Personnel Research: Freedom in Philadelphia - Leveraging Differences and Diversity in the IT Workforce*, (SIGMIS-CPR '03), 123-129.

[10] Woszczynski, A., Beise, C., Myers, M., and Moody, J. 2003. Diversity and the Information Technology Workforce: An Examination of Student Perceptions. *Proceedings of the 2003 SIGMIS Conference on Computer Personnel Research: Freedom in Philadelphia- leveraging Differences and Diversity in the IT Workforce* (SIGMIS-CPR '03), 117-122.

[11] Cain, C. 2012. Underrepresented groups in gender and STEM: the case of black males in CISE, *Proceedings of the 2012 ACM SIGMIS Computers and People Research Conference* (SIGMIS-CPR '12), 97-102.

[12] Trauth, E.M. 2013. The Role of Theory in Gender and Information Systems Research. *Information and Organization,* 23, 4, 277-293.

[13] Kvasny, L. 2006. Let the Sisters Speak: Understanding Information Technology from the Standpoint of the 'Other'. *The DATA BASE for Advances in Information Systems,* 37, 4, 13-25.

[14] Kvasny, L., Trauth, E.M. and Morgan, A. 2009. Power Relations in IT Education and Work: The Intersectionality of Gender, Race and Class. *Journal of Information, Communication and Ethics in Society Special Issue on ICTs and Social Inclusion* 7, 2/3, 96-118.

[15] Morgan, A. and Trauth, E. 2013. Socio-economic Influences of Health Information Searching in the US: The Case of Diabetes, Information Technology and People, 26, 4, 324-346.

[16] Snider, J. 2014. Yahoo Tech Diversity, *USA Today,* June 17. Retrieved July 1, 2014 from http://www.usatoday.com/story/tech/2014/06/17/yahoo-lack-of-diversity/10718789.

[17] Harper, S. 2012. *Black male student success in higher education: A report from the national Black male college achievement study.* Report. University of Pennsylvania, Center for the Study of Race and Equity in Education. Retrieved October 9, 2014 from https://www.gse.upenn.edu/equity/sites/gse.upenn.edu.equity/files/publications/bmss.pdf.

[18] Moore, J. 2006. A Qualitative Investigation of African American Males' Career Trajectory in Engineering: Implications for Teachers, School Counselors, and Parents," *Teachers College Record,* 108, 2, 246-266.

[19] Kvasny, L., Joshi, K.D., and Trauth, E.T. 2011. The Influence of Self-Efficacy, Gender Stereotypes and the Importance of IT Skills on College Students' Intentions to Pursue IT Careers. *Paper presented at iConference,* Seattle, WA.

[20] Mendoza, M. 2014. Google Admits it's Overwhelmingly White and Male, *Huffington Post.* Retrieved June 1, 2014 from http://www.huffingtonpost.com/2014/05/28/google-google-diversity-white- male_n_5407338.html.

[21] US Department of Labor. 2012. *The African-American Labor Force in the Recovery.* Report. US Department of Labor. Retrieved June 1, 2014 from http://www.dol.gov/_sec/media/reports/BlackLaborForce/BlackLaborForce.pdf.

[22] Rosen, R. 2014.Why is the African American Unemployment Rate so High?, *The Atlantic,* June 12. Retrieved October 9, 2014 from http://www.theatlantic.com/business/archive/2014/06/why-is-the-African American-unemployment-rate-so-high/372667.

[23] Jones, J. and Schmitt, S. 2013. *Has Education Paid Off for African American Workers?* Report. Center for Economic and Policy Research, Washington DC. Retrieved October 9, 2014 from http://www.cepr.net/documents/publications/black-good-jobs-2013-06.pdf.

[24] Hargittai, E. 2002. Second Level Digital Divide: Differences in People's Online Skills,"*First Monday,* 7, 4. Retrieved October 9, 2014 from http://firstmonday.org/article/view/942/864.

[25] Hargittai, E. 2008. The Digital Reproduction of Inequality, in *Social Stratification: Class, Race, and Gender in Sociological Perspective*, David B. Grusky, Manwai C. Ku and Szonja Szelényi (Eds.), Boulder, Colo.: Westview Press, pp. 936– 944.

[26] Kvasny, L. 2006. The Cultural (Re)production of Digital Inequality, *Information, Communication and Society*, 9, 2, 160-181.

[27] DiMaggio, P. and Hargittai, E. 2001. From the Digital Divide to Digital Inequality: Studying Internet use as Penetration Increases, Working Paper #15, *Center for Arts and Cultural Policy Studies, Princeton University*. Retrieved October 9, 2014 from http://www.princeton.edu/~artspol/workpap15.html.

[28] Kvasny, L. and Keil, M. 2006. The Challenges of Redressing the Digital Divide, *Information Systems Journal,* 16, 1, 23-53.

[29] Smith, A. 2014. African Americans and Technology Use, *Pew Internet*. January 26. Retrieved June 1, 2014 from http://www.pewinternet.org/2014/01/06/african-americans-and-technology-use.

[30] Steyaert, J. 2002. Inequality and the Digital Divide: Myths and Realities. *Advocacy, Activism and the Internet,* Chicago: Lyceum Press, 199-211.

[31] Murdock, G., Hartmann, P., and Gray, P. 1992. Contextualizing Home Computing: Resources and Practices, in *Consuming Technologies,* E. Hirsch (Ed.), New York: Routledge, 146-160.

[32] Hargittai E. and Hinnant, A. 2008. Digital Inequality: Differences in Young Adults' Use of the Internet, *Communication Research*, 35, 5, 602–621.

[33] Hargittai, E. and Walejko, G. 2008. The Participation Divide: Content Creation and Sharing in the Digital Age, *Information, Community and Society,* 11, 2, 239-256.

[34] Lent, R.W., Brown, S.D., and Hackett, G. 1994. Toward a Unifying Social Cognitive Theory of Career and Academic Interest, Choice, and Performance, *Journal of Vocational Behavior*, 45, 79-122

[35] Owens, E. W., Shelton, A. J., Bloom, C. M., and Cavil, J. K. 2012. "The Significance of HBCUs to the Production of STEM Graduates: Answering the Call," *Educational Foundations*, 26, 33-47.

Does Competitor Grade Level Influence Perception of Cybersecurity Competition Design Gender Inclusiveness?

Jason M. Pittman
California State Polytechnic University,
Pomona
3801 West Temple Ave.
Pomona, CA 91768
+1(805)-907-5313
jmpittman@cpp.edu

ABSTRACT

Lack of gender diversity is a recognized issue within STEM. As a result, much effort has been invested in alternative means of recruitment and education. One example are cybersecurity competitions serving as popular training mechanisms. Yet, earlier research found that competitors perceive these competitions to be designed in a non-gender inclusive manner. The prior work did not consider potential biases in competitors however. Motivationally, future competition design may be misguided if competitors' perceptions were skewed due to exposure and social desirability. This led to the general question of whether grade level is related to identification of such competitions as non-gender inclusive in design. Accordingly, this study measured if U.S. collegiate upperclassmen and underclassmen participating in competitions are equally likely to identify cybersecurity competitions as non-gender inclusive. To that end, a chi-square statistic was used to compare the rates of identification of competition design gender inclusiveness amongst 104 cyber competitors. The results of the analysis indicated that upperclassmen are no more likely than underclassmen to identify a cybersecurity competition as non-gender inclusive. Thus, gender non-inclusiveness of competitions may be inherent in the design of such as opposed to a subjective experience of competitors.

Categories and Subject Descriptors

K.3.2 [**Computers and Education**]: Computer and Information Science Education – *Curriculum, Information systems education*

General Terms

Design, Security

Keywords

Cybersecurity, cybersecurity competitions, gender, gender inclusive, design, STEM

1. INTRODUCTION

Gender diversity and equality are of great interest in science, technology, engineering, and mathematics (STEM) education [12][24]. Effort has been made to build understanding of why female participation is disproportionately low in computing fields in general [26][27]. Other research has extended the gender equality investigation to include the STEM field of cybersecurity specifically [2][20]. Likewise, there has been recognition of limited gender diversity from non-academic sources. All [1] reported that some cybersecurity competitions focus on developing security knowledge in underrepresented groups such as women. In the same article [1], Skoch stated that CyberPatriot has, "...about 17 percent female representation, and our goal is to get to 30 percent within three years." (para 7).

Indeed, cybersecurity competitions are an area of high interest since competitions are increasingly used to recruit and educate students [8][11][15]. Many efforts are underway to expand cyber competitions in both scope and availability [17][19]. The expansion in scope is to facilitate a wider array of real world objectives. The expansion in availability is to increase the number of competitions annually as well as the number of participants engaging in each competition.

While research [4][7] has considered the overall design of cybersecurity competitions, there has been limited examination into whether those designs include gender equal design elements. Meanwhile, gender equal game design elements are well defined outside of the cybersecurity field [9][13][25][28]. These design elements fall into one of four categories.

Gender equal design elements can be categorized as role, incentive, scoring, and play strategy [14][22][25]. Role, in the context of a game, equates to a function of behavior such as (male) *do better than everyone* or (female) *help everyone*. With incentive, socialization and group learning in-game opportunities are markedly female while mastery and domination are definitively male. Further, how a game is scored can manifest a variety of manners but tends to isolate down to either zero-sum (male) or non-zero sum (female). These scoring dynamics may also be represented in discrete leader boards (e.g., first place, second place and so forth) that define player placement (male) or normalized scoring where no definitive player placement occurs (female). Moreover, play strategy tends to be expressed in within two modalities: trial-and-error (female) or defined repeatable processes (male).

Within cybersecurity competition literature, prior work [21] revealed that the same gender equal game design element categories map appropriately to how competition participants prefer to play. Further, the same study found that participants identified cybersecurity competitions as definitively *non-gender inclusive* in design [21]. Concurrently, the participants overwhelmingly identified cybersecurity competitions as *male-centric* [21]. While those results indicate a perception of cybersecurity competition design, such do not account for potential biases that might lead competition participants to view the design as non-gender inclusive. Although a variety of individual biases might contribute to competition participants' perceptions, this study focused on potential effects of exposure [5]. This focus was motivated by two observations. First, cyber competitors are increasingly exposed to calls-to-action for gender equality in the field and, therefore, may over-value what are considered desirable. Second, while the original study [21] examined (a) distribution of male and female competitors across U.S. collegiate grade levels and (b) number of competitions completed, that work did not consider how exposure to higher numbers of competitions might bias perception.

To that end, the purpose of this study was to measure if collegiate upperclassmen (juniors and seniors) and underclassmen (freshmen and sophomores) are equally likely to identify cybersecurity competitions as non-gender inclusive. Measuring the potential relationship between collegiate grade level and gender inclusiveness identification holds significance for cybersecurity competition designers and educators alike. The results may guide competition designers during future efforts in developing cybersecurity competitions (particularly as educational tools). Concurrently, educators will benefit as well since understanding how grade level is related or not related might influence non-competition based pedagogy.

2. METHOD
2.1 Participants
The total population size of collegiate cyber competitors in the United States is unknown. Although an estimate for the number of annual competitions is known, because team size varies from competition to competition, some competitions permit multiple teams per institution, the total numbers of teams vary between competitions, and some competitions do not prohibit external help, estimating a total population would be difficult. According to [10] when population size is unknown or difficult to estimate, setting the population to a high number is appropriate. Therefore, the total population for the purposes of this study was set at 10,000.

In comparison, as of 2014, there were approximately 200 NSA/DHS designated Centers of Academic Excellence (CAE) in Information Assurance Two Year, Information Assurance Education and Research, as well as Cyber Operations [6]. Further, according to the National Science Foundation [18], approximately 500,000 students earned an undergraduate degree in a science and engineering. Isolating computer science, the estimate drops to 38,500. Yet, based on observation, not all computer science students compete in cybersecurity competitions. Along those lines, participation in competitions from non-engineering disciplines is not at all uncommon.

More known is the structure of undergraduate academics in the US. Thus, a stratified sampling strategy was deemed appropriate due to the use of collegiate grade levels as a variable in the study and gender as a sample constraint [16][23]. Although gender was not included in this study as an operational variable, there was an importance to maintaining a representative sample. Estimates in existing STEM research [3] suggested that the ratio of women to men is approximately 20% and 80% respectively. Grade level, as an operational variable, was bounded to the U.S. definition of four-year college or university *freshmen*, *sophomore*, *junior*, and *senior*. Pilot testing found that use of credit hours completed to determine collegiate grade level resulted in confusion amongst study participants. Therefore, grade level was defined as the last full academic level completed with sample strata established in 25% segments. Twenty-five percent segments were utilized because such ensured that each grade level was uniformly represented and individual segments could be summed into the operational variable groups. Furthermore, as individual grade levels were recruited to the study, the ratio of female and male participants was maintained as well.

Participants were recruited through an email sent to a list of 300 college and university students from six schools in the United States. The host colleges and universities were selected from the list of CAEs known to have cybersecurity competitors. Prior discussion with faculty at those CAE resulted in approval to solicit competitors at those institutions. The email contained informed consent information and a hyperlink to a web-based questionnaire. Clicking on the hyperlink allowed participants to complete a mix of Likert items and multiple-choice question covering demographic information, identification of game elements in cybersecurity competitions, and perception of competition design pertaining to gender inclusiveness. The questionnaire did not collect personally identifiable information.

2.2 Sample

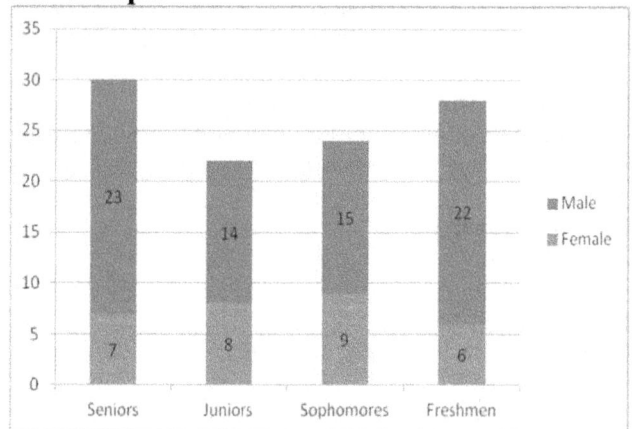

Figure 1. Distribution of sample by gender and grade level.

Based on the estimated population size, a total sample of 300 was desired with a stratification of (a) 20% female and 80% male and (b) 25% freshman, 25% sophomore, 25% junior, and 25% senior. One hundred and thirty individuals started the survey (i.e., finished at least one question) with 104 participants completing all questions. Such represents a 35% response completion rate.

The final sample size produced a 9.6% margin of error with a 90.4% confidence interval. The sample total included 31 participants identifying as female and 73 identifying as male. The grade level ratios (Figure 1) were 29% seniors, 21% juniors, 23% sophomores, and 27% freshmen. The geography of the sample included participants from six different states within the United States.

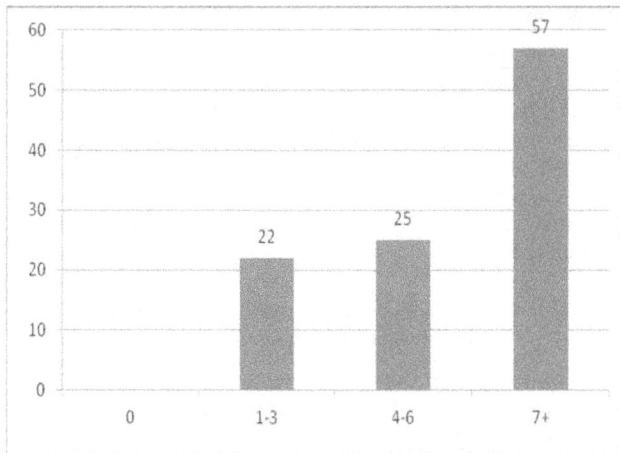

Figure 2. Distribution of the number of cybersecurity competitions completed by participants

Further, to ensure that study participants could accurately describe cybersecurity competitions, the questionnaire asked the population sample to identify the number of completed competitions. As seen in Figure 2, the majority of study participants identified as having completed between one and three competitions ($N=57$). Twenty-five participants identified as having completed between four and six competitions. The remaining participants ($N=22$) reported as having completed seven or more competitions.

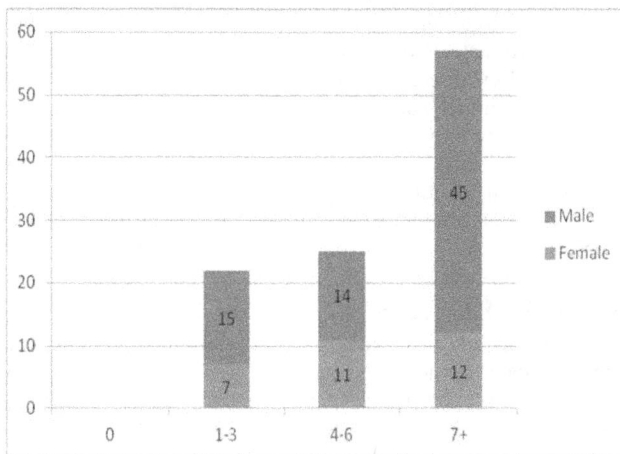

Figure 3. The number of cybersecurity competitions completed by participants by gender.

Additionally, this study examined distribution of gender, by grade level, across the number of competitions completed (Figure 3). Doing so established that both participant groups (female and male) were reasonably distributed over the number of competitions completed. Thus, data should be resilient to potential skewing due to, by gender, experiential difference.

Distribution of completed competitions across the U.S. collegiate grade levels was also identified (Figure 4). There was no stratification of the number of completed competitions prior to data collection because completed competitions did not serve as an operational variable. However, understanding the distribution of completed competitions across study participants was relevant when drawing conclusions based on results.

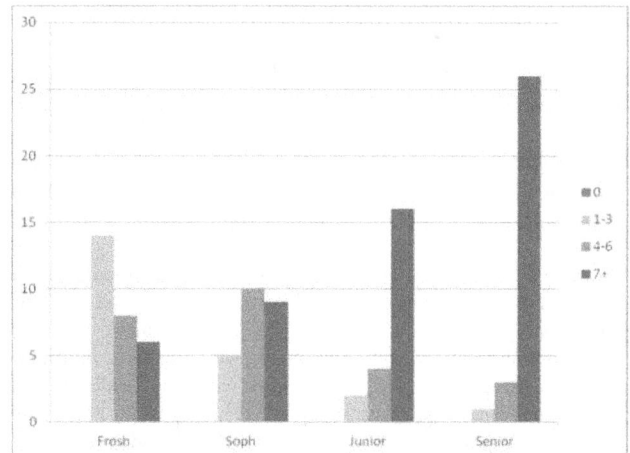

Figure 4. Distribution of the number of competitions completed by collegiate grade level

2.3 Research Design

This study included a single research question: are collegiate upperclassmen (juniors and seniors) more likely to identify cybersecurity competitions as non-gender inclusive than underclassmen (freshmen and sophomores). To answer these questions, a correlational research design was employed to test a single null hypothesis (Table 1). The premise of the research conjecture was that grade level would be directly related to identifying non-gender inclusiveness in cybersecurity competitions. Thus, if true, identification of non-gender inclusiveness may not be related to the design of the competition alone. On the other hand, if grade levels are not directly related to identification such may indicate that (a) competitions are indeed not designed to be gender inclusive; (b) there is some other variable related to non-gender inclusiveness not included in the scope of this research.

Table 1. Listing of the null and research hypotheses

Hypothesis Type	Hypothesis
Null	Upperclassmen are not more likely than underclassmen to identify cybersecurity competitions as non-gender inclusive.
Research	Upperclassmen are more likely than underclassmen to identify cybersecurity competitions as non-gender inclusive.

The study included one independent variables and one dependent variable. Participant grade level served as the independent variable. The dependent variable was identification of the gender-inclusiveness of cybersecurity competition design.

2.3.1 Instrumentation

Data were collected using a web-based questionnaire. The questionnaire consisted of five multiple-choice questions and a

Likert scale comprised of six items. The Likert scale questions consisted of five options: Strongly Agree, Agree, Neutral, Disagree, and Strongly Disagree. These options were nominally mapped to values of one, two, three, four, and five respectively. Multiple-choice questions included between two and six responses. Accordingly, nominally mapped values for the multiple choice responses ranged from one to six (relative to the total response size). All questions were bounded and descriptive in nature.

An IRB deemed the instrument ethical and sound. Participant consent was implied. Anonymity of participants was maintained at all times as no personally identifiable information was collected. Furthermore, participants had the ability to opt-out of the questionnaire at any time. Participants were numerically coded (e.g., P1, P2 and so forth) to aid in data analysis.

Reliability and validity of the instrument were affirmed through pilot testing. Ten cyber competition participants were selected for pilot testing. Pilot participants provided feedback on the instrument design, in particular clarity of questions, question order and grouping, as well as question wording. Feedback was incorporated into the instrument before release to the study sample participants. Pilot data were used to validate the data analysis procedures. However, data from pilot participants were not included in the final data set.

3. RESULTS

Based on the research design and instrumentation, data were considered nominal. Data analysis consisted tabulating data into a contingency table and then computing the chi-square test statistic .including *degrees of freedom* and a *p* value). An alpha level of five percent was selected as is customary. Data analysis was conducted using the *R* statistical computing language.

Table 2. Contingency table of grade levels and identification of gender inclusiveness

Grade Level	Identification of gender inclusiveness		
	Non-inclusive	Inclusive	Total
Senior	22	8	30
Junior	16	6	22
Soph	14	10	24
Frosh	15	13	28
Column Total	67	37	104

Data tabulation consisted of four steps. The research instrument collected data that indicated how individual participants identified cybersecurity competitions (i.e., as gender inclusive or non-gender inclusive). With grade level per participant appended, these data were entered into a simple matrix and the number of discrete identifications counted. The next sub-tabulation step summed participant gender inclusiveness counts into a four by two matrix according to grade level. Thus, all freshmen-inclusive results were tabulated, all freshmen-non-inclusive, all sophomores and so on (Table 2). The third step summed grade levels into the final variable groupings. Freshmen and sophomore frequencies were summed to underclassmen. Junior and senior counts were summed to upperclassmen (Table 3).

Table 3. Contingency table of grouped grade level and identification of gender inclusiveness.

Grade Level	Identification of Gender Inclusiveness		
	Non-Inclusive	Inclusive	Total
Upperclassmen	38	14	52
Underclassmen	29	23	52
Column Total	67	37	104

The final data analysis step was to execute the chi-square statistic and test our null hypothesis. The output of this step (Table 4) consisted of the chi-square value and a *p* value. Additionally, *degrees of freedom* was computed. The chi-square value was then compared to a chi-square distribution table to check the probability level.

Table 4. Results from the test statistic showing level of significance and chi-square value.

Statistic	df	Chi-square value	*p* value
Chi-square	1	3.4	0.065
Note: significant at p < 0.05			

These data indicated that there was no statistically significant difference in the identification of non-inclusive cybersecurity competition design between upperclassmen and underclassmen ($p > 0.05$). Meaning, the variables of grade level and identification of cybersecurity competition gender inclusive design were not related. Thus, there was no basis for rejection of the null hypothesis.

4. LIMITATIONS

This study had certain limitations. The study considered U.S. collegiate cybersecurity competitors only. This limitation was necessary due to restrictions in travel and access to a non-U.S. population. Moreover, the foundational study [21] was bounded to the United States. Comparison to or repetition of the study with international cybersecurity competitors of equivalent grade level would have further added to the conclusions of this study. As well, this study only considered a narrow range of biases. The study did not include controls for perception skewing due to sexism, sexual identity or any form of socioeconomic factors. Thus, the results are limited to cognitive gender identification and simple biases related to exposure or social desirability.

5. CONCLUSION

The purpose of this study was to measure if collegiate upperclassmen (juniors and seniors) were more likely than underclassmen (freshmen and sophomores) to identify cybersecurity competitions as non-gender inclusive. To affect this purpose, a questionnaire was administered to 104 study participants. The study included a single research question along with a pair of hypotheses (i.e., null and research). Data were analyzed using a chi-square statistic within the scope of a correlational research design. Results indicated that collegiate upperclassmen are no more likely than underclassmen to identify cybersecurity competitions are non-gender inclusive. There were several conclusions and ideas for future work based on these results.

Foremost, the results support the conclusion that collegiate grade level is not related to identifying cybersecurity competitions as non-gender inclusive. This means that competitors view competitions as non-gender inclusive irrespective of grade levels. The conclusion is significant as designers may begin to incorporate gender inclusive elements into competitions without concern that such elements are dependent upon educational level. Further, competitions designed with gender inclusive principles may be equally beneficial to all grade levels rather than favoring upperclassmen.

Concurrently, the results do not support any causative conclusions. While there may not be a relationship between grade level and identification, there may be other, unmeasured variables that are dependent and either individually or collectively lead to competitors identifying competitions are non-gender inclusive. The operational assumption is that these heretofore unmeasured variables are in fact game design elements. Even as an assumption though, competition designers and educators may benefit as there is now a reduced probability space of characteristics that can lead to a competitions being identified as non-gender inclusive.

Tangentially, the demographics analyzed in this study show that cybersecurity competitions are a force that reach across collegiate grade levels and participant genders. While not a direct mark of significance to competition developers and educators using competitions, the demographics may demonstrate a basis for the continued investment of time, labor and resources into cybersecurity competitions.

6. FUTURE WORK

Further study into the gender equal design of cybersecurity competitions is necessary. While the results of this study indicate that grade level is not related to identifying competitions as non-gender inclusive, and prior work [21] established that female and male competitors overwhelmingly describe competitions as non-gender inclusive, there are substantial areas of cybersecurity competition design left to investigate.

A rationale next step would be to develop a model to guide gender inclusive development of cybersecurity competitions. The fields of video game design and software development may be fertile sources for such a model. Additionally, focus groups comprised of competitors and designers may generate data that is additive to the literature present in these other fields. The resultant model would be exploratory in nature and constructed on a theoretical basis.

On an applied basis, the field may benefit from examining specific design elements and the potential mappings between gender inclusive game design principles and existing cybersecurity competitions. Such could be achieved independent from, or subsequently to, development of the exploratory model. The output of such research would contribute to an overall understanding if the presence of specific design elements (or lack thereof) affect the gender inclusiveness of cybersecurity competitions. Furthermore, work could begin on incorporating relevant and necessary gender inclusive elements into active cybersecurity competitions.

7. REFERENCES

[1] All, A. (2014, November 14). Programs aim to fill cybersecurity skills gap. *eSecurity Planet*. Retrieved from http://www.esecurityplanet.com/network-security/programs-aim-to-fill-cybersecurity-skills-gap.html

[2] Bagchi-sen, S., Rao, H. R., Upadhyaya, S.J., & Sangmi, C. (2010). Women in Cybersecurity: A Study of Career Advancement. *IT Professional*, 12(1). 24-31. doi: 10.1109/MITP.2010.39

[3] Beede, D., Julian, T., Langdon, D., McKittrick, G., Khan, B., & Doms, M. (2011). Women in STEM: A gender gap to innovation. ESA Issue Brief 04-11.

[4] Boe, B., Cavallaro, L., Cavedon, L., Childers, N., Cova, M., Egele, M., & Vigna, G. (2010). Organizing large scale hacking competitions. In *Detection of intrusions and malware, and vulnerability assessment 7th International Conference, DIMVA 2010, Bonn, Germany, July 8-9, 2010. Proceedings*. Berlin Heidelberg: Springer-Verlag.

[5] Bornstein, Robert F.; Crave-Lemley, Catherine (2004). "Mere exposure effect". In Pohl, Rüdiger F. *Cognitive Illusions: A Handbook on Fallacies and Biases in Thinking, Judgement and Memory*. Hove, UK: Psychology Press. pp. 215–234.

[6] Centers of Academic Excellence Institutions. (n.d.). Retrieved March 24, 2015, from https://www.nsa.gov/ia/academic_outreach/nat_cae/institutions.shtml

[7] Chapman, P., Brumley, D. (2013). picoCTF: Teaching 10,000 high school students to hack. Retrieved from http://www.cs.cmu.edu/~pmchapma/docs/picoctf.pdf

[8] Cheung, R. S., Cohen, J. P., Lo, H. Z. & Elia, F. (n.d.) Effectiveness of cybersecurity competitions. Presented at *The 2012 International Conference on Security and Management*. Retrieved from http://josephpcohen.com/papers/seccomp.pdf

[9] Cooke, Jedeikin, & Lepar (). MyWord: Testing female preferred gaming criteria (Technical Report). Retrieved from http://pubs.cs.uct.ac.za/archive/00000167/01/article.pdf

[10] Creswell, J. (2012). *Educational research : planning, conducting, and evaluating quantitative and qualitative research*. Boston: Pearson.

[11] Gavas, E., Memon, N., & Britton, D. (2012). Winning cybersecurity one challenge at a time. *Security & Privacy*, 10(4). 75-79. doi: 10.1109/MSP.2012.112

[12] Hill, C., Corbett, & St. Rose, A. (2010). Why so Few? Women in Science, Technology, Engineering , and Mathematics (Research Report). Retrieved from http://www.aauw.org/files/2013/02/Why-So-Few-Women-in-Science-Technology-Engineering-and-Mathematics.pdf

[13] Ibrahim, Wills, & Gilbert (2010). Degendering games: Towards a gender inclusive framework for games. Presented at *IADIS International Conference: Games and Entertainment Technologies part of the IADIS Multiconference on Computer Science & Information Systems (MCCSIS 2010)*.

[14] Innholt, K. (2009). *Designing videogames for women* (Master's thesis). Retrieved from

https://www.duo.uio.no/bitstream/handle/10852/10115/Innh olt.pdf?sequence=1&isAllowed=y

[15] Koch, S., Schneider, J., & Nordholz, J. (2012). Disturbed playing: Another kind of educational security games. In *Proceedings of the 5th USENIX Conference on Cyber Security Experimentation and Test*. USENIX Assoc., Berkeley, CA, USA.

[16] Lohr, S. (2010). *Sampling : design and analysis*. Boston, Mass: Brooks/Cole.

[17] Manson, D. (2013). National cybersecurity sports federation. Presented at *NIST NICE Workshop 2013*. Gaithersburg, MD.

[18] National Science Foundation (2012). *Science and engineering indicators 2012*. Retrieved from http://www.nsf.gov/statistics/seind12/c2/c2s2.htm

[19] Novak, H, Likarish, D. M., & Moore, E. (2013). Developing cyber competition infrastructure using the SCRUM framework. In Dodge, R. and Futcher, L. (Eds), *Information assurance and security education and training 8th IFIP WG 11.8 World Conference on Information Security Education, WISE 8, Auckland, New Zealand, July 8-10, 2013, proceedings, WISE 7, Lucerne, Switzerland, June 9-10, 2011 and WISE 6, Bento Gonçalves, RS, Brazil, July 27-31, 2009, revised selected papers*. Berlin New York: Springer.

[20] Outlay, C., Ambrose, P., & Chenoweth, J. (2012). Overcoming gender stereotype entry barriers to computing degree programs: the cybergirlz program experience. *Journal of Computing Sciences in Colleges, 28*(1). 33-38. Retrieved from http://dl.acm.org/citation.cfm?id=2379703.2379710

[21] Pittman, J. (2013). Attitudes on the gender equal design of collegiate cybersecurity competitions. Presented at the *NIST NICE Workshop 2013*. Gaithersburg, MD.

[22] Ray, S. (2004). *Gender inclusive game design expanding the market*. Hingham, Mass: Charles River Media.

[23] Salkind, N. (2010). *Encyclopedia of research design*. Thousand Oaks, Calif: Sage.

[24] Singh, K., Allen, K. R., Scheckler, R., & Darlington, L. (2007). Women in computer-related majors: A critical synthesis of research and theory from 1994 to 2005. *Review of Educational Research, 77*(4), 500-533.

[25] Thomas, A., & Walkerdine, V. (2000). Girls and computer games. Presented at the *4th European Feminist Research Conference: Body gender subjectivity crossing disciplinary and institutional borders*. Bologna Italy.

[26] Varma, R. (2009). Gender differences in factors in influencing students towards computing. *Computer Science Education, 19*(1). 37-49. Retrieved from http://www.unm.edu/~varma/print/CSE_Computer%20Intere st.pdf

[27] Varma, R. (2010). Why so few women enroll in computing? Gender and ethnic difference in students' perception. *Computer Science Education, 20*(4). 301-316. Retrieved from https://www.unm.edu/~varma/print/CSE_Few%20Women.p df

[28] Yatim, M.H.M., Nacke, L., & Masuch, M. (2006). Improving game design by understanding the gender differences: The cognitive approach. In *Proceedings of the International Conference on Gender in Educational Games and Gender Sensitive Approaches to E-Learning 2006*. Donau University Krems: Austria.

Characterizing the Traits of Top-Performing Security Personnel

Jordan Shropshire
University of South Alabama
Mobile, Alabama
jshropshire@southalabama.edu

Art Gowan
James Madison University
Harrisonburg, VA
gowanja@jmu.edu

ABSTRACT
Organizational information security is a talent-centric proposition. Information assurance is a product of the combined expertise, attention-to-detail, and creativity of an information security team. A competitive edge can be obtained by hiring the top information security professionals. Therefore, identifying the right people is a mission-critical task. To assist in the candidate selection process, this research analyzes the enduring traits of top security performers. Specifically, it evaluates the Big Five Model of personality and the Six Workplace Values. In a laboratory study, 62 undergraduates majoring in information assurance completed a series of simulations which assessed their ability to solve various information security problems. The characteristics of top information security performers were contrasted against the rest of the cohort. In terms of personality, the top performers have high levels of conscientiousness and openness. With respect to workplace values, the top performers have a stronger preference for theoretical endeavors such as the pursuit of truth.

Categories and Subject Descriptors
K.6.5 [**Security and Protection**]: Unauthorized access – *management of computing and information systems*

General Terms
Security

Keywords
Security, performance, personality, employee attitudes.

1. INTRODUCTION
Information security professionals are a critical talent group with disproportionate influence on global economic activities [1]. A team of information security professionals who proactively secure information resources and respond to incidents provides a decisive business advantage [2]. Developing platforms for new ecosystems, switching technologies, retiring legacy systems and operating ahead of the curve is less risky for organizations with advanced in-house security capabilities. These firms have the assurance that if a zero day exploit is uncovered, their information security team will rapidly render a solution. This translates into first-mover advantage, lower overhead costs, reduced stagnation, increased flexibility, and an entrepreneurial mindset [3]. Therefore, attracting and hiring the best candidates for

information security positions is a primary concern among chief information security officers and other business executives.

The purpose of this research is to identify the enduring characteristics of top information security performers. Specifically, it focuses on personality traits and workplace values. These characteristics were selected because they have been identified as significant determinants of employee performance [4]. Further, personality and values are long-lasting characteristics of individuals. In early research they were found to be useful predictors of long-term employee performance [5]. This research conceptualizes personality using the big five model, which includes openness, agreeableness, conscientiousness, neuroticism, and extraversion. It conceptualizes workplace values and motivation using the six workplace values. This abstraction includes theoretical, utilitarian, social, individualistic, aesthetic, and traditional values as discrete constructs.

The personalities and values of top performing information security professionals are expected to differ from those of mediocre performers. Specifically, the personalities of top performers are expected to be characterized by high levels of conscientiousness and openness. Further, top performers are expected to value economic and theoretical pursuits. These hypotheses are evaluated using a laboratory study. Some 61 subjects completed a series of information security simulations. The simulations are used to assess subjects' abilities to detect and respond to security problems. Subjects also complete various psychological inventories. This information is used to identify high achievers and to enumerate their defining characteristics.

The results of this research provide useful indicators of top information security performers. Organizations seeking to hire information security professionals can use this information to inform their hiring process and seek out candidates that will provide the best value over the long run. The remainder of this manuscript is organized as follows: The following section outlines the big five model of personality. Section three covers workplace values. It delineates the components of the six workplace values model. Section four conceptualizes the hypotheses. Section five covers the research methods. It describes the subjects, measures, and procedures. Section six describes the analysis. Section seven interprets the results in terms of the research hypotheses. Finally, section eight provides conclusions.

2. PERSONALITY
Of the many characteristics of employees, personality has long ranked among the most considered [4]. Personality's appeal is based on the long-term applicability of its constructs. Compared with attitudes and emotions, personality traits are considered to be permanent psychological features. They are slow to change [6]. Thus, they are often used for predicting individual temperament and disposition well into the future. There are five broad

Permission to make digital or hard copies of all or part of this work for personal or classroom use is granted without fee provided that copies are not made or distributed for profit or commercial advantage and that copies bear this notice and the full citation on the first page. To copy otherwise, or republish, to post on servers or to redistribute to lists, requires prior specific permission and/or a fee.
SIGMIS'15, June 4–6, 2015, Newport Beach, CA, USA.
Copyright 2015 ACM 1-58113-000-0/00/0010 …$15.00.
http://dx.doi.org/10.1145/2751957.2751971

dimensions of personality traits [7]. They are: openness, conscientiousness, extraversion, agreeableness, and neuroticism. Together, these traits provide comprehensive framework of non-overlapping elements. The big five model is commonly measured using personality questionnaires. The five personality dimensions have been independently confirmed by several sets of researchers. Occasionally, these traits are called the Big Five Model or the Five Factor Model. However, it should be noted that the big five is not theoretically derived but was discovered through empirical analysis.

The first dimension is openness to experience. This is a general appreciation for creative works, emotion, adventure, new ideas, imagination, and variety of experience [8]. Those who are open to experience are intellectually curious, receptive to emotion, sensitive to aesthetics, and willing to try new things. One study found that there is a connection between politically-liberal worldviews and openness to experience, however this finding has not been confirmed by other researchers [9].

The second personality dimension is conscientiousness. This is a tendency to show self-discipline, act dutifully, and aim for achievement against common measures of social conformity [5]. Conscientiousness is often considered a general predictor of job performance, while the other big five traits predict job performance in specific fields [10]. It is related to things such as achievement, perseverance, organization, and responsibility [11]. It governs the way in which people control, regulate, and direct their impulses.

The third dimension is extraversion. Extraverts enjoy talking, interacting with others, and are high-energy. They are the life of the party, enjoy being the center of attention, feel comfortable around people, easily start conversation, and like to mingle at parties. Extraverts often excel at sales, marketing, and communications positions [12]. Individuals high in extraversion prefer to do more things with more people than focus deeply on one thing. It includes traits such as sociability, activity, assertiveness, and positive emotionality. Extraversion is often associated with leadership behavior.

The fourth dimension is agreeableness. This dimension indicates a disposition to help others. It is another interpersonal construct. It reflects a general concern for social harmony. Agreeable individuals value group cohesion and getting along with others [9]. They are considered kind, generous, considerate, trusting, helpful, and willing to compromise in their interests. Agreeableness was been found to predict transformational leadership skills, good teamwork, and pro-social behavior [11].

The fifth dimension is neuroticism. This trait is characterized by a tendency to experience negative emotions such as anger, anxiety, vulnerability and depression [13]. It may also be called emotional instability. This dimension tends to be viewed negatively and is associated with worry, self-pity, self-consciousness, emotional outbursts, and vulnerabilities. Those who score high in neuroticism are emotionally reactive and vulnerable to stress [5].

3. WORKPLACE VALUES

The link between workplace values and employee performance has been studied repeatedly over the past decades [14]. Although numerous value measures have been developed over the years, most trace back to a model developed over 80 years ago [15]. The model holds that the essence of a person is best captured by understanding the individual's value-philosophy. It purports six types of ideals: theoretical, economic, political,

aesthetic, social, and religious [16]. Operationally, these six values are measured using a forced choice among pairs and quartets of choices. The values are presented in scenarios which are meant to represent core human experiences like choosing spouses and careers. This measure of human condition is valuable because of its relative permanence. People are slow to change their values. Thus, the values for which an employee is hired will be relevant long after his or her attitudes change [17].

The first of the six values is theoretical. It is defined as an interest in the discovery of truth through reasoning and systematic thinking. The theoretical person is primarily interested in cognitive pursuits. Those who value truth above all make excellent researchers, scientists, analysts, and health care providers [18]. The second value is economic. It is classified as an interest in usefulness and practicality. It includes the accumulation of wealth. The economic person is most focused on that which has utility. These persons are practical and are often successful at business [19]. The third value is aesthetic. It derives from interest in beauty, form, and artistic harmony. The aesthetic person places highest value on form and harmony. These persons believe life is a series of events that are to be enjoyed for their own sake [20].

The fourth value is social. It is described as an interest in people and human relationships. The social person seeks love and most values relationships with other people. Individual with social values are strong teammates. They are willing to sacrifice to ensure the success of the organization or the group [21]. The fifth value is political. It is defined as an interest in gaining power and influencing other people. The political person's dominant drive is power. These individuals excel at convincing others to act or behave in such a way that supports their own motives [14]. The sixth value is religious. It is conceptualized as an interest in unity and understanding the cosmos as a whole. Religious persons place the highest value on unity. They seek to understand and experience the world as a unified whole.

4. HYPOTHESES

Given that the purpose of this research is to identify the defining characteristics of top performing information security personnel, this section proffers four hypotheses. With respect to personality, it is predicted that the top InfoSec workers will have higher levels of conscientiousness and openness. In terms of values, the top information security performers are presumed to place greater emphasis on theoretical and economic values.

In general, high levels of conscientiousness are associated with better on-the-job performance. Conscientious employees have greater attention to deal, do not accept substandard work, and rarely overlook or ignore errors [22]. These attributes are critical for information security professionals, who operated in a detail-oriented field [23]. These workers must consider multitudes of technical specifications when making decisions. A conscientious information security professional will check and confirm facts before modifying systems and settings. Thus:

H1: The top information security performers will have higher levels of conscientiousness.

Beyond conscientiousness, it is expected that top performers will also report higher levels of openness. People who are open to new experience are generally more creative, imaginative, and willing to think outside the box [12]. These are important traits for information security professionals because they must think like hackers in order to anticipate potential attacks. System weaknesses are often observed by testing and manipulating variables such communication streams, files, data, and packets

[1]. Information security professionals must not only understand the inner workings of their respective systems but also be able to view them through the eyes of a hacker [24]. Therefore, the following hypothesis is offered:

H2: The top information security performers will have higher levels of openness.

In terms of work values, it is assumed that the top information security professionals place a greater emphasis on theoretical ideals. Previous research suggests that this group will be interested in the pursuit of truth. Their cognitive interests will lead to experimentation, testing, learning, and new perspectives on system vulnerabilities [16]. These are important qualities for information security professionals, because they lead to the identification of zero-day threats and previously-unidentified vulnerabilities [10]. Thus, the following hypothesis is extended:

H3: The top information security performers will place greater emphasis on theoretical values.

Finally, this research holds that the top information security performers will place greater emphasis on economic values. An information security analyst may multiple days or even weeks auditing new software for potentially exploitable weaknesses [18]. It becomes easy to lose track on the main goals and pursue less critical or non-essential endeavors. Previous studies report that analysts and researchers who are focus on abstract goals for long periods of time are motivated by extrinsic factors [22]. Therefore, a final hypothesis is presented:

H4: The top information security performers will place greater emphasis on economic values.

5. METHODS

In order to evaluate the proposed hypotheses, a laboratory style-test was performed. The purpose of the test was to identify the top performers in a cohort of information security workers and allow for a comparison of top performers' personality traits and values against those of less impressive workers.

5.1 Subjects

In order to control for factors such as age, prior experience, and education, a homogenous sample was constructed. The sample consisted of undergraduate students. At the time of the study, the subjects had completed their third year in an information technology degree program. These individuals had already taken courses in system security, and network assurance. This provided hands-on experience with enterprise-grade hardware, software, and systems. Thus, although the subjects lacked long-term information security work experience, they had the necessary technical training to perform entry-level work. Some 77 subjects were recruited in-class. Of these, 61 subjects attended the testing session, performed the evaluations, and completed the survey.

5.2 Measures

In order to measure candidates' workplace values, a cohesive new measure was implemented [25]. This pen and paper measure contained 45 items. This metric yields 120 scores, 20 from each value domain. The first 30 items are couplets while the last 15 items are quartets. Mean scores for all six domains are computed. A higher mean score is indicative of a stronger value preference. This measure was designed to be completed in 20 minutes. The five personality traits were operationalized using a shortened version of the original NEO inventory developed by Costa and McCrae [26]. This measurement consisted of 60 items, 12 for each domain. This instrument was designed to be completed in 15 minutes.

5.3 Procedure

In order to test the proposed hypotheses, it is necessary to identify the top information security performers. Because long term performance evaluations aren't feasible, a series of three simulations were conducted in order to gauge subjects' responses. The simulations revolved around activities which an entry-level information security professional could reasonably be expected to perform. Each involved identifying a potential vulnerability and applying an appropriate remedy. The simulations were performed on virtualized servers and overlay networks – infrastructure comparable with cloud computing systems. Each scenario was designed to incorporate a single vulnerability and had one clear solution. The study used three different computing ecosystems (i.e. Ubuntu Server, Windows Server 2012, and Cisco IOS) to create a level basis for comparison. For each scenario, subjects were judged according to how long it took to identify the security problem and implement a feasible solution. The time to complete each scenario was summed into a composite measure for each subjected. Those with shorter times are considered better performers. Time is considered to be an essential element of incident response. A rapid recovery minimizes exposure and provides a shorter path to back to normal operations. After completing the security simulations, subjects were also asked to complete pen-and-paper questionnaires containing the personality and values measures and provide demographic information.

6. ANALYSIS

On completion of the tests, all data was inputted into spreadsheet software for further analysis. Demographic data is depicted in Table 1. Individuals' survey responses were matched with their scores from the simulations. The 61 subjects were sorted according to their composite performance measures. The top information security performers were defined as individuals with the lowest composite time metrics. This category was restricted to the 1/3 lowest scores. This demarcation was based a previous study in which the classification of "top employees" were limited as a third of the workers in any given organization [27].

Table 1: Demographic Data		
Parameter	**Summary**	**Value**
	Mean	21.4
Age (years)	Median	21
	Range	20-22
	Male	57
Gender	Female	3
	Unreported	1
	Caucasian	49
	Black	8
Ethnicity	Hispanic	2
	Asian	1
	Other	1

The personality and values attributes of top information security performers were compared against the rest of the sample (see Tables 2 for personality and Table 3 for values). For each personality dimension and workplace value, a t-test of significant differences was performed. The purpose of this test is to compare and contrast tope information security performers with regular information security performers on an item-by-item basis.

Table 2: Mean Personality Dimension Scores

	Top Performers		Rest of Cohort	
	Mean	Std. Dev.	Mean	Std. Dev.
Openness	47.88	8.35	44.55	7.92
Conscientiousness	51.20	7.48	48.90	7.16
Extraversion	39.92	6.49	41.27	6.98
Agreeableness	36.59	8.03	36.68	7.45
Neuroticism	28.73	7.24	29.74	6.01

Table 3: Mean Workplace Value Scores

	Top Performers		Rest of Cohort	
	Mean	Std. Dev.	Mean	Std. Dev.
Theoretical	41.79	7.39	38.03	6.38
Economic	48.38	6.65	47.98	7.05
Social	42.67	5.78	44.98	7.17
Political	38.73	6.98	39.97	6.94
Aesthetic	37.98	7.04	38.69	5.80
Religious	36.31	5.49	39.42	6.17

7. RESULTS

The purpose of this research is to isolate top information security performers and identify traits which can be used to distinguish them from regular information security workers. Permanent traits are of interest because they will be valid over long periods of time. Thus, this research focused on personality and workplace values. With respect to personality, it was predicted that top performers will exhibit higher levels of conscientiousness and openness. In terms of workplace values, it is expected that top performers will place a greater emphasis on theoretical and economic ideals. For testing, a series of information security simulations was conducted in order to identify individuals who are better at identifying and reacting to vulnerabilities. These individuals are now empirically compared against regular information security workers.

With respect to the first hypothesis, H1, it was found that top performers have significantly higher levels of conscientiousness. This finding confirms early expectations that close attention to detail will be an important factor in auditing systems. The second hypothesis, H2, presumed that top information security performers will report higher levels of openness. The results suggest that these individuals have significantly higher levels of openness. The third hypothesis, H3, holds that the best InfoSec professionals will place a greater emphasis on theoretical values. The results confirm this expectation. Top performers are interested in the pursuit of truth. This is an asset because it encourages more in-depth analysis. Finally, the fourth hypothesis (H4) assumes that top information security professionals will place a greater emphasis on economic values. This hypothesis was based on the assumption that top workers will be influenced by economic incentives and rewards. However, the results indicate

that this is not the case. It appears that information security workers do not differ according to their interest in economic values.

Table 4: Results of Hypothesis Testing

	Description	Sig.	Result
H1	Top performers will have higher levels of conscientiousness	.027	Supported
H2	Top performers will have higher levels of openness	.041	Supported
H3	Top performers will place greater emphasis on theoretical values	.046	Supported
H4	Top performers will place greater emphasis on economic values	.114	Not supported

8. CONCLUSION

With the rise in global hacking teams and increases in major security breaches, organizations cannot ignore the need for better information system security. Executives have placed a premium on securing the most talented information security professionals. However, identification of the top talent can be difficult. Individuals with equivalent technical skills may have vastly different work ethics, perspectives, and goals. To assist in the hiring process, this research explored the characteristics of top information security performers. It focused on personality and workplace values because these attributes are likely to endure over the course of an individual's employment. To distinguish between top and average information security performers, this research conducted a laboratory study. Individuals completed a series of simulated security activities such as event response. Participants also completed questionnaires which assessed their personality traits and workplace values. The results of the study indicate that the top performers have higher levels of conscientiousness and openness to experience and place a premium on theoretical pursuits. Given that the sample consisted of 62 undergraduates, the results cannot be considered definitive. Studies which integrate supervisors' ratings of individual performance would provide a more authoritative study. However, the early results point to an important finding: long-term attributes such as personality and workplace values make useful predictors of future performance.

9. REFERENCES

[1] R. Baskerville, P. Spagnoletti, and J. Kim, "Incident-centered information security: Managing a strategic balance between prevention and response," Information & Management, vol. 51, pp. 138-151, 2014.

[2] R. Ruefle, A. Dorofee, D. Mundie, A. Householder, M. Murray, and S. Perl, "Computer Security Incident Response Team Development and Evolution," IEEE Security & Privacy, vol. 12, pp. 16-26, 2014.

[3] I. Tøndela, M. Lineb, and M. Jaatun, "Information security incident management: Current practice as reported in the literature," Computers & Security, vol. 45, pp. 42-57, 2014.

[4] T. Judge, C. Higgins, C. Thoresen, and M. Barrick, "The Big Five Personality Traits, General Mental Ability, and Career Success Across the Life Span," Personnel Psychology, vol. 52, pp. 621-652, 1999.

[5] [M. Mount, M. Barrick, and G. Stewart, "Five-Factor Model of personality and Performance in Jobs Involving Interpersonal Interactions," Human Performance, vol. 11, pp. 145-165, 1998.

[6] M. Barrick, M. Mount, and T. Judge, "Personality and Performance at the Beginning of the New Millennium: What Do We Know and Where Do We Go Next?," International Journal of Selection and Assessment, vol. 9, pp. 9-30, 2001.

[7] L. Goldberg, "An alternative "description of personality": The Big-Five factor structure," Journal of Personality and Social Psychology, vol. 59, pp. 1216-1229, 1990.

[8] R. McCrae and P. Costa, "Validation of the five-factor model of personality across instruments and observers," Journal of Personality and Social Psychology, vol. 52, pp. 81-90, 1987.

[9] J. Salgado, "The five factor model of personality and job performance in the European Community," Journal of Applied Psychology, vol. 82, pp. 30-43, 1997.

[10] S. Seibert and M. Kraimer, "The Five-Factor Model of Personality and Career Success," Journal of Vocational Behavior, vol. 58, pp. 1-21, 2001.

[11] R. McCrae and O. John, "An Introduction to the Five-Factor Model and Its Applications," Journal of Personality, vol. 60, pp. 175-215, 1992.

[12] P. Heslin, "Conceptualizing and evaluating career success," Journal of Organizational Behavior, vol. 26, pp. 113-136, 2005.

[13] S. Hogan and L. Coote, "Organizational culture, innovation, and performance: A test of Schein's model," Journal of Business Research, vol. 67, pp. 1609-1621, 2014.

[14] R. Kolodinsky, R. Giacalone, and C. Jurkiewicz, "Workplace Values and Outcomes: Exploring Personal, Organizational, and Interactive Workplace Spirituality," Journal of Business Ethics, vol. 81, pp. 465-480, 2008.

[15] P. Vernon and G. Allport, "A test for personal values," The Journal of Abnormal and Social Psychology, vol. 26, pp. 231-248, 1931.

[16] J. Eccles and A. Wigfied, "Motivational Beliefs, Values, and Goals," Annual Review of Psychology, vol. 53, pp. 109-132, 2002.

[17] A. Geare, F. Edgar, and I. McAndrew, "Workplace values and beliefs: an empirical study of ideology, high commitment management and unionisation," The International Journal of Human Resource vol. 20, pp. 1146-1171, 2009.

[18] C. Jurkiewicz and R. Giacalone, "A Values Framework for Measuring the Impact of Workplace Spirituality on Organizational Performance," Journal of Business Ethics, vol. 49, pp. 129-142, 2004.

[19] S. Goodman and D. Svyantek, "Person–Organization Fit and Contextual Performance: Do Shared Values Matter," Journal of Vocational Behavior, vol. 55, pp. 254-275, 1999.

[20] P. van Beurdan and T. Gossling, "The Worth of Values – A Literature Review on the Relation Between Corporate Social and Financial Performance," Journal of Business Ethics, vol. 82, pp. 407-424, 2008.

[21] J. Milliman, A. Czaplewski, and J. Ferguson, "Workplace spirituality and employee work attitudes: An exploratory empirical assessment," Journal of Organizational Change Management, vol. 16, pp. 426-447, 1988.

[22] B. Horne, "On Computer Security Incident Response Teams," IEEE Security & Privacy, vol. 12, pp. 13-15, 2014.

[23] M. Whitman, "Enemy at the gate: threats to information security," Communications of the ACM, vol. 46, pp. 91-95, 2003.

[24] C. Vroom and R. von Solms, "Towards information security behavioural compliance," Computers & Security, vol. 23, pp. 191-198, 2004.

[25] R. Kopelman, J. Rovenpor, and M. Guan, "The Study of Values: Construction of the fourth edition," Journal of Vocational Behavior, vol. 62, pp. 203-220, 2003.

[26] R. McCrae and P. Costa, "A contemplated revision of the NEO Five-Factor Inventory," Personality and Individual Differences, vol. 36, pp. 587-597, 2004.

[27] T. Mitchell, B. Holtom, and T. Lee, "How to keep your best employees: Developing an effective retention policy," Academy of Management Perspectives, vol. 15, pp. 96-108, 2001.

Lessons from the Strategic Corporal - Implications of Cyber Incident Response

Antoine Lemay
École Polytechnique de Montréal
2500, Chemin de Polytechnique
Montréal, Québec, CANADA
+1(514)340-4711
antoine.lemay@polymtl.ca

Sylvain Leblanc
Royal Military College of Canada
Electrical and Computer Engineering
Department - RMC
PO Box 17000, Station Forces,
Kingston, Ontario, CANADA
+1(613)541-6000 Extension 6355
Sylvain.Leblanc@rmc.ca

Tiago De Jesus
Carleton University
Infrastructure Resilience Research
Group (IR2G)
1125 Colonel By Drive
Ottawa, Ontario, CANADA
Tiagodejesus@gmail.com

ABSTRACT

With the rise of cyber espionage the role of cyber incident responders is becoming more complex, but the personnel profile of incident handlers has remained constant. In this new environment, the strategic position of companies is being affected by operation personnel, including cyber incident responders, who have little to no awareness of the strategic implications of their technical decisions. In recent decades, the military has gone through a similar situation and has dubbed this new reality the "Strategic Corporal". This paper analyzes cyber incident response through the theoretical framework of the Strategic Corporal to argue that today's cyber incident responders fit that profile. The paper looks at three solutions put forward by the military, namely training, communication of the commander's intent and embracing decentralization, and shows that these are viable solutions to make cyber incident responders ready to meet the current challenge.

Categories and Subject Descriptors

K.6.1 [**Management of computing and information systems**]: Project and people management – *Training*.

General Terms

Management, Security, Human Factors.

Keywords

cyber incident response, strategic impact of cyber decisions, cyber responder training, management of cyber responders.

SIGMIS-CPR '15, June 4-6, 2015, Newport Beach, CA, USA.
© 2015 ACM. ISBN 978-1-4503-3557-7/15/06...$15.00.
DOI: http://dx.doi.org/10.1145/2751957.2751965

INTRODUCTION

With the rise of Advanced Persistent Threat (APT) actors, who are often state-sponsored hackers dedicated to electronic espionage, the role of cyber incident responders has become more complex; it is no longer acceptable to just clean up compromises and move on. The personnel profile of incident handlers, namely their qualifications, skills and approach to incidents, has not changed since the days of Internet worms. How then, can we ensure that today's incident handlers are able to tackle the challenges introduced by APT-related incidents, in a manner that is consistent with a company's organizational objectives?

To answer this question, we can look to other fields that have successfully navigated similar changes in operating environments, and gain inspiration from their reflections. We propose the lessons learned from military forces, which have gone through similar a change in recent decades. While initially designed for traditional war fighting, military forces have increasingly been relied upon for operations other than war such as peacekeeping and humanitarian assistance. This paper argues that cyber incident response is undergoing a similar shift in operating environment. In this new environment, the strategic position of companies can be greatly influenced by operation personnel with little to no awareness of the strategic implications of their technical decisions.

The paper examines the operating environment in which companies must carry out cyber security, discussing the impact of operational decisions with a particular emphasis on incident response. This is explored through three case studies, namely incident response, the preservation of forensic evidence and the attribution of an incident to an APT. The paper then presents the Three Block War analogy, and discusses the implications of the Strategic Corporal in this complex and dynamic environment. The paper then looks at the solutions adopted by the military to empower the Strategic Corporal to operate effectively and suggests parallels for cyber incident response, followed by a brief conclusion.

1. THE OPERATING ENVIRONMENT OF CYBER SECURITY

The cyber security profession is one where practitioners are involved in an adversarial relationship. Like other I.T. professionals, cyber security practitioners make decisions based on criterion intrinsic to technology, such as scalability, performance and speed. In addition, cyber security professionals must also consider how their adversaries will react to security efforts. The cyber security profession must therefore evolve alongside its adversaries if it is to stay relevant.

Cyber security professionals perform a wide range of duties because of their involvement in technical matters and through the nature of the adversarial relationship with attackers. It may be possible for a professional to be deploying patches in the morning, extracting emails for an investigation in the afternoon and combating hackers hired by a nation-state in the evening. All of this must be done while minimizing impact on core organizational operations.

This wide range of tasks requires cyber security professionals to have a varied skill set. Some tasks may require in-depth technical skills while other tasks may require the ability to communicate risk to management. Unfortunately, the skills required for the former do not always suit the latter. Individuals imbued with a detail-oriented mind that is best suited for the technical aspects may lack the ability to see the bigger picture. Similarly, people with a knack for writing reports and speaking to management often lack the skills required to keep up with daily technical tasks.

In order to address this dichotomy, cyber security professionals are often categorized along this technical/non-technical divide. Technical cyber security professionals, whom we will dub tactical personnel, deal with the day-to-day operations and technical tasks. Professionals mainly tasked with producing deliverables for management, which we will dub strategic personnel, oversee the tasks related to compliance, reporting and governance. This separation is intended to allow each type of personnel to apply its strengths where it is most effective.

Unfortunately, the distinction between tasks having tactical and strategic impact is becoming increasingly blurry. This creates a skills mismatch between the skill set of current cyber professionals and the skill sets required to deal with the requirements of the new cyber security landscape.

1.1 Impact of Operational Decisions

To situate the discussion, we adapt the definitions of the operational levels of war [1] to the realm of cyber security in a business environment. The strategic level deals with the organization's long-term vision. The operational level deals with the organization's day-to-day operations. The tactical level refers to those minute-to-minute actions taken by personnel in the performance of their duties.

Most tactical tasks have limited impact. For example, the choice to encrypt data with either AES or RSA may yield different vulnerabilities, but is unlikely to significantly affect the risk faced by the enterprise. That risk is affected by the strategic decision about whether or not to encrypt the data.

However, some tactical level technical decisions can have strategic impact. Let us consider the release of a patch for a web application vulnerability that is being actively exploited. The decision to take down the web store for emergency maintenance can have strategic impact. Tactical personnel should be able to refer such a decision to strategic personnel, but that is not always the case.

With the rise APT actors, the number of incidents where technical decisions show a strategic scope has increased. In most APT cases, the ultimate goal of the attacker is to steal intellectual property for the purpose of economic and industrial espionage [2]. This is ultimately an inherently strategic concern, as intellectual property often offers a company its competitive edge. As such,

decisions taken in the handling of an APT incident can have a direct strategic impact. As an example, let us consider a company involved in a merger deal, where an APT actor has infiltrated the company and gained the ability to read internal emails, allowing them to steal the details of the deal. Should the incident response team inform the deal negotiators that their position may be known to a third party? Should the incident responders put a stop to email communication companywide even if it may prevent the deal negotiators from doing their jobs? Should they contain the problem as fast as possible or should they preserve evidence for an eventual court case? All of these questions can have a strategic impact for the organization.

In this new operating context, the strict division of labor between tactical personnel and strategic personnel cannot hold. Tactical personnel are routinely making decisions with strategic impact without the oversight or even knowledge of their management. This is most evidenced in incident response, which we discuss in more detail below.

1.2 Incident Response

Current cyber incident responders are working in an uncertain environment fraught with decisions that can have a strategic impact. The cyber incident response community however, has yet to incorporate this notion in its training or even in its processes.

In fact, most discussions in cyber incident response are still focused on technical aspects, such as how to best make use of a new forensic technique or how to apply indicators of compromise at scale. Even the literature for incident response against APT is dominated by tactical considerations; this is the case whether the literature is strategic guidance to incident responders [3], reports on APT incidents [4] or scholarly articles designed to foster research [5]. Cyber incident response is a complex technical task with many open challenges. But while this literature contributes to the advancement of cyber incident response capabilities, it is not sufficient to do a task correctly if that task is not the right thing to do.

Ideally, it would be possible for management to closely supervise the technical specialists performing incident response. Operational constraints however, often make it impractical to offer such direct supervision to cyber incident responders. As such, the technical personnel handling incidents at the technical level have to shoulder the strategic burden of the decisions themselves.

One of the first constraints preventing direct supervision is the amount of supervision that would be required. If we take the example of the detection step of the PICERL model [6], each event is analyzed to determine if an incident has occurred. While most of these evaluations are benign, some, such as the exfiltration of company secrets, may have serious strategic impact. Having a manager over the shoulder of every analyst in case a given event proves to be of strategic importance is not feasible.

A second constraint is the skills mismatch between most managers and technical incident responders. Even if a manager possesses an I.T. background, it is unlikely that he can keep abreast of the latest development in digital forensics, of the significance of the change of given registry keys and of current attack techniques, in addition to carrying out management duties. Similarly, technical personnel that are spending all their time trying to root out incidents can very well lose sight of the bigger picture. As such, it is seldom the case that a manager can clearly enunciate controls to ensure the operational team maintains strategic vision; conversely, technical personnel often have difficulties communicating the strategic implications of technical intricacies to the management.

A third constraint is the time available to make decisions. Because of the adversarial nature of the incident response process, it is often impossible to wait for management feedback. A cyber security professional working in the Security Operation Center at 3 A.M. who finds an active hacker in a company system may not have time to wait for the manager to answer his phone or to show up at the office before having to take action. The problem is further compounded by the speed at which cyber incidents can occur.

We discuss two cases where tactical decisions making from cyber incident responders have clear strategic implications.

1.3 Case Study: Preserving Forensic Evidence

In a paper presented in their CIO journal [7], Deloitte makes the case for an increased preservation of forensic evidence in cyber incidents. They illustrate their point by making a parallel with the first officer at a murder scene who takes care to secure the scene and avoid contaminating evidence. This is in contrast to the usual behavior of tactical I.T. personnel whose priority, when responding to incidents, is to quickly restore service and move on to other matters. As such, the authors argue for increased presence of forensics experts in incident response teams to act as guardians of evidence. We argue that these parallels can be problematic.

First, a murder investigation is typically not an adversarial process. The victim is dead, the murderer is gone and no one is actively attempting to erase traces of the crime. In such a situation, a well defined procedure can be followed and the decisions taken by first responder seldom have strategic impact. The first responder can take her time with little or no cost; she may refer to her chain of command and wait for backup to arrive. This is not the case in cyber incident response where any delay can increase the damage caused by the attackers.

Because there is a cost to gather forensics evidence in cyber incidents, the decision to engage in that procedure is a risk-reward calculation. The risk of increased damage should be weighed against the value of the evidence that is to be gathered. The preservation of the evidence only has value if the evidence will be used in legal action. Let us take the example of a botnet operated by a faceless cyber criminal from outside of the jurisdiction of the victim. Will collecting forensic evidence help with legal action? Will capturing evidence deter the criminal from further attacks? In such a case the reward for collecting evidence is low. Should the criminal be a disgruntled employee, pressing charges may prevent further incidents, and the collection of evidence may be worth the risk of continued exposure to the threat.

In other fields, risk-reward calculations are tightly overseen by management because it represents an important strategic decision. One would be very surprised to see the cashier at the local bank handing out loans without the direct approval of his supervisor. Yet, this is the kind of decision that tactical employees cleaning virus infection are implicitly empowered to make, often unbeknownst to them.

1.4 Case Study: Determining if an Incident is Linked to an APT

In their APT1 report [4], Mandiant revealed that APT1 maintained their presence in victim networks for a year on average, and that many of the victims were notified of the presence of the APT actor by third parties. This is a potential failure of two steps of the PICERL model: Detection if the attackers were never identified, or Eradication if the attackers were identified but never fully removed from the network.

The detection of an APT incident can be difficult. For example, when starting a spear phishing campaign, the APT actor will attempt to mimic a legitimate communication in order to appear innocuous. Even with this concealment effort, clues can point to the existence of an APT campaign. Someone might notice that the communication does not originate from the supposed sender or the attacker might make a mistake and trigger a technical detection mechanism (such as an IDS). When the detection occurs, it is critical for the responder to decide on the severity of the incident. If the incident is mislabeled as a common malware infection attempt instead of part of an APT campaign, the particular piece of malware may be neutralized, but no effort will be made to eradicate the APT campaign as a whole. This will allow the adversary to pursue his goals, which can cause strategic damage.

Determining if a given incident is linked with an APT actor is usually a technical decision carried out at the tactical level. For example, the code may present similarities to code typically used by a given APT actor, the infrastructure for remote access might be commonly used by a given actor or the style of the spear phishing emails might be re-used across multiple campaigns. As such, the person that is most likely to make that decision to attribute the event to an APT is the one that is most closely involved in the day-to-day technical operation of the given system. The attribution decision however, can result in significant resource allocation implications. If the incident involves common malware, the responder simply restores service, by following the removal procedure or re-imaging the machine, and carries on with his other tasks. If the incident is potentially linked with an APT, an in-depth investigation has to occur to ascertain if the attackers have managed to establish a foothold in the organization and to determine the extent of their presence. Given that significant effort must be invested just to confirm the presence of an APT, it is normal to only commit resources if the incident is likely linked with an APT.

The problem arises because the person that makes the initial determination seldom has strategic visibility to properly weigh the risks of committing resources against the value of the attribution to an APT; because of the other task they must perform, incident responders are often actively disincentivized from making a decision that would require the investment of more resources. After all, the incident responder will probably be the one saddled to perform the additional investigation work. In other words, when an incident is really linked with an APT, the negative consequences of the wrong decision are often externalized (i.e. affecting the organization as a whole), while the negative consequences of the correct decision are internalized (i.e. affecting the individual). Given this imbalance, the dismal statistics presented in the Mandiant report are not surprising.

The question then becomes, how can we ensure that cyber incident responders correctly take into account strategic level considerations when making technical decisions at tactical level? To answer this question, we consider how a similar problem was solved in another realm, namely how the military helps its tactical personnel consider the strategic implications of their actions.

2. THE THREE BLOCK WAR AND THE STRATEGIC CORPORAL

The complexity and fluid nature of modern military operations put an increasingly strategic burden on the decision making of troops at the lower levels of the chain of command. This section details the "Three Block War" analogy used to illustrate this new operating environment and exposes the strategic corporal, the new reality of boots on the ground personnel.

2.1 Three Block War

The rise of non-conventional conflicts following the end of the Cold War introduced new complexity in the work of armed forces. Forces that were trained to fight conventional war actions were suddenly tasked with keeping angry factions apart and escorting humanitarian expeditions. Naturally, the task of keeping the peace requires a different mindset than the task of waging war.

One way to address these different tasks is to create specialist forces that are trained to handle a specific mission very well. For example, a peace keeping force that is trained to interact with the local population rather than in war fighting. Unfortunately, in adversarial situations, the nature of operations can change drastically, in a very short time or in a small geographical area. The forces have to be able to adapt to any situation so it is generally seen as impractical to have forces that are not equipped for the entire spectrum of conflicts [8].

The metaphor most often used to illustrate this concept is the "Three Block". Krulak [9] defines the concept as such:

The [Marine] Corps has described such amorphous conflicts as -- the three block war -- contingencies in which Marines may be confronted by the entire spectrum of tactical challenges in the span of a few hours and within the space of three contiguous city blocks.

In other words, a military force could find itself fighting a conventional warfare action in a city block while it forcibly keeps apart combatants in the next city block and assists with humanitarian operations in a third. The fluid nature of this type of conflict puts an increased burden on tactical level troops, who must operate in varied contexts and usually under intense scrutiny from the local population and the media. This gives rise to the so-called Strategic Corporal.

2.2 Strategic Corporal

In a complex situation such as the Three Block War, each individual tactical decision, no matter how apparently benign, can have strategic repercussions. Let us consider a soldier at a checkpoint interacting with a Muslim woman wearing a niqab. Forcing her to remove the niqab might anger a local tribe and push them in the opposing camp, letting her through unchecked might allow for the smuggling of material that will be used to commit an attack and further decrease popular support for the war which is deemed essential to sustain the mission.

The fact that tactical decisions made by soldiers at the lower echelon of the chain of command, such as a corporal, must take into account strategic realities that used to be purview of the higher levels of the chain of command has lead to the coining of the term "Strategic Corporal".

In traditional warfare, the corporal is not expected to incorporate strategic information in his decision making process. The entire command and control apparatus is designed to free him from that

level of complexity. However, as Barcot points out [10] "corporals often lead their teams and squads on patrols in dangerous places that are at times far from direct supervision. Corporals have to make quick decisions, some of which can carry strategic implications". It is often impractical to consult the chain of command either because of the amount of supervision required (in the checkpoint example), because of technical constraints (in a forward deployment where communications are difficult) or because of the decision is time critical. There are direct parallels between these restrictions on the supervision of military personnel and the arguments we brought forth in our discussion of the impact of cyber operational decisions in preceding sections.

In those situations, it becomes critical for the commander to make sure that the Strategic Corporal is taking the right decisions to prevent the trading of long term strategic losses for short term tactical gains. Such devolution of strategically impacting decisions to tactical personnel is not the sole purview of the military; they also apply to cyber incident responders. These similarities will be explored in the following section where we also examine how armed forces have evolved to deal with this new reality.

3. SOLUTIONS

Based on their now decades-long experience fighting so-called Three Block Wars, armed forces have reflected on how to address the issue of the Strategic Corporal. This section looks at three solutions put forth by the military, namely training, commander's intent and decentralized decision making, and use them as guides to develop solutions in a cyber security context.

3.1 Training

The first proposed solution is to enhance training. The goal is to give the people making tactical decisions the tools they need to take into account the additional factors introduced by the complexity of the operational context. In his original paper on the Three Block War [9], Krulak states "*An institutional commitment to lifelong professional development is the second step [after recruitment which remains unchanged] on the road to building the Strategic Corporal.*" Showing the importance of training to adapt the toolset of the tactical level troops to the new reality.

In order to do so, Stringer argues in his paper "Educating the Strategic Corporal" [11] that the education has to be redesigned. In particular, the scope of training has to be broadened to include language education, cultural knowledge, cooperation with agencies and so on. In other words, provide an education that does not solely focus of the core technical competency, but that also provides an awareness of the complexities of the operational context. That awareness will then be able to get leveraged at the moment of decision to integrate that context.

While the specific skill set put forth by Stringer is probably not appropriate for cyber incident responders, the idea to broaden the scope of training seems to be equally applicable to the cyber context. For example, providing first responders such as system administrators and help desk technicians with a basic understanding of the court system would enable them to understand when it is important to preserve evidence. This also means that organizations can no longer be satisfied with hiring technical experts that are "fully trained". Companies must invest time and resources in the training of their technical personnel beyond the technical realm in order for them to gain a strategic understanding of the organization's business environment.

We tested this proposition during a series of training scenarios for cyber incident responders at the National Energy Infrastructure Test Center [12]; this training session serves as the basis for our assertion. A major goal of the sessions was to see if students could distinguish APT threats from common cyber crime. To do so, the emphasis was placed on providing students insight into what each actor is trying to achieve, rather than focusing on specific indicators. The defensive tools are then presented as means to prevent the adversary from achieving his goal, providing students with a context in which to use these tools. Hands-on training is provided on emulated networks that resemble their own networks, which ensures that their new understanding of the operational context transfers easily to operations. Based on comments obtained from feedback forms, students seem to appreciate this approach, reporting am increase in learning, even compared to other professional training programs that have objectively more content, but do not present that content in an operational context.

3.2 Mission Command

A second avenue to tackle the increased reliance on the bottom of the chain of command for strategic decision making is to improve on the methods used by commander to communicate to their subordinates what they are expected to do. This instruction must be at the same time specific enough so that the correct job gets done and open-ended enough so that the subordinate may adapt the method for the realization of the job to the realities on the ground. As such, the commander writes his orders not as a task list, but as statement of his intent leaving the particulars to the subordinate in what is termed "Mission Command".

This way of communicating management preference provides a concise description of the general goal toward which the subordinate is expected to progress. In turn, this enables the subordinate to keep this orientation in mind when he makes decision without having to explicitly refer back to the chain of command. This empowers the subordinate to use judgment to make appropriate decisions in the Three Block War.

Ultimately, this type of management is key to how the military sees the conduct of operations in the future, especially when explicit coordination through direct command and control is not possible. The Mission Command white paper [13] states the following:

[The commander] must clearly translate his intent to his subordinates. The missions given subordinates must be within their capabilities; the commander must understand what his subordinates can do, and trust - but not blindly - them to do it. In its highest state, shared context and understanding is implicit and intuitive [...] enabling decentralized and distributed formations to perform as if they were centrally coordinated.

This type of management seems very appropriate to address the problem of the strategic cyber incident responder. Not only does it empower cyber incident responders to make judgment calls based on greater situational awareness, it also helps bridge some of the management constraints identified in the Operating Environment of Cyber Security section of the paper such as the technological skills and knowledge gap between managers and technical personnel. Because Mission Command does not rely on listing tasks, the manager does not require as much technical expertise to properly frame a mission for a subordinate. He only needs enough expertise to be able to gauge the capabilities of the subordinate and his adequacy for fulfilling the mission.

Ironically, the tendency to have I.T. managers with strong backgrounds in I.T. is a hurdle to achieving Mission Command. Because of their specialist knowledge, such managers are often reluctant to trust implicitly their subordinates and avoid providing detailed task lists, resulting in micro-management. Furthermore, such technically inclined managers often lack the skills required to state their intent in something other than technical language. While some research is being done to provide tools to transmit commander's intent for cyber incident response such as [14], these approaches are immature and not yet sufficient for use in an industrial context.

3.3 Decentralized Decision Making

To operate in the very dynamic environment of the Three Block War, military forces reorganized decision making to a decentralized process without sacrificing the unity of purpose obtained through centralized command and control. This is seen as the only way to adapt to complex and rapidly changing situations, which are also characteristic of adversarial interactions such as those involved in cyber incident response. As such, military forces embraces rather than fears the concept of the Strategic Corporal. In his paper The Strategic Corporal [10] states that:

The truth is modern military experience, particularly in combat, is often characterized by rapid decision making in autonomous environments. While militaries function through chains of command, most units have decentralized leadership that places enormous amounts of responsibility in the hands of young men and women.

In a follow up paper to Strategic Corporal titled "Cultivating Intuitive Decision Making"[15], Krulak argues that the ability of subordinates to make decisions should be cultivated. This is done not only through enhanced training and better transmission of commander's intent, but also by fostering what he calls "a "culture" of intuitive decision making throughout the Corps". This is done by encouraging subordinates to make decisions and avoiding the application of harsh penalties for wrong decisions. This is in stark contrast to typical management structures where the incentives are organized for repeatability of process.

4. CONCLUSION

This paper has discussed how the tactical decisions of technical personnel can have strategic impact on an organization. Based on the experience of the post Cold War low intensity conflicts, military forces developed the concept of the Strategic Corporal to underline that tactical complexity and fluid operating environment can have strategic impacts. Military forces realized that a centralized command and control structure was not well suited for this type of environment and had to rethink their structure to embrace a more decentralized approach.

The characteristics of the three block war - complexity of the environment, the adversarial characteristics and the strategic implications of tactical decisions - can also be seen in the context of cyber incident response. In that sense, incident handlers are Strategic Corporals, often without realizing it. This was explored through an examination of case studies in incident handling, such as the preservation of forensic evidence and the attribution of an incident to an APT campaign.

While recognizing the problem of the strategic incident responder is an important step, solutions have to be developed to help the current incident workforce react to the new strategic reality. The paper looked at solutions advanced by the military for the development of their Strategic Corporals, namely broadening the scope of the training beyond core technical skills, developing the ability of managers to convey intent and embracing a decentralized decision processes. While much work remains to be done, we argue that the solutions espoused by military forces provide suitable avenues of research for solutions to the strategic cyber incident responders.

5. REFERENCES

[1] C. v. Clausewitz, On War, M. Howard and P. Paret, Eds., Princeton: Princeton University Press, 1989.

[2] R. Sloan, "Advanced Persistent Threat," *Engineering & Technology Reference*, vol. 1, no. 1, 2014.

[3] A. Baykal, "Incident Response in the Age of APT," 16 May 2012. [Online]. Available: http://doa.alaska.gov/ets/security/StrategicPlanning/MS-ISAC_IncidentResponse.pdf. [Accessed 19 December 2014].

[4] Mandiant, "APT1 - Exposing One of China's Cyber Espionage Units," February 2013. [Online]. Available: http://intelreport.mandiant.com/Mandiant_APT1_Report.pdf. [Accessed 8 August 2013].

[5] B. J. Nikkel, "Fostering Incident Response and Digital Forensics Research," *Digital Investigation*, vol. 11, no. 4, pp. 249-251, 2014.

[6] M. Pokladnik, "An Incident Handling Process for Small and Medium Business," 2007. [Online]. Available: http://www.sans.org/reading-room/whitepapers/incident/incident-handling-process-small-medium-businesses-1791. [Accessed 19 12 2014].

[7] Deloitte, "Computer Forensics: Preserving Evidence of Cyber Crime," 3 December 2014. [Online]. Available: http://deloitte.wsj.com/cio/2014/12/03/computer-forensics-preserving-evidence-of-cyber-crime/?KEYWORDS=security. [Accessed 19 December 2014].

[8] National Defence Canada, "Canada's Army," 1998.

[9] C. Krulak, "The Strategic Corporal: Leadership in the Three Block War," *Marine Corps Gazette*, vol. 83, no. 1, pp. 18-23, January 1999.

[10] R. Barcot, "The Strategic Corporal," *Harvard Business Review Spotlight*, 21 October 2010.

[11] K. D. Stringer, "Educating the Straegic Corporal - A Paradigm Shift," *Military Review*, pp. 87-95, September-October 2009.

[12] A. Lemay, J. Fernandez and S. Knight, "An isolated virtual cluster for SCADA network security research," in *1st International Symposium for ICS & SCADA Cyber Security Research 2013 (ICS-CSR 2013)*, Leicester, 2013.

[13] M. E. Dempsey, "Mission Command white paper," 3 April 2012. [Online]. Available: http://www.dtic.mil/doctrine/concepts/white_papers/cjcs_wp_missioncommand.pdf. [Accessed 20 December 2014].

[14] A. Lemay, S. Knight and J. M. Fernandez, "Preparation of the Cyber Environment (IPCE): Finding the High Ground in Cyberspace," *Journal of Information Warfare*, vol. 13, no. 3, pp. 47-56, 2014.

[15] C. Krulak, "Cultivating Intuitive Decisionmaking," *Marine Corps Gazette*, May 1999.

What Skills do you Need to Work in Cyber Security?
A Look at the Australian Market

Leigh Ellen Potter
Griffith University
170 Kessels Road
Nathan, Queensland, Australia
+61 7 3735 5191
L.Potter@griffith.edu.au

Gregory Vickers
Griffith University
170 Kessels Road
Nathan, Queensland, Australia
+61 7 3735 4847
G.Vickers@griffith.edu.au

ABSTRACT

The demand for cyber security professionals is rising as the incidence of cyber crime and security breaches increases, leading to suggestions of a skills shortage in the technology industry. While supply and demand are factors in the recruitment process for any position, in order to secure the best people in the security field we need to know what skills are required to be a security professional in the current cyber security environment. This paper seeks to explore this question by looking at the current state of the Australian Industry. Recent job listings in the cyber security area were analysed, and current security professionals in industry were asked for their opinion as to what skills were required in this profession. It was found that each security professional role has its own set of skill requirements, however there is significant overlap between the roles for many soft skills, including analysis, consulting and process skills, leadership, and relationship management. Both communication and presentation skills were valued. A set of 'hard' skills emerged as common across all categories: experience, qualifications and certifications, and technical expertise. These appear to represent the need for a firm background in the security area as represented by formal study and industry certifications, and supported by solid experience in the industry. Specific technical skills are also required, although the exact nature of these will vary according to the requirements of each role.

Categories and Subject Descriptors

H.1.2 [**User/Machine Systems**]: Human Factors

General Terms

Security, Human Factors.

Keywords

Cyber security, skills, security professional.

1. INTRODUCTION

The demand for cyber security professionals to protect companies from perceived threats is rising as the incidence of cyber crime and security breaches increases. Between 2012 and 2013, Australian Government departments and networks have experienced a 21 per cent increase in cyber threats (Cyber Security Operations Centre, 2014). Internationally, cyber crime has become increasingly prevalent, and is exacerbated by the prevalence of new technology and mobile technology (Symantec, 2014).

Rapid change in both the technology and security sectors means requirements for meeting the challenge are also changing. Individuals with security credentials are in increasing demand. Major companies in Australia are participating in initiatives designed to garner potential security specialists, such as the Cyber Security Challenge Australia. The FBI has described individuals with cyber expertise as it's most sought-after candidates", and is currently seeking to hire "highly talented, technically trained individuals" to become cyber agents (FBI, 2014).

The problem however is availability of talent. Part of the remit for the Cyber Security Challenge Australia 2014 was "to address a skills shortage in the number of cyber security professionals in Australia" (CySCA, 2014). A major Australian university has tried to appoint an IT Security manager for the past three years, to date unsuccessfully. Demand appears to outstrip supply.

While supply and demand are clear factors in the recruitment process for any position, in order to secure the best people in the security field we need to know what skills are required to be a security professional in the current cyber security environment. This paper seeks to explore this question by looking at the current state of the Australian Industry. We will analyse recent job listings in the cyber security area and present responses from current security professionals in the technology industry giving their opinion as to what skills are required by a security professional. Through this process we aim to generate an initial list of key skills required by a security professional.

We will present an overview of the skill situation from current literature, and then outline the approach we took for this study. The key data gathered in the study will be presented and discussed, in order to provide the security professional skill list.

2. CONCEPTS

Studies specific to the skills required by a modern security professional are sparse. Many studies exist looking at techniques and the broad technology professions, such as software engineering or business analysis, however work looking specifically as security professional skills are few.

Palmer (2012) stresses the importance of a mix of hard and soft skills, with hard skills represented in such tasks client/desktop support, programming and PC maintenance, and soft skills identified as communication, problem solving, and decision making. He also describes the qualifications and certifications that a network security engineer should possess, describing a background in information technology, information security, networking and engineering. He lists lifelong learning in order to keep up with new technology and new security solutions as important, and outlines a basic risk management approach as crucial for this position. He considers that a network security engineer should be capable of developing security policies and business continuity and disaster recovery strategies, and be able to test their developed plans and solutions prior to implementation.

Casper and Papa (2012) argue that current security degrees focus on network security and information assurance, and that this focus leads to "serious gaps in the mentality and abilities of the security engineer, and this hole in ability results in significant holes in the armor of the security design of a system." They suggest that skills from multiple disciplines are needed to address this problem, and specifically cite the importance of skills from the usability field.

Caldwell (2013) discusses a cyber security skills gap, and while she is not explicit as to specific skills, she does discuss issues such as "a mismatch between the expectations of employers and the needs of technically skilled employees" and that organisations may need to adjust their views in order to attract the right personnel. She also raises the challenge of junior security professionals gaining the experience they need for the industry.

The Cybersecurity Workforce Competency report (University of Phoenix & (ISC)2 Foundation, 2014) acknowledges a need to standardize a "set of industry-aligned professional competencies can help in educating, recruiting, developing, and retaining the caliber of talent that the industry needs." It identifies three gaps that hinder the progress of both security professionals and the profession itself: a competency gap between the proficiency level an individual possesses and that which an organisation desires, a professional experience gap, and an education speed-to-market gap where tertiary institutions are unable to adapt subject material in line with the speed of the changing security environment.

3. APPROACH

To identify the skills needed to work in cyber security, we conducted an analysis of a set of job advertisements and deployed a questionnaire to a group of cyber security professionals. These will now be described, together with the analysis process used.

Job advertisements from a major Australian internet job site (Seek.com.au) were gathered using a keyword search of "cyber security" with no constraints on classification, location (within Australia) or salary. The search was conducted in January 2015, with listings dated from December 2014 to early January 2015. This search returned 60 job listings, which was reduced to 33 listings with the removal of duplicate listings (the same job listed in multiple categories) and non-cyber security jobs. These 33 listings came from 18 separate employers, with the majority of listings from major Australian companies, and international companies with Australian offices. One employer listed 8 individual positions. Employers represented a broad range of

industries, including finance, small and large consultancy companies, and the government sector. The majority were large companies The final 33 job listings were analysed according to the skills listed as required or desirable for the job.

A questionnaire was sent in November 2014 to a group of seven Queensland Information Technology security professionals whose core role involved ensuring the security of the information technology networks of large, complex organisations asking them to describe the skills they felt were required to work in this field. Five professionals responded. The questionnaire included four open questions, and simply asked respondents to list and describe the key technical skills and personal skills that someone would need to be a good IT security professional, and which skills they felt were most important.

Both the job listings and questionnaire responses were then analysed using the computer assisted qualitative data analysis software NVivo 10 to code each skill or characteristic in the listing or response to a theme. These themes were identified as they emerged from the data itself, resulting in a set of skills that were common across both data sets, and additional skills for specific situations. These skills will now be discussed.

4. RESULTS

The 33 job listings covered a broad range of jobs, and based on the job titles these fell broadly into six security categories: Analyst, Consultant, Engineer, Security Assessor / Advisor, Manager, and Sales. The skill requirements were analysed for each category, and while there was significant overlap between some categories, each category resulted in an individual list of required skills.

4.1 Analyst

Four full time jobs were advertised as Analyst positions. These position descriptions involved "advice and subject matter expertise to stakeholders", "problem solving skills", "supporting the team with cyber security incidents", "risk management activities" and "security related support and incident management services". In one case, a job also listed "Any other duties as required". Analysis of the job descriptions yielded nine required skills for these positions: Analysis, Innovation, Motivation, Process creation, Team Work, able to work independently, Qualifications and certifications, Experience, and Technical expertise.

Analytical skills and "a sharp eye for detail" were listed, together with "innovative skills". One job asked for someone "highly motivated with a strong sense of ownership\responsibility and a keen passion for learning". Another asked for someone capable of the "development of incident handling, detection and threat mitigation procedures", who has "experience in working in geographically dispersed teams along with being able to work independently."

The remaining three skills were listed as critical in all positions. All positions required tertiary qualifications, with a degree in computer science or related field preferred, or the equivalent combination of education and experience. Three positions asked for industry certifications, and two asked for security clearance. All positions asked for applicants with experience, either in terms of cyber security experience ("3+ years of experience supporting cyber security or information security initiatives"), or experience with specific technologies required for the job. The final skill of technical expertise is listed with the greatest amount of detail in the listings, with all listings including specific technologies, frameworks, or expertise required for the role

4.2 Consultant

Nine jobs were listed with 'Consultant' in the title in both junior and senior positions. These were described as roles involving independent work and assistance to teams, analysis and "complex technical investigations", the identification, development, and management of customer relationships and opportunities, and the development of solutions. The twelve skills listed for consultancy jobs were the ability to work independently, process skills, leadership, presentation skills, time management, risk management, analysis, communication, consulting, qualifications and certifications, experience, and technical expertise.

Working independently was stated in one listing and implied in several others as "the consultant is responsible and accountable for…" the specific tasks in the job listing. Process skills refer to the ability to either establish or follow and maintain a framework of processes and procedures that support the organisation in meeting its goals, and this was included in the job listings. The more senior consultancy positions included management and leadership skills, together with the ability to report findings in formal presentations. Several jobs required skills in risk management and security risk management, and analytical skills were highly valued as consultants needed to "use their initiative and experience to analyse, plan, review and adjust priorities and work activities to meet business outcomes." Most positions required "Excellent communication (including written and presentation skills)" regardless of the seniority of the position. Unsurprisingly, these positions asked for the "ability to consult with business and technical representatives and to balance security and business requirements."

As with analysts, the most commonly sought skills were qualifications, certifications, experience, and technical expertise. Computer Science, ICT Security related degrees, and post-graduate qualifications were an advantage, however industry certifications such as CREST (security testing), CISSP (Certified Information Systems Security Professional), and CISM (Certified Information Security Manager) certifications were more commonly requested. One role asked for "Participation and membership of relevant industry associations." All jobs asked for industry experience as either mandatory or desirable, with specific experience requested by some listings as relevant for the listed position. This varied from the more general "industry experience or knowledge" to quite specific requirements, such as "five years of professional experience", and "seasoned experience". The area of technical expertise was again the most specific, with most listings requesting specific technical skills specific to the job, such as vulnerability assessment, threat and risk assessment, and expertise with specific technologies, frameworks and standards.

4.3 Engineer

One listing for multiple positions was listed for a Security Engineer. This will still be discussed separately as the term "security engineer" is an established title: a subsequent job search was conducted using only this title with a return of fifteen job listings, which were not included in this "cyber security" analysis. The position of Security Engineer has a technical focus dealing with network security, incident response, intrusion detection, and vulnerability assessment. The listing reflects this with a focus on analytical skills, experience, qualifications, and technical expertise.

Analysis in this case is the technical analysis of elements such as network traffic and log files. A Bachelor's degree in Information Security was desirable, as were industry certifications, in this case technical certifications including Cisco and security testing together with CISSP. "Four or more years of experience in network, host, data and/or application security" was essential for this position, with experience in a very specific list of technical skills relevant to the position requested in the listing.

4.4 Security Assessor / Advisor

Ten job listings were included in the Assessor / Advisor category with a focus on security assessment and advice. This category includes roles "for conducting security assessments including penetration testing and vulnerability assessments, and design tasks". The ten key skills identified for this category include consulting, analysis, process skills, relationship management, motivation, presentation skills, communication skills, experience, qualifications, and technical expertise.

One job listed consultancy skills in order to "balance security and business requirements when managing information security incidents". Analytical skills are listed, either directly ("possess advanced analytical and problem solving skills") or indirectly ("the ability to capture and articulate testing results"). This category includes process skills, such as "following a systematic methodology" and skills in governance. Relationship management is important in terms of relationships within teams and with the client. Motivation to perform the job appears to be key, with statements such as "You will display a passion for cyber security", "a passion for security, particularly Penetration testing", and "You will be passionate about technology and willingly engage in self-learning and security research as part of your daily life." Both presentation and communication skills appear to be important in this role with inclusion in multiple listing, as clearly articulated in the criteria for "Strong presentations skills including an ability to interpret and communicate complicated topics to all levels of stakeholders" and "Excellent presentation and communication skills are a must."

As with the earlier categories, the most commonly included skills are qualifications and certifications, experience and technical expertise. Computer Science or Information Technology degrees are most commonly requested. Industry certifications are more frequently listed than tertiary qualifications, with the more general certifications such as CREST, CISSP and CISM most commonly listed. All of the job listings require experience, either generally ("3 years", "we expect you will have recent experience") or specifically ("you MUST have a strong and indepth background in Endpoint Protection"). As with previous listings, by far the most detailed requirements are for technical expertise, with all of the job listings giving specific criteria for the position. In this category, these skills primarily relate to vulnerability assessment and penetration testing, with security framework understanding and competence highly valued.

4.5 Manager

Seven jobs were listed as managerial positions including Operations manager, executive manager, and cyber security manager. These roles involved management of teams, units, or security centres and resulted in the largest number of skills, with fourteen identified from the descriptions. These are event/Incident management, presentation skills, innovation, leadership, risk management, project management, process creation, process management, consulting skills, team management, qualifications and certifications, experience, technical expertise and relationship management.

A range of management roles were included in the listings, with some requiring the management of specific scenarios, such as "identified security events and incidents through to resolution". The ability to present to "C level executives" and "various other stakeholders" was desirable. The ability to innovate, be a "thought leader", and "bring a fresh perspective to the way we do things" was valued, as was the ability to inspire a team to "innovate and deliver value". The positions were often described as "leadership position(s)", with the ability to "influence the whole enterprise". Risk management skills were valued and listed in several positions, as were project management skills. The "demonstrated ability" to develop and maintain "key operational processes and procedures" was included in most of the positions, with both the creation of processes, and the implementation and maintenance of processes key requirements. "High level consulting" skills were listed in most of the positions, with the "ability to consult with business and technical representatives" and "the ability to advise clients, from a vendor agnostic perspective" identified as required. Perhaps not surprisingly, all but one of the listings included team management as a required skill, in terms of management of specific security operations teams, or more generally as an "experienced people leader keen to inspire, mentor and motivate large teams" or "proven people management experience."

Qualifications were only listed for three positions, with a requirement of "tertiary qualifications in Computer Science or related discipling", and "relevant industry certifications" were listed for only two positions. Three positions requested "Participation and membership of relevant industry associations." Experience appeared to be more valued, appearing in most of the job listings. In the manager category, experience in a management position and an "understanding and previous involvement with Cyber Security technologies and processes" were valued. Technical expertise was listed in all positions, however the descriptions of technical skills were more general than the other position descriptions. Skills required included a "strong level of technical security knowledge", an understanding of "security architecture and the pitfalls around different technologies", and "familiarity with modern attack systems and methodologies."

Relationship management appears to be the most valued skill in this category, appearing in every listing in a range of forms. Relationship management was included at several levels, including the management of internal teams, "maintenance of a close working relationship with other members of the client's teams", "maintaining and enhancing a good working relationship with the PSO (Principal Security Officer) Business Owners", and "managing stakeholders to effect change, including strong influencing skills."

4.6 Sales
Two job listings were sales positions: a Business Development Manager and a Security Bid/Proposal Engineer. The Security Bid/Proposal Engineering position included development of security solutions, and "working on Bids, Proposals and RFP responses." The Business Development Manager was "responsible for developing and growing a range of key Enterprise accounts" in the cyber security area. The skills listed

for these positions include Innovation, presentations skills, relationship management, communication, certifications, experience, and technical expertise.

The manager position listed an "innovative, lateral and pragmatic thought process" as a requirement. Both positions included the ability to present ideas. The manager position also included "exceptional relationship management" and "negotiation" skills as required. Both jobs required communication skills, with the manager position listing the "ability to communicate to all levels of key stakeholders" and the engineer position citing "strong writing and oral skills".

Only the engineer position requested formal qualifications, stating that an applicant should be a "Certified Information Systems Security Professional." Experience was more valued in both positions, with sales experience listed for both roles. The manager position asked for "an understanding of security, hacking or cyber espionage", but also stated that "a background in Security Software is an advantage but not essential." The engineer position requested specific security experience, as well as "experience supporting proposal development and capture activities." Specific technical expertise was required for the engineer position, with a list of general security skills such as intrusion detection, log monitoring, and security management and reporting listed.

4.7 Skills identified in Questionnaires
The skills identified in the questionnaire responses were not targeted at an identified position, and included both general and specific skills. These included the ability to learn, leadership, management, problem solving, communication, the ability to deal with people, analysis and motivation. These responses also included experience and technical expertise.

"Drive and the ability to learn" was cited as a valuable skill, as was the ability to inspire and lead. Management was seen as important, with one response in particular listing "PM skills, time management, vendor management, management management (seriously!)." For a security professional, "problem solving is key", with both research and analysis included as required skills. Communication is vital, with a requirement for the "ability to present data and reports to middle and senior management, with a business focus, without getting lost in the minutia of IT Security", and the "ability to communicate with people in a clear manner - when talking with a user, a manager, or a senior manager, the message has to be clear and well understood."

The ability to deal with people was clearly identified, with responses stating that a security professional should "get along with people", and have "the ability to interact with a user or users when establishing the situation that you are investigating - this has to be a respectful and honest conversation." Analytical skills were important to making this happen, as accurate information informs these relationships. The most commonly listed analytical skills given in the responses were technical, in terms of "log management and investigation into that data", and the "ability to integrate data from many sources and provide a reasonable, evidence based summary."

The motivation of the individual was seen as important for a security professional. Responses listed attributes such as being "hungry to learn anything and an independent learner", "drive and the ability to learn", and "curiosity" as important, as was someone who "wants a deeper understanding of how attacks/defense work."

While formal qualifications or certifications were not included in the questionnaire responses, both experience and technical expertise were. Responses included skills such as "a broad knowledge of networking, storage, system administration", "log data management and investigation into that data", and the "ability to integrate data from many sources and provide a reasonable, evidence based summary." One response was very specific, citing "Strong experience in two or more of the following: Coding/Scripting, Network Management, Server Administration (Windows and Linux), and Management of Core Services (DNS,Mail, DBA, ect..)" as important.

4.8 Security Professional skills

A set of skills suitable for six categories of Security Professional emerged as the job advertisements were analysed. Analyst positions needed nine skills: Analysis, Innovation, Motivation, Process creation, Team Work, able to work independently, Qualifications and certifications, Experience, and Technical expertise. Consultants needed twelve skills: the ability to work independently, process skills, leadership, presentation skills, time management, risk management, analysis, communication, consulting, qualifications and certifications, experience, and technical expertise. An engineer requires analytical skills, experience, qualifications, and technical expertise, however this list is limited by the single job listing analysed. Security advisors and assessors need ten key skills: consulting, analysis, process skills, relationship management, motivation, presentation skills, communication skills, experience, qualifications, and technical expertise. Managers require the largest skillset with fourteen listed: event/Incident management, presentation skills, innovation, leadership, risk management, project management, process creation, process management, consulting skills, team management, qualifications and certifications, experience, technical expertise and relationship management. Sales positions included seven skills: innovation, presentations skills, relationship management, communication, certifications, experience, and technical expertise.

Analysis of the questionnaire results revealed that current security professionals view eleven skills as core to the profession: the ability to learn, leadership, management, problem solving, communication, the ability to deal with people, analysis and motivation. These responses also included experience and technical expertise.

These skills represent a blend of both soft skills and technical skills. Soft skills that were included in many job listings across the categories included analysis, consulting skills, leadership, process skills, and relationship management. Both communication skills and presentation skills were valued. Experience and technical skills are critical, and included in all job listings and the questionnaire responses. The specific technical skills vary, depending on the characteristics of the job, however it is interesting to note that these were still cited in the questionnaire responses even though these responses were not addressing a specific position.

While not mentioned in all categories, motivation to do the job appears to be a valued trait. "Highly motivated", a "keen passion for learning", a "passion for cyber security", "passionate about technology", and a willingness to make "self-learning and security research as part of your daily life" were all listed in different job advertisements. In questionnaire responses, attributes such as "hungry to learn", "drive" and "curiosity" were all discussed. This reflects findings by Potter, von Hellens, and Nielsen (2009) suggesting that motivation is a key driver for an individual to both enter and remain in the Information Technology profession.

4.9 What's in a name?

In searching for jobs with the general search term of "cyber security", and in gathering responses from security professionals currently working in the IT industry, we observed a phenomenon that occurs in some other IT industries such as within information systems and the user experience field. Terms and labels for positions within the security field can be ambiguous, with different labels applied to very similar positions. Very few of the 33 job advertisements that we analysed had the same job title: we saw eighteen separate job titles advertised within this simple search. In some cases the same role was advertised with very different titles: for example, the titles penetration tester, security assessor, risk consultant, and security advisor were all used for a role that fit the description of penetration tester.

This was reflected in the diverse job titles of the questionnaire respondees, with Security Engineers, Security Specialists, and Security Project Manager among the titles given, despite all questionnaire responses coming from people tasked with very similar roles. The problem appears to not just be a variety of different names, but also the understanding of specific titles. One response stated that "a Security Engineer in one organisation could have a vastly different role to that at another." Confusion around the naming of roles within the security sector further complicate the question of skill requirements.

5. CONCLUSION

This paper asked what skills does a security professional need in the current information technology environment, and explored this question by looking at the current state of the Australian industry. Recent job listings in the cyber security area were analysed, and current security professionals in industry were asked for their opinion as to what skills were required in this profession.

It was found that each security professional role has its own set of skill requirements, however there is significant overlap between the roles for many soft skills. Analytical and consulting skills were valued as supporting interaction with clients, processing of complex data, and provision of the information generated back to the client. Leadership skills were valued as a means of dealing with other security specialists and promoting security work. The ability to create a process or procedure was valued for senior roles, and the ability to follow an established process or procedure was valued for many roles. Relationship management was seen as an important skill, supporting the interaction of the security professional with peers, clients, and senior management. The questionnaire responses took this a step further to suggest that security professionals need to be able to manage many competing demands, including time, priorities, and the technical aspects of the role.

Security professionals need to be good communicators, and many roles require the applicant to be able to present their ideas and findings in a formal setting. The ability to communicate was further emphasized in the questionnaire responses, with the ability to deal with people and an enthusiasm to learn was highly valued.

A set of skills emerged as common across all categories: experience, qualifications and certifications, and technical expertise. These appear to represent the core 'hard' skills of all security professionals, in terms of a solid background in the area as represented by formal study and industry certifications, and supported by solid experience in the industry. Specific technical skills are also required, although the exact nature of these will vary according to the requirements of each role.

6. REFERENCES

[1] Caldwell, T. (2013). Plugging the cyber-security skills gap. *Computer Fraud & Security, 2013*(7), 5–10.

[2] Casper, W. D., & Papa, S. M. (2012). A Multi-Disciplined Security Engineering Education Approach. In *SAM 2012* (pp. 243–248).

[3] Cyber Security Operations Centre. (2014). *The Cyber Security Picture 2013*. Canberra, ACT.

[4] CySCA. (2014). Cyber Security Career Opportunities.

[5] FBI. (2014). Most Wanted Talent: FBI Seeking Tech Experts to Become Cyber Special Agents. Retrieved December 31, 2014, from http://www.fbi.gov/news/stories/2014/december/fbi-seeking-tech-experts-to-become-cyber-special-agents

[6] Palmer, I. (2012). How to become a network security engineer. *Infosec Institute*. Retrieved from http://resources.infosecinstitute.com/network-security-engineer/

[7] Potter, L. E. C., von Hellens, L. A., & Nielsen, S. H. (2009). Childhood interest in IT and the choice of IT as a career. In *Proceedings of the special interest group on management information system's 47th annual conference on Computer personnel research - SIGMIS-CPR '09* (p. 33). New York, New York, USA: ACM Press. doi:10.1145/1542130.1542138

[8] Symantec. (2014). *2013 Norton Report* (p. 28).

[9] University of Phoenix, & (ISC)2 Foundation. (2014). *Cybersecurity Workforce Competencies: Preparing tomorrow's risk-ready professionals* (p. 16).

The Missing Circle of ISMS (LL-ISMS)

Masoud Hayeri Khyavi
Research Institute for ICT
North Karegar St .Tehran –Iran
+982184977718
m.hayery@itrc.ac.ir

Mina Rahimi
Research Institute for ICT
North Karegar St .Tehran –Iran
+982184977830
rahimi7@itrc.ac.ir

Abstract

Information security management (ISMS) subject is a new area which has been discussed in various companies and organizations and many large and small security companies also are thinking of investigating on this topic. However experience has shown that imitation of a scientific and technological issue and its implementation at the national level not only showed best real effect of that ever(but also) has caused a huge waste of resources. In this paper, we have an idea for localization of ISMS which in regard to ISO standards and importance of this subject, prepares the facility and best area for research and work on ISMS. In this essay we introduce a new circle which cover a new level in ISMS subject.

Categories and Subject Descriptors

H.1.m [Information Systems]: Models and Principle-Miscellaneous

General Terms

Management; Security.

Keywords

Information Security Management System, Security, PDCA Circle, Personnel, Risk

1. Introduction

Information highway, in regard to variety and huge amount of technologies which are growing fast, is a very dangerous road. We are living in a world where a movement can change the achievement of one person, one family, one organization or even one society. This movement (intentionally or unintentionally) would be very simple such as disconnecting a connecting cable from a sensitive socket in critical area of a network, unplugging an electrical cable or being aware of an important secret key or simpler than all example, hearing one word. We cannot ignore all attacks on home computer via cyber which contain hacking, virus and etc. If all these examples and threats happen in a serious moment, in critical area and on an important instrument, will bring irreversible effects. Security management and planning are the fundamental infrastructure for security layout in organizations. In today modern life we are witnessing the transferring of huge amount of data and information that can be very important or vice versa nonsense data. Information security management system or ISMS is a critical and management system which prepare a secure layout for information transferring and exchange, saving data and processing. [1]

SIGMIS-CPR '15, June 04 - 06, 2015, Newport Beach, CA, USA
Copyright 2015 ACM 978-1-4503-3557-7/15/06...$15.00
http://dx.doi.org/10.1145/2751957.2751972

In this paper we are trying to introduce a new vision about ISMS with this hope that governmental and private companies visit this area from new perspective with using new practical ideas resulting to have better knowledge about information and management systems and with wider vision implement them. Imitation without enough knowledge not only cannot solve security problem, but also imposes more cost and added more problems to previous one.

2. ISMS and its Framework

As we mentioned before ISMS is a management method which has special standards. This method considers all the security aspects with management view and based on standards which certified by ISO, distinguish the best way for designing, implementing, running and managing them. In this system all assets (tangible and intangible), vulnerabilities, risks, threats and controls would be considered and based on that a new security comprehensive scheme would be presented. Due to implementing this plan we should be careful enough to assess if this standardize method has this ability to run in a country and if we can trust on the first hand result of this implementation.

2. 1 PDCA Circle

The circle of Plan, Do, Check and Act (PDCA) In ISMS is a model and framework which in fact covers the circle of planning, executing, evaluating and running; this circle should be continuously done with the protection and positive force from management side. [2]

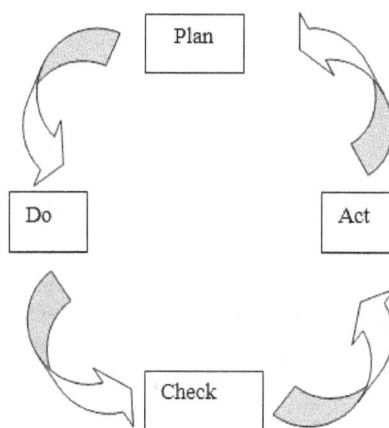

Figure 1- PDCA Circle

In Plan phase, Information security management system is implemented, in Do phase his system is used, in Check phase this system would be evaluated. At the end in Act phase, system is performed and maintained. [2]

The circle is complete and durable. But there is an important question that what is happening to personnel and people who are not in top level but are working in the heart of company? Is and information security management system complete without them? One of the biggest fault in security corporation returns to top level management and managers who focus just only on management and their view are limited to this area, we know management isn't far from fault and unfortunately the effects of the fault is too vast. Implementing of information security management system in organization or just in small part of organization will create constraints and limitations for colleagues and coworkers which almost bring dissatisfaction and negative view for both personnel and customers who are dealing with organization. From psychological point of view, unintentionally a resistant power would be appear against this constraints and limitations. So preparing just an information security management system cannot solve all the problems and is not such a guarantee for security challenges.

For instant the writers of this essay for ISMS design and implementation in some organizations confronted many challenges which was such a barrier for us and we couldn't make a progress, so at the end running ISMS did by much delay.[8]

2. 2 Systems Thinking

The essence of systems theory is that a system needs to be viewed holistically—not merely as a sum of its parts—to be accurately understood. A holistic approach examines the system as a complete functioning unit. Another tenet of systems theory is that one part of the system enables understanding of other parts of the system. "Systems thinking" is now a widely recognized term that refers to the examination of how systems interact, how complex systems work and why "the whole is more than the sum of its parts."2Systems theory is most accurately described as a complex network of events, relationships, reactions, consequences, technologies, processes and people that interact in often unseen and unexpected ways. Studying the behaviors and results of the interactions can assist the manager to better understand the organizational system and the way it functions. While management of any discipline within the enterprise can be enhanced by approaching it from a systems thinking perspective, its implementation will certainly help with managing risk. The success the systems approach has achieved in other fields bodes well for the benefits it can bring to security. The often dramatic failures of enterprises to adequately address security issues in recent years are due, to a significant extent, to their inability to define security and present it in a way that is comprehensible and relevant to all stakeholders. Utilizing a systems thinking approach to information security management will help information security managers address complex and dynamic environments, and will generate a beneficial effect on collaboration within the enterprise, adaptation to operational change, navigation of strategic uncertainty and tolerance of the impact of external factors.

Although systems thinking can contribute to these beneficial outcomes, it is important to note that the Business Model for Information Security, which is based on systems theory, should be treated as part of the strategic plan for the information security program, not as a quick-fix solution for a broken program. Systems thinking should be seen as a long-term exercise that will ultimately aid the enterprise in achieving business goals. In fact, it may help to think of it as a key to organizational maturity. The maturity of the information security program is often related to the maturity of the enterprise, which is linked to the degree systemic thinking is used in the organization. Systemic thinking paves the way for systemic processes [9].

2. 3 Challenges which Lead the ISMS Project to be Failed

Here are various challenges that awaits ISMS implementers. Among them that NISER have observed during the pilot program implementation are [6]:

2-3-1 Fear / Resistance to change

By implementing such an extensive management system in the workplace, changes are definitely going to be made, either in the working process, alterations in personnel responsibilities and many other areas. We observed that some organizations are quite reluctant to make major changes without elaborate justifications in place as it will impact the operations of their business.

2-3-2 Increased cost

By implementing ISMS, either directly or indirectly, it will definitely cause an increase in the costs incurred especially when implementing the controls identified to mitigate the known risks. We discovered that some of the organizations simply did not have adequate budget to allocate the funds and/or resources to implement such a system.

2-3-3 Inadequate knowledge as to approach

Many organizations still do not have the know-how on proper ISMS implementation and they may not have personnel who are qualified subject matter experts in the area. Thus this may lead to the delay or avoidance on the implementation.

2-3-4 Seemingly huge task

Depending on the scope, ISMS can sometimes be such a huge task to complete. Besides the extensive documentations that are required to be prepared, the other activities that needs to be done such as managing resources, user training and awareness and many others may prove to be too daunting to be completed by some of the participating organizations.

2-3-5 Limit Knowledge

One of the problematic criteria for managers is accepting the idea of technical expert while they themselves don't have enough technical knowledge on that area. They accept the idea without consulting or speaking with ordinary personnel. Information technology management in a best way depends on humans, their characters and besides, depends on process and technical considerations.

The managers of information security are going to change their view with researching aspect same as university which contains end user and discussion and making decision with the help of them whit concerning their view about information security.

The research shows these two view somehow is going to be complex which brings many trouble for end users. Information security managers are aware about internal problem but it needed to make balance between managerial power and the view of workers who play an important role in the organization. If their attention more focused on end users with research approach after sometimes the probability of happening the mistakes would be higher.

Making balance between two sides needs more finance which in first step it would be accepted by managers. Some interview with managers cleared that they are concentrating more on speak, presentation and idea developments instead of being curious about end users perspectives. [7]

What is the solution? Which approach minimize these challenges? The result of our research and experiences for preparing RFP and supervising a huge project in this area [8] were the causes of new circle beside the main circle of ISMS which we called that non-management layer or the missing circle of ISMS.

2. 4 Non-Management Layer or Missing Circle of ISMS

We are trying to definite other circle beside PDCA circle which is called ISMS "missing circle". This circle is related to non-management layer and is the ISMS sub-level or low-level- ISMS (LL-ISMS).

LL-ISMS is the complement of main ISMS and in regards of organizational goal can be installed inner ISMS or beside that which personnel and customers would be the main directors. Moreover customers and personnel are effective in running the main ISMS so would be accepted by them much easier in flexible way. Furthermore, with this new circle distinguishing risks and threats in organization would be easier and faster, besides, control enforcement and reaction against threats would be quicker, so in other hand, risk management would be improved. Each of the functions of LL-ISMS (internal or external) has interactional structure with main ISMS. We defined four phase for LL-ISMS with the names of **Do'**, **Feel**, **Think** and **Help**.

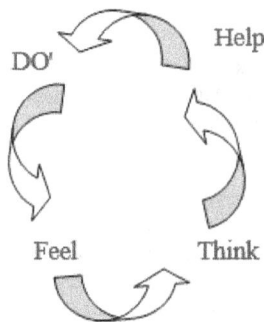

Figure 2- LL-ISMS circle

With attention to figure 2, in phase **"Do' "**, we are defining all the definition which we ran in management layer, in Feel state we are concerning on all the changes which have been made by personnel and customers. In Think State we focus deeply on changes and at the end in Help state all beneficial ideas and thought will be used for management level of ISMS.

"Do' " in LL-ISMS is an state between "Plan" and "Do" which all personnel and customers with previous knowledge and training with security system management planning are going to prepared for Do phase. What is more they are aware and ready for any change in system and relation in organization, besides, they are completely acknowledged about the situation. With this

description do phase in PDCA will be done with power and coherence and cohesion.

"Feel" is a state between "Do" and "Check" in PDCA circle where placed after **"Do' "** in LL-ISMS. In this phase personnel and customers feel the changes, how these changes be in positive way or negative (here being effective or non-effective is not the only element cause this view returns to management view, some happening may be known effective in manager's view while the same one is negative in customer or employee's view, such this event might be the reason of security problem in future). Whereas management in low level was active from first step and influenced by any subject so would be sensitive about any new action and act as a sensor for central management due to prepare the organization to enter the Check phases and be successful with much accuracy.

The **"Think"** phase is a state between "Check" and "ACT" in PDCA which is located after **"Feel"** State in LL-ISMS. In this plane, Personnel and employees will think about the results of their acts and behavior and prepare all which should be done to enter the next phase which is called ACT.

The final state in LL-ISMS is **"Help"** phase which in the middle of "ACT" and "Plan", plays the role of Auxiliary arm. Here the ideas and the results of the personnel in each layers, tangible or intangible will be transfer to the upper layer so all the vulnerabilities and defects which have not been observed before or after ACT state(however in small details) will appear and the system with suitable speed will enter to Plan phase Further.

During time of ISMS implementation, while workers enter to "Check" phase with enough enthusiasm, they will know themselves part of PDCA circle so they will put their best foot forward, In consequence, employee would think on what he has done and what is best to do in "Think" phase which all have come from previous positive sense. Gaining international certification or higher ranking is not an initiative factor for employees unless they have positive internal feeling of personal achievement which is the aim of "feel" phase.

In final step which is "help" phase, personnel who received glamorous experiences from previous steps in ISMS implementation in different cases such as work hardships, results and so on, know themselves as a success key in progress of project. Their feedback in technical and operational aspects surely is essential and beneficial for improvement of project.

As mentioned in advance, LL-ISMS due to internal nature and being aside (with regard to PDCA circle) has interactive structure with main ISMS.

In figure 3 and 4, LL-ISMS are being seen inner and beside PDCA circle.

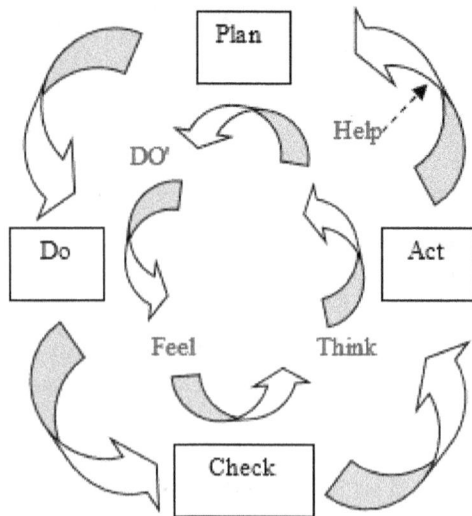

Figure 3- LL-ISMS in inter side of ISMS

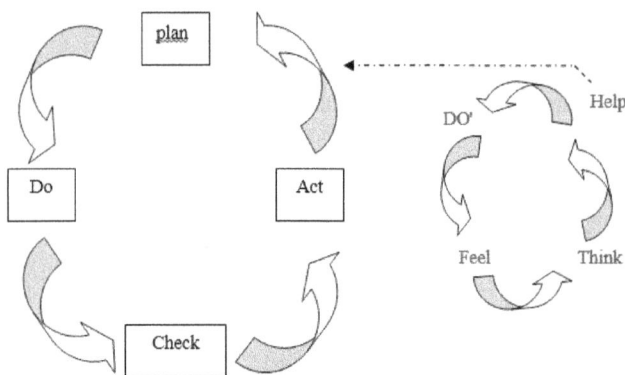

Figure 4- LL-ISMS beside ISMS

Preparing trust, reserve it and promoting is the most significant role of security, while the root of trust returns to the true and strong belief between two different parts. Belief is an internal sense and when you trust someone completely that belief on him/her and are sure about the accessible goals.

For implementing ISMS, usually routine process of PDCA is eye-catching so the main concentration of organization would be gaining the Certification of ISO 27001, meanwhile the important role of personnel, just are considered in terms of their knowledge or career levels or job ranking and their holistic view toward special tasks which include their sense and their feeling are omitted.

In the project we worked on as a supervisor, one problem we faced continuously was about personnel's worry in time of assessment security in their department. Person who was responsible in the particular department was cooperating due the job duty not because of enough motivation or constructive working atmosphere. In some cases we were witness of even Interruption in the process of project which needed to be solved by head manager or consultant. In this situation "positive feeling" is critical because of its effects on all aspect of job. We want to

insist that managers of organization who persuade workers in scientific subject, besides should have psychological view; in other word we need to implement new culture on working places.

3. Conclusion

The success of an Information Security Management System (ISMS) lies in the best combination of People, Policies, Procedures, Compliances, Standards, Processes, Products and Technology.

Information security management is a continuous process. The ISMS along with policies, procedures and compliances should be reviewed and updated to match with the latest market trends and requirements. The cycle of review, gap analysis and update will ensure the long term benefits to the organization by protecting its IT assets in the most effective manner. Understanding the importance of security implementation is very crucial. If employees do not understand the necessity of it, they may not take part in the implementation wholeheartedly and it may lead to failure of the project or delay in achieving results. The senior management, being the prime sponsor and motivator of the project, plays an important role in this matter from the very beginning. The security solution should be carefully designed to achieve cost-effectiveness and return-of-investment (ROI) adding business values, apart from satisfying the compliance regulations keeping in mind that the investment on information security is an insurance cost which will protect organization's information from loss or destruction, avoiding downtime and thus increasing productivity[10].

Concerning a complete circle which connects management level with non-management levels, will further consolidate the security system and will minimize the challenges especially in ISMS implementation. LL-ISMS will brings benefits and advantages such as:

ISO standards and other security standards suggest all requirements [3] and recommendations [4], but surely it is not a force to limit yourself in obligations without presenting any other advice.

Security standards have been prepared with thinking of their authors and supporters and have been presented trough an "overall solution". ISMS scheme via standards, plays the backbone and infrastructure for security body of an organization and following that in wider area such as country, but all conditions and areas are not the same, so the skeleton should be compatible in special manner which in any condition tolerates the pressure and guaranties the highest reliability.

With the suggestion idea from the authors of this essay, we are able to find a suitable answer for each of security requirements, cause the personnel of the lower layer in organization with the states of Feel and Think would recognize the reason of each of them by themselves and perhaps in some cases with their suggestions and new ideas increase the efficiency of security scheme and decreases the cost. With this idea we are going to localize the ISMS. Furthermore this new circle (figure 5) will bring an invisible connection between security management level and its subsets which advantages in trust and confidence in the firm.

In this presented scheme with Cost prediction and presenting a basic dynamic plan, this new ISMS are much prone to beneficial cost, energy and time in implementation and execution.

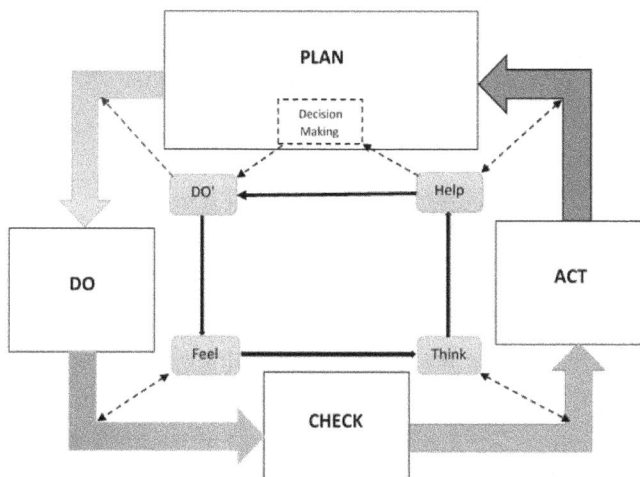

Figure 5- Connection between "missing circle" and the larger circle (PDCA)

Other merits of these two circle near each other are interconnection between different management levels, flexibility, personnel's responsibilities and customers' commitments for themselves and for their firms (they know themselves effective in their organization) and etc. the most important gift which this circle brings as a new subject in security area is "security near each other with mutual trust beside".

4. References

[1] S. AbuZineh. *Success Factors of Information Security Management: A Comparative Analysis between Jordanian and Finnish Companies.* http://www.pafis.shh.fi/graduates/samabu04.pdf, 2006

[2] V. K. Puthuseeri. www.infosecwriters.com/text_resources/pdf/ISMS_V Kumar.pdf, January 2006.

[3] ISO/IEC. *ISO 27001: Information technology-Security techniques-Information security management systems-Requirements*, 2005.

[4] ISO/IEC. *ISO17799: Information technology - Security techniques - Code of practice for information security management*, 2005.

[5] NISCC Briefing 08/a. *Social engineering against information systems: what is it and how do you protect yourself.* www.niscc.gov.uk/niscc/docs/SocialEngineering08a0 6.pdf, June 2006.

[6] S. Abdul Jalil, R. Abdul Hamid. *ISMS Pilot Program Experiences: Benefits, Challenges &Recommendations.* http://www.cybersecurity.my/en/knowledge_banks/ar ticles/main/detail/2372/index.html

[7] F. Heyrani http://www.douran.com/DesktopModules/News/New sView.aspx?TabID=1&Site=douranportal&Lang=fa-IR&ItemID=1724&mid=15226&wVersion=Staging. ISMS Sector. Douran Group

[8] *ISMS Plan and Implementation in Telecommunication Company of Khorasan-e-Razavi.* IRAN, 2006

[9] ISACA Knowledge Center. *An Introduction to the Business Model or Information Security.* ISACA Computer Organization. USA, 2009

[10] M. Dey. *Information Security Management - A Practical Approach.* IEEE Conference Publications; Page(s): 1 – 6. AFRICON 2007.

IT Surveillance and Social Implications in the Workplace

Mohammad Mohammad
University of Western Sydney
Parramatta, NSW
mohammad.phd@hotmail.com

ABSTRACT

The workplace is where most adults spend roughly half of their waking hours. It is not surprising, therefore, that employment practices affect a broad range of privacy rights. With the exception of polygraph testing, there are few areas of workplace activities that are covered by the American constitution or privacy laws. Accordingly, employers have a great deal of leeway in collecting data on their employees, regulating access to personnel files, and disclosing file contents to outsiders. In addition to the issue of personnel files, workplace privacy involves such practices as polygraph testing, drug testing, computer and telephone monitoring, and interference with personal lifestyle. All of these practices stem from a combination of modern employer concerns employee theft, drug abuse, productivity, courtesy and the protection of trade secrets and technological advances that make it more economical to engage in monitoring and testing. The result for employees, however, is a dramatic increase in workplace surveillance. Unprecedented numbers of workers are urinating into bottles for employer run, drug-testing programs. Thousands of data entry operators have their every keystroke recorded by the very computers on which they are working. Surveillance is so thorough in some offices that employers can check to see exactly when employees leave their work stations to go to the bathroom and how long they take. A significant step toward resolving these issues can be taken by considering the possibilities and limitations posed by the extended use of surveillance and developing a model to balance these competing concerns. The model is proposed a master plan entitled "Monitoring Process Model (MPM)" showing the employers and employees and their inter-related activities. Which uses a thorough examination of the research literature, thus far to advocate the use of justifications for surveillance that Weigh Company interests against a notion of transactional privacy a form of privacy that focuses on trust and relationships.

Categories and Subject Descriptors

K.4.1 [**Public Policy Issues**]: Privacy; K.4.2 [**Social Issues**]: Employment; K.5.2 [**Governmental Issues**]: Regulation.

General Terms

Legal Aspects, Performance, Security, Measurement.

Keywords

surveillance, monitor, privacy, trust.

1. INTRODUCTION

In a time when businesses conduct more and more of their business communications through advanced telecommunications technologies like the Internet, blackberries, and smart phones, the surveillance of employees has become a more frequent topic of concern, both among employers and employees. Employee communications form the backbone of business, and they carry with them the ability to sell a product or service, create a hostile work environment, or leak company secrets.

As such the success of these communication environments is crucial not only to the success of individual companies, but also to the overall success of U.S business, since all business must negotiate the complex legal and financial issues associated with employee actions. Consequently, finding ways of monitoring and filtering these communications in a manner acceptable to the law and the business environment remains a high priority. In addition, significant legal issues must be understood and taken into account. Employees have an expectation and right to privacy, and businesses have a legitimate interest in preventing employee communications from harming business profits or opening the business to legal action.

The purpose of this research is to establish and analyse how researchers have understood the issue of workplace surveillance, its benefits and its problems, and the suggestions they have for improving the viability and justifications for monitoring regimes. Through the research, an investigation is carried out regarding the process and warrants for monitoring, as well as the legal stakes involved in any monitoring regime (from no monitoring to intense surveillance). Finally, as a result of this research will make a recommendation about the best method for framing and conducting workplace surveillance.

2. ANALYSIS OF INSTITUTIONAL VALUE OF SURVEILLANCE

Prior to the explosion of Internet communications and the increasing role they play in the business environment, workplace surveillance held a limited significance. With computers now pervasive in many workplaces, and with the provision of Internet access now conventional requirement for workplace productivity, employee communications have taken on a whole new dimension of complexity. In addition, the use of personal mobile devices, including iPads and iPhones, has created a porous workplace environment that further complicates the possibility and desirability of workplace surveillance. Nevertheless, studies show that almost 77.7% of major companies in the United States already engage in workplace surveillance activity (Holmes, 2003). This number is likely to increase as communications technologies continue to evolve and more and more company interactions and strategy sessions take place in conjunction with telecommuting and online interactions. As more and more companies consider the nature and extent of their workplace surveillance, they will need to better understand the issues that prompt and are prompted by various workplace surveillance regimes.

3. REASONS FOR SURVEILLANCE

Surveillance does not take place on an ad hoc, random basis; rather specific warrants are given and particular policies are adopted. Already, an impressive amount of businesses are enacting surveillance policies in an effort to monitor employee communications (Holmes, 2003; Watson, 2002), for two good reasons. First, there are obvious benefits for workplace productivity. An estimated one out of eight workers spends up to two hours a day on non-work related activity (Buss, 2001), and some companies have needed to start monitoring simply to understand why all their bandwidth is disappearing and slowing down legitimate business communications.

The drain this places on overall productivity is a serious concern. Not only does it reduce overall hours spent working on workplace-related tasks, it may also impede actual efforts by other employees to complete their respective workloads by slowing down or interfering with their communications efforts. Not only can surveillance serve to curb this drain, the ability to determine who is and is not working can actually boost productivity. (Lee & Kleiner, 2003) for example, argue that surveillance can help to motivate employees to work hard. Managers argue that they can fairly evaluate employees' performance because monitoring gives employers a clear picture of which employees are hard workers and which are unproductive. Because their efforts on the job directly reflect on performance appraisals, workers become more commit¬ted. This argument may not manifest in the workplace, but it indicates the potential for combining incentives with surveillance programs as a means of encouraging employees. Then again, this potential may be limited. (Lee & Kleiner, 2003) offer little empirical support for their claim, and many employees may find the idea that surveillance would be tied to incentives rather thin. After all, outcome based incentives provide a far more reasonable, fair, and more accurate reflection of the value of an employee's overall contribution.

Monitoring also serves a more functional purpose employees may not practice e-mail safety and thus open up company servers to hacking or viruses. Monitoring communications in and out can make these occurrences significantly less likely (Watson, 2002). Given the high costs (in time and money) of disruptions to a company's information infrastructure, a compelling business interest exists in limiting vulnerability by controlling employee communication rights.

Second, there are substantial legal risks that surveillance can address. Surveillance technologies offer the possibility of that preemptive policy decisions can ward off or limit any legally prescribed restitution from infractions in federal or state law. Employees that send e-mails out of a malicious sense of humour jokes or stories that derive their humorous implications from making fun of sex or ethnicity can place the entire company at risk for harassment and equal protection claims. (Buss, 2001) notes "Because of the unprecedented sensi¬tivity toward harass¬ment in today's work¬place, the legal pitfalls created by this prob¬lem nearly eclipse the productivity issue." (Buss, 2001) tells the story of Peter Chung, a finance employee at the world-famous Carlyle Group, who used a corporate e-mail account to boast of his sexual conquests. Carlyle fired Chung when the e-mail became public, but that publicity may have already cost

them in reputation and resources. "More e-mails like Peter Chung's could be used to paint a pic¬ture of a 'hostile environment' toward women," (Buss, 2001) "which is the basis for many of today's sexual harass¬ment lawsuits. In 1995, for example, Chevron Corp. paid four female plaintiffs $2.2 million to settle a suit over just that alle¬gation when an inter¬nal e-mail reached them about 'why beer is better than women.'" (Buss, 2001) may be exaggerating the risks, as his collection of anecdotes are not backed by corresponding statistical analysis, but he is right to hype the liability that such unmonitored e-mails and communications carry with them. With payouts like the one from Chevron, companies may want to err on the side of caution (Panko & Beh, 2002), describe similar legal concerns. The legal ramifications from sexual harassment claims, to take just one example, can be particularly difficult for companies who fail to engage in monitoring/surveillance regimes.

While a single inappropriate e-mail, like Chung's, is rarely sufficient enough an infraction to provide an actionable case, companies that fail to monitor internal communications may be unaware that multiple instances have been circulating among employees:

An employer's lax attitude toward Internet and e-mail use and abuse may allow racially offensive or sexually explicit material to pervade the work environment and create or contribute to a hostile work environment (Panko & Beh, 2002).

Under existing employment law, employers must take proactive steps to prevent such a degradation of the work environment, and a failure to enact a clear and effective monitoring regime can put the entire business at risk for legal action. (Panko & Beh, 2002) are not entirely clear about what the damage of such action might be, and given the brevity of their case review, the legal history seems as of yet undecided as to the specific standards by which monitoring effectiveness and consent are to be measured. To this extent, their piece raises more questions than it answers though the questions it does ask are the ones companies should be asking themselves, the ones that address the possibility of workplace-based litigation.

The legal risks do not end with harassment. The possibility of corporate espionage, the trading of company secrets, or the inadvertent disclosure of confidential information, can have disastrous effects on a company's financial outcomes. Employees are typically asked to sign confidentiality agreements, but these cannot resolve all issues that may arise, either due to accident or maliciousness, and they still only allow a post hoc recourse, which means that the damage has already been done.

Fortunately, the Electronic Communications Privacy Act, which governs the expectation of privacy for any and all electronic exchanges, has built in exceptions which allow for monitoring as a result of these two risks. The first is the provider exception, which states that the provider can monitor communications on its own systems, so many companies are now providing their own servers and Internet services, so that they can better monitor communications for the risk factors noted above. The second exception is even more specific and is called the "ordinary course of business" exception. It says that the "employer may monitor employee communications to ensure such legitimate business objectives as assur¬ing quality control, preventing sexual harassment, and preventing unauthorized use of equipment, such as excessive telephone or e-mail usage." (Nord & McCubbins, 2006). The standards for proving that any curtailment of employee communication meets this "ordinary course" are unclear, though so far the courts have shown considerable deference to the employer side of the equation. In Smith v. Pillsbury, for example, a "court in Pennsylvania held that an employer could discipline and discharge an employee for sending inappropriate e-mail...even in contravention of a promise not to monitor e-mail" (Panko & Beh, 2002). Still, there are exceptions and further ambiguities. In Restuccia v. Burk Technology, for example, an employer searched computer backups in order to ascertain details about an employee's e-mail habits. This time, rather than simply defer to the employer's rights under the ECPA, the Massachusetts court "plaintiffs had a reasonable expectation of privacy in their e-mail messages" and left the merits of the invasion as a matter for trial. These were different cases with different facts in different jurisdictions, obviously, but the inconsistency tells us that there remains some important limits on the deference awarded to employers' monitoring rights.

4. PROBLEMS CAUSED BY SURVEILLANCE REGIMES

A number of problems can be caused by the adoption of a workplace surveillance policy. The first and major concern is that employees will feel a lack of trust and respect on the part of management, and develop a desire "pushback" against what they consider unnecessary or authoritarian monitoring programs. This tendency may be more significant if the work environment is especially porous, with various telecommunications devices requiring worktime outside of work space.

I'm spending the whole weekend taking cell calls for you, and now you're telling me I can't spend 15 minutes at my desk surfing the Web to try to make dinner reservations for me and my wife? (Panko & Beh, 2002).

Faced with a situation wherein work consistently invades the home, employees may feel less incentive to meet employee expectations, or may actively seek alternative employment. In some situations, employees may simply circumvent surveillance methods using their own devices, which would mean that surveillance fails to increase productivity. The author explains that employers may need to compromise somewhat and adopt common sense policies that allow reasonable personal use of workplace communication facilities. If this does not happen, employees will increasingly turn towards using their own communications at work for personal business (Watson, 2002).

This point cannot be overstated. Employers can monitor communications, but they have the capacity to monitor only the communications they provide. Should employees begin carrying a second cell phone, or using an alternate form of text messaging, or should they actively attempt to circumvent surveillance through anonymous routers, encryption, or domain masks, employers will lose more than mere control over information flow; they will also lose the time and work that employees spend on these acts of circumvention. One can imagine an escalating game of communications espionage, with companies installing audio and video taps in office areas to catch employees, who in turn begin generating white noise or positioning objects to obstruct recording, and so on and so forth.

In addition, other legal issues come into play that will not benefit company interests. (Holmes, 2003) notes that although courts have routinely limited the scope of employee privacy rights. This tendency seems likely to continue (Wilczeck & Prokott, 2005) as

corporate lobbies and lawyers continue to influence both legislative policy definition and subsequent judicial interpretation. Nevertheless, this tendency remains just that, and so the chance exists that courts may in fact find in favour of the employee given certain situations or facts. Given this possibility, employers need to be aware that stricter surveillance policies may actually increase the legal risks to the company as they can create an incentive for lawsuits by employees who feel company monitoring has been done unfairly, with prejudice, or done in a manner that has violated their privacy. Companies that monitor certain classes of employees (men more than women, African Americans more than European Americans, or as might be the case these days, Arab Americans more than the rest of employees) may find themselves on the wrong end of a discrimination lawsuit, or if enough employees feel adversely and disproportionably affected by a surveillance regime, these companies may face class action or even criminal charges. Other problems may arise at the level of the work environment. The sense of community and fun that makes business creativity and cooperative success possible may be diminished by overly zealous surveillance policies. (Oravec, 2002) argues that surveillance policies that reduce online recreational time misunderstand how workplace creativity and job enthusiasm gets fostered. She argues that the small meetings and fun that used to be had during workplace face-to-face encounters is increasingly being found in online interactions, and that if channeled and encouraged within particular limits, this constructive recreation may actually be more productive than simply forcing workers to carry on pretence of committed work. One can imagine a situation in which employees feel so scrutinised and limited by workplace monitoring that they take up alternate, less productive forms of recreation, or that their productivity tapers off as the day progresses, as they wait for their release at the end of the business day.

5. JUSTIFICATIONS AND SURVEILLANCE REGIMES

Many employers considering solidified, enhanced, or introductory surveillance regimes are aware of the negative attitudes held towards such regimes by their employees. The rather reasonable desire to be able to get through a work day without the possibility of being constantly monitored means that many employees may be unwilling to see the inherent value of such policies, believing that their freedom to work should not be assaulted by corporate oversight in its pursuit of profit and reduced liability. As a consequence, employers will need to develop justifications for their surveillance policies that employees will find willing to accept, as that acceptance can mitigate negative reactions to changes in the workplace monitoring policies.

6. EMPLOYEE TRUST AND SURVEILLANCE

Much of the literature agrees that the difficult negotiation between the needs of the employer and the privacy and desires of employee centres around the question of trust. Three factors influence the possibility that trust can be maintained during surveillance regimes. First, employees tend to believe that monitoring is more necessary and thus acceptable if employers can provide reasonable justifications for implementing monitoring procedures. The quality of the justifications will matter, and some evidence shows that employees make well-reasoned assessments of the viability of employer justifications (Stanton & Weiss,

2003). However, the standards for "reasoned" assessment remains unclear in Stanton and Weiss, and while it seems appropriate to presume that employees are capable of making sophisticated value judgments, the degree to which this capacity exists in reality will likely depend upon a number of factors not touched upon in (Stanton & Weiss, 2003) study: the employee's identification with their employer, the financial incentives provided by their employment, the degree of interference that surveillance regimes produce, and the overall value placed on individual freedom relative to corporate interest.

Employee personalities will also influence the reception of surveillance policies. Extraverts will be less concerned with monitoring overall, whereas more introverted employees will have a high initial objection to monitoring (Zweig & Webster, 2003). This finding is obviously not surprising, but it is beneficial to have the certainty provided by statistical research. (Zweig & Webster, 2003) have also shown that these objections can be reduced if adequate information is given about the nature of the monitoring and if some control over the implementation of monitoring can be given to employees. Their work suffers from a lack of specificity, in that the definition of "adequate" remains rather ill-defined, and the idea of giving "some" control over monitoring policies to employees may be ill-advised and counterproductive if the goal of the surveillance regime is to curtail likely behaviour on the part of employees. Assuming the assessed need for such surveillance has any basis in reality, those same employees will then use their newly awarded control to mitigate the value of any monitoring system. Nevertheless, their research points to one way that employers can approach the question of surveillance without simultaneously violating employee trust.

Third, having workplace surveillance policies correspond to legal standards can maximise employee trust. The author suggests that businesses should follow GAO (General Accounting Office) standards when defining their monitoring policy, and that they should make explicit that: company computing sys¬tems are provided as tools for business and all information created, accessed, or stored using these systems are the property of the company and subject to monitoring, audit¬ing or review (Holmes, 2003). (Holmes, 2003) is right to suggest this, but the article overstates the relationship between standardisation and employee trust. No evidence is provided, for example, that employees are aware of or approve of the GAO definition, and so the argument for trust must be predicated on the appeal of a legal standard in general rather than a particular standard in particular (Holmes, 2003) does not provide the data to justify this degree of specificity. One might make an alternate case that an employer who wanted to appear even more sensitive to their employee's privacy rights would go to lengthy to differentiate themselves from the accepted standard and instead stress how progressive and unique is their monitoring policy. (Holmes, 2003) is right that legal standards have value, without a doubt, but there is no reason to believe that the value will be inherently persuasive to employees.

7. FAIRNESS AS A STRATEGY FOR JUSTIFICATION

This fairness and/or justice provide interesting alternatives to the conventional justifications of legal liability and workplace productivity, though this alternative remains relatively unexplored compared to the more 'normative approaches' means relating to

an ideal standards of surveillance or model. (Introna, 2000) provides perhaps the most striking theoretical outline of this approach. His argument begins by noting that questions of legal rights (i.e. privacy rights) fail to offer a reasonable metric for formulating monitoring policies, since the private/public split is meaningless in a workplace, since wages and salaries are paid-for work time and not personal time. In such a situation, a claim for privacy protection seems ill-founded, or at least unsustainable.

For (Introna, 2000), this situation sets the stage for a more pernicious problem, namely an imbalance of power between the employer who monitors and the employee who is subject to surveillance. This power difference explains theoretically the phenomenon of "pushback" and the concomitant legal abreactions that accompany it. Because employees fear the decisions that employers will make with the information provided by surveillance, they are unlikely to start from a position of trust; the power differential is too great. Stressing legal arguments about the nature of privacy, and noting the courts' deference to employers, only makes the situation less resolvable, since such justifications this would include even the standardised legal language only reinforces the notion that the fundamental power differential marks the entire system as unfair and/or unjust.

As an alternative, (Introna, 2000) argues that privacy be thought as a value not in terms of its legal foundation, but rather as a crucial concept in what, drawing on philosopher Rawls, which (Leiden, 2013) noted he calls a model of "distributive" justice. This model would attempt to balance an understanding that an individual derives benefit and security from privacy with an understanding that a collective (a company/employer, in this case) derives security from transparency. The balance would be determined by thinking through a "veil of ignorance," a hypothetical situation in which the interested parties devise a plan without knowing which end of the power dynamic they would occupy after the position is in place. The author explains:

A fair set of rules for this distribution would be a set of rules that self-interested participants would choose if they were completely ignorant about their own status in the subsequent contexts where these rules will be applied (Introna, 2000). In this model, deference would be provided to the employees because the employees already suffer from a substantial power and control, even before any implementation of surveillance mechanisms in the workplace. So a fair regime of, surveillance would provide the employee with the following:

• Avoid monitoring unless explicitly justified by the employer.

• Provide mechanisms for the employee to have maximum control over the use of monitoring data (Introna, 2000).

This claim, supported by the above warrants and the philosophical grounding (Leiden, 2013) noted that in Rawls theory of justice, echoes the empirical data provided by (Zweig & Webster, 2003) though it suffers from the same ambiguities. Still, the theoretical grounding provides more hope than does the empirical data that prompts (Zweig & Webster, 2003) to suggest a similar approach, namely (Introna, 2000) offers a way of framing the justification for surveillance based on a sound and more persuasive appeal of fairness/justice, rather than choosing an option that advocates surveillance based on what seems most productive and least troublesome for the employee. (Zweig & Webster, 2003) by contrast, functionally advocate that employees should consider strong justifications for surveillance alongside certain concessions regarding the control of monitored data only because it makes introverted employees less likely to cause problems in response to a particular monitoring regime.

8. PHILOSOPHICAL PRETEXTS

Privacy suffers almost as much philosophical ambiguity as it does legal ambiguity. In a lengthy review of, the different conceptualization of privacy, (Walters, 2001) notes three basic views on privacy. The first view believes that privacy is a claim or a right; in other words, privacy is an actionable concept by which one individual can invoke a distance between them and some other person or collective. This is the conception of privacy most obviously affiliated with the legal grounding discussed previously, but it suffers from several theoretical flaws. First, it begs the question of its own moral worth (Walters, 2001) a claim serves as a vehicle to an end, it says nothing about the nature of the claim itself nor the value of the end achieved. In addition, it assumes that one maintains a degree of autonomy, intent, and "will" that may not be true in a concrete social situation. This may not be the case, for example, in an employment situation structured by pre-existing power imbalances.

The second conception of privacy is that of control; here the individual maintains a sense of ownership over the information they themselves produce. The author notes this definition also suffers a fairly serious flaw: A person shipwrecked on a deserted island or lost in a forest has certainly lost control over personal information, but we cannot say they have no privacy; in fact, they have too much privacy. Similarly, a person who wilfully discloses everything about herself to others cannot be said to have lost control over personal information (Walters, 2001). As with the first definition, this too requires a belief in will and autonomy, and that belief may not match reality.

The final definition treats privacy as a state of limited access. (Cozzetto & Pedeliski, 1997) offer a similar formulation of privacy as "personal space." Here the individual neither controls information nor makes actionable claims; rather privacy instead means a presumed limit on the ability of a person or collective to gather information from some other individual. Interestingly, privacy is here thought as a social relation rather than as something that gains its status from a legal system (a claim) or the individual (control). As such, this definition shares much in common with the one that animates (Introna, 2000) discussion of justice as justification.

9. MONITORING PROCESS MODEL (MPM)

9.1 Organizations: Monitoring/Programs

t Generally, employers have a right to monitor company's network and other technologies associated with it, such as PCs, wireless devices and e-mails in accordance with any relevant policies or procedures. An employee may strongly object to monitoring, yet perceive little real opportunity to change the situation. Such an employee is likely to remain in the current position despite strong negative feelings to monitoring. (Cozzetto & Pedeliski, 2003) in 'Privacy and the workplace: Technology and public employment' agree that although an organization may inform its workers when they are being monitored, the degree to which employees can truly choose whether

to submit to monitoring may be severely limited by external factors. However, an ethical organization must inform prospective employees that it performs electronic monitoring, what types of monitoring it conducts, and how the information obtained from monitoring is used by the organization or third party.

9.2 Identifying the Issues/Problems Related to (Employers and Employees)

Managers are most likely sensitive to the legal requirements imposed by electronic personnel monitoring. However, focusing on what one can and cannot legally do does not address the underlying ethical concerns associated with electronic monitoring of employees. For this purpose, a model for the framework has to be developed taking into consideration all the factors and activities involved. The MPM attempts to provide such a framework taking into consideration what have been experienced due to surveillance in the workplace from both sides' employers and employees. Employers are always feeling exposed to theft, vandalism and misconduct, to reduce security risks and legal liability, as an employer, you need to use other forms of security and supervision. On the other hand, employees see its potential dehumanize their workplace environment.

Underlying the debate is a belief about employee and employer rights. To address these concerns directly, we must explicitly consider this conflict of rights and how best to manage it. I believe attributes allow both employers and employee concerns to be addressed: moderating monitoring and disclosing monitoring. Employers need to carefully identify important key elements:

• what they need to monitor and why.

• also need to clearly convey this information to their employees.

(Introna, 2000) reframing of the privacy issue, away from legal standing and toward a mechanism of justice, hints at the fundamental importance of privacy as a value in negotiating any surveillance policy. Of course, privacy has always been a contested issue, especially in the American legal system. While no portion of the constitution expressly outlines a "right" to privacy, the prevailing belief is that certain portions of the constitution often cited that amendments require an implicit right to privacy in order to function. While this view has steady purchase in today's legal environment, the ambiguous legal grounding for privacy provides a significant degree of leeway in interpreting specific instantiations of that right. As a consequence, it is worth considering more thoroughly the value of privacy within the context of this research.

The recuperative move in Walters's article comes later, however, when he turns to (Fried, 1984) treatment of privacy as a relational function, one that enables basic interactions like respect and trust. Fried, 1984) continues to believe in a public/private split that, following (Introna, 2000) does not provide a foundation for privacy in the workplace.

Nevertheless, one can take the notion of privacy as a relational device what might be called transactional privacy and see in this a more solid value upon which to justify the employee's concerns over surveillance and to return the debate over surveillance justifications to the model espoused by (Introna, 2000). Instead of, claiming that privacy is a right or that individuals should be left alone and therefore, free from surveillance an argument that cannot win. Given the legal and financial forces pressuring employers the notion that privacy must be respected to earn and enable trust has a reasonable chance or curtailing and limiting the invasiveness of surveillance regimes. As this review has shown, trust remains fundamental to eliminating 'pushback' and enabling company success

9.3 Productivity/ Employees' Performance

time: These organizations could not function effectively until employees performance were measured and assessed the nature of, their ability, or quality, so as to identify those who were fit for workplace. Using score points scale to identify good and poor performance is important. But on the other hand, surveillance is also important because it can identify not only those who are failing to achieve the organization goals but those who can achieve them, and provide a good customer service and beyond.

profit/cost: Surveillance has social costs (Rosen, 2000) and of course, it does not necessarily ensure that improvements to employee performance and productivity, implementing standardized work processes to ensure Return On Investment (ROI). For example, create employee to-do-list and identify whether those tasks have been successfully completed within the required timeframe. Once the time, cost and profit measured effectively against productivity.

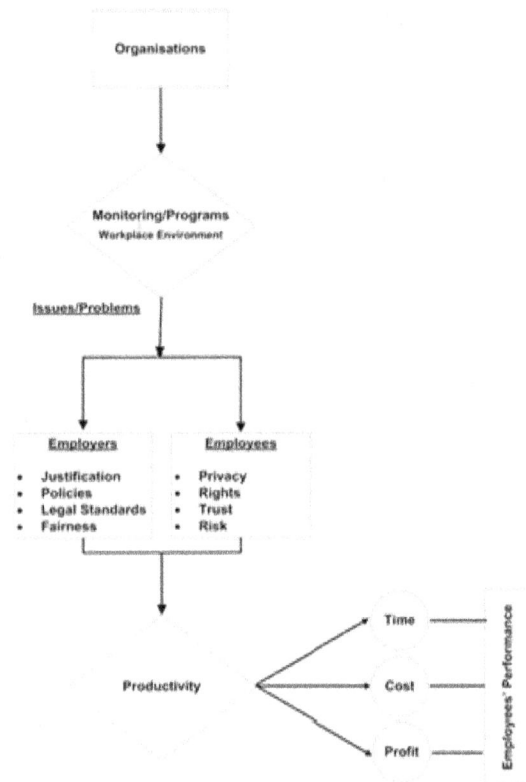

Figure 1. Monitoring Process Model (MPM).

10. BALANCING PRIVACY AND SECURITY

'Transactional privacy' is information processing for business transactions involving the collection, modification and retrieval of all transaction data. Which offers a way of negotiating the surveillance regime, but lest the balance shift to far toward the employee, it remains important to stress the very real security concerns that animate the onset of monitoring in the first place. As notes previously, the historical record and empirical data show that companies have much to lose in terms of profit and liability if they do not monitor their employees electronic communications. A variety of solutions exist. (Walters, 2001) proposes that employees be given opt-in/opt-out rights for any regulatory regime. This would give employees more control over the data accumulated on them, but would continue to allow companies to keep surveillance apparatus in place. Unfortunately, the social pressures being what they are, it seems unlikely that employees would ever opt out. Employees would be concerned that failure to opt-in would indicate a lack of trustworthiness and could adversely affect future employment prospects. Nevertheless, social pressure is not the same as legal pressure, and the illusion of choice may provide a greater level of trust and sense of control than simply informing employees that they are now subject to strict observation. (Walters, 2001) also proposes the use of PETs, or 'privacy enhancing technologies' can help to design information and communication systems and services in a way that minimizes the collection and use of personal data and facilitate compliance with data protection rules. though most of the examples he provides do not touch upon the employer/employee relationship.

In the end, there are no quick and universal solutions to determine the proper balance between security and privacy, just as there is no quick and universal means of defining privacy. Instead, the varied perspectives in the research stress that any balancing, while necessary, will need to be done between specific employers and their specific employees.

11. CONCLUSIONS & FUTURE WORK

Employee interests will continue to be difficult to perform, and even more difficult if not impossible to resolve with any finality. Nevertheless, this research provides solid evidence for two conclusions: first, that surveillance will be both increasingly 'normative' believes that laws are decided as a consensus based on the norms and values of society and increasingly necessary for companies concerned with legal risks and worker productivity, and second, that the negative consequences of surveillance can be mitigated through an attention to trust and fairness, as well as a demonstrable attention to the employee's need for constructive recreation and respect from their employer. The exact means by which this attention can be demonstrated, and the exact balancing point between these competing interests will likely vary in each case, but companies should strive to take into account the need for this balancing act when they decide upon the need and means for monitoring their employees. Crucial to this balancing act will be a discourse about the nature of privacy, and for that discourse to be productive, a critical review of the research points to a transactional appreciation of privacy, one that encourages fairness and trust.

12. REFERENCES

[1] Anonymous. 2015. Canadian Employment Law Today. *Carswell Publishing*. Vol.1, No. 1: pp.1

[2] Buss, D. 2001. Spies Like Us. *Training*. Vol. 38, No. 2: pp. 44-48.

[3] Cozzetto, D. A. and Pedeliski, T. B. 1997. Privacy and the Workplace: Technology and Public Employment. *Public Personnel Management*. Vol. 26, No. 4: pp. 515-527.

[4] Fried, S. 1984. Philosophical Dimensions of Privacy. *Yale Law Journal*. Vol. 12, No. 7: 475-493.

[5] Grant, I. 2008. Can you trust your staff?. *Computer Weekly*. Vol. 7, No. 1: pp.1

[6] Halpern, D., Reville, P. J., and Grunewald, D. 2008. Management and legal issues regarding electronic surveillance of employees in the workplace. *Journal of Business Ethics*. Vol. 80, No. 2: pp. 175-180.

[7] Holmes, J.D. 2003. Will Big Brother Cause Your Company to Be Sued? *Information Systems Security*. Vol. 12, No. 3: pp. 39-44.

[8] Introna, L.D. 2000. Workplace Surveillance, Privacy and Distributive Justice. *Computers and Society*, Vol. 30, No. 4: pp. 33-39.

[9] Kotyk, J. 2013. What is a reasonable expectation of privacy in the information contained on a workplace computer?. *Education Law Journal*. Vol. 22, No. 2: pp. 223-229.

[10] Kozlowski, J. 2009. Privacy, please! Parks & Recreation. *Technical report*, NJ.

[11] Lee, S. and Kleiner, B.H. 2003. Electronic Surveillance in the Workplace. *Management Research News*. Vol. 26, No. 2: pp. 72-81.

[12] Leiden, N.L.D. 2013. John Rawls, A Theory of Justice Available from: ProQuest ebrary. [12 March 2015].

[13] Lyon, D. 2001. Facing the Future: Seeking Ethics for Everyday Surveillance. *Ethics and Information Technology*, Vol. 3, No. 3: pp.171-181.

[14] Martin, A. 2008. WORKER watching. Hairdressers. *Journal International*, Vol. 3, No. 1: pp. 72-73.

[15] Nord, G.D., McCubbins, T.F., and Nord, J.H. 2006. E-monitoring in the Workplace: Privacy, Legislation, and Surveillance Software. *Communications of the ACM*. Vol. 49, No. 8: pp. 73-77.

[16] Oravec, J.A. 2002. Constructive Approaches to Internet Recreation in the Workplace. *Communications of the ACM*, Vol. 45, No. 1: pp. 60-63.

[17] Palm, E. 2009. Securing privacy at work: The importance of contextualized consent. *Ethics and Information Technology*, Vol. 11, No. 4: pp. 233-241.

[18] Panko, R.R. and Beh, H.G. 2002. Monitoring for pornography and sexual harassment. *Association for Computing Machinery*, Vol. 45, No.1: pp. 84-96.

[19] Piotrowski, C. 2012. From workplace bullying to cyberbullying: The enigma of harassment in modern organizations. *Organization Development Journal*, Vol. 30, No. 4: pp. 44-53.

[20] Premji, S., Casebeer, A., and Scott, R.E. 2012. Implementing electronic health information systems in local community settings: Examining individual and organizational change experiences in the Philippines. *Electronic Journal of Information Systems Evaluation*. Vol. 15, No. 2: pp.186-197.

[21] Stanton, J.M. and Weiss, E.M. 2003. Organizational databases of personnel information: contrasting the concerns of human resource mangers and employees. *Behavior & Information Technology*. Vol. 22, No. 5: pp. 291-304.

[22] Walters, G.J. 2001. Privacy and security: an ethical analysis. *Computers and Society*. Vol. 31, No. 2: pp. 8-23.

[23] Watson, G. 2002. E-mail surveillance in the UK workplace a management consulting case study. *Aslib Proceedings: New Information Perspectives*. Vol. 54, No. 1: pp. 23-40.

[24] Wilczeck, D.G. and Prokott, D.G. 2005. Tape Recorders at Work. *Computer and Internet Lawyer*, vol. 22, 9, pp. 26-29.

[25] Zweig, D, and Webster, J. 2003. Personality as a moderator of monitoring acceptance. *Computers in Human Behavior*. Vol. 9, No. 4: pp. 479-491

Exploring Green IT Awareness and Adoption Among Indian Students

Rajendra K Bandi
Associate Professor, IIM Bangalore
Bannerghatta Road
Bangalore, India
+919742221336
rbandi@iimb.ernet.in

Anik Bose
Doctoral Scholar, IIM Bangalore
Bannerghatta Road
Bangalore, India
+918884322992
anik.bose13@iimb.ernet.in

Ashay Saxena
Doctoral Scholar, IIM Bangalore
Bannerghatta Road
Bangalore, India
+919901727520
ashay.saxena@iimb.ernet.in

ABSTRACT

The effect of global warming on our environment has shifted the focus to green technologies worldwide. Subsequently, multiple research studies have attempted to assess awareness around the concept of 'Green IT' in different countries. This study explored Green IT awareness, adoption and practice of Green IT among the Indian students' at leading universities and colleges. This study also explored the willingness of Indian students to pay for Green IT. Descriptive statistics, independent-samples t-test and Factor analysis were used to analyze the data. Findings suggest that Indian students are adequately aware of the terms related to Green IT and the specific reasons for its adoption. Moreover, results suggest that Indian students follow Green IT practices; largely dominated by those practices which promote 'reducing paper consumption'. However, there exist a significant percentage of Indian students who are willing to adopt Green IT, but the relatively higher cost of adoption seems to be an inhibitor.

Categories and Subject Descriptors

H.m [**Information Systems**]: Miscellaneous

General Terms

Management and Human Factors.

Keywords

Green IT; Awareness; Adoption; Practices; Willingness to Pay.

1. INTRODUCTION

Advancement in computing and mobile technologies has resulted in a significant increase in information and communication technologies (ICT) adoption. Information Technology (IT) has become all pervasive in the last decade largely due to the multiple forms in which it has been made available to the consumer.

Currently, IT is available to the consumers in the form of mobile devices like tablets, smart phones and laptops, and also in form of immobile desktop computers. This has altered the way in which consumers use IT for their daily activities. The advancement in technology coupled with the multiple forms in which IT is available has driven the growth of IT and has also altered the way in which consumers use IT for their daily activities. According to Gartner[1] and Reuters[2], personal computer (PC) users worldwide have crossed the 1 billion mark in 2008 and were forecasted to cross the 2 billion mark this year (2014).

Around 40% of the world population is connected to internet today[3] and the number has increased significantly over time with a growth rate of 220% in the past decade[4].This trend continues to grow at an accelerated rate, with one billion internet user mark reached in ten years in 2005, while the next two billions were added in another five and four years respectively3. Devices used to connect to internet have also changed with users from China[5] and USA[6], which are among the top three countries worldwide in internet usage, largely shifting from personal computers to mobile phones as the primary mode of connectivity. Users from India, which is the third ranked country in internet usage, are also showing trends to move in the same direction[7]. Thus, mobile phone devices today play a significant role in the growth of IT and have a huge potential in near future. Statistics show that the developing nations currently have an internet penetration less than 50% and if the internet penetration in countries India and China were to reach the level of developed countries, the number of potential users will massively increase, given the population densities in these countries.

The affordability of ICT devices has improved with the advancement in technology, and ICT devices have become ubiquitous in nature influencing all aspects of life. We are surrounded by Information and Communication Technologies

---

[1] http://www.gartner.com/newsroom/id/703807

[2] http://www.reuters.com/article/2008/06/23/us-computers-statistics-idUSL2324525420080623

[3] http://www.internetlivestats.com/internet-users/#trend

[4] http://www.statista.com/statistics/273018/number-of-internet-users-worldwide/

[5] http://thenextweb.com/asia/2014/07/21/in-china-more-people-now-access-the-internet-from-a-mobile-device-than-a-pc/

[6] http://money.cnn.com/2014/02/28/technology/mobile/mobile-apps-internet/

[7] http://trak.in/tags/business/2012/05/02/indian-mobile-vs-desktop-internet-web-usage/

(ICTs) devices, be it the set-top box for our television, the automated traffic signal, the surveillance camera used for security, or the smart phones we carry, the laptops we work on or the printer we use. Life without ICT devices is unimaginable in the present times. However, the lifetime of all these devices is reasonably short and people tend to change these devices either due to technology obsolesce or as a lifestyle statement or simply due to non-usability of the product resulting in large number of ICT devices being discarded across the world on a daily basis. These discarded ICT devices contribute to electronic waste, which is highly toxic in nature with materials like cadmium, lead, mercury, plastic etc. being non-environment friendly (Appendix 1 contains a list of pollutants in discarded ICT devices or electronic waste(e-waste) and their negative influence). The total e-waste generated in 2012 was 53.9 million tons[8] and this is expected to increase by one-third in 2017[9].

IT-based industries are considered much 'cleaner' worldwide compared to other industries due to lack of physical cues of pollution like emission, but they contribute significantly to environmental pollution, albeit indirectly. A study by Juniper Research in 2014 suggested that the world was generating around 6.4 megatons of greenhouse gases (GHG) from Smartphone charging alone[10]. This indicates the high extent of pollution generated due to Smartphone alone. GHG emission due to ICT devices is not only restricted to the energy consumption by them during usage but also during its raw material excavation and production process. According to a magazine report[11], the transfer of one gigabit information (around 500 minutes of call) consumes the same amount of energy equivalent to that of driving a car for 200 km thereby suggesting that ICTs are energy intensive. Apparently, ICT, as a whole, contributes to 2.5 percent of global carbon emission which may not seem too much but is actually at par with the airline industry (now it seems serious, isn't it?)[12].Thus, the statistics give us an alarming picture of how disastrous the situation is with regards to ICT contribution to environmental pollution and emphasize the importance of understanding and practicing the responsible use of ICT given the immense growth potential which can make situation worse. Despite the negative impacts of ICTs on environment, it is recognized that ICTs can also have positive impact in terms of energy savings, provided, one adopts responsible green IT practices. Hence, the emphasis is on consumers to ensure that proper environmentally sustainable practices are followed which can considerably reduce the negative impact of ICT devices.

Against this backdrop, it seems imperative that awareness about the 'Green' practices and also willingness to implement them would act as a prerequisite for promoting sustainable ICT usage practices. Prior research has looked at awareness about green IT practices in many countries like Indonesia (Widjaja et al. 2011), Mauritius (Dookhitram et al. 2012),Bangladesh (Ansari et al. 2010) etc., to understand the extent of knowledge of the citizens

---

[8] http://www.step-initiative.org/index.php/overview-world.html

[9] http://www.theverge.com/2013/12/15/5208626/step-initiative-global-ewaste-map

[10] http://www.cnet.com/news/smartphone-charging-spews-out-megatons-of-greenhouse-gases/

[11] http://www.lowtechmagazine.com/2008/02/the-right-to-35.html

[12] http://www.huffingtonpost.co.uk/roger-keenan/green-tech_b_5646977.html

(or students) regarding the negative impact of IT on environment. In this paper, we report the results of a study conducted to assess the awareness about Green IT, the prevailing practices around it and the willingness to adopt Green IT among the students in leading Indian universities and colleges.

The remainder of the paper is organized as follows: In the next section, we present a review of the relevant literature on the concept of 'Green IT'. We then present and discuss the research study. This is followed by a discussion on data collection and data analysis. Finally, we conclude with the implications of the findings from this study.

2. LITERATURE REVIEW
2.1 Green IT Concept
Green IT has been the focus of only a handful of studies in Information Systems Management and even in these studies there has been a lack of uniformity in defining the concept. 'Green IT' and related concepts have been defined in a number of ways, varying in terms of the scope of the definition and the goals for its implementation. It has been variedly labeled as Green IT (Chen et al. 2011; Dedrick 2010; Molla et al. 2011; Molla et al. 2009; Widjaja et al. 2011), Green IS (Chen et al. 2011; Dedrick 2010; Gholami et al. 2013), Green Computing (Chow et al. 2009), IT for Green (Molla et al. 2011) and IT for environmental sustainability (Elliot 2011; Thatcher 2007). Refer to Appendix-2for a complete list of definitions.

There has been a variation in nomenclature used for environmental sustainability ICT practices and the concepts. Chow et al. (2009) have defined *green computing* as "The study and practice of using **computing resources** efficiently and that the main objective is **to minimize the pollutions of environment.**" Thus the authors included only usage of computing resources like PCs, servers etc. in their definition and stated the main goal to be pollution prevention while being silent on the scope of the definition in terms of life cycle stages of the computing resource. *Green IT* is defined by Dedrick (2010) as "the study and practice of **designing, manufacturing, using, and disposing** of **computers, servers, and associated subsystems**–such as monitors, printers, storage devices, and networking and communications systems – **efficiently and effectively with minimal or no impact on the environment.**" In this definition, the author expands the applicability of green concepts to the entire lifecycle of the IT and communication products with the aim of increasing energy efficiency and reduce pollution. Thus in these two definitions, we find different nomenclature for similar concepts of environmental sustainability with the definition differing in three main aspects- the products considered for Green IT practices, the life stage of the product at which Green IT practices are applicable and the goal achieved by Green IT. A summary of the different definitions from literature is presented in Table 1 based on these aspects.

Table 1. Green IT Definition from certain aspects

Products taken into consideration	Goal of implementation
IT Resources (46%)	Improve energy-efficiency (24%)
IT Hardware (18%)	Reduce emission and waste (24%)
Network Systems (9%)	Improve cost-effectiveness (11%)
IS products: Software (27%)	Enhance sustainability (29%)
	Pollution prevention (6%)
	Product Stewardship (6%)

There isn't much variation among the definitions on the aspect of the life stage of the products at which Green IT is applied. Around 90% of the definitions argue for consideration of the entire lifecycle of the products.

While conceptualizing sustainable practices or related concepts, most definitions are comprehensive in looking into the entire lifecycle of the products from design to disposal, and accordingly this paper does so while formulating the working definition for the study.

Majority of IS researchers have considered IT resources for their definition of Green IS/IT. 'IT resources' includes all forms of IT devices like monitors, printers and laptops and network devices like servers, modems and routers. Although it includes network devices but it is a little different from the Network and Communication Systems segment since IT Resources doesn't include communication device like mobile phones etc.

The scope of 'Green IT' definition will surely include IT resources but whether communication devices should also be included in definition is a contested idea. The line between an IT device and a communication device is blurred in present times. E-mail for instance, an often used communication medium in many organization sand in our daily life is an IT innovation and can be accessed from computers (IT device) as well as from mobile devices (communication device). Besides, IS researchers have studied the impact of communication devices in developmental studies. Hence, it seems appropriate to understand the environmental impact of communication devices as well.

There is a wide variation in Green IT definitions on the goal for its implementation. In line with prior research, the main constructs explored are *energy-efficiency, pollution prevention, product stewardship, cost effectiveness, emission reduction,* and *sustainability.*

The concept of eco-sustainability seems closest to defining most of these terms collectively and has been used by many researchers earlier in environmental sustainability research. It has been described by Hart in three stages, namely 'pollution prevention', 'product stewardship' and 'clean technology' (Hart 1997). The first stage, pollution prevention, focuses on minimizing or eliminating polluting emissions and effluents before they are created. The next stage, product stewardship, focuses on product design considering the environmental impacts throughout the entire life-cycle of the product, including raw-material sourcing, product design and development processes. The final stage, clean technology, requires investment in technologies of the future which can cause significant changes in the production process with a view to reducing the level of environmental impact along a product's life cycle from design to consumption.

'Pollution prevention' and 'product stewardship' are the stages of eco-sustainability and the former also incorporates the concept of 'emission reduction'. 'Sustainability' as a construct is very close to the definition of 'clean technology' and is also a goal of eco-sustainability. The concept of 'energy efficiency' has been discussed by Chen et al. (2011) which defines three goals of eco-sustainability: eco-efficiency, eco-equity and eco-effectiveness. Hence, 'eco-sustainability' as a goal can take care of most of the identified goals of Green IT and hence has been included in our definition.

For the purpose of this study, we therefore define Green IT as:

"An implementation process of environmentally sustainable practices to the entire lifecycle of information and communication technology devices to achieve eco-sustainability."

2.2 Green IT Practice

With the threat posed by the expanding ICT usage, Green IT has become a priority for many governments as well as organizations across the world. In the past two decades, IS researchers have also focused on Green IT. Ehrlich and Holden have defined environmental impact as a function of population, affluence (levels of consumption) and technology (impact per unit of resource used) (Ehrlich et al. 1971). IT is heavily used in the business world and also highly impacts the life of the people and therefore can be attributed as a major contributor to the technology part in definition of environmental impact. The impact of IT can be positive on environment or negative depending on its usage and hence it is important to understand the level of awareness among the people on Green IT. There have been some studies in a few countries where researchers have assessed the level of awareness.

Environment quality has been recognized as a very important aspect by organizations, business, government and citizens alike. The first step toward environmental sustainability as identified by Chou et al. (2012)in their Green IT value model is awareness. Ahmad et al. (2013) have explored the awareness of green computing among the students in Malaysian university and found that majority of the students lack awareness about the terms, factors and the issues related to green commuting. The authors also found that students with some prior education related to ICT have greater awareness as compared to non-ICT background students, thereby concluding that education forms a firm step in creating awareness. Another awareness study conducted among students in Mauritius by Dookhitram et al. (2012) concluded that students have moderate level of knowledge about green computing. The paper also concluded that irrespective of moderate knowledge, the practices around green computing were very less but the students have a positive attitude towards adopting it. Another awareness study conducted by Widjaja et al. (2011) on IT professionals in Indonesia have found a strong concern among them for IT-related environment issues though they have moderate knowledge about Green IT. This study found a strong support for Green IT practices and personal commitment to it among the IT professionals.

3. RESEARCH STUDY

3.1 Research Context

This study has been done in the Indian context. We focus on India which, with its 290 million internet users by the end of 2014, is second in the world in terms of number of internet user. With the population of India being1.25 billion and internet penetration around 19%, which amounts to approx. 250 million users in absolute numbers, the country has very high scope of ICT expansion[13] in near future. According to an article in Livemint[14], 74% of users in India access internet via mobile devices. With

---

[13]http://beebom.com/2014/07/indian-social-media-mobile-and-internet-usage-stats-2014

[14]http://www.livemint.com/Politics/RPQoGQAAhIP8ZwmECrChpK/India-to-have-213-million-mobile-Internet-users-by-June-Rep.html

mobile devices getting cheaper and affordable for larger sections of Indian population, this user base is rapidly expanding. The growth in internet user base in India was 42% in 2013 and is predicted to grow in a similar if not a higher rate over the coming years primarily riding on the mobile internet users[15]. India, with such large growing ICT user base, seems to be an appropriate setting for the study of awareness and practices about environment friendly usage of these devices.

As compared to Smartphone penetration of 14%[16], around 70% of the Indian students currently own a Smartphone[17]. Various state governments in India are promoting computer education by distributing tablet devices[18] and PCs[19] among the students. The present government in India also emphasizes on education through IT devices and is building schools with basic IT setup to promote computer education. Moreover, India's educational settings, viz. universities and colleges, are taking large strides in moving towards being a part of the 'digital society' with proper infrastructure and facilities in place to promote usage of IT. These clearly suggest that students form a significant, perhaps the largest base of IT users, in India. Thus it seems appropriate to focus on the students of leading universities and colleges for this study; given that they seem to constitute the largest group of IT users and seem more likely to be a part of 'digital society' in India.

3.2 Survey Instrument

In this study, we have looked to understand the general sense of awareness regarding Green IT as well as willingness to pay for it among IT users, primarily students at leading colleges/universities in India. Survey instrument, used for the purpose of this study, was built largely from the literature. Survey instrument covered four major sections- Green IT Awareness, Green IT Adoption, Green IT in Practice, and Willingness to Pay for Green IT. Green IT in Practice section was further divided into two sections – (1) to determine individual Green IT practices and (2) to check for organizational Green IT practices. Green IT awareness related scale was adopted from Cai et al. (2013); Chen et al. (2011); Molla (2009) and Molla et al. (2011) to assess the Indian students' ability to relate various computing related vocabulary items to Green IT. Green IT adoption related scale primarily attempted to assess the students' views on adoption of Green IT and was adopted from Cai et al. (2013) and Dedrick (2010). Green IT in practice related scale was adopted from Cai et al. (2013), Chen et al. (2011), Molla et al. (2011), Jenkin et al. (2009) and Widjaja et al. (2011) to assess adopted Green IT practices of Indian students and Green IT practices in organizations as perceived by those with prior work experience. A scale was developed to analyze willingness to pay for Green IT among the Indian students. It

comprised of a few scenario based questions to measure preference among Indian students for buying mobile phones with varying degree of green features such as recyclability, durability, upgradability and ease of repair. In general, responses were sought largely on a five-point Likert scale with a response of 1 for 'Strongly Agree' and 5 for 'Strongly Disagree'. Likert-type scales have been used in most of the previous surveys on Green IT.

3.3 Data Collection

The survey was administered over web. Participants were reached through e-mails and social networking sites. Participants were asked to consider each statement in the survey instrument and indicate the degree to which they agreed or disagreed with it. The sampling method used to determine the sample to administer our questionnaire was based on convenience sampling. We have collected data from students at leading colleges/universities with variability in terms of the discipline of study and the level of degree they are currently pursuing. We received survey responses from 205studentsacross all disciplines. Of the 205 responses obtained, 40 were not deemed usable because of incomplete responses. In addition, two of the cases were outliers as response to every construct was similar and therefore deleted. This reduced the usable number of responses to 163.Non-response bias was tested by dividing the responses into early and late respondents and t-testing their mean responses to 10 randomly selected survey questions(Armstrong et al. 1977).

3.4 Demographics

Our survey respondents constituted 40% Female and 60% Male. About 45% of them are aged below 21 years. In terms of degree of discipline currently being pursued, survey respondents' cut across various disciplines – largely dominated by Commerce (37%) and closely followed by Management (31%) and Engineering (26%). The number of graduate level students (55%) was slightly higher than those enrolled in under-graduate programs (45%). A little less than half of the survey respondents (41%) have prior work experience. Of these respondents, nearly 50% had experience in banking and financial services sector. Responses from students with different kind of prior work experience in sectors like Manufacturing, IT and Retail also constitute part of the data for this study.

4. DATA ANALYSIS AND FINDINGS

In this section, we present the findings from analysis of survey responses. Factor analysis technique has been used to explore underlying factors for Green IT awareness and Green IT in practice - organization related scales. Moreover, Descriptive statistics and t-tests have been used to draw inferences from survey responses.

4.1 Reliability of Scales

The reliability of scales was tested with Cronbach's alpha, one of the most popular reliability statistics in use today (Cronbach 1951). Cronbach's alpha determines the internal consistency or average correlation of items in a survey instrument to gauge its reliability. It is an index of reliability associated with the variation accounted for by the true score of the "underlying construct". Construct is the hypothetical variable that is being measured (Hatcher 1994). As a rule of thumb, before using an instrument, Cronbach's alpha value greater than 0.60 is considered satisfactory (Nunnally Jr 1970) whereas value greater than or equal to 0.70 is desirable (Bland et al. 1997).

---

[15] http://www.thehindubusinessline.com/economy/india-to-have-243-million-internet-users-by-june-2014-iamai/article5630908.ece

[16] http://www.statista.com/statistics/257048/smartphone-user-penetration-in-india/

[17] http://gadgets.ndtv.com/mobiles/news/70-percent-students-use-smartphone-in-india-survey-381068

[18] http://www.bgr.in/news/government-to-invest-rs-8000-crore-to-distribute-free-tablets-to-over-20-million-students/

[19] http://www.ndtv.com/article/india/akhilesh-yadav-s-govt-to-purchase-15-lakh-laptops-for-students-321294

In our questionnaire instrument, all the constructs met the desirable criteria. Cronbach's alpha value for various scales has been highlighted in the Table 2 below.

Table 2. Reliability Statistics

Scale	Cronbach's Alpha
Green IT Awareness	0.85
Green IT Adoption	0.75
Green IT in Practice – Individual	0.70
Green IT in Practice – Organization	0.86

Since all the values are greater than or equal to desirable value, we are comfortable about the reliability of our instrument.

4.2 Green IT Awareness - Individuals

Figure 1 below shows the percentage distribution of students who were able to or not able to relate several computing vocabulary items with Green IT. Interestingly, the respondents seem to be quite aware of the relatedness of most of these items to Green IT. The awareness on the relatedness of server virtualization, storage virtualization, desktop virtualization, storage consolidation and use of IT in logistics with Green IT is comparatively lesser (15% - 32% unaware) than the awareness of the relatedness of the other concepts (less than 10% unaware) with Green IT. The above mentioned five concepts are typically handled by the system administrators and users are not directly involved, and hence it is likely that the users have a lower awareness on these concepts in comparison to other concepts.

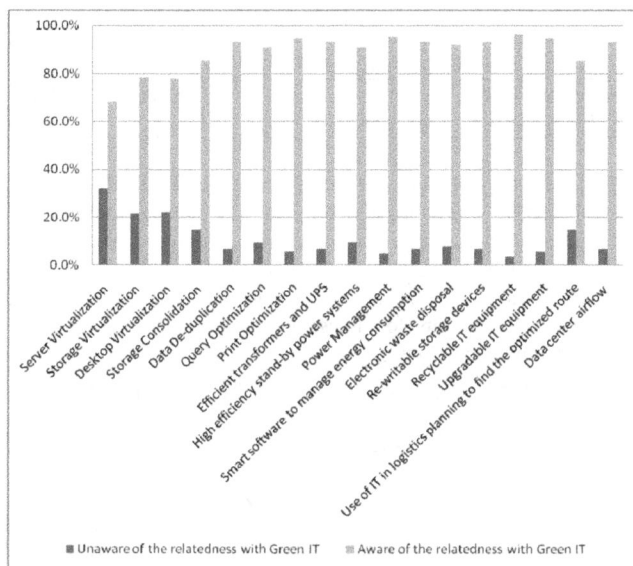

Figure 1: Green IT Awareness

Green IT awareness related scale, which comprised of the 17 items presented in Figure-1, was analyzed to assess factors associated with various items. Factor analysis revealed three underlying factors (represented in different shades in Table-3) – (1) Green technologies, (2) Green processes and (3) Green Accessories – for Green IT awareness. The first factor, viz. Green technologies comprises of virtualization related items such as Server virtualization, Storage virtualization, Storage consolidation and Desktop virtualization. The second factor, viz. Green processes comprises of process related matters such as Query

optimization and Data de-duplication. The third factor, viz. Green accessories broadly comprises of hardware items such as recyclable IT equipment, upgradable IT equipment, recyclable storage devices, smart software to manage energy consumption and e-waste disposal.

Table 3. Respondents' assessment of various concepts relatedness to Green IT

	Somewhat related	Neutral	Highly related
Server Virtualization	26.1%	33.3%	40.5%
Storage Virtualization	16.4%	33.6%	50.0%
Desktop Virtualization	24.4%	26.8%	48.8%
Storage Consolidation	16.5%	23.7%	59.7%
Data De-duplication	9.2%	19.7%	71.1%
Query Optimization	12.8%	18.2%	68.9%
Print Optimization	11.0%	12.3%	76.6%
Efficient transformers and UPS	12.5%	11.2%	76.3%
High efficiency stand-by power systems	8.8%	17.6%	73.6%
Power Management	7.7%	13.5%	78.7%
Smart software to manage energy consumption	3.9%	13.2%	82.9%
Electronic waste disposal	8.7%	12.0%	79.3%
Re-writable storage devices	9.2%	12.5%	78.3%
Recyclable IT equipment	9.6%	8.3%	82.2%
Upgradable IT equipment	7.1%	20.8%	72.1%
Use of IT in logistics planning to find the optimized route	9.4%	18.7%	71.9%
Data center airflow management	11.8%	17.1%	71.1%

Table 3 also shows the details of the responses of those students who are aware of the relatedness of these terms to Green IT. A greater number of respondents were able to relate the items – smart software to manage energy consumption, e-waste disposal and recyclable IT equipment to Green IT than the other items. There is a growing awareness among the Indian citizens on the general concept of 'green' with focus on the phrase 'reduce, reuse and recycle' which typically emphasizes reducing consumption reusing products, and recycling used materials. This growing general green awareness seems to be the likely reason that respondents are more aware of these three items (smart software to manage energy consumption, e-waste disposal and recyclable IT equipment) as compared to the other items. The items in 'green technologies' factor are perceived by fewer number of respondents to be related to Green IT, compared to the other two factors viz. 'green processes' and 'green accessories'. From table-3, it is clearly evident that the items which form 'green technologies' factor are less known to Indian students with most of them not able to relate them to Green IT.

The next step in our analysis, measures the influence of the level of education and gender on the ability of the respondents to relate the items with Green IT. This was established by computing the average score of the students on the seventeen Green IT awareness items and running two independent samples t-tests on the average score by the level of education and gender.

The t-test results (see Table 4 below) suggest that gender doesn't have any influence on the ability to relate these items to Green IT although female students have marginally higher mean score. Results also suggest that the level of education has a statistically significant influence on the respondents' assessment of these items, with graduate students being more able to relate the items with Green IT in comparison to the under-graduate students.

Table 4. Influence of level of education & gender on student's ability to relate to Green IT

Respondents	N	Mean	Std. Deviation	t	p-value
Level of Education:					
Graduates	90	3.7244	.78902	2.983	0.003*
Under-graduates	73	3.3584	.76706		
Gender:					
Male	97	3.5576	.76385	-.055	0.956
Female	66	3.5647	.85176		

*significant at p<0.05

4.3 Green IT Adoption - Individuals

Descriptive statistics regarding the respondents' belief towards Green IT adoption is presented in Table-5 below. Based on survey responses, around 20% of the respondents were not sure about cost of adopting Green IT. Moreover, one-third of the respondents, who had some idea about the cost implications, were neutral in their opinion. This suggests that Indian students seem to have low awareness on financial implications of adopting Green IT.

Table 5. Respondents' view on adoption of Green IT

Adoption of Green IT...	Disagree	Neutral	Agree
Gives No Benefits	72%	16.11%	12%
Enhances Social Image	8.39%	23.78%	67.83%
Is a Statutory Requirement	16.91%	31.62%	51.47%
Is Ethical	6.67%	20.67%	72.67%
Is Just a sensation by intellectuals	50.35%	22.70%	26.95%
Fits with my personal values	6.71%	14.77%	78.52%
Is my responsibility towards environment	2.72%	12.24%	85.03%
Is non-alluring due to high cost	28.68%	33.33%	37.98%
Is important because others are adopting	42.66%	33.57%	23.78%

From the table above, it is clearly evident that respondents largely consider adoption of Green IT as their responsibility towards environment with the specific item 'Adoption of Green IT is my responsibility towards environment' being the most agreed upon item. With the three items viz. Green IT gives no benefits (12%), Green IT being sensation created by few intellectuals (27%) and Green IT adoption being important because others are adopting (24%) being least agreeable, it can be implied that respondents have clearly discarded these three reasons of Green IT adoption. It seems reasonable to believe that Indian students are concerned

about environment related matters. Moreover, it can be inferred from Table 5 that Green IT's fit with the personal values of Indian students' and its ethical considerations are strong reasons for Green IT adoption by Indian students.

4.4 Green IT in Practice – Individuals

Descriptive statistics regarding the adopted Green IT practices of the respondents are displayed in Table 6 below. It is clearly evident from the table below that practices concerning 'saving paper' are being followed by students'. Close to 90% of respondents print on both sides of paper and only when necessary indicating that 'saving paper' takes priority among them. This could be due to the fact that 'saving paper' has direct cost implications to the students, whereas the other Green IT practices do not directly affect them.

Table 6. Respondents' View on Green IT Practice

	Disagree	Neutral	Agree
Print on both sides of paper	5.52%	4.90%	89.58%
Take print-out only when necessary	3.70%	6.13%	90.18%
Turn-off my computer when I am not using it	11.70%	9.20%	79.14%
Use Screen-saver	26.99%	15.34%	57.67%
Use Monitor-sleep	14.12%	11.65%	74.23%
Reduce the amount of time spent in using computers	28.00%	25.00%	47.00%
Use re-writable storage media	6.14%	14.72%	79.14%
Dispose used IT equipments in e-waste recyclable bins	23.32%	25.15%	51.53%
Prefer recycled IT equipments for my own personal use	25.00%	31.00%	44.00%

Moreover, the influence of gender and level of education is established by computing the students' average scores on all the nine items and running two independent-samples t-tests on the average scores by gender and level of education. Level of education did not reveal any significant influence on practicing Green IT. The results for assessing gender based influence are presented in table below.

Table 7. Influence of Gender on Green IT practice

Respondents	N	Mean	Std. Deviation	T	p-value
Male	97	3.7015	.57322	2.551	.012
Female	66	3.9273	.52598		

The t-test results on the groups' mean scores show a statistically significant impact of gender on Green IT practice in favour of female students. Female students obtained a higher score on the scale (M=3.93, SD=0.52) than did males, suggesting that practice of Green IT among female students is slightly higher compared to males.

4.5 Green IT – Personal Willingness to Pay

Respondents were presented with features of four mobile phones with similar specifications but varying on the following five features- recyclability, upgradability, easy to repair, durability and price (see details in Appendix - 3). Respondents were presented with hypothetical question to assess their personal buying preference of mobile phone among the four available options.

Figure 2 indicates their preference with an astounding 73% of the respondents opting for Phone-C which though is most expensive, is recyclable, durable, upgradable and is easily repairable. This indicates an enormous market for green products among Indian students.

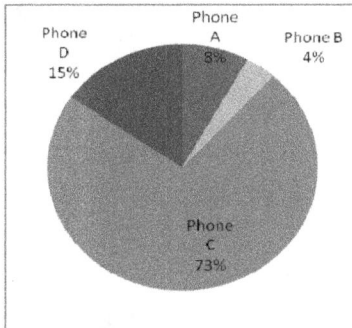

Figure 2. Preference of Mobile Phone among respondents

The respondents were also asked to relatively rank the five features on which the mobile phones are distinguished. Among the respondents who have recognized price as the most or second-most important factor, 73% have not considered recyclability to be important. 85% of those who consider recyclability as important don't consider price as an important factor. This is possibly because the respondents consider price and recyclability to be two ends of a continuum with the price conscious consumer not preferring recyclability probably due to its expected high price, whereas people who prefer to buy recyclable product not getting deterred by a high price tag.

Referring to Table-6 presented earlier, 44% of the respondents believe that they prefer recycled IT items for their personal use. However, results in this section show that recyclability in comparison to other features is still important to only 55.55% of these students. This indicates that though people consider using recyclable product as a Green IT practice yet it seems to have less importance with respect to other features.

4.6 Green IT in Practice – Organization

In addition to conducting the study which looked at understanding the individuals' awareness, adoption and personal willingness to pay for Green IT, survey also sought responses of participants on their awareness of organizational level initiatives to promote Green IT based on their experiences with the last organization worked for. Only those respondents (63) who had prior professional work experience in an organization, viz. 40% of the overall respondents, were considered for the purpose of this analysis. Table-8 represents the level of awareness of these individuals about the Green IT initiatives in the organization they had been part of. It is evident from the table that the respondents were more aware of the organizational initiatives to encourage teleconferencing facility, videoconferencing facility, online collaboration tools and reduced power consumption by IT equipments, than the other items. Usage of conferencing facilities and online collaboration tools, are typically the basic necessities in most organizations. Hence, it seems reasonable to assume that this could be a reason for greater awareness among the respondents on these items.

Table 8. Awareness on organizational initiatives for Green IT

My organization...	Not Aware	Aware
Encouraged enhanced use of teleconferencing facility	3%	97%
Encouraged enhanced use of videoconferencing facility	6%	94%
Encouraged enhanced use of online collaboration tools	3%	97%
Had a separate budget allocated for sustainability practices	21%	79%
Encouraged reducing power consumption by IT equipments	5%	95%
Rewarded Green IT initiatives undertaken by employees	11%	89%
Provided facilities for e-waste disposal	10%	90%

Green IT in practice – organization related scale was analyzed to assess factors associated with various items. Factor analysis revealed two underlying factors related to individuals' understanding of organizational Green IT initiatives (represented in different shades in Table-8) – (1) Work-related initiatives and (2) Additional measures. The first factor, viz. Work-related initiatives comprises of organizational initiatives like encouraging use of teleconferencing facility, video conferencing facility and online collaboration tool, which directly impact the work of the employees and give direct cost benefit to the organization. The second factor is termed 'additional measures' since it comprises of initiatives which requires extra effort and commitment from organization like allocating separate budget for sustainability practices, encouraging power savings by IT usage, rewarding Green IT initiatives and providing e-waste disposal facility.

Figure-3 below represents the respondents view on organizational initiatives for Green IT. The respondents, who are aware of these initiatives, felt that their organization encouraged and supported work-related initiatives which encouraged Green IT practices but comparatively speaking they felt that there was not as much support from the organization on additional Green IT initiatives.

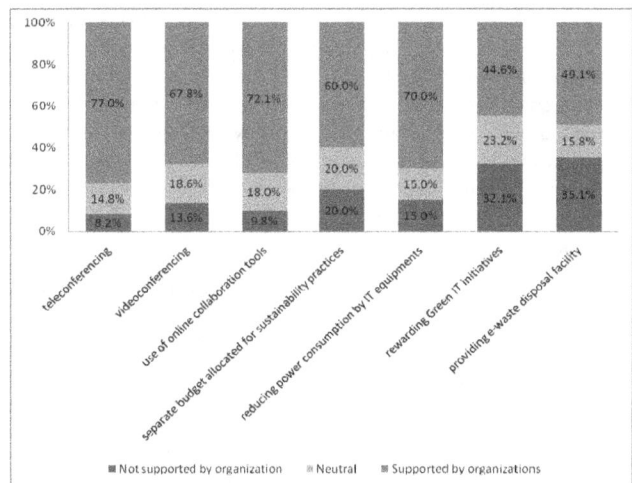

Figure-3: Respondents' View on Organizational initiatives for Green IT

5. Conclusion and Future Work

In this study, we explored the Green IT awareness, adoption & practices and also willingness to pay for Green IT among the Indian students.

At a broad level, results suggest that Indian students are reasonably aware of the vocabulary and concepts associated with Green IT. As for Green IT adoption, Indian students seem to be aware of most of the reasons ranging from responsibility towards environment to ethical considerations of adopting Green IT. Results also suggest that Indian students follow Green IT practices, largely dominated by practices like 'reducing paper consumption' etc. There exists a need for students' to look beyond these and follow some of the practices concerning power savings with IT usage as well as proper e-waste disposal etc.

Finally, a significant percentage of Indian students are willing to adopt Green IT, but the relatively higher cost of adoption seems to be an inhibitor. In our analysis of the preference of green features for IT product, though recyclability and price are perceived as opposite end of continuum by the Indian student, yet there seems to exist an ambiguity in terms of relative preference of other green features such as durability, upgradability and ease of repair. Future research needs to address this ambiguity through conducting in-depth studies which address the notion of willingness to pay for Green IT.

Moreover, given that the students, participants of this study, would be part of the productive work-force in near future, it is reasonable to expect that Green IT practices in organizations would be significantly shaped by their awareness of Green IT. We hope that the seemingly higher level of awareness regarding Green IT would positively enhance the extent of Green IT practices in organizations. Future research need to establish this link between impacts of high level of Green IT awareness among individuals on organizational practices.

As stated earlier, prior research has analyzed Green IT awareness among students/ IT professionals in Mauritius, Bangladesh, Indonesia, etc. However, it seems difficult to compare the results of these studies with our study primarily due to lack of uniformity in measuring the notion of 'Green IT awareness' across all the studies. This presents a future need to conduct systematic studies across different countries so that results can be comparable.

This paper has attempted to assess awareness, the first component of Green IT value model proposed by Chou et al. (2012). Translation, comprehension and Green IT value are the subsequent component in the Green IT value model. Besides assessing awareness among the Indian students, this study also assessed the adoption and practices in Green IT which partially contributes to the second component of the value model – translation. Future studies need to evaluate the other two components of value model.

Green IT is in a nascent stage in Information Systems literature and has enormous scope for contribution. Researchers need to go beyond Green IT awareness and also focus on several factors like adoption and practices concerning Green IT. Another fruitful avenue of research would be an attempt to study the transition among citizens of a particular demography from Green IT awareness to its adoption. Longitudinal studies to address this research could pave way for further contributions to the stream of Green IT literature.

6. REFERENCES

[1] Ahmad, T., Badariah, T., Bello, A., and Nordin, M. S. 2013. "Exploring Malaysian university students' awareness of green computing," GSTF International Journal on Education (1:2), pp 92-102.

[2] Ansari, N. L., Ashraf, M., Malik, B. T., and Grunfeld, H. 2010. "Green IT awareness and practices: results from a field study on mobile phone related e-waste in Bangladesh," in Proceedings of the 2010 IEEE international symposium on technology and society : social implications of emerging technologies : 7-9 June 2010, University of Wollongong, New South Wales, Australia, K. Michael (ed.), IEEE: Piscataway, N.J., pp. 375-383.

[3] Armstrong, J. S., and Overton, T. S. 1977. "Estimating nonresponse bias in mail surveys," Journal of marketing research), pp 396-402.

[4] Bland, J. M., and Altman, D. G. 1997. "Statistics notes: Cronbach's alpha," Bmj (314:7080), p 572.

[5] Bose, R., and Luo, X. 2011. "Integrative framework for assessing firms' potential to undertake Green IT initiatives via virtualization – A theoretical perspective," Journal of Strategic Information Systems.

[6] Cai, S., Chen, X., and Bose, I. 2013. "Exploring the role of IT for environmental sustainability in China : An empirical analysis," Intern. Journal of Production Economics (146), pp 491-500.

[7] Chen, A. J., Watson, R. T., Boudreau, M.-c., and Karahanna, E. 2011. "An Institutional Perspective on the adoption of Green IS & IT," Australasian Journal of Information Systems (17), pp 5-27.

[8] Chou, D. C., and Chou, A. Y. 2012. "Awareness of Green IT and its value model," Computer Standards & Interfaces (34), pp 447-451.

[9] Chow, W. S., and Chen, Y. 2009. "Intended Belief and Actual Behavior in green computing in hong kong," Journal of Computer Information Systems).

[10] Cronbach, L. J. 1951. "Coefficient alpha and the internal structure of tests," psychometrika (16:3), pp 297-334.

[11] Dedrick, J. 2010. "Green IS : Concepts and Issues for Information Systems Research," Communications of the Association for Information Systems Volume (27).

[12] Dookhitram, K., Narsoo, J., Sunhaloo, M. S., Sukhoo, A., and Soobron, M. Year. "Green Computing : An Awareness Survey among University of Technology , Mauritius Students," International Conference on Higher Education and Economic Development, Mauritius, 2012, pp. 1-8.

[13] Ehrlich, P. R., and Holdren, J. P. 1971. "Impact of population growth,").

[14] Elliot, S. 2011. " Transdisciplinary perspectives on environmental sustainability: a resource base and framework for IT-enabled business transformation," MIS Quarterly (35:1), pp 197-236.

[15] Gholami, R., Binti, A., Ramayah, T., and Molla, A. 2013. "Senior managers ' perception on green information systems (IS) adoption and environmental

performance : Results from a field survey," Information & Management (50), pp 431-438.

[16] Hart, S. L. 1997. "Beyond Greening: Strategies for a Sustainable World," Harvard Business Review), pp 66-76.

[17] Hatcher, L. 1994. A step-by-step approach to using the SAS system for factor analysis and structural equation modeling, (

[18] Jenkin, T., and McShane, L. Year. "Green Information Technologies and Systems in Organizations: The State of Practice," Academy of Management Annual Meeting2009, pp. 7-11.

[19] Molla, A. 2009. "Organizational Motivations for Green IT : Exploring Green IT Matrix and Motivation Models," in PACIS.

[20] Molla, A., and Abareshi, A. 2011. "Green IT Adoption : A Motivational Perspective," in PACIS.

[21] Molla, A., Cooper, V. A., and Pittayachawan, S. 2009. "IT and Eco-sustainability : Developing and Validating a Green IT Readiness Model," in International Conference on Information Systems.

[22] Nunnally Jr, J. C. 1970. "Introduction to psychological measurement,").

[23] Thatcher, M. E., Pingry, D. E. 2007. "Modeling the IT value paradox," Communications of the ACM (50:8), pp 41-45.

[24] Widjaja, N., Mariani, M., and Imam, K. 2011. "IT Professionals Awareness: Green IT International Comparison Study," Communications of the IBIMA (2011), pp 1-15.

Appendix-1: : Long-term and Short-term effects of Pollutants in Discarded ICT Devices

Pollutant	Effect	
	Short-term/ Less amount	**Long-term/ Heavy dosage**
Arsenic	Lead to various diseases of the skin and decrease nerve conduction velocity. Can also cause lung cancer and can often be fatal.	
Barium	Brain swelling, muscle weakness, damage to the heart, liver and spleen	Not known.
Beryllium	Causes skin diseases, lung diseases and cancer in extreme cases.	
Brominated flame retardants (BFRs)	Causes severe hormonal disorders, cause of cancer, harm reproductive and immune system	
Cadmium	Flu-like symptoms of weakness, fever, headache, chills, sweating and muscular pain. Also is believed to cause pulmonary emphysema and bone disease.	Lung cancer and kidney damage.
CFCs (Chlorofluorocarbons)	Accumulate in the stratosphere and have a deleterious effect on the ozone layer. Increased incidence of skin cancer and genetic damage	
Chromium (VI)	Irritating to eyes, skin and mucous membranes.	Permanent eye damage. May also cause DNA damage.
Lead	Appetite loss, abdominal pain, constipation, fatigue, sleeplessness, irritability and headache.	Blood anemia, kidney damage, severe stomach aches, muscle weakness and brain damage.
Mercury	Affects the central nervous system, kidneys and immune system. It impairs fetus growth and harms infants through mother's milk.	

Appendix-2: Concepts of Environmental Sustainability in ICT from Literature and their Definitions

Concept	Definition	Author
The impacts of IT on the environment	"First-order effects are direct impacts from IT hardware during the product lifecycle, including *production, use and disposal of computer equipment.*" "Second-order effects are the *effects of ICTs on other processes* such as transportation or industrial production, influencing their environmental impacts." Third-order effects "occur when widespread use of ICTs leads to changes in lifestyles and economic structures."	(Dedrick 2010)
Green IT	Green IT is a systematic application of environmental sustainability criteria to the *design, production, sourcing, use and disposal of the IT technical infrastructure* as well as within the human and managerial components of the IT infrastructure in order *to reduce IT, business process and supply chain related emissions and waste and improve energy efficiency*.	(Molla et al. 2009)
Green IT	"Green IT refers to the using of IT resources in an energy-efficient and cost-effective manner."	(Bose et al. 2011)
Green IT	"The study and practice of *designing, manufacturing, using, and disposing* of computers, servers, and associated subsystems—such as monitors, printers, storage devices, and networking and communications systems-*efficiently and effectively with minimal or no impact on the environment*."	(Dedrick 2010)
Green IS	"The use of information systems to enhance sustainability across the economy."	(Dedrick 2010)
Green IS & IT	"*IS & IT products* (e.g., software that manages an organization's overall emissions) and *practices* (e.g., disposal of IT equipment in an environmentally friendly way) that aims to *achieve pollution prevention, product stewardship, or sustainable development*."	(Chen et al. 2011)
Green computing	"The study and practice of using *computing resources* efficiently and that the main objective is *to minimize the pollutions of environment*."	(Chow et al. 2009)
Green IT and IT for green	"The first-order effect refers to the negative environmental impact of IT production, use, and disposal. This perspective considers IT as negatively impacting eco-sustainability. Thus making *IT production, use and disposal greener* refers to Green IT.'' ''The second-order effect refers to the positive impact of using IT on business and economic processes. This perspective considers IT as part of the solutions to **eco-sustainability**. Thus using IT to make enterprises greener refers to IT for Green."	(Molla et al. 2011)
Green IS	"which can reduce the environmental impact of firm's actions, and how it can contribute to environmental sustainability"	(Gholami et al. 2013)
Green IT	Green IT appears to be the right element to connect both corporate innovation and environmental integration during **development, production, usage, and disposal phase** of the product.	(Widjaja et al. 2011)
IT for environmental sustainability	IT for environmental sustainability refers to activities to **minimize the negative impacts and maximizes the positive impacts of human behaviour** on the environment through the use of IT and IT-enabled products and services throughout their **life cycle**.	(Elliot 2011)
IT for environmental sustainability	IT for environmental sustainability is a broad concept which subsumes efforts and initiatives to use energy in a more **effective, efficient, and sustainable way** so as to make our **environment more sustainable**, with regard to use of IT.	(Thatcher 2007)

Appendix – 3: Mobile phone features for measuring Willingness to Pay

The table below gives the characteristics of four mobile phones, all of which have similar specifications (Screen Size, Resolution, Camera, Processor Speed etc.)

	Recyclable	Upgradable	Easy to Repair	Durability	Price
Phone A	Yes	No	No	Low	Medium
Phone B	No	No	No	Medium	Low
Phone C	Yes	Yes	Yes	High	High
Phone D	No	No	Yes	Medium	Medium

Recyclable – Raw material used to manufacture it can be extracted and used as a raw material for some other product.

Upgradable - Features (memory size, data storage space etc.) can be updated at a later stage to meet the user requirements.

Easy to Repair – Spare parts are readily available and the cost associated is fairly low.

Durability –Does not wear out easily and lasts for considerably long period of time.

Is Managing IT Security a Mirage?

Conrad Shayo
California State University
5500 University Pkwy
San Bernardino, CA, 92407
+1(909) 537-5798
cshayo@csusb.edu

Javier Torner
California State University
5500 University Pkwy
San Bernardino, CA, 92407
1(909) 537-7262
jtorner@csusb.edu

Frank Lin
California State University
5500 University Pkwy
San Bernardino, CA, 92407
1(909) 537-5787
flin@csusb.edu

Jake Zhu
California State University
5500 University Pkwy
San Bernardino, CA, 92407
1(909) 537-5068
jzhu@csusb.edu

Joon Son
California State University
5500 University Pkwy
San Bernardino, CA, 92407
1(909) 537-5778
json@csusb.edu

ABSTRACT

The purpose of this panel is to provide a forum to discuss the main IT security issues confronting organizations today. The panelists and attendees will discuss the existing gap between current IT security practices vs. best practices based on survey trends on IT security for the past 5 years, explore popular models used to justify IT security investments, and showcase some of the most popular hacking tools to demonstrate why it is so easy to compromise organizational IT security assets. The panel will conclude by discussing the emerging IT security standards and practices that may help deter, detect, and mitigate the impact of cyber-attacks. As the title suggests, we posit the question: **Is Managing IT Security a Mirage?**

Categories and Subject Descriptors

D.4.6 [**Security and Protection**]: access controls, authentication, invasive software, cryptographic controls. K.6.5 [**Security and Protection**]: physical security, unauthorized access, insurance. C.2.0 [**Computer - Communication Networks**]: firewalls, security and protection.

General Terms

Management, Performance, Reliability, Security, Human Factors, Standardization, Verification

Keywords

Cyber-attacks; ransomware, hacking; cyber security; information security; cyber-terrorism; IT vulnerability; information system security; secure IT infrastructure

SIGMIS-CPR'15, June 4–6, 2015, Newport Beach, CA, USA.
ACM 978-1-4503-3557-7/15/06.
http://dx.doi.org/10.1145/2751957.2751970

1. INTRODUCTION

Organizational IT security breaches are on the rise [1], [2], [3]. The more spectacular breaches in 2014 include J.P. Morgan (83 million customers), Home Depot (56 million), Target (40 million), Montana Department of Public Health (1.3 million), and Sony Pictures (6,000 employees). Reports are that even companies that have high IT security budgets such as Target became victims. The conclusion is that there is no such thing as 100% IT security [4], [5]. And given the disastrous impact an IT security breach can have on the very survival of an organization, the only option left is to anticipate cybercrime and prepare to ward-off cyber-attacks.

Granted that security breaches are on the rise, why are so many organizations caught off-guard? Why are organizations reactive and not proactive? What are the best practices? The purpose of this panel is to provide a forum to discuss the main IT security issues confronting organizations today. The panelists and attendees will: (a) discuss the existing gap between current IT security practices vs. best practices based on global and national survey trends on IT security for the past 5 years, (b) explore popular models used to justify IT security investments, and (c) showcase some of the most popular hacking tools to demonstrate why it is so easy to compromise organizational IT security assets. The panel will conclude by discussing the emerging IT security standards and practices that may help deter, detect, and mitigate the impact of cyber-attacks [6], [7]. As the title suggests, we posit the question: **Is Managing IT Security a Mirage?**

2. PANEL TOPIC AREAS

Strategies for Securing and Protecting Organizational Information Systems and Network Infrastructure: Lessons from Higher Education Institutions [Javier Torner]. Javier will share his wealth of experience in securing and protecting information systems and computer network in institutions of higher learning. He will focus on the realities of IT security challenges facing institutions of higher learning, lessons learnt from mutually sharing IT security risk information among an alliance a few institutions, and the challenges of building an ongoing organizational culture that values the importance of information security in institutions of higher learning.

Summary of Cyber Security Trends for the past 5 years [Frank Lin]. A number of organizations provide yearly national, regional and global surveys on the state of cyber security. Frank will provide an aggregate view of responses provided in the cyber security surveys for the past 5 years. Focus will be on the issues and main trends provided by the respondents. The surveys include the: Global Information Security Survey (GISS) by EY-Global Security, SANS Survey on Application Security Programs and Practices by SANS, PwC's The Global State of Information Security Survey. Respondents to the surveys comprise of top management (e.g., CIOs, CSOs, and CEOs) and IT practitioners.

Recent Cybercrimes, Perpetrators, Motivation and Impact. [Conrad Shayo]. Conrad will discuss ten (10) most recent cybercrimes, who the perpetrators were, stated/speculated motivation, and impact. The motivations of cyber attackers will depend on who they are and what they are seeking. Attackers include: national state actors, technology companies, telecommunication companies, domestic intelligence services, hackers, hacktivists, current or former employees, customers, organized crime, hobbyists, and supply chain partners. The impact could range from mild to devastating. Some of the motivations sited in the literature include: financial gain, sabotage, embarrassment, theft of (IP addresses, blueprints, M&A data, R&D data, strategy documents, pricing information) and espionage.

Demonstration of popular hacking techniques and how to prevent them. [Jake Zhu]. Jake will demonstrate popular hacking techniques for computers and smart phones and how you can prevent them. Focus will be on how easy it is to access the tools and preventive, detective and corrective measures.

The future of IT Security: Emerging IT security standards and practices [Joon Son]. Jon will present emerging IT security standards and practices and discuss the future of the IT security industry. Focus will be on cooperation among members of the IT security ecosystem including private-public partnerships, supply chain collaboration, international cooperation, heightened end user computing vigilance, and better dynamic IT security monitoring, detection and corrective devices.[7], [8].

3. REFERENCES

[1] CyberSource Corporation (2014). *CyberSource 2013 Online Fraud Survey Report, 14th Annual Edition.* DOI = http://www.slideshare.net/joshuaenders/cyber-source-2013onlinefraudreport [Last Accessed, February 10th, 2015].

[2] Schneider, B. (2014). 5 huge cybersecurity breaches at companies you know. *Fortune Magazine.* DOI = http://fortune.com/2014/10/03/5-huge-cybersecurity-breaches-at-big-companies/ [Last Accessed, February 10th, 2015].

[3] Weise, E. (2014). "Massive data breaches: Where they lead is surprising" *US Today.* DOI = http://www.usatoday.com/story/tech/2014/10/02/home-depot-data-breach-credit-card-fast-food/16435337/ [Last Accessed, February 10th, 2015].

[4] Diana, A. (2014). "Montana Health Department Hacked" *Information Week.* DOI = http://www.informationweek.com/healthcare/security-and-privacy/montana-health-department-hacked/d/d-id/1278872 [Last Accessed, February 10th, 2015].

[5] Cisco Annual 2014 Security Report (2014). http://www.cisco.com/web/offer/gist_ty2_asset/Cisco_2014_ASR.pdf [Last Accessed, February 10th, 2015].

[6] Gelbstein, E. & Kamal, A. (2002). *Information insecurity: A survival guide to the uncharted territories of cyber-threats and cyber-security.* United Nations ICT Task Force and the United Nations Institute for Training and Research. [Last Accessed, January 10th, 2015].

[7] NIST Cyber Security Framework. DOI = http://www.nist.gov/cyberframework [Last Accessed, February 10th, 2015].

[8] Phillips, C.E. Jr.; Ting, T.C. & Demurjian, S.A. (2002). "Information Sharing and Security in Dynamic Coalitions", SACMAT'02, June 3-4, Monterey, California, USA. DOI = http://www.princeton.edu/~rblee/ELE572Papers/p87-phillips.pdf [Last Accessed, March 31st, 2015)

[9] Weiss, N.E. (February 2015). Legislation to Facilitate Cybersecurity Information Sharing: Economic Analysis, Congregational Research Service. DOI: http://fas.org/sgp/crs/misc/R43821.pdf [Last Accessed, March 31st, 2015.

Cybersecurity Competitions in Education: Engaging Learners through Improved Game Balance

David H Tobey, PhD
Holy Cross College
5415 State Road 933 North
Notre Dame, IN 46556-0308
dtobey@hccenter.org

Portia Pusey, EdD
Cybersecurity Competition Federation
3801 West Temple Avenue
Pomona, CA 91768
edrportia@gmail.com

Josh Chin
Net Force
P.O. Box 90083
City of Industry, CA 91715-0083
+1 (708)-888-0778
josh.chin@net-force.net

ABSTRACT

In this presentation we will present models and research findings related to characteristics of competitions including: game balance, engagement, frameworks, and difficulty.

Categories and Subject Descriptors

K..3. [**Computers and Education**]: Miscellaneous

General Terms

Measurement, Human Factors

Keywords

Competitions; VUCA; Cybersecurity; Engagement; Competency; Assessment

1. Summary

The difficulty of gamification of education is to provide pathways to mastery where the challenges are just within reach of a learner's ability to solve them so that competition activities remain "pleasantly frustrating" for the learner [1]. However, "pleasantly frustrating" is difficult to achieve. Players, or learners, have diverse competencies (i.e., knowledge, skill and abilities) and we lack information about which competencies a specific game (e.g., cybersecurity competition) objective requires for successful performance. Matching player competence with game objectives, called game balance, is a critical requirement cybersecurity competitions are to engage learners to increase their learning and encourage their pursuit of cybersecurity as a profession.

A project funded by the Department of Homeland Security Science and Technology (S&T) Directorate demonstrated the value and need for an evidence-based approach to understanding game balance in cyber competitions [2]. The results of this exploratory study revealed that little is known about the: challenges that are included in a competition; what competencies are required to perform well in each challenge; degree to which the difficulty of task performance is reflected in the score; alignment or adjustment of competition difficulty to competency level; effectiveness of the competition in engaging students.

The dynamic nature of cyber threats and attack patterns require that mission-critical roles and task assignments are continually updated based on evidence gathered from the latest tactics, techniques and procedures used in cybersecurity incidents. To infuse this "dynamic" ground truth into workforce training requires that cybersecurity competition challenges are mapped to standards, constantly adapted and based on critical computer security incident stories. Thus, embedded within critical incident stories that have multiple process paths and levels of cognitive loads (distractors), we use semantic templates [3] built from community-developed and reviewed enumerations of weaknesses and attack patterns to determine the concept coverage within a training and simulation exercise.

The panel will present models and research findings related to:

1. Exploring methods for designing cybersecurity competition challenges that balance participant competency and incident difficulty

2. Applying design elements that lead to the development of efficacy and career engagement in competitors

3. Mapping cybersecurity challenges to established competency models, such as the NBISE Operational Security Testing Job Performance Model, NICE Workforce Framework, and the Electric Sector-Cybersecurity Capability Maturity Model (ES-C2M2)

4. Develop a validated method for identifying competition characteristics, including:

   a. Description of challenges that are included in a competition

   b. List of competencies are required to perform well in each challenge

   c. Measurement of the degree to which competition scores accurately measure the difficulty of task performance

5. VUCA and the ability of the competition to align or adjust of competition difficulty to player competency level

SIGMIS-CPR'15, June 4–6, 2015, Newport Beach, CA, USA.
ACM 978-1-4503-3557-7/15/06
http://dx.doi.org/10.1145/2751957.2751969

2. References

[1] Gee, J. P. (2005). *Why video games are good for your soul: Pleasures and learning.* Melbourne, Australia: Common Ground.

[2] Assante, M. J., Tobey, D. H., & Vanderhorst, T. J. (2013). *Mission Critical Role Project* (No. Award Number FA8750-10-2-0234). Washington, D. C.: Department of Homeland Security HSARPA, Cyber Security Division.

[3] Yan, W., Gandhi, R.A, and Siy, H., *"Using Semantic Templates to Study Vulnerabilities Recorded in Large Software Repositories"* Proc. of The 6th International Workshop on Software Engineering for Secure Systems (SESS'10) at the 32nd International Conference on Software Engineering (ICSE 2010), South Africa, Cape Town. 2010

Insider Threat: Language-action Cues in Group Dynamics

Shuyuan Mary Ho
Florida State University
School of Information
Tallahassee, FL 32306-2100
smho@fsu.edu

Hengyi Fu
Florida State University
School of Information
Tallahassee, FL 32306-2100
hf13c@my.fsu.edu

Shashanka S. Timmarajus
Florida State University
Computer Science
Tallahassee, FL 32306-2100
st13f@my.fsu.edu

Cheryl Booth
Florida State University
School of Information
Tallahassee, FL 32306-2100
clb14h@my.fsu.edu

Jung Hoon Baeg
Florida State University
School of Information
Tallahassee, FL 32306-2100
jhb6536@my.fsu.edu

Muye Liu
Florida State University
Computer Science
Tallahassee, FL 32306-2100
ml11an@my.fsu.edu

ABSTRACT

Language as a symbolic medium plays an important role in virtual communications. Words communicated online as action cues can provide indications of an actor's behavioral intent. This paper describes an ongoing investigation into the impact of a deceptive insider on group dynamics in virtual team collaboration. An experiment using an online game environment was conducted in 2014. Our findings support the hypothesis that language-action cues of group interactions will change significantly after an insider has been compromised and makes efforts to deceive. Furthermore, the language used in group dynamic interaction will tend to employ more cognition, inclusivity and exclusivity words when interacting with each other and with the focal insider. Future work will employ finely tuned complex Linguistic Inquiry and Word Count dictionaries to identify additional language-action cues for deception.

Categories and Subject Descriptors

H.1.2. [**User/Machine Systems**]: Human information processing; I.2.7. [**Natural language processing**]: Text analysis.

General Terms

Design, Human Factors, Language, Security.

Keywords

Trusted human-computer interaction; online deception; insider threat detection; language-action cues.

1. INTRODUCTION

In the physical world, people assess the behavioral intent of others through various physical cues – such as subtle facial expressions, appearance, and body language [1, 2]. However, in

a virtual environment where communication is limited to written exchanges (i.e. texts, e-mails), written language is the only available means of assessing behavioral intent and gaining insight into an actor's intimate "feelings," "thoughts," and "intentions" [3, p. 40]. Language becomes the medium of communication through which an actor expresses his or her behavioral intent – whether explicitly or implicitly [4].

When the expressed behavioral intent of an actor is given effect with consistent action, trust will arise. Jones and Marsh [5] assert that group trust is of critical importance to effective group interactions – particularly where group members are relying on each others' actions and information to achieve specific outcomes. This efficacy can be undermined by anything that undermines group trust – and particularly when a member (or members) of the group engages in deception. This paper discusses a sociotechnical study to investigate this "insider threat" scenario, simulated in an online game environment through examination of language-action cues within the impacted virtual team. The study seeks to address the research question: *How do language-action cues in group interactions change when a compromised actor engages in a deceptive act?*

The uniqueness of this study is three-fold. First, we set up online game experiments using Google+ Hangout to study information behavior. Second, we simulate and study group interactions in an insider betrayal scenario. Third, language-action patterns and cues of groups' interactions are carefully analyzed to decipher changes in communicative intent.

2. STUDY FRAMEWORK
2.1 Trust in Virtual Team Interaction

Trust is widely acknowledged as being the most important factor in the effectiveness of virtual team [5-8]. Trust in the context of this discussion is not just a "...global feeling of warmth or affection...", but refers to the conscious decision of one actor to be dependent on another to various degrees based on circumstances [13]. Effective communication and trust can improve not only a team's task-specific performance outcomes [7, 9], but also the social dynamics among members [10-12] including conflict management, motivation, confidence building, cohesiveness, and coordination [9]. Zand [13] illustrates the interactive relationship of trust with information flow, the willingness to influence and be influenced by others, and the desire to control others within dynamic groups. Klimoski and Karol [14] suggest that people in high trust groups tend to be more willing to share opinions, suggestions and information than those in groups with lower levels of trust – making trusting groups more effective. When trust is absent, communication within virtual teams breaks down.

2.2 Insider Threats in Global Information Systems Context

Modern information systems are confronted by a variety of threats. Attacks originating from outside, such as hacking attempts or viruses, have gained a lot of publicity recently. But in fact, insider threats pose a significantly greater level of risk [15]. By definition, *insider threat* refers to situations where a member of an organization behaves against the interests of the organization, in an illegal and/or unethical manner [16]. A malicious insider has the distinct advantage of understanding the corporation's information assets, processes and infrastructure. Further, the insider has legitimate and often privileged access to resources and information, having knowledge of other team members and work in progress. All of the foregoing factors make the insider better positioned to cause damage to an organization than an external attacker.

Within a virtual setting, the problem of insider threats becomes more complex due to today's mobility of storage, communication media, and technology as enabled by distributed, grid, and cloud computing. The controls and tools that are used for the protection of the information systems (IS) from externally initiated attacks (e.g. firewalls and intrusion detection systems) are generally not effective in preventing insider threats [15]. Research on insider threats has generally focused on categorizing and modeling [17]. For example, some researchers have proposed models that enable analyzing and detecting the insider misuse phenomenon [18, 19]. Schultz [20] defined a set of cues that can be used to predict insider attack, including deliberate markers, meaningful errors, preparatory behavior, correlated use patterns, verbal behavior, and personality traits. Magklaras and Furnell [21] focused on the capability and opportunity factors to propose a model of end user sophistication, which could be embedded in an insider threat prediction tool.

2.3 Language-action Cues in Detection

"Language-action cues" refers to linguistic styles, phrases, patterns, or actions in an actor's written expression and manifested as an indirect or subtle signal to other actors. In online communications, people must rely on fairly simple evidence (e.g. words and actions) to decide whether or not to trust another party. Untruthful and deceitful communication has destroyed basic trust in our society [22]. Lacking traditional face-to-face (FtF) visual cues, the virtual setting has made it easier for individuals to misrepresent themselves. In virtual environments, deceptive communication cues that are common in FtF contexts are not available, but certain communication cues can still be observed [23, 24]. For example, research from Zhou et al [25] suggests that deceivers use more modal verbs and less individual references, and further that deceivers have a lower imagery ratio and may tend to use more sensory, spatial, and temporal words. Hancock et al [26] found that deceivers generally use more words, sense-based words, other-oriented pronouns, and fewer self-oriented pronouns. Toma and Hancock [27, 28] similarly found that users who were highly deceptive in online profiles used fewer self-references, fewer negations, more motion-related words, but fewer words overall, when compared to less deceptive profiles.

However, previous research has not studied how group members interact and react when a deceptive actor is present. We hypothesize that group members may be able to sense the psychological states of other group members, and will tend to use words showing cognitive process as well as inclusivity and exclusivity when they perceive an untrustworthy or deceptive actor is present. Accordingly, we hypothesize that:

> Hypotheses 1 (H1): *The language-action features of communication within groups containing a deceptive actor will be significantly different from those in groups without a deceptive actor.*

We further hypothesize that group interaction will change significantly after an incentive for deception has been introduced to a critical actor in the team. As a result, the group's language-action features may reflect a subtle reduction in their willingness to work with the deceiver, as well as a dampening of the overall team's mood in the categories of affective and emotions.

> Hypotheses 2 (H2): *The language-action features of a group's interactions will change after an actor within the group has accepted an incentive for deception.*

3. METHOD

3.1 Research Design and Data Collection

We designed and deployed an experimental game platform using Google+ Hangout to maximize the collection of data points (Figure 1). Datasets were collected during 2014. This experiment consisted of six virtual teams' (three control groups, and three treatment groups) collaborating in an asynchronous game environment. Each team was composed of randomly assigned participants, including a randomly assigned focal actor. Participants were volunteers - geographically dispersed across the United States. A total of 27 students participated in this study; 17 were males and 10 were females. Players' names were replaced with pseudo-names to protect participants' privacy. Ages ranged from 18 to 65 years old.

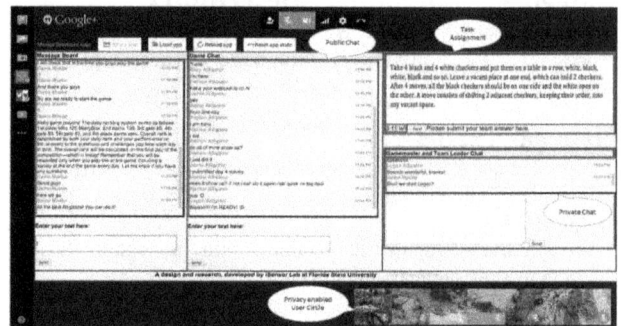

Figure 1. Illustration of an online game designed and developed as for data collection.

To frame the research problem, an online game was developed. The game environment included message boards for announcements, and chat forums for interactive discussion. The game engaged teams to solve logic puzzles in a series of 30-minute sessions over 5 consecutive days. A member of the research group served as Game Master, and interacted directly with a focal team leader on each team. Because the game structure and functionality is complex, the following is intended to provide only a brief description and overview.

Of the six total teams, three were treatment groups and three were control groups, each with an average of three to four team members plus one focal team leader. The primary responsibility of the focal team leader was to submit his/her team's puzzle answers on behalf of the team to the Game Master using a built-in submission function. Through this private chat function, the Game Master offered incentives to the focal actors in the treatment groups, using a micropayment system. Specifically, a financial incentive was offered to each focal leader at the end of Day Two. But this incentive came with two conditions: (1) the deal must be kept a secret from their team; (2) if their team won, the focal actor would be required to split the incentive with all team members, but if their team did not win, the focal actor had no obligation to distribute the incentives to their teammates. By introducing this financial incentive, the focal actors in the treatment groups were presented with an ethical dilemma: whether to share the incentives with the team members, or to sabotage the team effort and keep the incentives. All conversations between team-members (including focal actors) and between the focal actors and Game Master were logged in the MySQL database. These logs recorded focal actors from three treatment groups that betrayed the team and kept the incentive. These logs also record the interactions of the focal actors and his/her respective team members in each treatment group (pre- and post- incentive) and each control group, allowing for comparison of information behaviors within and between the various groups as well as capturing relevant language-action cues.

3.2 Data Analysis

A total of 5,850 lines of conversation logs were collected, cleaned, and processed. Linguistic Inquiry and Word Count (LIWC) was used to identify relevant language-action cues (selected categories noted below). The raw transcripts were first tokenized and cleaned to correct common spelling mistakes. This improved the overall accuracy of LIWC in assigning words to selected categories. An independent samples test was used to identify those language-action cues that differed between the treatment groups and the control groups. The coding schema of the language-action cues is set forth in Table 1, along with some general examples of words in each category.

Table 1. LIWC categories and examples.

Category	Examples	Coding Schema
Achievement	earn, hero, win	Ach
Cognitive process	cause, know, ought	Cog
Affective process	happy, cried, abandon	Aff
Positive emotion	love, nice, sweet	PoEmo
Negative emotion	hurt, ugly, nasty	NegEmo
Discrepancy	should, would, could	Dis
Causation	because, effect, hence	Cau
Tentative	maybe, perhaps, guess	Ten
Negation	no, not, never	Neg
Insight	think, know, consider	Ins
Certainty	always, never	Cert
Inclusivity	and, with, include	Incl
Exclusivity	but, without, exclude	Exc

3.3 Hypothesis Testing and Results

Hypothesis 1 stated that the language-action features of groups containing a deceptive actor will be significantly different than groups without a deceptive actor. A comparison of the differences in language-action features between the treatment group(s) (i.e. the group(s) with a deceptive actor) and the control group(s) (i.e. the group(s) without a deceptive actor) shows statistically significant differences in several language-action

features e.g., cognition, inclusivity, exclusivity, and achievement (Table 2) between treatment groups and control groups.

The positive t value in Table 2 shows that, overall, the control group actors used more words of cognition, inclusivity and exclusivity than treatment groups. In other word, the groups without a deceptive actor employ more words in cognition, inclusivity, and exclusivity than groups with a deceptive actor. The negative t values indicate that achievement words were used more often in treatment groups than in control groups, implying that players in treatment groups were more active and more concerned about wining the game as a team after a team leader had seemingly gone "rogue". These results indicate that the interactions within the treatment groups may have been indirectly influenced by the fact that the focal (deceptive) actors were offered financial incentives, and decided to keep them.

Table 2. Independent samples t-test (H1).

Independent Samples Test

			t-test for Equality of Means		
	t	df	Sig. (2-tailed)	Mean Difference	Std. Error Difference
Cog	2.990	25	.006	3.41264	1.14153
	2.994	24.970	.006	3.41264	1.13967
Inc	3.614	25	.001	1.27522	.35285
	3.594	23.816	.001	1.27522	.35485
Exc	2.535	25	.018	1.00236	.39540
	2.500	21.030	.021	1.00236	.40096
Ach	-2.119	25	.044	-.60665	.28634
	-2.143	23.842	.043	-.60665	.28311

Hypothesis 2 stated that the language-action features of a group's interaction will differ significantly after an incentive for deception has been accepted by an actor. A comparison of the differences between a treatment groups' interactive behavior before and after the introduction of financial incentives revealed statistical differences in language-action cues within the categories of affective process and positive emotions (Table 3). In other words, the increased usage of words in the affective process and positive emotion categories suggests that group players displayed more amicable behavior in their chat. This implies that the groups containing a deceptive actor displayed more affective process of positive and negative emotions, including anger, anxiety and sadness in their group interaction after the bait was introduced to the deceptive actor, and that the actor has betrayed their team.

Table 3. Paired samples t-test (H2).

		Differences Std. Dev.	Sig. (2-tailed)
Pair 1	Aff - Aff	1.95652	.001
Pair 2	PoEmo – PoEmo_2	1.90621	.001

Although the affective language cues for the treatment groups are statistically significant, this result may have been influenced by some passively angry players in the groups, or the intensity of the puzzle solving. This shows that team players can indeed sense subtle changes in the behavior of the focal actor (i.e. after an incentive was offered to him/her).

4. CONCLUSION AND FUTURE WORK

This study suggests promising results for using online gaming as a research system to investigate the dynamics of communicative intent through language-action cues from the perspective of group interaction with the focal actor.

It can be challenging to identify subtle changes in behavior in a CMC environment due to the limited number of data points and lack of overall insight into the team's dynamic interaction. Our future work includes a computational approach that automatically discerns deceptive language-action cues with the aid of machine learning for regression modeling and neural networks. We will further investigate the heuristic mechanisms used to detect subtle changes in deceptive behavior, as well as group interaction in online collaborative settings.

5. ACKNOWLEDGMENTS

The authors wish to thank the National Science Foundation EAGER grants #1347113 & #1347120, 09/01/13–08/31/15, the Florida Center for Cybersecurity Collaborative Seed Grant 03/01/15–02/28/16, and the Florida State University CRC Planning Grant #034138, 12/01/13–12/12/14.

6. REFERENCES

[1] Ekman, P., *Telling lies: Clues to deceit in the marketplace, politics, and marriage.* 2009. New York, NY: W. W. Norton & Company. ISBN: 978-0393337457.

[2] Ekman, P. and M. O'Sullivan. *Who can catch a liar?* American Psychologist, 1991. **46**(9): 913-920.

[3] Austin, J.L., *How to do things with words*, 2nd ed. 1962. Cambridge, MA: Harvard University Press.

[4] Habermas, J., *The theory of communicative action*. Reason and the Rationalization of Society. 1981. Boston, MA: Beacon Press.

[5] Jones, S. and S. Marsh. *Human-computer-homan interaction: Trust in CSCW.* ACM SIGCHI Bulletin, 1997. **29**(3): 36-40. doi: 10.1145/264853.264872.

[6] Jarvenpaa, S.L. and D.E. Leidner. *Do you read me? The development and maintenance of trust in global virtual teams*, in *INSEAD Working Paper Series*, edited by Austin, U.o.T.a., 1997: Fontainebleau, France. 1-44.

[7] Jarvenpaa, S.L. and D.E. Leidner. *Communication and trust in global virtual teams.* Journal of Computer-Mediated Communication, 1998. **3**(4): 0. doi: 10.1111/j.1083-6101.1998.tb00080.x.

[8] Jarvenpaa, S.L. and D.E. Leidner. *Communication and trust in global virtual teams.* Organization Science, 1999. **10**(6): 791-815.

[9] Mathieu, J., M.T. Maynard, T. Rapp, and L. Gilison. *Team effectiveness 1997-2007: A review of recent advancements and a glimpse into the future.* Journal of Management, 2008. **34**(3): 410-476.

[10] Hsu, M.H., T.L. Ju, C.H. Yen, and C.M. Chang. *Knowledge sharing behavior in virtual communities: The relationship bewteen trust, self-efficacy, and outcome expectations.* International Joural of Human-Computer Studies, 2007. **65**(2): 153-169.

[11] Mooradian, T., B. Renzl, and K. Matzler. *Who trusts? Personality, trust and knowledge sharing.* Management Learning, 2006. **37**(4): 523-540.

[12] Panteli, N. and S. Sockalingam. *Trust and conflict within virtual inter-organizational alliances: A framework for facilitating knowledge sharing.* Decision Support Systems, 2005. **39**(4): 599-617.

[13] Zand, D.E. *Trust and managerial problem solving.* Administrative Science Quarterly, 1972. **17**(2): 229-239. doi: 10.2307/2393957.

[14] Klimoski, R.J. and B.L. Karol. *The impact of trust on creative problem solving groups.* Journal of Applied Psychology, 1976. **61**(5): 630-633. doi: 10.1037/0021-9010.61.5.630.

[15] Ho, S.M. and J. Hollister. *Cyber insider threats in virtual organizations.* In Encyclopedia of Information Science and Technology, edited by Khosrow-Pour, M.E. 2015. Information Resource Management Association: Hershey, PA. 1517-1525.

[16] Ho, S.M. *Behavioral anomaly detection: A socio-technical study of trustworthiness in virtual organizations*, in *Information Science & Technology*, 2009. Syracuse University: Syracuse. 1-457.

[17] Stanton, J.M., K.R. Stam, P. Mastrangelo, and J. Jolton. *Analysis of end user security behaviors.* Computers & Security, 2005. **24**(2): 124-133.

[18] Dhillon, G. and S. Moores. *Computer crimes: Theorizing about the enemy within.* Computers & Security, 2001. **20**(8): 715-723.

[19] Wood, B. *An insider threat model for adversary simulation.* in *Research on Mitigating the Insider Threat to Information Systems.* 2000. 1-3.

[20] Schultz, E.E. *A framework for understanding and predicting insider attacks.* Computers & Security, 2002. **21**(6): 526-531.

[21] Magklaras, G.B. and S.M. Furnell. *A preliminary model of end user sophistication for insider threat prediction in IT systems.* Computers & Security, 2005. **24**(5): 371-380.

[22] Sengupta, S. Trust: Ill-advised in a digital age, The New York Times Sunday Review, August 11, 2012.

[23] Hancock, J., J. Birnholtz, N. Bazarova, J. Guillory, J. Perlin, and B. Amos. *Butler lies: Awareness, deception and design.* in *CHI 2009*. 2009. Boston, MA: ACM.

[24] Wright, R.T. and K. Marett. *The influence of experiential and dispositional factors in phishing: An empirical investigation of the deceived.* Journal of Management Information Systems, 2010. **27**(1): 273-303.

[25] Zhou, L., J.K. Burgoon, D.P. Twitchell, T. Qin, and J.F. Nunamaker Jr. *A comparison of classification methods for predicting deception in computer-mediated communication.* Journal of Management Information Systems, 2004. **20**(4): 139-165.

[26] Hancock, J., L.E. Curry, S. Goorha, and M. Woodworth. *On lying and being lied to: A linguistic analysis of deception in computer-medicated communication.* Discourse Process, 2008. **45**(1): 1-23. doi: 10.1080/01638530701739181.

[27] Toma, C. and J. Hancock. *Reading between the lines: Linguistic cues to deception in online dating profiles.* in *International Conference on Computer Supported Cooperative Work (CSCW 2010)*. 2010. Savannah, Georgia: ACM. doi: 978-1-60558-795-0/10/02.

[28] Toma, C. and J. Hancock. *What lies beneath: The linguistic traces of deception in online dating profiles.* Journal of Communication, 2012. **62**: 78-97. doi: 10.1111/j.1460-2466.2011.01619.x.

An Efficient Approach to Develop an Intrusion Detection System Based on Multi Layer Backpropagation Neural Network Algorithm

Rinku Sen
NSHM College of Management & Technology
Kolkata, India
+91-9433705691
rineelsen@gmail.com

Manojit Chattopadhyay
Indian Institute of Management - Raipur
Raipur, India
+91-8718054788
mjc02@rediffmail.com

Nilanjan Sen
Pailan College of Management & Technology
Kolkata, India
+91-9433170778
nilanjansenin@yahoo.co.in

ABSTRACT

The key success factor of the business depends upon correct and timely information. The vital resources of the organization should be protected from inside and outside threats. Among many threats of network security, intrusion has become a crucial reason for many organizations to incur loss. Many researchers are trying their level best to handle the different types of intrusion affecting the business. To detect such a type of intrusion, our initiative is to us a very popular soft computing tool namely back propagation neural network (BPNN). We have prepared a flexible BPNN architecture to identify the intrusion with the help of anomaly detection methodology. The result we obtained is better than or at per with many best research paper in this field of study. We have used KDD dataset for our experiment.

Categories and Subject Descriptor

I.2 ARTIFICIAL INTELLIGENCE
I.2.6 Learning:Connectionism and neural nets; Parameter learning

Keywords

Intrusion Detection System; Artificial neural network; BPNN; KDD CUP 99 dataset; Anomaly detection.

1. INTRODUCTION

Information security is procedures or measures taken so that one can prevent unauthorized access, destruction, theft or damage to information system in an organization. If these issues are not handled properly, it can lead to increase in cost and can also affect the quality of productivity of an organization, thereby affecting organization's objective of increasing efficiency and productivity (Choobineh 2007).

Accurate resource estimation is essential, but handling resource is a complicated task as it depends on three factors:

- Scale and complexity of the organization
- Interdependencies between resources
- Dynamic nature of resource estimation

Whitman (2003) categorized different types of attacks occurring in an organization. He calculated ranking based on responses received in each category. The important fact is that, threats are not only from outside the organization (like disabling the firewalls, or imitation of legitimate packets by the intruder), it can be from inside also.

Different neural network approaches have been used to solve the problem of intrusion detection, but till date no robust intrusion detection mechanism has been devised that will built a completely secure system. Out of different types of intrusion detection i.e. anomaly and misuse intrusion detection, our paper tries to focus on anomaly detection because it has been found that anomaly detection is capable in identification of new unseen attacks. On the negative side, anomaly detection also detects normal new packets as attack and vice versa, thereby raising false alarm rate. In our work, we have tried to develop an efficient BPNN architecture which will reduce false positive rate in an anomaly based Intrusion Detection System (IDS). The actual response obtained from the proposed model is better than the responses of linear and neuro-fuzzy models as well as the neural network with purely nonlinear hidden node activation function and linear hidden node activation function in terms of detection rate and accuracy.

2. PROPOSED WORK

Our present work is the extended work of our previous work which had been published in an IEEE conference (Sen et al. 2014). Our research goal is to search for a better BPNN architecture which will yield higher accuracy and detection rate for anomaly based intrusion. We have used normalized 20% KDD CUP 99 data set for our experiment.

The experiment is divided into two phases:

1. The training phase: In this phase, our BPNN architecture is trained using the known attacks.

2. The Testing phase: In this phase, we have verified how the same architecture is working in case of unknown attacks.

- We have used 40 features of the KDD CUP 99 dataset.

- 1000 epochs have been used every time to perform our experiment. The Mean Square Error is calculated along with the execution time.

- The "Confusion matrix" is generated from the result obtained in training phase. Based on the data obtained from the confusion matrix, the accuracy and detection rate is calculated.

- In our experiment, the dataset has been split into two halves. One half is used for training phase and the other half is used for testing phase. We have used 3 percent splits of the data set for our experiment, viz. 60-40 percent split, 70-30 percent split and 80-20 percent split.

3. RESULTS AND DISCUSSION

We have experimented with different combinations of hidden layers and different neurons in each hidden layers. Same combination of hidden layers and neurons are used for the 3 different percentage split of the KDD dataset. Depending upon the outcomes of our experiments, we have drawn several graphs to show the relationship between the different parameters and have found the following results:

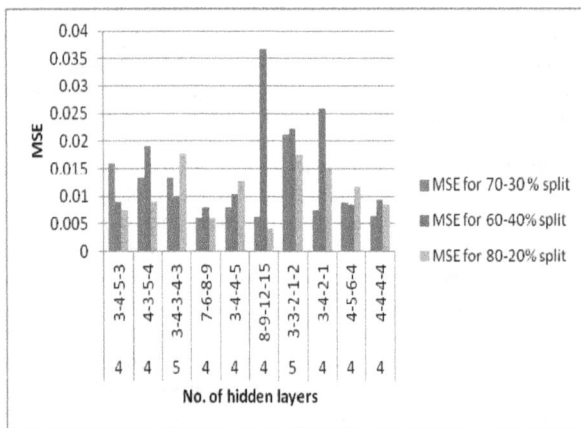

Graph 1. Mean Square Error versus Number of Hidden Layers in different percentage split

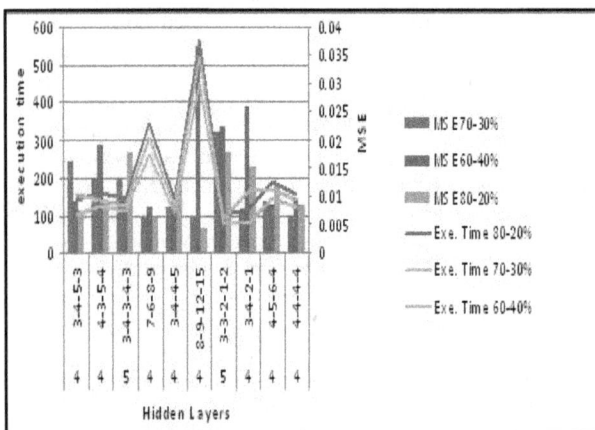

Graph 2. The relationship between Mean Square Error, Hidden Layer and execution time in different percentage split

After considering all parameters such as high testing accuracy, high testing detection rate, lowest false positive rate, smaller execution time etc., we have come to the conclusion that the BPNN architecture with 4 hidden layers with neurons combination of 3-4-5-3 performs well using 70-30% split of

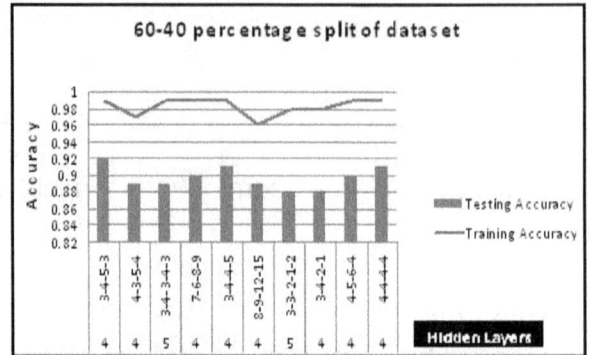

Graph 3. The relationship between testing and testing accuracy obtained in different hidden layers in 60% training and 40% testing dataset

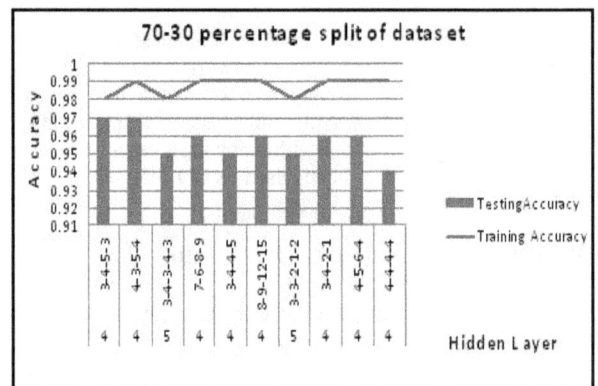

Graph 4. The relationship between testing and testing accuracy obtained in different hidden layers in 70% training and 30% testing dataset

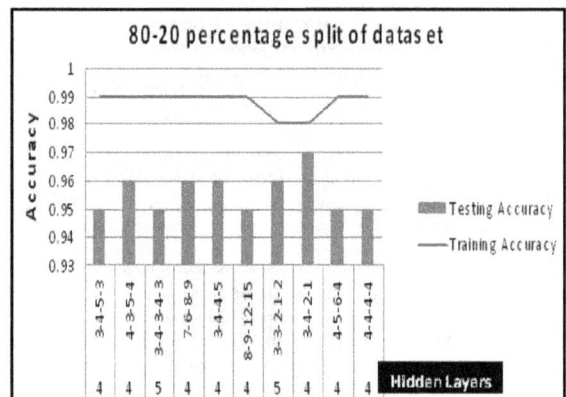

Graph 5. The relationship between testing and testing accuracy obtained in different hidden layers in 80% training and 20% testing dataset

KDD dataset compare to other two splits. This finding matches with our previous finding and reinforce our proposed BPNN architecture (Sen et al. 2014).

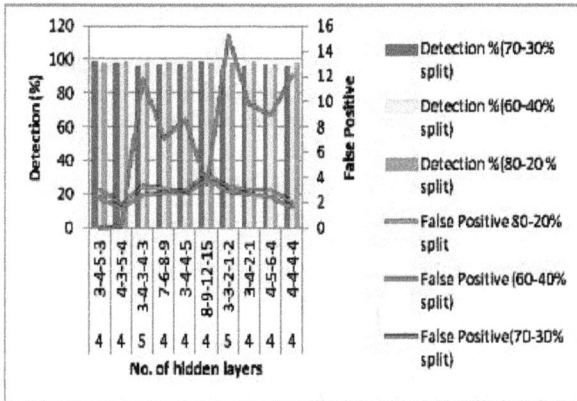

Graph 6. The relationship between false positive and testing detection (%) for 3 different percentages split

We can summarize the characteristic features of the proposed architecture as under:

- The mean square error (MSE) is less in 80-20 percentage split, but worst in 60-40 percentage split in dataset in the architecture consisting of 4 hidden layers, with 8, 9, 12 and 15 hidden nodes respectively.

- The MSE is more or less same and less than 0.01 for all the three split datasets in the architecture consisting of 4 hidden layers with 7, 6, 8 and 9 hidden nodes respectively. But at the same time the execution time is lowest in 60-40 percentage split dataset, moderate in 70-30 percentage split dataset and worst in 80-20 percentage split dataset.

- The False Positive rate is highest in 70-30 percentage split dataset with 5 hidden layers, but the same split dataset has the lowest rate in the two architectures with 4 hidden layers each, containing 3-4-5-3 and 4-3-5-4 hidden nodes respectively. Whereas the other two split datasets have the moderate range of false positive rate but not as good as the first one.

- The testing detection rate of our proposed model is 98.97% which is higher than the detection rate obtained by the model proposed by Naoum et al. (2012) and Sindhua et al. (2012), the testing accuracy is 97% and the execution time is 156.3 sec. which is better than the model proposed by Kuanf et al., (2012) and Mukkamala et al., (2002). Moreover Kuanf et al. (2012) obtained testing accuracy rate 99.2% at the cost of 407.92 sec in execution times.

- In the proposed architecture we have kept the number of hidden layers and the nodes in each hidden layer flexible so that we can find out the optimal combination of hidden nodes.

- The activation function used for each hidden node is also flexible, though in our experiment we have confined it to sigmoid and hyperbolic tangent function. We have seen

that, by using the sigmoid and hyperbolic tangent function interchangeably, we have got good result in terms of accuracy and detection.

- Last but not the least, by keeping the learning rate flexible, we can compare the performance measure of the architecture for each dataset.

Table 1 given below is depicting our result compared to other related works in the field of intrusion detection. Some fields of the table are left as blank due to the unavailability of the data. It is seen that our work is better than or at per with the best performance achieved by others. The table is the extended version of the table used in (Sen et al. 2014).

Table 1: Comparison between our proposed model and other related works

Refe-rence	Detection rate		Accuracy		Exec. time (Sec.)	Dataset used
	Trai-ning %	Test-ing %	Trai-ning %	Test-ing %		
Kuanf et al. (2012)	-	-	99.98	99.20	407.92	KDD (Train: 4000; Test: 2000)
Naoum et al. (2013)	-	94.7	-	-	-	KDD
Sindhua et al. (2012)	-	98.38	-	-	-	KDD
Mukka-mala et al. (2002)	-	-	99.48 (with 41 fea-tures)	-	1800	KDD (Train: 14000; Test: 7000)
Deva-raju and. Rama-krishnan (2011)	-	-	-	97.50	-	KDD
Mukho-padhyay et al. (2011)	-	-	73.90	-	-	KDD
Our proposed approach	99.58	98.97	98	97	156.38	KDD 20% dataset

4. MANAGERIAL IMPLICATIONS

Leading information security issues by the top level management is a complex one in the organization. It necessitates the top level managers to comprehend the interactions among vital assets, the organizational setting and the technical know-how since they manage the identification of assets, measuring the risks, maintaining management setting and accomplishing stability between the investment and profit.

Additionally to defile an organization's reputation, the intrusion detection has direct operational impact by making organization and its assets as vulnerable through exposure of lawful or financial implications.

Therefore, the research is necessary for attraction, retention and development of cyber security professionals to cope up the organizational implications for generating alarm against vulnerabilities through proactive implementation of intrusion detection system. How they should work to effectively control and detect intrusion is a mere technical question as management concern is always significant than a technical design of organizational assets in the network warfare using future cyber professional soldiers.

5. CONCLUSIONS AND FUTURE WORK

Since the aim of this research was to get better accuracy of anomaly attacks using Back Propagation Neural Network, we have succeeded in achieving our objective by using the BPNN algorithm to classify the data accordingly. In this paper, by applying BPNN we have developed an architecture which can be used for anomaly based IDS. After comparing our model with existing works, we can conclude that our model performs better in terms of execution time and detection rate.

The future enhancement and directions of the present research are followings:

- To develop more superior architecture that will identify the attacks more accurately and efficiently.

- Computation time as well as execution time can be minimized by eliminating the irrelevant links between the nodes of different layers of the proposed BPNN architecture.

- BPNN has the potential to be adapted to an incremental learning algorithm. However the present BPNN has been developed for batch training. The intrusion detection system can be developed as an automatic modified system to identify the attacks more accurately and minimize false alarm on attacks.

6. REFERENCES

[1] Choobineh J., Dhillon G., Grimaila M. R., and Rees J. 2007. Management of Information Security: Challenges and Research Directions. *Communications of the Association for Information Systems*, 20, (Dec. 2007), 958-971.

[2] Devaraju S., and Ramakrishnan S. 2011. Performance analysis of intrusion detection system using various neural network classifiers. *In Recent Trends in Information Technology, International Conference on, IEEE,* (Jun. 2011), 1033-1038.

[3] Kuanf F., Xu W., Zhang S., Wang Y., and Liu K. 2012. A novel Approach of KPCA and SVM for Intrusion Detection. *Journal of Computational Information Systems,* (Apr. 2012), 8, 8, 3237–3244.

[4] Mukhopadhyay I., Chakraborty M., Chakrabarti S., and Chatterjee T. 2011. Back propagation neural network approach to Intrusion Detection System. *In Recent Trends in Information Systems, 2011 International Conference on, IEEE,* (Dec. 2011), 303-308.

[5] Mukkamala S., Janoski G., and Sung A. 2002. Intrusion detection using Neural Networks and Support Vector Machine. *International Joint Conference on Neural Network, IEEE,* (May. 2002), 1702 – 1707.

[6] Naoum R. S., Abid N. A., and Al-Sultani Z. N. 2013. An enhanced Resilient backpropagation artificial neural network for Intrusion detection. *International Journal of Computer Science and Network Security*, (Mar. 2013), 13, 3, 98-104.

[7] Sen N., Sen R., and Chattopadhyay M. 2014. An Effective Back Propagation Neural Network Architecture for the Development of an Efficient Anomaly Based Intrusion Detection System. *Sixth International Conference on Computational Intelligence and Communication Networks, IEEE,* (Nov. 2014), 1054 – 1058.

[8] Sindhu S. S. S., Geetha S., and Kannan A. 2012. Decision Tree Based Light Weight Intrusion Detection Using a wrapper Approach. *Expert Systems with Applications, Elsevier,* (Jan. 2012), 39, 1, 129–141.

[9] Whitman M. E. 2003. Enemy at the gate: Threats to Information Security. *Communications of the ACM,* (Aug. 2003), 46, 8, 91-95.

The Cybersecurity Competition Federation: Promoting and Connecting Competitions into a Developmental Learning and Enrichment Experience

Daniel Manson, PhD
Cal Poly Pomona
Computer and Information Systems
Department
3801 West Temple Avenue
Pomona, CA 91768
dmanson@csupomona.edu

Portia Pusey, EdD
Cybersecurity Competition
Federation
3801 West Temple Avenue
Pomona, CA 91768
edrportia@gmail.com

Mark J. Hufe, EdD
Wilmington University
320 N. DuPont Highway
New Castle, DE 19720
mark.j.hufe@wilmu.edu

James Jones
Mid-Pacific ICT (MPICT) Center
City College of San Francisco
50 Phelan Avenue
Science Hall 107/Box S107
San Francisco, CA 94112
jjones@mpict.org

Daniel Likarish
Regis University
6380 S Fiddlers Green Cir
Greenwood Village, CO 80111
dlikaris@regis.edu

Jason Pittman, PhD
Cal Poly Pomona
1223 N. Kraemer Blvd.
Placentia, CA 92870
jmpittman@cpp.edu

David H Tobey, PhD
Holy Cross College
5415 State Road 933 North
Notre Dame, IN 46556-0308
dtobey@hccenter.org

ABSTRACT

In a time of global crisis in cybersecurity, competitions and related activities are rapidly emerging to provide fun and engaging ways of developing and assessing cybersecurity knowledge and skills. However, there is no neutral organization that brings them together to promote collective efforts and address common issues. This paper will describe the rationale and process for developing the Cybersecurity Competition Federation (CCF) (National Science Foundation Award DUE- 134536) which was created to facilitate a community that promotes cybersecurity competitions and related activities. CCF's vision is to maintain an engaged and thriving ecosystem of cybersecurity competitions and related activities to build career awareness and cybersecurity skill to address a global shortage of cybersecurity professionals.

Categories and Subject Descriptors

K.3.2. **[Computers and Education]** Information Systems

SIGMIS-CPR'15, June 4–6, 2015, Newport Beach, CA, USA.
ACM 978-1-4503-3557-7/15/06
http://dx.doi.org/10.1145/2751957.2751980

General Terms

Human factors; Management

Keywords

Competency model; Job Performance Model; Critical incident; Vignette; Cyber Defense Competition; Aptitude; KSA; Game balance; Talent management

1. INTRODUCTION: The Problem

According to Cisco Systems, there is already a shortage of a million cybersecurity workers [1]. When one considers that most computing jobs require the capacity to apply cybersecurity concepts, there is an additional projected shortfall of a million workers between now and 2020 [2]. This is a national economic and workforce development crisis and an important strategic issue facing all industries. This is critical as our nation increasingly relies on our cyber infrastructure, information, tools, and intellectual property for efficiency and competitive advantage [13,16]. What's more, those who attack our infrastructure are well trained and armed; many cybercriminals are backed by robust criminal organizations and rogue nation states [2]. To secure the nation's infrastructure, financial system, and intellectual property, we need millions of trained individuals who have been tested in high-fidelity simulations [4]. The formal education system will not produce the number of cybersecurity professionals we need to mitigate the several million worker shortage estimate stated above [15]. We desperately need to build awareness and interest in cybersecurity careers and accelerate our technical workforce development. Cybersecurity competitions have emerged as a method for identifying talent and addressing the worker shortfall [9]. Manson and Pike describe several professional development and awareness outcomes of competitions which are often anecdotally expressed [10]:

- Improves the skills of talented individuals

- Provides a competitive outlet for individuals

- Enriches learning with practice

- Supports the development of 21st century skills and sense of cyber-citizenship

- Enables students a chance to excel in and out of the classroom with practice-based education

Players, coaches, employers and even spectators often express their excitement to participate in competitions [10] and the players report that the events motivate them to acquire knowledge and skills to improve their scores [11]. Furthermore, the hands-on nature of cybersecurity competitions and games provides the opportunity for educators to integrate them into formal curriculum. Specialized competitions have been created which address the particular needs of educators [12,16]. These competitions provide support materials for instructors and a rigorous scoring system. Finally, a significant consideration for middle, high, and college school students provided by competitions is the legal and safe place to develop professional ethics and hone skills [10].

However, cybercompetitions are a new domain and are quickly evolving. There are a wide variety of silo-ed competitions, targeting different audiences, with different rules, and measurement systems. This limits the ability of the individual competitions to contribute to attracting and developing the cyber workforce on a larger scale. Furthermore, research suggests that competitions attract participants who are already engaged with the profession and may discourage novice competitors [14]. Collectively, competitions could contribute to research which could investigate methods for attracting and engaging diverse participants, supporting novice competitors, addressing cheating, and improving the rigor of scoring strategies. Strategically, the landscape needs a single organization to

- facilitate better promotion,

- coordination, collective advocacy,

- information sharing, and

- integration with education and workforce development systems.

This poster presentation describes a novel approach to addressing the cybersecurity workforce shortage, the formation of a community to promote cybersecurity competitions and related activities called the Cybersecurity Competitions Federation.

The Cybersecurity Competition Federation (CCF), funded by a grant from the National Science Foundation (DUE- 134536) was founded by academic, industry and government organizations with a common interest in building awareness and interest in cybersecurity careers and accelerating our technical workforce development by supporting cybersecurity competitions and the competitors they serve. CCF members share the common goal of increasing awareness, endorsing ethical standards, building a common understanding of diverse competition tasks, and helping those who oversee activities and competitions. The key to fulfilling the CCF mission to support the development of skill at a large scale is bringing cybersecurity competitions together to identify a developmental pathway of cybersecurity-based activities. As competitions provide the CCF information about their events the CCF website will help players of all ages and skill levels identify a point of entry into a continuum of cybersecurity competition experiences.

With a focus on communication and promotion the CCF maintains the autonomy of competition creators, supports their business models, and does not interfere with their sponsorship or funding sources. The communication and promotional functions of the CCF also serve an important function for prospective competitors by addressing the objections of administrators and parents. Cybersecurity competitions have an image problem. With media coverage focusing on the theft of data, disruptive activism by anonymous groups of "hackers", and extreme events such as DEF CON, parents and administrators are reluctant to encourage cybersecurity competitions for their children and students. Furthermore, there is a stereotype among teenagers that kids with strong computer skills are outsiders. The CCF has begun to produce informational videos and documents to elevate cybersecurity competitions to the same trustworthy status of other afterschool programs such as sports, music, scouts etc. Through the website, competition and member events, and conference presentations by members, the CCF will support collaboration among cybersecurity competitions and related activities which in turn will prepare players with widely needed cybersecurity knowledge and skills.

Ethics

Protecting the identity and privacy information of cybersecurity competitors affirms a priority expressed by the current CCF membership; the CCF should serve as a model for ethical practice in cybersecurity. However, it is difficult to identify other opportunities for the CCF to demonstrate ethical leadership. Issues of enforceability, monitoring, boundaries and limits resulted in a consensus decision to avoid any unilateral, judgmental determinations including a required ethical policy for all members. Furthermore, some competitions provide experiences which are counter to educational institutions' acceptable-use policies, state and federal laws. Yet, these competitions are an accurate simulation of the work of cybersecurity professionals. The debate remains, should these competitions be included or excluded in the CCF?

Despite this challenge, work is being done to identify models of ethical policies which could be adopted by member competitions and competitors. In order to identify the essential ethical considerations among existing competitions a CCF team searched the large and growing list of competition websites for ethical policies or statements. Additional sources for ethical statements included professional security societies, and user groups (ACM, IEEE, ISC2, EC-Council etc.) The ethical statements were compiled into a single document. The next step will be to determine if there is an identifiable common lexicon with which to develop a shared taxonomy.

1.1 Pathways

Developing a common lexicon is necessary for the diverse set of activities and events that constitute the current landscape of cybersecurity competitions. Over the course of the CCF workshops, many types of competitions were identified including:

- Capture the Flag
- Inherit/Defend, Forensics
- Hack-a-thon, Attack/Defend
- "Build-it, Break-it, Fix it"
- Coding, Build & Defend
- Networking, Jeopardy
- Quiz Bowl, and Coding

However, the implementation of each event varies from competition to competition. The CCF team has begun to study the characteristics that could be used to define the varied events and activities. Lists of characteristics that typify each type of competition will be classified so that common definitions can be shared with the community.

The study of the mechanics and rules of the competitions supports the development of a searchable continuum of experiences aligned with player interests, capabilities and goals. The CCF is studying methodologies for developing a pathway framework which will support a self-sustaining cybersecurity competition ecosystem. The pathway framework will need to include a schema for a continuum of tasks that are differentiated by interests, career/educational goals and difficulty. The personalized pathways will also include links to resources which provide tutorials on game mechanics, and media to support training.

The challenge of this task is to develop and maintain an up-to-date database of competitions and the evolving list of skill inputs, outputs, and new technologies. Examples of information that can aid the CCF in providing a continuum of contiguous experiences include:

- Knowledge: level of conceptual understanding (proficiency)
- Skill: level of task accomplishment (performance)
- Ability: level of aptitude to learn and create (adaptability)
- Fields: computer science, forensics, IT, penetration testing
- Participation: team, individual
- Eligibility: novice, professional, grade, age, education, certification

Finding a competition that aligns with an individual's competency and interests among the myriad of competitions is a material obstacle to cybersecurity competition growth. The CCF website will facilitate matchmaking between the players' or educators' abilities/goals and the competitions' missions and requirements. Further, plans include the ability to query the pathway information to design a personalized sequence of competitions. This successful matchmaking may support learning and encourage career engagement [5,6,14].

The challenge in implementing the pathway concept is in simplifying the information that is required of competitions. Current lists of characteristics are not detailed enough to anticipate changes to the competition landscape. At the same time, the list is sufficiently long that there are concerns about the amount of time a competition organizer would spend filling out the information form. Feedback and suggestions will be collected to help the CCF identify essential information that stakeholders would require to select a competition that meets their interests, abilities and goals.

1.2 Learning Objectives

For education-focused competitions in both higher education and K-12, there may be a relationship between the cyber competition and learning objectives that can be leveraged in curriculum. Competitions used in formal learning environments are different because educators must be able to measure growth in their students' knowledge, skills or abilities. This can only happen if the score of a competition is aligned with identified learning objectives, and the scoring system provides valid and reliable results that can be used as a grade. Including these competitions and their objectives in the CCF database will help to support hands-on learning and performance objectives in formal cybersecurity instruction nationwide.

However, it is important to note that not all competitions are geared towards education or specific objectives; some are just for fun, prioritize career awareness, or emphasize the critical thinking and problem solving that occurs in a free-for-all environment. Furthermore, some career development-focused competitions may be geared to measure performance objectives necessary to complete professional tasks. It was suggested the CCF assist competitions who would like to serve an educational competition to identify learning objectives for their events [11].

2. Conclusion

The key to the mature CCF is a proven business plan which can sustain changes in leadership, and fund the work which supports the vision and mission. A mature CCF should have a stable, long-term membership which values and supports its vision and mission, a history of successful advocacy and information sharing which has expanded the scale and value of cybercompetitions, games and events, a well-developed set of resources for all of its stakeholder groups, and a widely adopted set of ethics, nomenclature, game classifications, data sharing and information. Above all, a mature CCF should be able to claim without controversy that its efforts have benefited cybercompetitions, games and events and accelerated cyber workforce development in the U.S.

3. REFERENCES

[1] Cisco (2014). *"Cisco 2014 Annual Security Report"*. http://www.cisco.com/web/offer/gist_ty2_asset/Cisco_2014_ASR.pdf

[2] Cluley, G. (June 26, 21012). State-sponsored cybercrime on "industrial scale" says MI5 chief. https://nakedsecurity.sophos.com/2012/06/26/state-sponsored-cybercrime-on-industrial-scale-says-mi5-chief/

[3] code.org (n.d.). *"Promote Computer Science"*. http://code.org/promote

[4] Cybersecurity Research &Development: Hearing before the Subcommittee on Research and Science Education: (2009). House of Representatives, 111th Congress. http://science.house.gov/sites/republicans.science.house.gov/files/documents/hearings/061009_damico.pdf

[5] Dede, C. (2009). Immersive interfaces for engagement and learning." *Science*. Vo. 323, No. 5910: pp. 66--69.

[6] Hong, E., Milgram, R., and Whiston, S. (1993). "Leisure activities in adolescents as a predictor of occupational choice in young adults: A longitudinal study," *Journal of Career Development*. Vo. 19, No. 3: pp. 221-229.

[7] Lubinski, D. and Benbow, C. (2006). "Study of mathematically precocious youth after 35 years: Uncovering antecedents for the development of math-science expertise." Perspectives on Psychological Science. Vo.1, No. 4: pp. 316--345.

[8] Manson, D. & Pike, R. (2014). The case for depth in cybersecurity education. *ACM Inroads: Special Section on Cybersecurity Education*. Vo. 5, No.1, pp. 47-52.

[9] Paulsen, C., McDuffie, E., Newhouse, W., Toth, P. (2012). "NICE: Creating a Cybersecurity Workforce and Aware Public", *IEEE Security & Privacy*. Vo.10, No. 3: pp. 76-79.

[10] Pusey, P. (2013). "Summary of NCSF Workshop: August 2013". Unpublished Report, Department of Computer Information Systems, Cal Poly Pomona, Pomona, California.

[11] Pike, R. E. (2013) "The "Ethics" of Teaching Ethical Hacking," Journal of International Technology and Information Management: Vol. 22: Iss. 4, Article 4. http://scholarworks.lib.csusb.edu/jitim/vol22/iss4/4

[12] The National Cyber League (2015). http://www.nationalcyberleague.org/index.shtml

[13] The National Cybersecurity Initiative (n.d.). https://www.whitehouse.gov/issues/foreign-policy/cybersecurity/national-initiative

[14] Tobey, D. H., Pusey, P., & and D. Burley (2014). "Engaging learners in cybersecurity careers: Lessons from the launch of the National Cyber League". *ACM Inroads: Special Section on Cybersecurity Education*. Vo. 5, No.1, pp. 53-56.

[15] USM Cybersecurity Task Force (2011, May). Report of the Cyber Security Task Force to the University System of Maryland. http://www.usmd.edu/newsroom/news/987

[16] Weiss,R.; Locasto,M., Mache, J., & Nestler, V. (2013). Teaching cybersecurity through games: a cloud-based approach. 29(1):113-115.

Privacy Issues and Techniques in E-Health Systems

Tina Francis
BITS Pilani,
Dubai Campus, DIAC
Dubai
p2011002@dubai.bits-pilani.ac.in

Dr. Muthiya Madiajagan
BITS Pilani,
Dubai Campus, DIAC
Dubai
madiajagan@dubai.bits-pilani.ac.in

Dr. Vijay Kumar
BITS Pilani,
Dubai Campus, DIAC
Dubai
vijay@dubai.bits-pilani.ac.in

ABSTRACT

During the present era, mobiles and smart devices are in abundance. A number of services have been provided through these devices. Ubiquitous services is gaining popularity in the present era. Ubiquity in healthcare is a sector which has gained importance in the current decade, as medical costs are not affordable to the common man. Ubiquitous healthcare has scope in seamlessly monitoring patients and identifying their health conditions. However privacy is at risk when using ubiquitous healthcare as personal health data are given to third party individuals for monitoring, storage and retrieval. This paper proposes a privacy preserving model of an e-health system, so as to maintain the security of patient data across different domains in the e-health system.

Categories

C.2.4 [Cloud Computing], C.2.1 [Internet], K.7.2 [ACM].

General Terms

Distributed Applications, Network Security, E-Health Applications.

Keywords

Cloud computing; security; access controls; patterns; data encryption, cloud data security; cryptography; security monitoring, trusted computing; access control.

1. INTRODUCTION

With the development of smart devices such as smart phones, PDA's and other digital devices, a number of these devices were embedded with low cost sensors. Sensors are provided as means of getting data. Sensors are used in numerous sectors, such as oil & gas, healthcare, petro-chemicals and automobiles.

An E-health system obtains data from patients through sensors, monitors, devices and they analyze this information to obtain inferences. Such systems are described using a general terminology called ubiquitous healthcare applications. As data is information that can be used in a fruitful or malicious way, there should be ways to secure the data collected and transmitted on such systems. This paper focuses on remote health monitoring

using smart devices and the concerns of using it. In addition to remote health monitoring, cloud computing has been used with e-health systems to off-load services onto the cloud to increase scalability and performance of the system. 'Mednet' was designed by Microsoft to remotely monitor different health conditions of patients [4]. Cloud services put confidential health records at stake as their services are provided by third party vendors. The end-to-end architecture of an E-health system is given in Figure 1. From the architecture of the e-health system it is seen that the medical server/ emergency servers and the personal servers are the main entities responsible of authenticating the patients, care givers, commercial health care providers and professionals such as doctors and surgeons. This paper focuses on the privacy issues that affect e-health systems in following paragraph. Also some effective security techniques are proposed for an end-to-end E-health application. The last section gives a secure E-health application and the advantages of using this system.

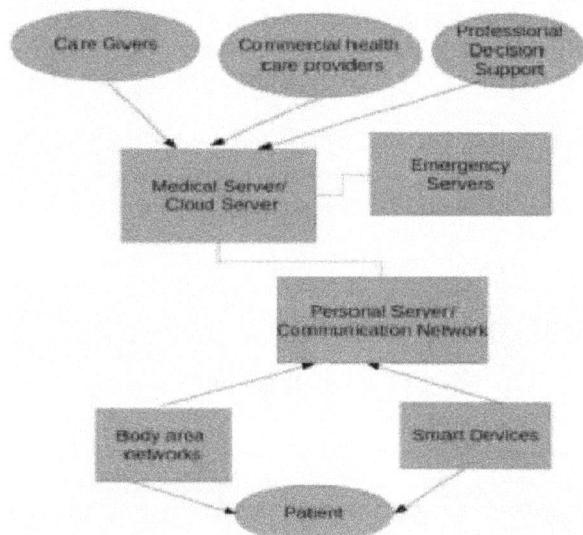

Figure 1: End-to-End Architecture of an E-Health System.

2. SECURITY ISSUES IN E-HEALTH SYSTEMS

E-health systems obtain patient data and give the information to doctors, nurses, etc. Unethical practices in using these systems can give rise to security issues of tampering with the medical data. For example a diabetic patient to undergo a surgery for knee replacement, e-health systems will give the past and present data of the patient. But his underlying mental conditions need not be mentioned to doctors. By tampering with the electronic health records, such potential sensitive information can be revealed. If this information is obtained by the company in which the patient is employed, or the insurance company that the patients have taken the policy, then it can have long term consequences. Hence maintaining the privacy and security of electronic health records in different e-health systems is very important. Many of the e-health systems offload services such as health care data management, storage, retrieval etc. to the cloud servers. Cloud services are provided by third party vendors, hence there are probabilities of security attacks from insiders, denial of service attacks (DOS), eavesdropping, health care data tampering and duplication of health care data [3]. This paper considers the privacy and security concerns in a basic e-health system, such as those that are networked between hospitals, patients and the cloud. This type of architecture is useful for health care providers such as hospitals, clinics, private practices, healthcare social networking sites (HSNS).

In order to overcome these security concerns, adequate precaution have to be taken at the cloud front and at the user front where health data is transmitted and stored. Network security based on public key cryptosystems, symmetric key cryptosystems are some of the techniques that are used to secure the networks. The next section focuses on the effective security strategies implemented when building an e-health system.

3. PRIVACY TECHNIQUES IN E-HEATLH SYSTEMS

Based on this survey, it is evident that E-health systems are subjected to many compromises in privacy. A few security strategies that are effectively used in E-health systems are at the data collection stage, transmission stage and storage stage. On the basis the following security stages in an E-health systems are identified.

3.1 Secured Data Collection

Wireless Body area networks collect streams of data such as pulse rate, blood pressure, ECG, EEG etc. which are then transferred to common transmission unit such as a home server/ mobile device etc. Hybrid encryption techniques such as ECC (Elliptic Curve Cryptography) are used as it offers security with smaller key sizes between Wireless sensor nodes and the connecting devices [2].

3.2 Secured Data Transmission/ Retransmission

Transmission and retransmission of e-health records are subject to different attacks. Access Controls and encryption are effective in securing health records. The author [6] proposes a multi-authority based weighed attribute encryption scheme for cloud encryption. The concept of weight in this scheme is given to different authorities accessing the secure data. Weights are decided based on the attributes.

3.3 Secured Data Storage

As data is stored in cloud servers, at different locations which may even be geographically diverse locations. Security is an important factor in geographically diverse locations due to impact of governmental rules and laws of the land [1].

Other than these security techniques employed at different stages in the e-health systems, on the whole an e-health system build

should employ the main cryptographic techniques for making the system seamless and secure. Also some health parameters that are acquired through continuous monitoring are ECG, heart rate etc. Sizes of some of these parameters are very huge for example ECG. Privacy preserving techniques for transmission of ECG signals are required. Encryption along with compression is used for large data such as ECG. The author [4] gives an efficient ECG encryption scheme using SPIHT (Set Partitioning in Hierarchical Tress) compression along with selective encryption which is used to maintain an energy efficient and high quality data transmission of ECG signals.

Hence with the above methods of securing the system the most appropriate end-to-end encryption strategy is the symmetric key encryption technique. Time complexity for execution of public key encryption algorithms are higher than other encryption standards. Many public key cryptosystems have modular multiplications and modular additions. Symmetric key cryptosystems use block ciphers. As mentioned in the above paragraph, security is already handled at the collection, transmission/ retransmission and at the storage end, by other public key encryption standards. Attacks at the channel such as denial of service (DOS) and snooping attacks can be handled by symmetric key ciphers. As there are probabilities that there can be a breach of trust among these entities through insider attacks, a central authority is included in the system. To maintain the security of the entire system cloud computing/ e-health portal provider has an important role to identify the key distribution center for different users in the system. The owner of the health record shares the master key with the entity maintaining the e-health system. This authority maintains an identity for all the entities participating in the e-health system. A combination of symmetric key and public key encryption is used in the entire E-health system. The central authority has the public key for all the entities in the system and enables key exchange among the entities and encryption is done using stream ciphers.

4. PRIVACY PRESERVING E-HEALTH SYSTEM
4.1 Secure E-Health System

After addressing the security factors in the last section, a central authenticating module is proposed to be included in the e-health system to authenticate patients, doctors and clients. The actors to be authenticated, identify themselves to this authority and provide their verification. The central authority acts as the key distribution center for cloud server/e-health server, patients, doctors etc. Session keys are maintained for different transaction timestamps using the symmetric key cryptosystems. Figure 2 shows the e-health architecture with a trusted central authority and figure 3 shows the Transmission/ Retransmission sequence diagram between patient and cloud server/e-Health server. The central authority maintains the master key to maintain secure communication between personal computer of patients and cloud server/e-health server. Thus from this architecture it is seen that patients are in controls of their health records through the trusted authority who acts as the mediator to maintain the security of their health records from commercial healthcare providers, care givers, doctors, decision support professionals. The security issues discussed in the second paragraph of this paper had been addressed through the use of access controls by the patients. Access controls are authenticated by trusted authority before providing data to other entities in the architecture.

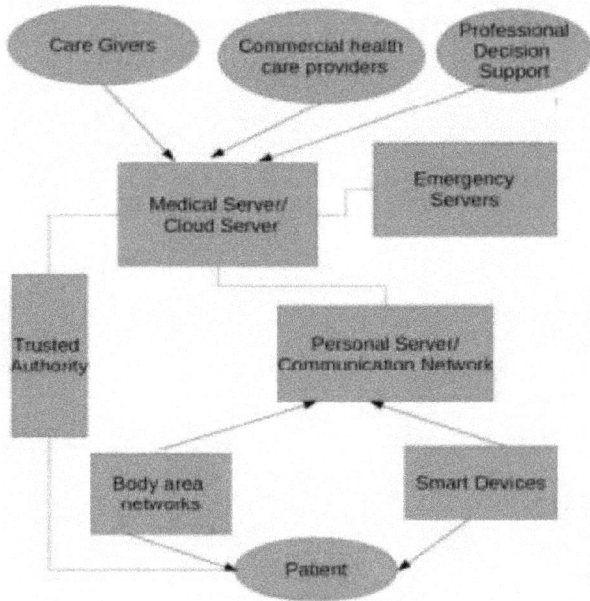

Figure 2 E-Health Architecture with trusted central authority

Figure 3: Secured Sequence Diagram for E-Health System

5. CONCLUSION

E-health systems are an emerging applications in ubiquitous computing. But securing the data transmitted and stored is the most important requirement in this system. There are a number of challenges in securing this data and maintaining its privacy. This paper identifies the different privacy issues in E-health systems. False practices and malicious users can tamper the privacy of E-health records that are personal to users. In order to overcome these issues this paper proposes a privacy preserving e-health system, which will rely on a trusted authority for key exchange and secure transmission of personal data. This helps patients maintain control of their health records, and deciding to whom access controls are to be given through this trusted authority.

6. ACKNOWLEDGMENTS

Our thanks to all the reviewers for their valuable suggestions.

7. REFERENCES

[1] Francis T. and Vadivel S., 2012. Cloud Computing Security: Concerns, Strategies and Best Practices. *International Conference Cloud Computing Technologies Applications and Management, pp 205 -207.*

[2] Li M., Lou W and Ren K., 2010. Data Security and Privacy in Wireless Body Area Networks, *IEEE Wireless Communication, Vol. 17, Issue 1*, pp 51-57.

[3] Lui, J. and Kyung, S. K., 2010. Hybrid Security mechanisms for Wireless Body Area Networks, *International Conference on Ubiquitous and Future Networks, Korea*, pp 98- 103.

[4] Ma T., Lal T., Hempel M., Peng D., Hamid S. and Hsiao C. 2012. Assurance of Energy Efficiency and Data Security for ECG transmissions in BASNs, *IEEE Transactions on Biomedical Engineering, Vol 59, No. 4*, pp 1014-1022.

[5] Mohan P., Marian D., Sulatan S. and Dean A. 2008. Mednet: Personalizing the self-care process of patients with diabetics and cardiovascular diseases using mobile telephony. *Engineering in Medicine and Biology Society, pp 755-758.*

[6] Wang Y., Zang D., Zong H., 2014 Multi Authority based weighed attribute encryption scheme in cloud computing, *10th International conference on Natural Computation*, pp 1033 -1038.

Professional Obsolescence in IT: The Relationships between the Threat of Professional Obsolescence, Coping and Psychological Strain

Tenace Setor
Nanyang Technological University
tenacekw001@e.ntu.edu.sg

Damien Joseph
Nanyang Technological University
adjoseph@ntu.edu.sg ·

Shirish C. Srivastava
HEC Paris
srivastava@hec.fr

ABSTRACT

Professional obsolescence has been recognized as one of the biggest threats confronting present day IT workers. Despite the imperative to understand the strategies for coping with this professional threat, research on the subject is relatively limited. Moreover, most studies on the subject till date are anecdotal. Clearly, theoretically grounded empirical research on the subject will not only help advance the understanding on professional obsolescence but will also provide actionable directions for IT professionals to work effectively.

With this end in view we first draw upon the mediational model of occupational stress to theorize the relationships between the threat of professional obsolescence and problem-focused and emotion-focused coping and their consequent impacts on psychological strain. Next, we test the hypothesized model via survey data collected in two waves from a sample of 738 IT professionals from a large Indian IT company. Results show that the threat of professional obsolescence is positively related to problem-focused coping but not emotion-focused coping. In addition, emotion-focused coping of professional obsolescence is associated with higher levels of psychological strain, but problem-focused coping of professional obsolescence is not significantly associated with psychological strain. We discuss the implications that the results of this study have for theory and practice.

Keywords

Professional Obsolescence, Problem-focused Coping, Emotion-focused Coping, Psychological Strain, Mediational Model of Occupational Stress.

1. INTRODUCTION

Due to rapid technological developments, current day IT workers, more than workers from other knowledge professions, face a constant threat of *professional obsolescence* (e.g. Ferdinand 1966; Glass 2000; Zhang et al. 2012). Professional obsolescence is defined as the erosion of worker's professional knowledge and skills required for successful performance (Dubin 1990; Ferdinand 1966; Glass 2000).

Professional obsolescence is an occupational stressor that requires adaptive responses from individuals in the form of cognitive and behavioral coping strategies (Rosen et al. 2010; Sonnetag et al. 2009).

Extant IT research has taken a disparate approach to examine how IT professionals cope with professional obsolescence. Some IT studies have exclusively examined updating behaviors (Joseph et al. 2011; Schambach 1999) as a form of coping with professional obsolescence. Other IT research have examined, piecemeal, specific coping mechanisms such as delegation of updating to others (Joseph et al. 2010; Rong and Grover 2009); and constriction of control and restriction of information processing (Joseph and Ang 2001). By contrast, the qualitative studies of Tsai et al. (2007) and Pazy (1994) have attempted to taking a grounded-theory approach to identify a broader range of cognitive and behavioral coping strategies utilized to cope with the threat of professional obsolescence.

However, to the best of our knowledge, no study till date has statistically tested the link between the threat of professional obsolescence and the broader coping strategies (see Tsai et al. (2007); Pazy 1994). Through this study we address this gap by building on the work of Tsai et al. (2007) and Pazy (1994). We examine how professional obsolescence is related to coping strategies, which in turn influence psychological strain.

By doing so, this study contributes to the literature on professional obsolescence in two ways. First, this study answers calls to examine the efficacy of coping strategies towards resolving the stress of professional obsolescence (see Tsai et al. 2004). Second, this study contributes to the growing body of literature by developing a theoretical stress-based model of professional obsolescence and empirically testing that model with a two-wave survey data collected from a large sample of IT professionals. The adaption of the mediational model of occupational stress within the context of professional obsolescence strengthens the model's generalizability.

The rest of the paper is organized as follows. First, we present our research model that explains the relationships between the threat of professional obsolescence, coping and psychological strain. Next, we provide a description of the methodology used to analyze the research model. Finally, we present the results and discuss the implication of our findings.

2. THEORETICAL FOUNDATION AND HYPOTHESES DEVELOPMENT

The current study utilizes a mediational model of occupational stress (Lazarus and Folkman 1984; Webster et al. 2011). Occupational stress refers to a process through which individuals appraise and respond to occupational demands that threaten their resources (Rosen et al. 2010). The element that triggers the stress process – a stressor – is appraised as a threat to individual resources (Hobfoll 1989; Lazarus and Folkman 1984). Threat appraisal, i.e. the threat of professional obsolescence in the case of current study (see Figure 1) induces psychological strains (Jex and Yankelevich, 2008). Psychological strain is defined as aversive and potentially harmful psychological reactions of the individual to stressful occupational work (De Croon et al. 2004).

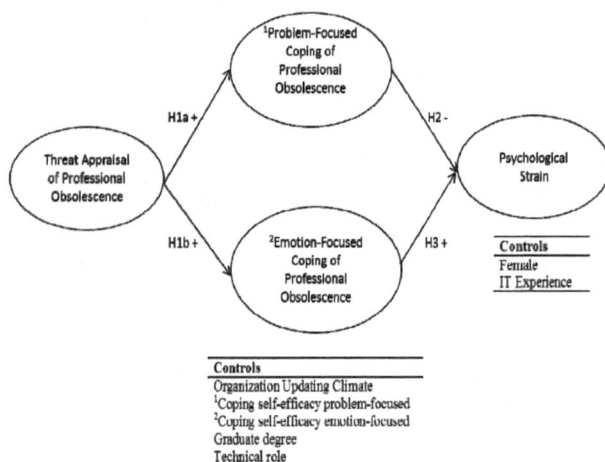

Figure 1: Mediational Model of threat of Professional Obsolescence

Within this model of stress, coping strategies are posited to mediate the impact of occupational stressors and levels of psychological strain (Folkman et al. 1986; Lazarus and Folkman 1984). Coping strategies are cognitive and behavioral efforts expended to manage a stressor (Lazarus and Folkman 1984). There are two general forms of coping – problem-focused coping and emotion-focused coping (Boyd et al. 2009; Lazarus and Folkman 1984).

Problem-focused coping refers to behaviors that directly address and/or change the problem causing the distress (Lazarus and Folkman 1984). Emotion-focused coping cognitively regulates negative emotions arising from distress (Lazarus and Folkman 1984).

2.1 Relationship between Threat Appraisal of Professional Obsolescence and Coping

Threat appraisal of professional obsolescence focuses on the negative implications of possessing devalued IT skills e.g. lower compensations and employability (Lazarus and Folkman, 1984; Tsai et al., 2007; Mithas and Krishnan 2008). IT professionals are motivated to preserve the currency of IT skills so as to avoid the negative implications of devalued IT skills (Hobfoll 1989). IT professionals preserve IT skills' currency by updating IT skills and knowledge.

Updating actions are problem-focused forms of coping with professional obsolescence (Tsai et al. 2004). Hence, we posit

Hypothesis 1a: Threat appraisal of professional obsolescence is positively related to problem-focused coping of professional obsolescence.

Threat appraisal of professional obsolescence induces negative emotions such as the disquietude of possessing devalued IT skills (see Lazarus and Folkman, 1984). Negative emotions deplete cognitive resources and individual motivations (Wright and Cropanzano 1998). As such, negative emotions demotivate IT professionals to engage in demanding activities; such as learning and updating (Carver and Scheier 1990; Pekrun 1992). Emotion-focused coping then becomes a favorable coping option because it is comparatively unexacting. The adoption of emotion-focused coping is intended to provide a sense of security from the distressing situation (Lazarus and Folkman 1984).

Hence we hypothesize,

Hypothesis 1b: Threat appraisal of professional obsolescence is positively related to emotion-focused coping of professional obsolescence.

2.2 Relationship between Coping and Psychological Strain

While the literature on professional obsolescence has classified the various coping strategies adopted into problem and emotion focused coping (e.g. Tsai et al. 2007), it has yet to theoretically and empirically link these forms of coping to psychological strain. Nonetheless, Tsai et al. (2007) provide initial evidence to suggest that IT professionals who enact problem-focused coping strategies are less likely to experience psychological strain. Problem-focused coping strategies maintain the currency of IT skills. IT professionals with up-to-date IT competencies will experience lower levels of anxiety whiles carrying out their work functions because of their updated skillsets. The argument that problem-focused coping reduces psychological strain is consistent with the extant stress literature. Generally, problem-focused coping has been found to be associated with lower levels of anxiety experienced on the job (Boyd et al. 2009; Latack 1986; Sears Jr et al. 2000).

Hence:

Hypothesis 2: Problem-focused coping of professional obsolescence is negatively related to psychological strain

In contrast to the aforementioned arguments, IT professionals who adopt more emotion-focused coping such as denial of the threat of professional obsolescence experience higher levels of distress on the job (see Tsai et al. 2007). Emotion-focused coping strategies do not augment IT professionals' abilities to deal with the realities of professional obsolescence. In other words, IT competencies remain out-of-date to the extent that IT professionals' ability to function effectively on the job. This is a worrying situation for IT professionals because their outdated competencies hold less value in the IT labor market (Mithas and Krishnan 2008). Hence we hypothesize:

Hypothesis 3: Emotion-focused coping of professional obsolescence is positively related to psychological strain.

3. RESEARCH METHOD

The heading of a section should be in Times New Roman 12-point bold in all-capitals flush left with an additional 6-points of white space above the section head. Sections and subsequent sub-sections should be numbered and flush left. For a section head and a subsection head together (such as Section 3 and subsection 3.1), use no additional space above the subsection head.

3.1 Data Collection Procedure and Sample

We collected survey data from a sample of IT professionals in a large multinational IT organization headquartered in India. Email invitations were sent to 1962 IT professionals within the organization to complete the survey questions.

Two waves of surveys were conducted six months apart to minimize common method (Podsakoff et al. 2003). We had 1193 responses in the first wave and 991 responses in the second wave. The final dataset comprised of 738 usable responses, which represents a final response rate of 37.6%.

The profile of respondents in the dataset is as follows: 78% are males; 67% held graduate degrees; 61% were in technical positions, including software developers and engineers; and 39% held managerial positions such as IT project managers.

3.2 Measures

Wherever possible, we used and adapted validated instruments from prior literature. For measures developed in this study (*e.g.* threat appraisal of professional obsolescence, problem-focused coping and emotion-focused coping dimensions), we followed the instrument development approach recommended by Clark and Watson (1995). Unless otherwise stated, all the items were measured on a 7-point Likert scale in which 1 represented "*strongly disagree*" and 7 represented "*strongly agree*".

Psychological Strain: This was measured by adapting six items of Warr's (1990) scale. A sample item is, "Thinking about the past few weeks, how much of the time has your job made you feel worried". Items were measured on a 7-point Likert scale in which 1 was "*All of the time*" and 7 was "*Never*".

Coping with Professional Obsolescence: The coping strategies examined in this study were operationalized from Pazy's (1994) study of how knowledge workers cope with professional obsolescence.

The coping measures and other measures developed for this study (*e.g.* threat appraisal of professional obsolescence), were developed by following religiously the instrument development approach recommended by Clark and Watson (1995).

Problem-focused coping and emotion-focused coping were specified as reflective second-order constructs. Conceptually, problem-focused coping and emotion-focused coping are multidimensional constructs as they consist of several distinct coping dimensions (Pazy 1994; Tsai et al. 2007):

Problem-Focused Coping: This second-order construct consists of *Knowing a Lot about Little* (KLOTL), *Knowing Little About a Lot* (KLLOT), and *Incremental Evolution* (IE) items. *Knowing a Lot about Little (KLOTL)*: Three items were developed to measure KLOTL. A sample item is "I cope with professional obsolescence by mastering a specific IT area related to my work". *Knowing Little about a Lot (KLLOT)*: Three items were developed to measure KLLOT. A sample item is "I cope with professional obsolescence by being familiar with a broad scope of diverse IT topics". *Incremental Evolution (IE)*: Three items were developed to measure IE. A sample item is "I cope with professional obsolescence by learning from time to time".

Emotion-Focused Coping: This second-order construct consists of *Vanishing Factor of Obsolescence, Shifting Focus from Oneself to the Unit* and *Temporarily Unchanging Bubbles* items. *Vanishing Factor of Obsolescence (VFO)*: Three items were developed to measure *VFO*. A sample item is "I cope with professional obsolescence knowing that updating is not a necessary ingredient of success". *Shifting Focus from oneself to the Unit (SFOU)*: Four items were developed to measure *SFOU*. A sample item is "I cope with professional obsolescence by knowing it is less important that I am up-to-date as long as someone in the organization keeps up-to-date with IT developments". *Temporarily Unchanging Bubbles (TUB)*: Four items were developed to measure *TUB*. A sample item is "I cope with professional obsolescence believing that it is not essential to pick up new IT knowledge and skills that are not needed for my current work".

Threat Appraisal of Professional Obsolescence: This construct was developed for the study using the approach described above and has five items. A sample item is "I perceive professional obsolescence to be a threat to my IT skills".

Control Variables: The following control variables were included to account for alternative explanations of the results. *Coping-Self Efficacy* was measured with ten items adapted from Chesney *et al.,* (2006). On a 7-point Likert scale (1 = *Not at all confident; 7 = Certainly Confident*), respondents were asked to rate how confident they were to employ problem-focused coping and emotion-focused coping. *Organization Updating Climate* was measured with eight items adapted from Kozlowski & Hults (1987). Education level and job role were both measured with dichotomous variables – *Graduate degree* ("*1*"; Post-graduate degree "*0*"), *Technical Role* ("*1*"; Managerial Role "*0*"). We also controlled for the possible effects of gender and IT experience on psychological strain. *Gender* was measured with a dichotomous variable *Female* ("*1*"; Male "*0*"). IT experience was measured as the number of years the respondent has worked in IT.

4. DATA ANALYSIS

A structural equation modeling (SEM) technique, using Rosseel's (2012) lavaan package (version 0.5-17) in *R*, was used to analyze the theoretical model. SEM technique is utilized to test the hypothesized paths of our research model.

4.1 Confirmatory Factor Analysis

Confirmatory factor analysis revealed the existence of items exhibiting lower factor loadings (cut-off of 0.60, MacKenzie et al. 2011). To test the measurement model, internal consistency (reliabilities) and the validity (convergent and discriminant) of the scales were examined. Results show that all scales were reliable, with Cronbach alphas greater than 0.70.

The resulting measurement model demonstrated a great fit to the data (χ^2 [1324] = 2130.82; χ^2/df = 1.61; CFI = .97; SRMR = .040; RMSEA = .029, 90% CI [.026, .031]) (Hair et al. 2010).

4.2 Structural Model

The structural model demonstrated a great fit to the data (χ^2 [932] = 1542.521; χ^2/df = 1.66; CFI = .97; SRMR = .046; RMSEA = .030, 90% CI [.027, .032]) (Hair et al. 2010).

Hypothesis 1a and 1b predicted that threat appraisal of professional obsolescence is positively related to problem-focused coping and emotion-focused coping of professional obsolescence respectively. The results indicate that threat appraisal is positively related to problem-focused coping of professional obsolescence ($\beta = 0.118$, $t = 2.476$, $p < 0.05$).

Thus, Hypothesis 1a is supported. Contrary to Hypothesis 1b, threat appraisal is negatively related to emotion-focused coping of professional obsolescence. Thus, Hypothesis 1b was not supported.

Hypothesis 2 predicted that problem-focused coping of professional obsolescence is negatively related to psychological strain. The results indicate that problem-focused coping of professional obsolescence is negatively related to psychological strain ($\beta = -0.024$, $t = -0.507$, $p = n.s.$) but the relationship is not significant. Thus, Hypothesis 2 is not supported

Hypothesis 3 predicted that emotion-focused coping of professional obsolescence is positively related to psychological strain. The results indicate that emotion-focused coping of professional obsolescence is positively related to psychological strain ($\beta = 0.173$, $t = 3385$, $p < 0.05$). Thus, Hypothesis 3 was supported.

For the control variables, the results indicate that organization update climate is positively related to problem-focused coping of professional obsolescence. This is consistent with prior research that suggests that IT professionals are likely to engage in direct updating actions when the organization climate encourages updating (Schambach 1994). Technical role is positively related to emotion-focused coping of professional obsolescence. This is also consistent with prior research that found that the different roles (technical and non-technical) performed by knowledge professionals have an influence on the way they cope with professional obsolescence (Pazy 1996).

5. DISCUSSION

This study, based on the mediational model of stress and coping, explicates the relationships between threat appraisal of professional obsolescence, coping and psychological strain. Specifically, the study proposed that threat appraisal of professional obsolescence is positively related to problem-focused and emotion-focused coping. We hypothesized that emotion-focused coping is positively related to psychological strain and problem-focused coping is negatively related to psychological strain.

Two of the above four hypotheses were not supported. Contrary to the hypothesis, threat appraisal of professional obsolescence was negatively associated with emotion-focused coping. One reason might be that the threat of professional obsolescence may not necessarily trigger negative emotions or require the regulation of it. Not all IT professionals perceive professional obsolescence in terms that are associated with negative emotions. Some IT professionals are shown to take a "pragmatic tone" towards the threat of professional obsolescence (Tsai et al. 2007. p. 399). In other words, the threat of professional obsolescence is seen as neither positive nor negative.

Given that prior IT research frames professional obsolescence as a threat, we call on future research to examine whether IT professionals have multiple conceptualizations of professional obsolescence. For example, professional obsolescence may be perceived as an opportunity for professional development. Professional obsolescence may be perceived as an opportunity to update for fun (Joseph et al. 2011). In such a case, IT

professionals may evoke less emotion-focused coping because they believe nothing needs to be done about professional obsolescence.

They may be awareness of effective coping strategies that can be enacted to deal with professional obsolescence.

The other hypothesis not supported by the results related problem-focused coping to psychological strain. Although the result found that that problem-focused coping of professional obsolescence is negatively related to psychological strain, this relationship was not significant. This finding suggests that some, but not all, IT professionals found problem-focused strategies unable to lower psychological strain. A possible explanation could be that problem-focused coping of professional obsolescence, which largely consists of updating actions, is challenging and difficult (Joseph et al. 2011; Pazy 2004; Tsai et al. 2007). Updating actions require cognitive effort and time. Some IT professionals might not have the capacity to update, given competing tasks at work (Schaubroeck et al. 2000; Van Vegchel et al. 2005) and life (Dierdorff and Ellington 2008).

As such, future research would serve IT professionals well by examining the competing demands of occupation (e.g. professional obsolescence), work (e.g. time pressures) and life (e.g. meeting family obligations). We do not know of any such study examining the interplay of demands across roles on the well-being of employees. Such a study would enrich the stress literature on how individual, organization and family resources are complemented or substituted towards meeting life's demands.

6. CONCLUSION

The present study is one of the first few studies to examine the relationship between threat appraisal of professional obsolescence and the general forms of coping – problem-focused and emotion-focused of professional obsolescence. We contribute to theory by adapting and testing the meditational model of occupational stress and coping in explaining the relationship between threat appraisals of professional obsolescence, coping and psychological strain.

The findings of the study contributes to extant research on professional obsolescence that has remained silent on the efficacy of the general forms of coping with professional obsolescence *i.e.* whether problem-focused coping and emotion-focused coping of professional obsolescence would result in lower levels of psychological strain.

6.1 Limitations

Notwithstanding the theoretical contributions made by the present study, there are limitations of this study that should be noted. The data we collected for the study are cross-sectional so other possible explanations of the results may exist. We controlled extensively for the possible confounding effects that may offer alternative explanations of our results. For example, we controlled for the possible effects of coping self-efficacy, organization updating climate and demographic variables such as level of education on emotion-focused and problem-focused coping of professional obsolescence.

Cross-sectional data are susceptible to the threat of common-method bias. We conducted two cross-sectional surveys within a six-month period to collect our data to minimize common-method bias that may result from variables measured concurrently (Podsakoff et al. 2003). In addition, we conducted a post-hoc analysis (unmeasured latent methods factor technique) to determine whether common-method bias was of significant concern. The results of the CFA and structural model, when we accounted for the effects of the latent common-method variance construct, remained the same as the original results (without latent common-method variance construct).

6.2 Suggestions for Future Research

The present study offers some avenues for future research. First, a longitudinal field experiment is warranted to establish causality and rule out possible confounding effects that may be present in studies using cross-sectional data. Objective updating activities of IT professionals could be tracked and measured over time following professional obsolescence appraisals in longitudinal field experiments. Such a study would provide more robust results on the causal directions of variables in the theoretical model.

Second, we call for future research to examine professional obsolescence from a two-dimensional perspective with regards to how IT professional professionals may appraise professional obsolescence. A distinction between threat and opportunity appraisals of professional obsolescence may have differential impacts on employee attitudes and behaviors such as coping.

6.3 Implications for Practice

The study makes important contribution to IT work and practice. First, though the study does not examine strain management practices, the study provides important insights that may be useful in managing strain on the job. IT professionals who engage in emotion-focused coping of professional obsolescence are more likely to experience strain on the job. Managers may put in place strain-reducing measures such as professional counseling for these IT professionals.

Second, managers should realize that IT professionals may have the motivation to engage in updating actions that builds new IT skills to combat professional obsolescence. Thus, managers may take advantage of this finding and provide the necessary tools and resources required for learning new technologies.

7. REFERENCES

[1] Agarwal, N. K. 2011. "Verifying Survey Items for Construct Validity: A Two-Stage Sorting Procedure for Questionnaire Design in Information Behavior Research," *Proceedings of the American Society for Information Science and Technology* (48:1), pp. 1-8.

[2] Boyd, N. G., Lewin, J. E., and Sager, J. K. 2009. "A Model of Stress and Coping and Their Influence on Individual and Organizational Outcomes," *Journal of Vocational Behavior* (75:2), pp. 197-211.

[3] Carmines, E. G., and Zeller, R. A. 1979. *Reliability and Validity Assessment*. Sage.

[4] Carver, C. S., and Scheier, M. F. 1990. "Origins and Functions of Positive and Negative Affect: A Control-Process View," *Psychological review* (97:1), p. 19.

[5] Chesney, M. A., Neilands, T. B., Chambers, D. B., Taylor, J. M., and Folkman, S. 2006. "A Validity and Reliability Study of the Coping Self-Efficacy Scale," *British journal of health psychology* (11:3), pp. 421-437.

[6] Clark, L. A., and Watson, D. 1995. "Constructing Validity: Basic Issues in Objective Scale Development," *Psychological assessment* (7:3), p. 309.

[7] Dierdorff, E. C., and Ellington, J. K. 2008. "It's the Nature of the Work: Examining Behavior-Based Sources of Work-Family Conflict across Occupations," *Journal of Applied Psychology* (93:4), pp. 883-892.

[8] Dubin, S. S. 1990. "Maintaining Competence through Updating," in *Maintaining Professional Competence,* S.L. Willis and S.S. Dubin (eds.). San Francisco: Jossey-Bass, pp. 44-48.

[9] Ferdinand, T. N. 1966. "On the Obsolescence of Scientists and Engineers," *American Scientist*), pp. 46-56.

[10] Folkman, S., Lazarus, R. S., Dunkel-Schetter, C., DeLongis, A., and Gruen, R. J. 1986. "Dynamics of a Stressful Encounter: Cognitive Appraisal, Coping, and Encounter Outcomes," *Journal of personality and social psychology* (50:5), p. 992.

[11] Glass, R. 2000. "On Personal Technical Obsolescence," *Communications of the ACM* (43:7), pp. 15-17.

[12] Hair, J. F., Black, W., Babin, B., and Anderson, R. E. 2010. "Multivariate Data Analysis (7th Ed.)," *Upper Saddle River*).

[13] Hobfoll, S. E. 1989. "Conservation of Resources: A New Attempt at Conceptualizing Stress," *American psychologist* (44:3), p. 513.

[14] Joseph, D., and Ang, S. 2001. "The Threat-Rigidity Model of Professional Obsolescence and Its Impact on Occupational Mobility of It Professionals," *Twenty-Second International Conference on Information Systems*, New Orleans: Association for Information Systems, pp. 567-573.

[15] Joseph, D., Boh, W. F., Ang, S., and Slaughter, S. A. 2012. "The Career Paths Less (or More) Traveled: A Sequence Analysis of It Career Histories, Mobility Patterns, and Career Success," *MIS Quarterly* (36:2), pp. 427-452.

[16] Joseph, D., Koh, S. K. C., and Foo, C. H. A. 2010. "Sustainable It-Specific Human Capital: Coping with the Threat of Professional Obsolescence," *International Conference on Information Systems 2010 Proceedings*, St. Louis, MO.: Association for Information Systems, p. Paper 46.

[17] Joseph, D., Tan, M. L., and Ang, S. 2011. "Is Updating Play or Work?: The Mediating Role of Updating Orientation in Linking Threat of Professional Obsolescence to Turnover/Turnaway Intentions," *International Journal of Social and Organizational Dynamics in IT* (1:4), p. 37.

[18] Kozlowski, S. W., and Hults, B. M. 1987. "An Exploration of Climates for Technical Updating and Performance," *Personnel Psychology* (40:3), pp. 539-563.

[19] Latack, J. C. 1986. "Coping with Job Stress: Measures and Future Directions for Scale Development," *Journal of Applied Psychology* (71:3), pp. 377-385.

[20] Lazarus, R. S., and Folkman, S. 1984. *Stress, Appraisal, and Coping*. New York, NY.: Springer.

[21] MacKenzie, S. B., Podsakoff, P. M., and Podsakoff, N. P. 2011. "Construct Measurement and Validation Procedures in Mis and Behavioral Research: Integrating New and Existing Techniques," *MIS quarterly* (35:2), pp. 293-334.

[22] Mithas, S., and Krishnan, M. S. 2008. "Human Capital and Institutional Effects in the Compensation of

Information Technology Professionals in the United States," *Management Science* (54:3), pp. 415-428.

[23] Moore, G. C., and Benbasat, I. 1991. "Development of an Instrument to Measure the Perceptions of Adopting an Information Technology Innovation," *Information systems research* (2:3), pp. 192-222.

[24] Neimeyer, G. J., Taylor, J. M., and Rozensky, R. H. 2012. "The Diminishing Durability of Knowledge in Professional Psychology: A Delphi Poll of Specialties and Proficiencies," *Professional Psychology-Research and Practice* (43:4), pp. 364-371.

[25] Pazy, A. 1994. "Cognitive Schemata of Professional Obsolescence," *Human Relations* (47:10), pp. 1167-1199.

[26] Pazy, A. 1996. "Concept and Career-Stage Differentiation in Obsolescence Research," *Journal of Organizational Behavior* (17:1), pp. 59-78.

[27] Pazy, A. 2004. "Updating in Response to the Experience of Lacking Knowledge," *Applied Psychology-an International Review-Psychologie Appliquee-Revue Internationale* (53:3), pp. 436-452.

[28] Pekrun, R. 1992. "The Impact of Emotions on Learning and Achievement: Towards a Theory of Cognitive/Motivational Mediators," *Applied Psychology* (41:4), pp. 359-376.

[29] Podsakoff, P. M., MacKenzie, S. B., Lee, J. Y., and Podsakoff, N. P. 2003. "Common Method Biases in Behavioral Research: A Critical Review of the Literature and Recommended Remedies," *Journal of Applied Psychology* (88:5), pp. 879-903.

[30] Rong, G., and Grover, V. 2009. "Keeping up-to-Date with Information Technology: Testing a Model of Technological Knowledge Renewal Effectiveness for It Professionals," *Information & Management* (46:7), pp. 376-387.

[31] Rosen, C., C., Chang, C.-H., Djurdjevic, E., and Eatough, E. 2010. "Occupational Stressors and Job Performance: An Updated Review and Recommendations," in *New Developments in Theoretical and Conceptual Approaches to Job Stress*. Emerald Group Publishing Limited, pp. 1-60.

[32] Rosseel, Y. 2012. "Lavaan: An R Package for Structural Equation Modeling," *Journal of Statistical Software* (48:2), pp. 1-36.

[33] Schambach, T. 1999. "Updating Activities of Older Professionals," in: *Proceedings of the Fifth Americas Conference on Information Systems,* W.D. Haseman and D.L. Nazareth (eds.). Association for Information Systems, pp. 505-507.

[34] Schambach, T. P. 1994. "Maintaining Professional Competence: An Evaluation of Factors Affecting Professional Obsolescence of Information Technology Professionals." Ann Arbor: University of South Florida, pp. 224-224 p.

[35] Schaubroeck, J., Lam, S. S. K., and Xie, J. L. 2000. "Collective Efficacy Versus Self-Efficacy in Coping Responses to Stressors and Control: A Cross-Cultural Study," *Journal of Applied Psychology* (85:4), pp. 512-525.

[36] Sears Jr, S. F., Urizar Jr, G. G., and Evans, G. D. 2000. "Examining a Stress-Coping Model of Burnout and Depression in Extension Agents," *Journal of Occupational Health Psychology* (5:1), p. 56.

[37] Sonnetag, S., Ganster, D. C., and Perrewe, P. L. 2009. *Research in Occupational Stress and Well Being.* Emerald Group Publishing.

[38] Tsai, H. P., Compeau, D., and Haggerty, N. 2004. "A Cognitive View of How It Professionals Update Their Technical Skills," *Proceedings of the 2004 SIGMIS conference on Computer personnel research: Careers, culture, and ethics in a networked environment*: ACM, pp. 70-73.

[39] Tsai, H. Y., Compeau, D., and Haggerty, N. 2007. "Of Races to Run and Battles to Be Won: Technical Skill Updating, Stress, and Coping of It Professionals," *Human Resource Management* (46:3), pp. 395-409.

[40] Van Vegchel, N., De Jonge, J., and Landsbergis, P. A. 2005. "Occupational Stress in (Inter)Action: The Interplay between Job Demands and Job Resources," *Journal of Organizational Behavior* (26:5), pp. 535-560.

[41] Warr, P. 1990. "The Measurement of Well-Being and Other Aspects of Mental Health," *Journal of occupational Psychology* (63:3), pp. 193-210.

[42] Wright, T. A., and Cropanzano, R. 1998. "Emotional Exhaustion as a Predictor of Job Performance and Voluntary Turnover," *Journal of Applied Psychology* (83:3), pp. 486-493.

[43] Zhang, X. N., Ryan, S. D., Prybutok, V. R., and Kappelman, L. 2012. "Perceived Obsolescence, Organizational Embeddedness, and Turnover of It Workers: An Empirical Study," *Data Base for Advances in Information Systems* (43:4), pp. 12-32.

Extending Moore's Exhaustion Model: Including Further Dimensions of Burnout and Investigating Their Influence on Turnover Intention Among IT Professionals

Christoph Weinert
Centre of Human Resources Information Systems
University of Bamberg, Germany
+49 951 8633918
christoph.weinert@uni-bamberg.de

Christian Maier
Centre of Human Resources Information Systems
University of Bamberg, Germany
+49 951 8633919
christian.maier@uni-bamberg.de

Sven Laumer
Centre of Human Resources Information Systems
University of Bamberg, Germany
+49 951 8632873
sven.laumer@uni-bamberg.de

Tim Weitzel
Centre of Human Resources Information Systems
University of Bamberg, Germany
+49 951 8632871
tim.weitzel@uni-bamberg.de

ABSTRACT

This research focuses on burnout as a driver of turnover intention amongst IT professionals. We extend Moore's exhaustion model by including further dimensions of burnout into the model, namely depersonalization and reduced personal accomplishment. The effect of stressors on these dimensions and the original dimension of emotional exhaustion is investigated, as is their influence on turnover intention among IT professional. Results based on a data sample of 154 IT professionals show that not only emotional exhaustion but also depersonalization leads to turnover intention. This outcome cannot be neglected when trying to reduce turnover intention in an organization in order to maintain competitive advantages. Moreover, while the stressors suggested by Moore influence emotional exhaustion, they only slightly explain the dimensions of depersonalization and reduced personal accomplishment. This indicates that these two dimensions of burnout are caused by additional factors, which represents a research gap worth investigating in future research.

Categories and Subject Descriptors

K.4.3 [**Organizational Impacts**]: Employment

General Terms

Management, Human Factors

Keywords

Emotional exhaustion; depersonalization; reduced personal accomplishment; burnout; turnover intention; IT professionals

1. INTRODUCTION

Research focusing on information technology (IT) professionals has increased over the past years [3, 10, 17, 20, 26]. These professionals are a crucial group of employees in the current knowledge driven economy [38]. In order to grow and remain competitive, firms depend on IT and in turn on the technical and business knowledge of IT professionals [1, 37]. Hence, to preserve the skills and capabilities of IT professionals, organizations must focus on managing their turnover intention. Recent research, therefore, focuses on understanding these intentions and thus providing organizations with fundamentals for implementing successful employee retention measures [38]. In this context, several investigations on IT professionals focus on the examination of work exhaustion as a source of turnover intention and acknowledge that IT professionals indicate a high level of burnout and thus a high level of intention to leave their job [2, 3, 37, 43].

Most of the information system (IS) research studies focus on emotional exhaustion as an example of employee burnout and predict turnover intention to a certain extent. However, psychological literature indicates that burnout is a combination of emotional exhaustion, as well as depersonalization and reduced personal accomplishment [33] and therefore pays extra attention to all of these aspects. *Depersonalization* occurs when a person feels distant towards their work, whereas *reduced personal accomplishment* occurs when an individual self-evaluates its productivity and achievements as low and feels incompetent [34]. *Emotional exhaustion* is the stress dimension of burnout. With the focus on employee exhaustion, prior IS research explains the drivers and consequences of this dimension of burnout well, however, it neglects the relationship individuals have with their work [34].

Therefore, in coherence with the research by Maslach and Jackson [33], we consider depersonalization and reduced personal accomplishment alongside emotional exhaustion as different dimensions of burnout in this paper. By doing so, we are able to place the individual burnout experience in the social workplace, which embodies both the person's self-perception as well as the perception of others [32]. This consideration of the three-dimensional burnout construct enables us to better understand and manage IT professional turnover. Specifically, an analysis and discussion is possible in regard to which characteristics are the cause of which dimensions and which dimensions are the cause of which consequences. Therefore, by considering all three dimensions of burnout among IT-professionals and by evaluating their impact on turnover intention, a research gap in IT personnel research can be filled. In order to do so, the present research aims to investigate the effect of stressors on emotional exhaustion, depersonalization and reduced personal accomplishment as well as their influence on turnover intention among IT professionals. Hence, the research question is:

What are causes of emotional exhaustion, depersonalization, and reduced personal accomplishment and what is their impact on IT professionals' turnover intention?

The present paper is organized as follows. In the beginning of the paper, we explain the theoretical background of burnout and describe prior literature on emotional exhaustion among IT professionals. Based on this, several hypotheses are developed and the research model is displayed. Subsequently, the methodology and research results are presented. Finally, we discuss the research results, show the theoretical and practical contributions and outline limitations as well as future research streams.

2. THEORETICAL BACKGROUND
2.1 Burnout
Burnout is a multidimensional construct, which comprises three different dimensions: emotional exhaustion, depersonalization, and reduced personal accomplishment [33]. The first, *emotional exhaustion, "arises from feelings of tension and frustration due to individuals' fears that they will be unable to provide previous levels of work performance"* [45, p. 488]. Symptoms are feelings of tension and depletion of one's emotional and physical resources [35]. *Depersonalization*, the second dimension of burnout, *"represents the interpersonal context dimension of burnout and refers to a negative, callous, or excessively detached response to various aspects of the job."* [34, p. 498]. The symptoms of depersonalization are among others cynicism, withdrawal through longer breaks, distance, and an unfeeling and impersonal response [24]. The third dimension of burnout is the *reduced personal accomplishment*. Individuals tend to evaluate themselves negatively, which leads to self-evaluative feelings of incompetence and lack of achievement at work. Individuals feel unhappy about themselves and dissatisfied with their accomplishments on the job [34]. Symptoms of reduced personal accomplishment are among others the perception of low competence, ineffective efforts, and feelings that suggest one is unappreciated [24].

As Figure 1 summarizes, the burnout construct consists of three dimensions: emotional exhaustion, depersonalization and reduced personal accomplishment, which are visible through different symptoms.

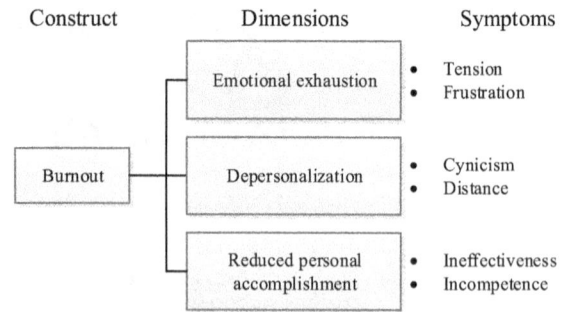

Figure 1. Conceptualizing of burnout [33, 35]

2.2 Prior Literature on Burnout Among IT Professionals
Prior literature focuses on the examination of burnout as a predictor of turnover. It thereby follows the causality of stressors, strains (in our case burnout) and consequences, as depicted in Figure 2. Research examines the cause of burnout, so-called stressors, as certain stimuli encountered by an individual [4, 46]. Stressors might trigger individuals to produce different individual responses in the form of strain [46], such as burnout. These strain responses lead to different consequences such as turnover intention. IT personnel literature shows that different strain responses, such as satisfaction, organizational commitment or burnout, are contributing factors of turnover intention. However, most of the IT professional examinations focus only on one of the three dimensions of burnout. These are described in the following.

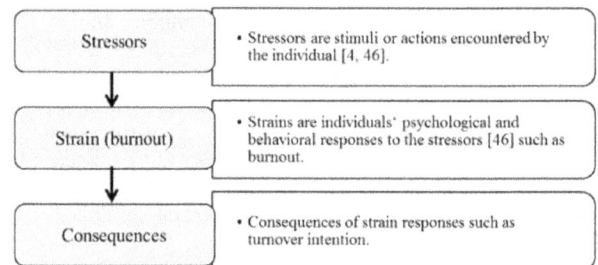

Figure 2. Stressor-strain-consequences dependencies

King and Sethi [25] investigate the moderation effect of organizational commitment on the relationship between role stressors and burnout in IT professionals. They focus on the emotional exhaustion dimension of burnout and reveal that role stressors influence exhaustion. Results show that affective commitment moderates the relationship between role stressors and emotional exhaustion. Moore [36] examines the concept of work exhaustion as one dimension of burnout. Findings of the study show that exhausted IT professionals indicate significantly lower job satisfaction, lower organizational commitment, and higher turnover intention in comparison to non-exhausted IT professionals. Two years later, Moore [37] examines the work exhaustion dimension of burnout in the context of IT professionals. She investigates the effect of workplace factors such as work overload, role ambiguity and conflict, lack of autonomy and rewards on the dimension work exhaustion and in turn on turnover intention. Results show that IT professionals experience higher levels of exhaustion and a higher intention to leave the job. The strongest contributor to work exhaustion is work overload among IT professionals. These results and the important role of work overload are confirmed in subsequent research [30]. Ahuja et al. [1] build on the turnover intention model by Moore [37] with the aim to examine the antecedents of turnover intention among IT road warriors, which they define as IT professionals who spend most of their work-week at a client's site. They extend the model by the workplace factors work-family conflict and organizational commitment. Findings indicate that work–family conflict, perceived work overload, fairness of rewards, and job autonomy influence organizational commitment and work exhaustion among IT road warriors. Thereby, work-family conflict acts as the major contributor on the work exhaustion dimension of burnout. Rutner et al. [43] investigate the influences of emotional dissonance of IT professionals on work exhaustion as a dimension of burnout. They also build upon the turnover intention model [37] and extend it by complementing job satisfaction and emotional dissonance. Results show that emotional dissonance predicts the work exhaustion to a higher extent than workload, role ambiguity and role conflict. The complemented construct, job satisfaction, is influenced by role ambiguity and work exhaustion and in turn, causes turnover intention among IT professionals. Armstrong and Riemenschneider [3] investigate multiple models of the antecedents of the emotional exhaustion dimension of burnout among IS workers. Findings show the mediating role of the demands within the IS profession. The effect of affective connections to the profession on emotional exhaustion is presented as well. Ford and Burley [18] investigate the relationship between work exhaustion, disengagement as a dimension of burnout and turnover intentions among IT professionals in a university setting. Results show that disengagement consistently showed a statistically significant, positive correlation with turnover intentions, whereas work exhaustion indicates inconsistent statistical significance in its correlation to turnover intentions. Weinert et al. [47] investigate teleworking-induced stress of IT professionals. They hypothesize that teleworking-induced stressors influence emotional exhaustion as a dimension of burnout as well as the discontinuous intention towards teleworking. Findings show that work overload, work-home conflict, information underload, and social isolation influence telework-exhaustion. A discontinuous intention towards teleworking is directly influenced by social isolation and exhaustion due to teleworking. Chang et al. [10] examine the effect of stressors and situational moderators on IS employees' work exhaustion as a dimension of burnout in the context of small- and medium-sized enterprises (SMEs). They propose a research model which hypothesizes that techno-stressors, role stressors, and work-related stressors influence work exhaustion, which are moderated by situational factors.

In summary, as seen in Table 1 several examinations consider the phenomenon of burnout among IT professionals. Different stressors such as work overload, role ambiguity, role conflict, autonomy, fairness of rewards, emotional dissonance and several consequences such as job satisfaction, organizational commitment and turnover intention have been studied. However, as Table 1 emphasizes most of the examinations consider only one of the three burnout dimensions. While emotional exhaustion is the most studied dimension, depersonalization and reduced personal accomplishment are neglected in IT personnel research. To address this shortcoming the present research considers all three dimensions of burnout and investigates the influence of several work stressors on all three dimension. Furthermore, this paper examines how turnover intention is predicted by the three dimensions of burnout.

Table 1. Prior literature

References	Stressors	Burnout dimensions	Consequences
King and Sethi 1997 [25]		Work exhaustion	
Moore1998 [36]		Work exhaustion	Job satisfaction, organizational commitment, turnover intention
Moore 2000 [37]	Work overload, role ambiguity, role conflict, autonomy, fairness of rewards	Work exhaustion	Turnover intention
Ahuja et al. 2007 [1]	Work overload, job autonomy, work-family conflict, fairness of rewards	Work exhaustion	Turnover intention, organizational commitment
Rutner et al. 2008 [43]	Work overload, role ambiguity, role conflict, autonomy, fairness of rewards, emotional dissonance	Work exhaustion	Turnover intention, job satisfaction
Armstrong and Riemenschneider 2011 [3]	Uncertainty, career family conflict, psychological contract violation	Emotional exhaustion	-
Ford and Burley 2012 [18]		Work exhaustion	Turnover intention
Chang et al. 2014 [10]	Techno-stressors, role ambiguity, role conflict, autonomy, fairness of rewards, work overload, work-family conflict	Work exhaustion	
Weinert et al. 2014 [47]	Work overload, work home conflict, information underload, social isolation	Exhaustion due to teleworking	Discontinuous intention towards teleworking

3. HYPOTHESES DEVELOPMENT

In the following, we develop our research model. In line with prior research [31], we follow the causality of stressors, strains (in our case burnout), and consequences as described in the previous section. We use the model by Moore [37] as a baseline model for our research and extend it by breaking burnout down into its three dimensions. Subsequently, we investigate the effect of the different stressors revealed by Moore [37] on the three dimensions of burnout and examine the influence of these dimensions on turnover intention among IT professionals. We start by looking at the stressors and hypothesizing the influences of stressors on the three dimensions of burnout. Afterwards the focus gears towards turnover intention, as we then explain why the three burnout dimensions influence turnover intention among IT professionals.

3.1 The Influence of Stressors on Burnout

3.1.1 Work overload
Work overload is *"the perception that assigned work exceeds an individual's capability or skill level"* [4, p. 834]. The results by Moore [37] show that work overload is a strong predictor of emotional exhaustion among IT professionals. We, therefore, adopt the assumption that work overload increases the emotional exhaustion (H1a). Furthermore, cynicism emerges due to the perception of work overload [35]. Individuals attempt to distance themselves from their work when faced with too much work which exceeds their capabilities [35], such that work overload might increase depersonalization (H1b). In addition, work overload is linked to a low level of self-esteem [16]. If individuals have too much to do and cannot get all of their tasks accomplished a self-evaluative feeling of incompetence might occur (H1c). In sum, we assume that:

H1: The higher the work overload (a) the higher the emotional exhaustion, (b) the higher the depersonalization and (c) the higher the reduced personal accomplishment among IT professionals.

3.1.2 Role ambiguity

Role ambiguity is the unpredictability of the consequences of one's role performance and the lack of information needed to perform the role [16]. Moore [37] shows that role ambiguity has a significant influence on emotional exhaustion in the IT profession, so that we align with her results (H2a). Prior studies reveal that role ambiguity is positively linked to depersonalization and reduced personal accomplishment [27, 44]. People might try to avoid role ambiguity at work by distancing themselves from their jobs, which leads to an even higher perceived level of role ambiguity, which in turn indicates a high depersonalization (H2b). The unpredictable performance and the lack of information needed to perform the job might increase the feelings of reduced personal accomplishment, because individuals think they cannot accomplish their tasks properly. For example, if IT professionals perceive a lack of information which is needed to perform the task a feeling of low reduced personal accomplishment might occur (H2c). All together, we assume that:

H2: The higher the role ambiguity (a) the higher the emotional exhaustion, (b) the higher the depersonalization and (c) the higher the reduced personal accomplishment among IT professionals.

3.1.3 Role conflict

Role conflict is *"an incompatibility between job expectations that may originate from one or more individuals with whom an employee interacts"* [43, p. 639]. Based on the results by Moore [37], we adopt the assumption that role conflict increases emotional exhaustion (H3a). Cooper et al. [16] state that several studies indicate a positive link between role conflict and burnout [27]. In psychological research the relationship between role conflict and depersonalization as well as reduced personal accomplishment is well established [23]. Since IT professionals have to work with coworkers on both the technical and business side, they are faced with role conflict, giving means for negative emotional reactions to occur which then lead to depersonalization as a coping mechanism and to a feeling of low reduced personal accomplishment. Hence, we assume that:

H3: The higher the role conflict (a) the higher the emotional exhaustion, (b) the higher the depersonalization and (c) the higher the reduced personal accomplishment among IT professionals.

3.1.4 Job autonomy

Autonomy is manifested by *"the ability to determine one's work methods, work schedules, and even issues such as breaks an vacations"* [16, p. 105]. Autonomy is expected to have a positive effect on burnout [16]. As before, we adopt the hypotheses by Moore [37] by assuming that autonomy reduces emotional exhaustion (H4a). People with high autonomy are able to schedule their work and can decide when to take a break [16]. If people are free in scheduling their time, they do not have to cope by avoiding work or withdrawing from it all together. Instead, they can simply take a break when needed. For example, if IT professionals are able to decide when to take a break, stressors are perceived less, thus decreasing the

consequence in terms of depersonalization (H4b). People with a high degree of autonomy are more satisfied [21]. Research reveals a high degree of autonomy in IT jobs [37], such that IT professionals enjoy a high degree of autonomy and perceive a lower reduced personal accomplishment (H4c). In sum, we assume that:

H4: The higher the job autonomy (a) the lower the emotional exhaustion, (b) the lower the depersonalization and (c) the lower the reduced personal accomplishment among IT professionals.

3.1.5 Fairness of rewards

Fairness of rewards is manifested by the distributive justice of rewards among employees [37]. Adopted from Moore [37] we assume that the fairness of rewards is the negatively linked with emotional exhaustion (H5a). Several investigations reveal that insufficient rewards might be the cause of burnout [34, 35]. The fairness of rewards is manifested in the equilibrium between the inputs (i.e., time, effort, and expertise) and outputs (i.e., rewards and recognition) [34]. If a person's input is higher than the output, they might cope with this situation through cynicism and withdrawal (H5b). A lack of recognition from others leads to feelings of inefficacy and fairness of rewards is perceived as more important than the favorableness of the outcome [34], such that fair rewards decrease reduced personal accomplishment (H5c). In sum, we assume that:

H5: The higher the fairness of rewards (a) the lower the emotional exhaustion, (b) the lower the depersonalization and (c) the lower the reduced personal accomplishment among IT professionals.

3.2 The Influences of Burnout on Turnover Intention

Prior literature shows that burnout has an influence on turnover intention [45]. We adopt the assumption from Moore [37] that emotional exhaustion among IT professionals leads to a higher turnover intention and assume that:

H6: The higher emotional exhaustion the higher the turnover intention among IT professionals.

Distance from work, which happens in the case of high depersonalization might be realized due to physically removing oneself from the work location [45]. Lee and Ashforth [27] state that people with a high depersonalization indicate a high turnover intention. As a result, IT professionals, which show a high level of depersonalization might distance themselves from work and thereby show a high turnover intention. We, therefore, assume that:

H7: The higher the depersonalization the higher the turnover intention among IT professionals.

Reduced personal accomplishment might cause turnover [45]. The perception of incompetence and inefficiency leads to avoidance of work or reduction of the effort [6]. IT professionals with great reduced personal accomplishment might decrease their efforts because of low feelings of effectiveness and grow turnover intentions instead. Therefore, we assume that:

H8: The higher reduced personal accomplishment the higher the turnover intention among IT professionals.

The overall research model is demonstrated in Figure 3.

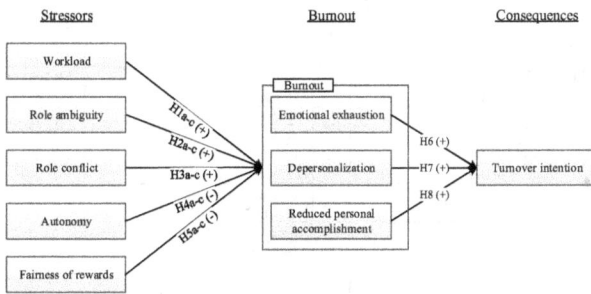

Figure 3. Research model

4. RESEARCH METHODOLOGY

For the validation of the research model, we develop an online survey. Our institute works together with a global career portal, with which we annually perform different recruiting studies. As part of one of these studies, an online questionnaire was promoted by the career portal. A hyperlink to the survey was mailed out to the members of the online career portal. We receive 185 responses, which we validate by discarding the responses with too many missing values. Furthermore, we consider only IT professionals, which we ensure by taking only participants in consideration who state that they see themselves as an IT professional and are at least characterized by one of the following attributes: has taken an IT position (96%), works at an IT driven or based company (71%), contains knowledge about IT and business (96%), has a degree in information systems or computer sciences (36%). Overall, we based our research on the answers of 154 individuals. For data analysis we used SmartPLS 3.1.6 [42] and SPSS. The demographics of all participants are displayed in Table 2.

Table 2. Study participants

Demographics		
Gender	Men	92.9 %
	Women	7.1 %
Age	25-34	26.6 %
	35-44	31.8 %
	45-54	33.1 %
	55-65	8.4 %

5. RESULTS

5.1 Common Method Bias

Perceived and subjective measures are used to capture individuals' responses to a certain situation. A potential issue with subjective measures is common method bias (CMB) [39]. To evaluate the extent of CMB, we utilize Harman's single factor test [22] and the procedure suggested by Williams et al. [48]. The results of the Harman's single factor test show that one factor explains 22.2 % of the variance, which is not the majority, such that we conclude that CMB is of no great concern. Furthermore, we follow the procedure suggested by Williams et al. [48], during which an additional factor is entered into the PLS model, which contains each indicator of the origin model. The remaining factors are transformed into single-item constructs and the ratio of R^2 with the CMB factor is compared with the R^2 without the CMB factor. The CMB factor explains an average R^2 of 0.004 so that a ratio of 1:185 is received. By comparing this ratio with the ratio of prior research using this approach [28], we can state that no signs of CMB influence are observed in consideration of the circumstances that this approach is subjected to several flaws [12].

5.2 Measurement Model

All constructs of the measurement model are measured by reflective indicators such that the four aspects – content validity, indicator reliability, construct reliability, and discriminant validity – have to be validated [5].

Content Validity. All measurement items used in the present research originate from prior research. The measurements of work overload, role ambiguity, role conflict, job autonomy, fairness of rewards as well as turnover intention are based on Moore [37]. Emotional exhaustion, depersonalization, and reduced personal accomplishment are measured on a 7 point Likert scale from strongly agree to strongly disagree based on the burnout scale by Maslach [33]. We use the original burnout items and do not adjust the questions such that reduced personal accomplishment is measured by reversed items. These validated and robust items are displayed in Table 4.

Indicator Reliability. The indicator reliability reflects the relation of the variance of one indicator that comes from the corresponding latent variables. In order to explain at least 50 percent of the variance of a latent variable by the indicators, values should be more than 0.707 [9]. To fulfill this condition, we used only items with values higher that 0.707, as shown in Table 3. All other items have been removed from the model. In addition, a bootstrap method with 5,000 samples is performed and shows significant levels of all loadings of at least 0.001.

Construct Reliability. The construct reliability reflects criteria to determine the quality at the construct level. Therefore, composite reliability (CR) should be higher than 0.7 and average variance extracted (AVE) should be higher than 0.5 [19]. Table 3 demonstrates that the CR as well as AVE criteria are fulfilled.

Discriminant Validity. Discriminant validity describes the extent to which measurement items differ from each other [8]. Discriminant validity is the degree to which a scale measures the variable it is intended to measure, rather than other variables, and it is indicated by low correlations between the measure of interest and the measure of other constructs [19]. The square root of the AVE for each construct is located on the diagonal of Table 3 and is higher for all constructs, such that these criteria are fulfilled.

Table 3. Measurement model

	Constructs	AVE	CR	Loadings	1	2	3	4	5	6	7	8	9
1	Work overload	0.723	0.886	0.789-0.907	0.723								
2	Role ambiguity	0.696	0.872	0.784-0.876	-0.412	0.696							
3	Role conflict	0.633	0.874	0.780-0.823	0.342	-0.324	0.633						
4	Autonomy	0.739	0.894	0.766-0.945	-0.093	0.136	0.004	0.739					
5	Fairness of reward	0.891	0.942	0.935-0.953	-0.117	0.097	0.029	0.083	0.891				
6	Emotional exhaustion	0.742	0.935	0.835-0.949	0.587	-0.351	0.214	-0.171	-0.318	0.742			
7	Depersonali-zation	0.702	0.875	0.734-0.883	0.381	-0.289	0.349	-0.161	-0.092	0.394	0.702		
8	Personal accomplish-ment	0.605	0.859	0.727-0.833	-0.367	0.308	-0.014	0.112	0.039	-0.382	-0.237	0.605	
9	Turnover intention	0.838	0.954	0.892-0.930	0.355	-0.136	0.19	-0.09	-0.333	0.419	0.309	-0.121	0.915
Note: Square root of AVE is listed on the diagonal of bivariate correlations.													

Table 4. Measurement items

Con-struct	Items
Work overload	I have to deal with a lot of unexpected problems, requests or complaints. (WO-1)
	The amount of work I do interferes with how well it is done. (WO-2)
	During my work I feel busy or rushed. (WO-3)
	During my work I feel pressured. (WO-4)
Role ambiguity	I know exactly what is expected from me during my work. (RA-1)
	I have a clearly defined role in my work group. (RA-2)
	Clear, planned goals and objectives exist for my tasks. (RA-3)
Role conflict	I do things that are apt to be accepted by one person and not accepted by others.(RC-1)
	I have to "buck" a rule or policy in order to carry out my tasks. (RC-2)
	I often receive incompatible requests from two or more people. (RC-3)
	I often get things done for two or more supervisors who appreciate a different way of working. (RC-4)
	In my work, I often have to balance two or more conflicting requirements. (RC-5)
Autonomy	During my work I usually do not ask my superiors before making a final decision.(A-1)
	My superiors do not have to give me permission before I can start with my tasks. (A-2)
	Instead of asking my immediate supervisor, I often make my own decisions about what to do at work. (A-3)
	During my work, I can do what I want without consultation with my supervisor. (A-4)
Fairness of reward	I think my level of pay is fair. (FR-1)
	Overall, the rewards I receive here are quite fair. (FR-2)
Emotional exhaustion	I feel emotionally drained from my work. (EE-1)
	I feel used up at the end of the workday. (EE-2)
	I feel fatigued when I get up in the morning and have to face another day on the job. (EE-3)
	Working with people all day is really a strain for me. (EE-4)
	I feel frustrated by my job. (EE-5)
	I feel burned out from my work. (EE-6)
	I feel I am working too hard on my job. (EE-7)
	Working with people directly puts too much stress on me. (EE-8)
	I feel like I am at the end of my rope. (EE-9)
Depersonalization	I feel I treat some people as if they were impersonal 'objects' (DEP-1)
	I have become more callous toward people since I took this job. (DEP-2)
	I worry that this job is hardening me emotionally.(DEP-3)
	I do not really care what happens to some people. (DEP-4)
	I feel recipients blame me for some of their problems. (DEP-5)
Reduced personal accomplishment	I can easily understand how my people feel about things. (PA-1) *
	I deal very effectively with the problems of other people. (PA-2) *
	I think I am positively influencing other people's lives through my work. (PA-3) *
	I feel very energetic. (PA-4) *
	I can easily create a relaxed atmosphere with people. (PA-5) *
	I feel exhilarated after working closely with my recipients. (PA-6) *
	I have accomplished many worthwhile things in this job. (PA-7) *
	In my work, I deal with emotional problems very calmly. (PA-8) *
Turnover intention	I often think about to cancel my contract in my current company. (TI-1)
	I plan to cancel my current contract. (TI-2)
	I am considering leaving my current employer. (TI-3)

Note: * reversed item

5.3 Structural Model

To validate the research model we use the coefficient of determination (R^2) and the significance levels of the path coefficients [11]. Table 5 shows that work overload has a significant effect on emotional exhaustion, depersonalization, and reduced personal accomplishment. Role ambiguity indicates a significant negative influence on reduced personal accomplishment and role conflict influences depersonalization and reduced personal accomplishment significantly. Job autonomy has no significant effect on one of the burnout dimensions, whereas fairness of rewards shows a negative effect on emotional exhaustion. With regard to emotional exhaustion 42.7 % of the variance is explain by the stressors, whereby 22.7 % of the variance of depersonalization and 19.3 % of the variance of reduced personal accomplishment are explained.

Referring to the consequences, results indicate that emotional exhaustion and depersonalization predict turnover intention significantly, which explain 20.4 % of the variance of turnover intention. Results show that hypotheses H1a-c, H2c, H3b-c, H5a, H6, and H7 are supported.

Table 5. Structural model

	Path coefficients			
	Stressor	→	Burnout	β
H1a	Work overload	→	Emotional exhaustion	0.502***
H1b	Work overload	→	Depersonalization	0.245***
H1c	Work overload	→	Reduced personal accomplishment	0.333***
H2a	Role ambiguity	→	Emotional exhaustion	-0.104[NS]
H2b	Role ambiguity	→	Depersonalization	-0.090[NS]
H2c	Role ambiguity	→	Reduced personal accomplishment	-0.222**
H3a	Role conflict	→	Emotional exhaustion	0.016[NS]
H3b	Role conflict	→	Depersonalization	0.238***
H3c	Role conflict	→	Reduced personal accomplishment	-0.173**
H4a	Job autonomy	→	Emotional exhaustion	-0.090[NS]
H4b	Job autonomy	→	Depersonalization	-0.123[NS]
H4c	Job autonomy	→	Reduced personal accomplishment	-0.053[NS]
H5a	Fairness of rewards	→	Emotional exhaustion	-0.242***
H5b	Fairness of rewards	→	Depersonalization	-0.052[NS]
H5c	Fairness of rewards	→	Reduced personal accomplishment	0.031[NS]
	Burnout	→	Consequences	
H6	Emotional exhaustion	→	Turnover intention	0.374***
H7	Depersonalization	→	Turnover intention	0.177**
H8	Reduced personal accomplishment	→	Turnover intention	-0.063[NS]

Note: [NS] $p > 0.05$; * $p < 0.05$; ** $p < 0.01$; *** $p < 0.005$; bold highlights mean that the hypothesis is supported.

	Coefficient of determination (R^2)	
Burnout	Emotional exhaustion	42.7%
	Depersonalization	22.7%
	Reduced personal accomplishment	19.3%
Consequence	Turnover intention	20.4%

5.4 Post-hoc Analyses

For further specification of the results, we next analyze the strength of effect of the stressors on the three dimensions of burnout and the effect of burnout on turnover intention. Furthermore, a mediation test is conducted in order to analyze whether or not emotional exhaustion, depersonalization, and reduced personal accomplishment act as mediators between stressors and turnover intention.

To determine the strength of effect we refer to Cohens f^2 measure [15]. As seen in Table 4, work overload shows the strongest influence on emotional exhaustion, whereas role ambiguity and fairness of rewards indicate a low effect. Concerning depersonalization, the results show that work overload, role conflict, and autonomy have a low effect. The main effect on reduced personal accomplishment is shown by work overload, whereby role ambiguity and role conflict also demonstrate a low effect. Turning to the consequences in terms of turnover intention it appears that emotional exhaustion indicates the main effect, whereupon depersonalization also has a low effect on turnover intention.

Table 6. Strength of effects

Dependent variable	Independent variables	f^2	Interpretation
Emotional exhaustion	Work overload	0.34	Medium
	Role ambiguity	0.02	Low
	Role conflict	0.00	None
	Autonomy	0.01	None
	Fairness of reward	0.10	Low
Depersonalization	Work overload	0.06	Low
	Role ambiguity	0.01	None
	Role conflict	0.06	Low
	Autonomy	0.02	Low
	Fairness of reward	0.00	None
Reduced personal accomplishment	Work overload	0.11	Low
	Role ambiguity	0.05	Low
	Role conflict	0.03	Low
	Autonomy	0.00	None
	Fairness of reward	0.00	None
Turnover intention	Emotional exhaustion	0.13	Low
	Depersonalization	0.03	Low
	Reduced personal accomplishment	0.00	None

Note: f^2 means effect size; Cohen [13] interprets effect sizes as follows: >.35 = high effect; >.15 = medium effect; > .02 = low effect

In order to validate whether emotional exhaustion, depersonalization, and reduced personal accomplishment mediate the influences of the stressors on turnover intention, we use a bootstrapping method as suggested by Preacher and Hayes [41]. The method suggests to calculate the 95 percent-bias-corrected confidence intervals (1,000 bootstrap resamples) of each independent variable. If the zero is not within the bias-corrected interval, the independent variable has an indirect effect through the mediator on the depended variable. As seen in Table 7 only the influences of work overload and fairness of rewards on turnover intention is mediated through emotional exhaustion. All other stressors indicate non indirect effects.

Table 7. Mediation effect

Independent variable (IV)	Mediator (M)	Dependent variable (DV)	Bootstrapping results		
			Lower	Upper	Indirect effect
Work overload	Emotional exhaustion	Turnover intention	0.182	43.075	Yes
Role ambiguity			-12.462	-0.159	No[1]
Role conflict			0.052	14.031	No[1]
Job autonomy			-3.021	0.420	No
Fairness of rewards			-22.118	-0.086	Yes
Work overload	Depersonalization		-25.185	0.015	No
Role ambiguity			-0.004	13.613	No
Role conflict			-18.909	0.259	No
Job autonomy			-0.187	5.475	No
Fairness of rewards			-6.640	0.040	No
Work overload	Reduced personal accomplishment		-1.0142	0.0113	No
Role ambiguity			-0.011	4.298	No
Role conflict			-0.585	0.009	No
Job autonomy			-0.104	0.575	No
Fairness of rewards			-1.897	0.068	No

Note: [1]This method identifies an significant indirect effect, but the 3-step approach by Baron and Kenny [7] suggest that no mediation exists as the direct influence of IV on M is insignificant as shown in Table 5.

6. DISCUSSION, IMPLICATIONS, AND FUTURE RESEARCH

The present research brings attention to burnout and extends Moore's [37] research model by including further dimensions of burnout into the model, namely depersonalization and reduced personal accomplishment and examining their influences on turnover intention among IT professionals. The research questions regarding the causes of emotional exhaustion, depersonalization, and reduced personal accomplishment and their impact on IT professionals' turnover intention should be answered. Prior research on IS personnel focused solely on emotional exhaustion and neglected depersonalization and reduced personal accomplishment, which are also core constructs of burnout (see Table 1). To address this shortcoming it is hypothesized that the work stressors, work overload, role ambiguity, role conflict, job autonomy and fairness of rewards influence emotional exhaustion, depersonalization, and reduced personal accomplishment. Additionally, an influence of the three burnout dimensions is hypothesized to predict turnover intentions in order to better understand and manage IT professionals' turnover intentions and maintain organizational competitive advantages. Results show that work overload has a significant influence of all three burnout dimensions and role conflict positively effects depersonalization. Job autonomy indicates no significant influences and fairness of rewards has a decreasing effect on emotional exhaustion. In contrary to our expectations role ambiguity and role conflict negatively influence reduced personal accomplishment, which might result from the different exactions from co-workers, which causes the perceptions that people have accomplished something because their co-workers have high expectations. With regard to turnover

intention, findings show that emotional exhaustion and depersonalization are contributing factors of turnover intention. Regarding the effect size results indicate that there is one medium effect of work overload on emotional exhaustion. Several other effects are low, however, this means only that the effect is smaller than the medium effect but not that the effect is trivial [14]. Based on that, we interpret our results which have several theoretical as well as practical implications, which are presented in the following paragraphs.

We extend the research model by Moore [37] by examining depersonalization and reduced personal accomplishment next to emotional exhaustion within the IT profession. By doing so, we contribute to literature (e.g., [1, 18, 36, 37, 43]) by demonstrating that not only emotional exhaustion determines turnover intention but also depersonalization indicates a significant effect on turnover intention among IT professionals. Furthermore, we reveal that work overload and fairness of rewards are mediated by emotional exhaustion and have an indirect effect on turnover intention. The extension of Moore's research model shows that turnover intention is strongly influenced by emotional exhaustion but also by other burnout dimensions, which cannot be neglected by investigating and understanding turnover among IT professionals.

By investigating the effects of work stressors on the three dimensions of burnout we find that work overload is the strongest contributing factor on emotional exhaustion and confirm the results of Moore [37]. By hypothesizing and validating the influences of different stressors on depersonalization and reduced personal accomplishment among IT professionals, we extend IT personnel literature (e.g., [1, 18, 36, 37, 43]). We identify work overload and role ambiguity as antecedents of depersonalization as well as work overload, role ambiguity and role conflict as antecedents of reduced personal accomplishment. A comparison of the coefficient of determination between the burnout dimensions indicates that the stressors suggested by Moore [37] are better predictors for the stress component of burnout, emotional exhaustion, rather than depersonalization and reduced personal accomplishment. Consequently, we identified a significant research gap by showing that the causes of the burnout dimensions differ and that they are insufficiently examined in IT professional research, which should be the focus of future research.

Besides theoretical contributions, the present research also contains practical implications. Companies depend on IT professionals in order to grow and remain competitive [1, 37]. By providing evidence that turnover intention among IT professionals is also influenced by depersonalization, human resource managers can manage the turnover of IT professionals better and might retain the organization's competitive advantages. In order to reduce turnover intention organizations should not only focus on emotional exhaustion but also on depersonalization. Organizations should support coping mechanisms which focus not only on emotional exhaustion but also on depersonalization in order to reduce turnover intention among IT professionals.

Like every empirical research, the present examination contains several limitations. The present study considers only the stressors suggested by Moore [37] and does not consider any additional stressors. Furthermore, we do not distinguish between different groups of IT professionals as suggested by Lo and Riemenschneider [29]. We are aware that the data sample contains clearly more males than females which possibility results from the heterogeneity of IT personnel [40]. Future research can extend the model by Moore et al. [37] by additional antecedence, which might better predict depersonalization and reduced personal accomplishment. The group of IT professionals can be divided into several subgroups such as developers or IT road warriors as suggested by Lo and Riemenschneider [29]. Furthermore, the influences of the three burnout dimensions on other different dependent variables such as job performance or productivity can be investigated. Moreover, the dependencies between the three burnout dimensions and the influences of different coping mechanisms on the three dimensions can be focus of future research.

7. CONCLUSION

The present research extends Moore's [37] research model by including further dimensions of burnout into the model, namely depersonalization and reduced personal accomplishment. We investigate the effect of stressors on all three burnout dimensions and examine their influence on turnover intention among IT professionals. Results based on a data sample of 154 IT professionals show that not only emotional exhaustion but also depersonalization lead to turnover intention, which cannot be neglected when trying to understand and reduce turnover intention among IT professionals to maintain organization's competitive advantages. In addition, the stressors suggested by Moore [37] influence emotional exhaustion and only slightly explain depersonalization and reduced personal accomplishment, which indicate that the investigation of additional antecedence of depersonalization and reduced personal accomplishment depicts a significant research gap.

8. REFERENCES

[1] Ahuja, M. K., Chudoba, K. M., Kacmar, C. J., McKnight, D. H., and George, J. F. 2007. It Road Warriors: Balancing Work--Family Conflict, Job Autonomy, And Work Overload to Mitigate Turnover Intentions. *MIS Quarterly* 31, 1, 1–17.

[2] Ang, S. and Slaughter, S. 2004. Turnover of information technology professionals. *ACM SIGMIS Database* 35, 3, 11–27.

[3] Armstrong, D. and Riemenschneider, C. 2011. The influence of demands and resources on emotional exhaustion with the information systems profession. *ICIS 2011 Proceedings*.

[4] Ayyagari, R., Varun, G., and Russell, P. 2011. Technostress: Technological Antecedents and Implications. *MIS Quarterly* 35, 4, 831–858.

[5] Bagozzi, R. P. 1979. The Role of Measurement in Theory Construction and Hypothesis Testing: Toward a Holistic Model. In *Conceptual and theoretical developments in marketing*, O. C. Ferrell, S. W. Brown and C. W. Lamb, Eds. Proceedings series - American Marketing Association. American Marketing Association, Chicago, 15–32.

[6] Bandura, A. 2007. *Self-efficacy. The exercise of control.* Recording for the Blind & Dyslexic, Princeton, N.J.

[7] Baron, R. M. and Kenny, D. A. 1986. The Moderator-Mediator Variable Distinction in Social Psychological Research: Conceptual, Strategic, and Statistical Considerations. *Journal of Personality & Social Psychology* 51, 6, 1173–1182.

[8] Campell, D. T. and Fiske, D. W. 1959. Convergent and discriminant validation by the multitrait-multimethod matrix. *Psychological bulletin* 56, 2, 81–105.

[9] Carmines, E. G. and Zeller, R. A. 2008. *Reliability and validity assessment.* Sage, Newbury Park, Calif.

[10] Chang, L.-M., Hung, S.-Y., and Hung, W.-H. 2014. Critical Stressors Affecting Work Exhaustion of IS Employees in SMEs. *Proceedings of the 35th International Conference on Information Systems - ICIS 2014*.

[11] Chin, W. W. 1998. The partial least squares approach for structural equation modeling. In *Modern methods for business research*, G. A. Marcoulides, Ed. Lawrence Erlbaum.

[12] Chin, W. W., Thatcher, J. B., and Wright, R. T. 2012. Assessing common method bias: problems with the ULMC technique. *MIS Quarterly* 36, 3, 1003–1019.

[13] Cohen, J. 1988. *Statistical power analysis for the behavioral sciences.* L. Erlbaum Associates, Hillsdale, N.J.

[14] Cohen, J. 1992. Statistical Power Analysis. *Current Directions in Psychol Sci* 1, 3, 98–101.

[15] Cohen, J. 2013. *Statistical Power Analysis for the Behavioral Sciences.* Taylor and Francis, Hoboken.

[16] Cooper, C. L., Dewe, P., and O'Driscoll, M. P. 2001. *Organizational Stress. A review and critique of theory, research, and applications.* Foundations for organizational science. Sage Publications, Thousand Oaks, Calif.

[17] Eckhardt, A., Laumer, S., Maier, C., and Weitzel, T. 2014. The effect of personality on IT personnel's job-related attitudes: establishing a dispositional model of turnover intention across IT job types. *Forthcoming in: Journal of Information Technology*.

[18] Ford, V. F. and Burley, D. L. 2012. Once you click 'done': Investigating the relationship between disengagement, exhaustion and turnover intentions among university IT professional. *Proceedings of the 50th annual conference on Computers and People Research*, 61–68.

[19] Fornell, C. and Larcker, D. F. 1981. Evaluating Structural Equation Models with Unobservable Variables and Measurement Error. *Journal of Marketing Research* 18, 1, 39–50.

[20] Gallagher, K. P., Kaiser, K. M., Simon, J. C., Beath, C. M., and Goles, T. 2010. The requisite variety of skills for IT professionals. *Communications of the ACM* 53, 6, 144.

[21] Hackman, J. and Oldham, G. R. 1976. Motivation through the design of work: test of a theory. *Organizational Behavior and Human Performance* 16, 2, 250–279.

[22] Harman, H. H. 1976. *Modern factor analysis.* University of Chicago Press, Chicago.

[23] Jawahar, I. M., Stone, T. H., and Kisamore, J. L. 2007. Role conflict and burnout: The direct and moderating effects of political skill and perceived organizational support on burnout dimensions. *International Journal of Stress Management* 14, 2, 142–159.

[24] Kalliath, T. J. and Beck, A. 2001. Is the path to burnout and turnover paved by a lack of supervisory support? A

structural equations test. *New Zealand Journal of Psychology* 30, 2, 72.

[25] King, R. C. and Sethi, V. 1997. The moderating effect of organizational commitment on burnout in information systems professionals. *European Journal of Information Systems* 6, 2, 86–96.

[26] Kollmann, T., Häsel, M., and Breugst, N. 2009. Competence of IT Professionals in E-Business Venture Teams: The Effect of Experience and Expertise on Preference Structure. *Journal of Management Information Systems* 25, 4, 51–80.

[27] Lee, R. T. and Ashforth, B. E. 1996. A Meta-Analytic Examination of the Correlates of the Three Dimensions of Job Burnout. *Journal of Applied Psychology* 81, 2, 123–133.

[28] Liang, H., Saraf, N., Hu, Q., and Xue, Y. 2007. Assimilation of enterprise systems: the effect of institutional pressures and the mediating role of top management. *MIS Quarterly* 31, 1, 59–87.

[29] Lo, J. and Riemenschneider, C. 2011. Heterogeneity of IT employees. *ACM SIGMIS Database* 42, 3, 71.

[30] Maier, C., Laumer, S., and Eckhardt, A. 2015. Information technology as daily stressor: pinning down the causes of burnout. *Journal of Business Economics*, 1-39.

[31] Maier, C., Laumer, S., Eckhardt, A., and Weitzel, T. 2014. Giving Too Much Social Support: Social Overload on Social Networking Sites. *Forthcoming in: European Journal of Information Systems*.

[32] Maslach, C. 1993. Burnout: A multidimensional perspective. In *Professional burnout: Recent developments in theory and research*, W. B. Schaufeli, C. Maslach and T. Marek, Eds. Series in applied psychology: Social issues and questions. Taylor & Francis, Philadelphia, PA, US, 19–32.

[33] Maslach, C. and Jackson, S. 1981. The measurement of experienced burnout. *Journal of Organizational Behavior* 2, 2, 99–113.

[34] Maslach, C. and Leiter, M. P. 2008. Early predictors of job burnout and engagement. *Journal of Applied Psychology* 93, 3, 498–512.

[35] Maslach, C., Schaufeli, W. B., and Leiter, M. P. 2001. Job Burnout. *Annual Review of Psychology* 52, 1, 397–422.

[36] Moore, J. E. 1998. Job attitudes and perceptions of exhausted IS/IT professionals. *Proceedings of the 1998 ACM SIGCPR conference on Computer personnel research* 1998, 264–273.

[37] Moore, J. E. 2000. One Road To Turnover: An Examination Of Work Exhaustion In Technology Professionals. *MIS Quarterly* 24, 1, 141–168.

[38] Niederman, F., Sumner, M., and Maertz JR., Carl P. 2007. Testing and extending the unfolding model of voluntary turnover to it professionals. *Human Resource Management* 46, 3, 331–347.

[39] Podsakoff, P. M., MacKenzie, S. B., Jeong-Yeon Lee, and Podsakoff, N. P. 2003. Common Method Biases in Behavioral Research: A Critical Review of the Literature and Recommended Remedies. *Journal of Applied Psychology* 88, 5, 879.

[40] Prasad, J., Enns, H. G., and Ferratt, T. W. 2007. One size does not fit all: Managing IT employees' employment arrangements. *Human Resource Management* 46, 3, 349–372.

[41] Preacher, K. and Hayes, A. 2004. SPSS and SAS procedures for estimating indirect effects in simple mediation models. *Behavior Research Methods* 36, 4, 717–731.

[42] Ringle, C. M., Wende, S., and Becker, J.-M. 2014. Smartpls 3.0. *SmartPLS*.

[43] Rutner, P. S., Hardgrave, B. C., and McKnight, D. H. 2008. Emotional Dissonance And The Information Technology Professional. *MIS Quarterly* 32, 3, 635–652.

[44] Schaufeli, W. B. and Buunk, B. P. 1996. Professional burnout. *Handbook of work and health psychology*, 311–346.

[45] Swider, B. W. and Zimmerman, R. D. 2010. Born to burnout: A meta-analytic path model of personality, job burnout, and work outcomes. *Journal of Vocational behavior* 76, 3, 487–506.

[46] Tarafdar, M., Tu, Q., and Ragu-Nathan, T. S. 2010. Impact of Technostress on End-User Satisfaction and Performance. *Journal of Management Information Systems* 27, 3, 303–334.

[47] Weinert, C., Maier, C., Laumer, S., and Weitzel, T. 2014. Does teleworking negatively influence IT professionals? *Proceedings of the 52nd ACM conference on Computers and people research*, 139–147.

[48] Williams, L. J., Edwards, J. R., and Vandenberg, R. J. 2003. Recent Advances in Causal Modeling Methods for Organizational and Management Research. *Journal of Management* 29, 6, 903.

Panel – Preparing the Next Generation of Computer Personnel

Leigh Ellen Potter
Griffith University
170 Kessels Road
Nathan, Queensland, Australia
+61 7 3735 5191
L.Potter@griffith.edu.au

Diane Lending
James Madison University
MSC 0203, 342 Zane Showker Hall
Harrisonburg, VA 22807
+1 540 568 3273
lendindc@jmu.edu

Michelle L. Kaarst-Brown
School of Information Studies
Syracuse University
Syracuse, NY 13244 USA
+1 315 443 1892
mlbrow03@syr.edu

ABSTRACT
The purpose of this panel is to explore different techniques and approaches that are currently in use within the tertiary sector to prepare students in the technology industry for the move to working in the industry. A growing demand from employers for soft skills, and from university bodies for positive graduate employment outcomes is leading to a re-imagining of our approach to coursework. Work integrated learning and industry involvement within coursework and assessment will be presented, together with approaches for encouraging students to engage with industry and the development of non-traditional course offerings.

Categories and Subject Descriptors
K.7.1 **The Computing Profession**: Occupations

General Terms
Human Factors.

Keywords
IT Workforce, assessment approaches, employability, industry readiness.

1. INTRODUCTION
Employability: "A set of achievements – skills, understandings and personal attributes – that makes graduates more likely to gain employment and be successful in their chosen occupations, which benefits themselves, the workforce, the community and the economy" (Knight & Yorke, 2003; The Higher Education Academy, 2014).

Despite a range of academic arguments, there has been a growing demand over the last fifteen years for the development of employability outcomes and industry readiness for university graduates (Lowden, Hall, Elliot, & Lewin, 2011). Most universities now embed employability aspects within their graduate outcomes. Within the Information Technology industry, this means producing graduates who have a broad base of technology knowledge, together with specific knowledge and

SIGMIS-CPR '15, June 04-06, 2015, Newport Beach, CA, USA
ACM 978-1-4503-3557-7/15/06.
http://dx.doi.org/10.1145/2751957.2756527

experience in one or more key areas, and an understanding of what will be required of them in the workplace. There is now a growing focus within technology schools and faculties on establishing what the technology industry requires in a potential graduate, and on what the student needs to know in order to satisfy those requirements.

Internationally, universities are meeting this challenge through the use of capstone programs, work integrated learning, and accreditation programs for students. There is room for greater innovation in this regard. This panel will present the key measures the presenters are using within their own local context, and open discussion for attendees to describe the approaches that they have found help or hinder. We will discuss the different elements that affect our approach, together with the lessons we have learned from our experience. We will outline our experience with both university colleagues and industry representatives.

The aim of this panel is to explore innovative practices and approaches for preparing students for working in industry, and to share these practices.

2. OVERVIEW OF PRESENTATIONS
Leigh Ellen Potter will present her experience teaching an undergraduate capstone course, and her work with industry engagement in undergraduate and masters level coursework. She will discuss the approach she has taken with work integrated learning, and the outcomes this has produced for students in terms of connections with industry, networking opportunities, skills development, and the development of student confidence. She will also outline her work incorporating 'real world' elements in the assessment pieces for second year courses, and student feedback regarding their experience with this approach.

Diane Lending will discuss getting students involved in the IS profession. She has made this a course objective for the first course that IS majors take in their junior year. The approach uses a combination of class work, a very active student organization, young alumni who want to give back to the university, and internships. She will discuss the outcomes that this has produced in terms of a program-industry partnership, student jobs, and growth of the major. She will also talk about potential pitfalls of this approach.

Michelle L. Kaarst-Brown will share how employer demands for "soft skills" are shaping non-traditional course offerings, employer engagement in designing academic courses, and view of certification. She has been engaged in new course creation for over twenty years, integrating practitioner views, experiential opportunities, and community and employer engagement in evaluating student performance outcomes. Her presentation will share several diverse examples of these types of courses, and cover key lessons learned in collaborating with employers. Michelle will also present some of the new opportunities how thinking beyond traditional MIS curriculum and basic certification training has increased students' career choices within and outside IT, added resume building experiences, and aided in building students' career networks within and outside the university.

3. PRESENTERS

Leigh Ellen Potter is a lecturer in the School of Information and Communication Technology, Griffith University in Australia. Her background is in industry, where she worked as a business analyst and user experience advocate prior to commencing her PhD. She completed her doctorate in Information Systems at Griffith University, exploring the attributes of IT professionals, and what draws them to the industry. Her research interests include user centred design and usability, and emerging technology. She is team lead for the Seek and Sign Project, a research project exploring how technology can support young Deaf children to learn sign language.

Diane Lending is the Capital One Information Security Scholar and a Professor of CIS at James Madison University in Virginia. Her research interests are in information systems education, the adoption of information technology, and assessment. Her doctorate is in Management Information Systems from the University of Minnesota. Dr. Lending has written papers published in several journals including the Journal of Information Systems Education; the Journal of Computer Information Systems; Computers, Informatics, Nursing; and Data Base. Prior to joining academia, she was a programmer, systems analyst, and manager of systems development projects.

Michelle L. Kaarst-Brown is an Associate Professor and former Director of the Professional Doctorate Program in Information Management at the School of Information Studies, Syracuse University. Much of her recent research has been in partnership with practitioners in government, industry, and education. Drawing upon prior management and consulting experience, her research studies how social, cultural, knowledge and generational factors influence IT governance and the IT workforce. Dr. Kaarst-Brown has published in a number of top academic and business journals including MIS Quarterly, Information Technology and People, the Journal of Strategic Information Systems, CIO Canada, and MISQ Executive.

4. REFERENCES

[1] Knight, P. T., & Yorke, M. (2003). *Assessment, Learning and Employability*. Maidenhead, Berkshire: Open University Press.

[2] Lowden, K., Hall, S., Elliot, D., & Lewin, J. (2011). *Employers' perceptions of the employability skills of new graduates* (p. 42).

[3] The Higher Education Academy. (2014). Employability. Retrieved April 10, 2015, from https://www.heacademy.ac.uk/workstreams-research/themes/employability

Factors Affecting Individual Information Security Practices

Santos M. Galvez
Trident University
577 Plaza Drive
Cypress, CA 90630
1-714-816-0366
santos.galvez@my.trident.edu

Joshua D. Shackman
Trident University
577 Plaza Drive
Cypress, CA 90630
1-714-816-0366
joshua.shackman@trident.edu

Indira R. Guzman
Trident University
577 Plaza Drive
Cypress, CA 90630
1-714-816-0366
indira.guzman@trident.edu

Shuyuan Mary Ho
Florida State University
142 Collegiate Loop
Tallahassee, FL 32306
1-850-645-0406
smho@fsu.edu

ABSTRACT

Data and information within organizations have become important assets that can create a significant competitive advantage and therefore need to be given careful attention. Research from industry has reported that the majority of security-related problems are indirectly caused by employees who disobey the information security policies of their organizations. This study proposes a model to evaluate the factors that influence the individual's information security practices (IISP) at work. Drawing on social cognitive and control theories, the proposed model includes cognitive, environmental, and control factors as antecedents of ISSP. The findings of this study could be used to develop effective security policies and training. They could also be used to develop effective security audits and further recommendations for organizations that are looking to make significant improvements in their information security profiles.

Categories and Subject Descriptors

K.6.5 Security and Protection

General Terms

Security, Human Factor, Standardization.

Keywords

Information Security Behavior; Mandatoriness; Social Cognitive Theory; Control Theory; Information Security Practices; Self-Efficacy; Security Standards; ISO27002.

1. INTRODUCTION

Researchers have realized that the majority of the problems in regards to information security are indirectly caused by

employees' disobeying the information security policies of their organizations (Warkentin, Shropshire & Johnston, 2007; Whitman & Mattord, 2008). As security threats have grown, the need to protect organizational data has become a corporate crucial need. Although some of these attacks originate externally, most of them are intentionally or unintentionally originated by internal employees (Dhillon & Backhouse, 2000).

Stanton et al., (2003) pointed out that information security research has focused more on technical aspects of information security while ignoring its human factors. According to Mackenzie (2006) "... more than half of all security breaches are due to social engineering and end users' careless behavior". This means that, even if the technical layer is efficient, the security position of organizations depends on users' behavior. Even though information security has been seen as a technical issue, its members are formed only with technicians (Collete & Gentile, 2006). In focusing on the technical side, information security has overlooked the human factor which is frequently called the weakest point of a security chain (Angel, 1993). Human errors can cause severe security breaches in organizations. Hence, human factors are important and have been picked up by both the research community, and Information Systems security practitioners (Parker, 1998, 1999; Peltier, 2000, Siponen, 2000a, 2000b; Straub 1990). For example, Hinson (2003) points out that simple configuration mistakes by humans in the area of information security can leave networks ports open, firewalls vulnerable and information systems completely unprotected. Many organizations evaluate their technology for security risks, evaluating new products and testing the systems. But very few assess risks in regards to their employees (Hinson, 2003).

2. SIGNIFICANCE OF THE STUDY

The problem is how to encourage good individual security practices at work. There are many naive user behaviors that can cause negative effects on information security unintentionally. To design and prepare a more efficient security program for individuals, it is necessary to understand the factors that encourage good individual behavior (Rhee, Kim & Ryu, 2009). Siponen et al. (2009) point out that if individuals understand how vulnerable their organization is to security threats, they are more likely to comply with information security policies. Individuals' compliance with information security policies is a psychological phenomenon, the theoretical model of this research was developed from behavioral theories such as social cognitive and control theory. These theories may shed light on factors influencing individual information security practices (IISP) at work.

In contrast to previous studies about information security that applied socio cognitive theory (SCT) using only one variable for Self Efficacy (Rhee et al., 2009), this study adopts the Compeau and Higgins (1995) model used in an information systems context. Compeau and Higgins (1995) took into consideration different factors of Social Cognitive Theory (SCT) such as "the encouragement of use by others", "the actual use of computers by others", and "the organizational support for computer use" that influence self-efficacy and outcome expectations. In this study, the researcher adopts the variables that were used by Compeau and Higgins (1995) and used in the information security practices model.

S. Boss, Kirsh, Angermeier, Shingler, and R. Boss (2009) used Control Theory in Information Systems to predict "precautions taken in information security" using items developed from professional security standards and from general information security best practices published by the National Cyber Security Alliance (2005). I include the variables used by Boss et al. (2009) for use in the information security practices model in addition to the ones used by Compeau and Higgins (1995) applied in computer usage.

In this research paper uses the well-known international standards in information security (ISO17799/27002) to measure the construct of individual information security practices (IISP) at work. By following the recognized and tested ISO17799/27002 standard, organizations will improve the efficiency of managing their information security endeavors. ISO17799/27002 has a group of published documents that offers guides to manage better information security. By referencing ISO 17799/27002, financial institutions will have access to a group of library controls that can be included in the development of security architecture. That architecture can be integrated with other technology processes in order to create policies, standards, and procedures that can be used as a part of the governance structure that need to be done in organizations (FFIEC, 2014).

This study will be beneficial for all kinds of organizations that want to develop better information security procedures with a more standard approach. Therefore, this study can explain security practices as expected by all companies whose security policies are based on ISO17799/27002.

3. BACKGROUND LITERATURE, MODEL, HYPOTHESES

The current model integrates Compeau and Higgins (1995) and Boss et al. (2009) models into one model by adapting some variables from both studies within the information security context to see the impact on the dependent variable, individual information security practices (IISP) at work based on ISO17799/27002.

This model should be examined to evaluate the weight and importance of each of the components of the model. Given that, an individual's compliance with information security policies is a psychological phenomenon. Hence, the theoretical model of this research was developed from behavioral theories such as social cognitive and control theory. These theories are important in understanding factors influencing individual information security practices (IISP) at work based on ISO17799/27002

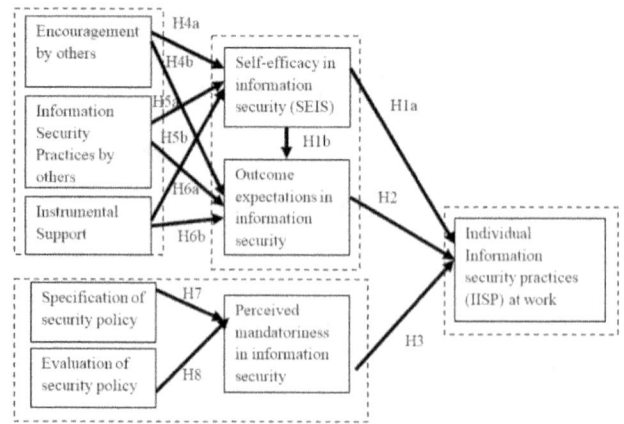

Figure 1 Research model.

3.1 Individual Information Security Practices (IISP) at work

Individual information security practices can be defined as preventive security behaviors (Straub, 1990) associated with desktop computer management, virus protection, and local-area-network security issues (Ryan, 2006). The repetition of an information security issue can show the way to regularity, structure, and knowledge transfer (Bartoli, Hermel &Ramis-Pujol, 2003) (As cited in Ryan, 2006, p.68). This results in a learned information security practice. In other words, IISP at work is the individual practices/behaviors that make the organizational information more secure.

Individual Information Security Practices (IISP) at work is related to guidelines and standards suggested by professionals in order to protect the assets of organizations (Ma & Pearson, 2005). The ISO27002 is the new name for ISO17799 standard and is the code of practice for information security (ISO, 2013). One of the best international standards well known in information security is ISO17799/27002. This standard provides good knowledge on information security in order to accomplish information security in organizations. According to Ma and Pearson (2005, p.4), information security professionals define best practices as guidelines, frameworks or checklists to protect the elements of the Information Systems. In addition, Theoharidou et al. (2005) point out that ISO17799/27002 is based on risk management which is accomplished via appropriate control measures to stop security threats. Given the flexibility and comprehensiveness of Information Security International Standard ISO17799/27002, it is taken as the basis of individual information security practices (IISP) at work.

3.2 Self-Efficacy in Information Security (SEIS)

There are different ways for individuals to show their efficacy. One of the effective ways that individuals expand to a more robust significance of efficacy is through experiences. Their performance accomplishments make them believe that they have the ability to perform a specific task well. Conversely, failures create self-doubts. To gain a sense of self-efficacy, individuals must overcome obstacles through effort. After individuals realize their capabilities through recurring successes, they can manage failures by being less negatively affected by them. Another way to strengthen self-belief is through modeling in which individuals partially judge their capabilities in comparison with others (Bandura, 1994).

Rhee et al. (2009) suggested that SEIS might help explain current security practices and the intention to persevere in that effort. They define security practice as an "individual's information security risk management behavior involving two aspects: the adoption of security technology and security conscious care behavior related to computer and Internet usage". One is related to the use of security tools and features such as anti-virus software, anti-spyware, pop-up blocking function etc., and the other is in reference to security compliance behavior in using a computer and the Internet. Rhee et al. (2009) conclude that people who practice security care behavior and adopt security tools lower the vulnerability of information security. Based on the discussion above, there is a relationship between self-efficacy and the use of security tools. In this research, the construct of individual information security practices (IISP) at work will be based on the standard ISO 17799/27002 particularly in the areas of access control, compliance and information security policy with the objective of creating better security policies in organizations. Therefore we predict that:

H1a: Individual's self-efficacy in information security (SEIS) is positively associated with individual information security practices (IISP) at work.

According to SCT, an outcome expectation is related to reward systems (Bartol & Srivastava, 2002) and is an important construct that can be used to explain and predict human behavior. It has three major forms: physical effects (i.e., pleasure, pain, and discomfort), social effects (i.e., social recognition, monetary rewards, power, and applause) and self-evaluation effects (i.e., self-satisfaction, self-devaluation). Therefore, human behaviors can be regulated by one of these different forms of effect (Bandura, 1997; Compeau & Higgins, 1995a). There are two types of outcome expectations (performance-related outcome expectations and personal outcome expectations) that deal with an individual's belief and reaction about the ability to proficiently use computers. Therefore we predict that:

H1b: Individual's self-efficacy in information security (SEIS) is positively associated with an individual's outcome expectations in information security.

3.3 Outcome Expectations in Information Security (OEIS)

An outcome expectation is an important construct that is used to explain and predict human behavior (Albion, 2001; Davis, 1989; Delcourt & Kinzie, 1993). Hence, it motivates individuals to carry on behaviors over extended periods of time if they believe their actions will generate desired results. According to Lent, Brown & Hackett (1994), outcome expectations are related to the anticipated outcomes of an action. For example, "If I regularly use my security tools, I will have more secure systems". In the context of information security, outcome expectations can motivate individuals to keep up information security behaviors if they believe their actions will generate a desired result. Thus,

H2: An individual's outcome expectations in information security is positively associated with individual information security practices (IISP) at work.

3.4 Perceived Mandatoriness in Information Security (PMIS)

According to Venkatesh and Davis (2000), mandatoriness is based on the individual's perceptions of forced use of technology. A major amount of studies in Information Systems describe mandate in different ways; as a black box where individuals decide whether to react positively or negatively to the mandate, as a one- time decision to obey or reject the mandate, and finally as orders that come from management (Chae & Poole, 2005).Markus (1983) explains how some users accepted and some resisted the implementation of a financial system whose use was mandated by management. Other authors such as Sussman and Siegal (2003) analyze the use of e-mail which is not directly mandated by management. They propose that the acceptance of email services is not voluntary for individuals at any modern organization. According to Brown et al. (2002), individuals respond accordingly to a continuous mandate when they consider a policy mandatory or voluntary. Boss et al. (2009) in their study describe mandatoriness as the "degree to which individuals perceive that compliance with existing security policies and procedures is compulsory or expected by organizational management".

Based on Ouchi (1977, 1979) (As cited in Boss et al., 2009, p.5), a control system needs to be implemented to observe and evaluate individual behavior against some standard. A mandate from management in regards to policy can persuade individuals to follow the code of practice for information security. According to D'Aquila (2001), management expectations play a big role on individual behavior. Therefore, if individuals perceive that the code of practice for information security ISO17799/27002 is mandatory, they are more likely to have a better individual information security practices (IISP) at work.

H3: The higher the individual's perceived mandatoriness of compliance with existing information security policies and procedures, the higher the individual information security practices (IISP) at work.

3.5 Encouragement by others (ENCO)

Keyvani and Mozafari (2009, p.4) state that encouragement is "a process that focuses on the individual's resources and potentials to enhance self-esteem and self-acceptance". In addition, encouragement focuses on any resource that can be turned into an asset or strength (Keyvani & Mozafari, 2009). According to Dreikurs (1981), people need encouragement in a way that plants need water.

The encouragement of others has to do with situations where an individual looks to find guidance on behavioral expectations. This might influence both self-efficacy and outcome expectations (Compeau & Higgins, 1995).

Compeau and Higgins (1995) found out that encouragement by others (family, friends and subordinates) to use computers did not represent an important source of persuasion as when persuasion came from peers and superiors.

Similarly, it is expected that encouragement by others (peers and superiors) may influence self-efficacy in information security (SEIS) and personal outcome expectations in information security related to the use of information security tools as hypothesized in this study.

H4a: High encouragements by others in the use of information security tools positively affects an individual's self-efficacy in information security (SEIS).

H4b: High encouragements by others in the use of information security tools positively affect individual's outcome expectations in information security.

3.6 Information Security Practices by Others (ISPO)

Compeau and Higgins (1995) point out that the use of technology by others can be applied as a foundation of information in forming self-efficacy and outcome expectations. From a psychological perspective, behavior acquisition is done through learning by observation (Latham & Saari 1979; Manz & Sims 1986; Schunk 1981). Bandura (1977) points out that an individual learns new information and behavior by watching other individuals. That process is called observational learning which is mainly based on live and verbal instruction. Live model has to do with the actual individual showing the behavior to others, and a verbal instruction model describes and explains the behavior. According to Bandura et al. (1977), learning by observation influences behaviors through the influence on self–efficacy, i.e. the more frequent the use of information security practices by others, the higher the individual self-efficacy in information security. And it also influences outcome expectations by revealing the possible consequences of the behavior (Bandura, 1971).

In the context of information security, it is expected that others' practice (peers and superiors) may influence SEIS and outcome expectations in information security with regards to the use of information security tools, which is hypothesized in this study.

H5a: The more frequent the Information Security Practices by others in one's reference group is, the higher the individual's Self-efficacy in information security (SEIS) will become.

H5b: The higher the Information Security Practices by others in one's reference group, the higher the individual's outcome expectations in information security.

3.7 Instrumental Support (ISUP)

Social Cognitive Theory (SCT) conceives support as one of the factors that positively affect self-efficacy (Compeau & Higgins, 1995). Organizations give computer support to individuals who need it. Therefore, individuals are supposed to enhance their ability and their perceptions of their ability to manage a specific task (i.e. computer use). Support can also influence outcome expectations meaning that the organization's posture toward individuals' behavior might answer questions about the possible consequences of computer use (Compeau & Higgins, 1995).

In terms of information security, the availability of assistance as a type of support improves the user's security behaviors that could significantly reduce the organization's size of security related overhead and drive down the level of severity of security incidents. Therefore we predict that:

H6a: The higher the instrumental support to individuals for information security in the organization, the higher the individual's self-efficacy in information security (SEIS).

H6b: The higher the instrumental support for information security in the organization, the higher the individual's outcome expectations in information security.

3.8 Specification of security policy (SOSP)

One of the features of practicing control is the specification of desired behaviors or outcomes that come regularly in the form of formal documented procedures (Eisenhardt, 1985; Kirsch, 2004). These policies give controllers flexibility to align desired behavior with organizational goals with the purpose of achieving a particular objective (Lorange & Scott-Morton, 1974; Kirsch, 2004). Understandable policies give a clear path to the individual with the target of achieving the desired behavior. For example, a security policy might say, "Employees are to log off their computers when not at their desks." Another well- specified information security policy could be "Report/forward any suspicious e-mails (ones that request personal or organizational data, called 'phishing') that are not caught by the organizations' spam filter to the IS security workers for assessment" (S. Boss, Kirsch, Angermeier, Shingler, &R. Boss, 2009). Schneider et al. (2005) point out that the action of specifying a desired behavior shows the way to perceptions of mandatoriness on the part of individuals. Based on the above discussion, I propose that the specification of the existence of corporate information security policy might be seen by individuals as a mandatory.

H7: The higher the specification of security policy is, the higher the perceived mandatoriness in information security will be.

3.9 Evaluation of security policy (EVSP)

Evaluation is an essential part of control that can be described as the analysis of collected data with the intention of evaluating individual's compliance with specific behaviors or outcomes (Jaworski, 1988; Kirsch, 2004). If management never evaluates compliance, policies will be disregarded by employees (Boss et al., 2009).

People in charge of evaluation decide if the result has been accomplished or whether the individual has demonstrated desired behaviors by following written policies. Evaluation is based on formal documentation that measures current status and makes modifications accordingly. Auditors usually evaluate individual's behavior based on the log file. Another type of evaluation is hands-on where personnel of the organization evaluate the individual's machine to check for compliance. The requirement is for individuals to perceive compliance with existing policies as crucial to management. In addition, management needs to show all individuals in the organization that they view compliance with the policy as mandatory (S. Boss, Kirsch, Angermeier, Shingler, & R. Boss, 2009).

H8: The higher the individual's evaluation of security policy, the higher the perceived mandatoriness of compliance with existing security policies and procedures.

4. RESEARCH DESIGN METHODOLOGY

4.1 Data Collection Procedure

The link of the online survey was distributed via e-mail to individuals who have experience working with Information Systems as end users.

4.2 Reliability and Validity

The measurement items suggested in this research study were selected from previous research studies, some items were used in their original form and others adapted for the information security context of this study. It is critical for each reflective measurement instrument that its reliability and validity Cronbach alpha coefficients were used to determine the internal consistency reliability of each instrument composed of multiple items. Content validity refers to whether the selected items capture the total scope of the construct as described by the construct's domain (Straub et al., 2000). Construct validity will be assured through literature review related to construct's domain (Peter et al., 2007).

The construct individual information security practices (IISP) at work was adapted from Ma and Pearson (2005) study of "best practices" with ISO17799. Ma and Pearson covered ten ISO17799/27002 security dimensions composing of 36 security practices for self-assessment, reassessing the information security practices of business partners, and the independent evaluation of information security management within the business organization. To my knowledge, no studies were done at the individual level using ISO17799/27002. After analyzing each question of the sections of ISO11799/27002, I managed to adapt twenty five questions covering five different security areas applied to the individual level. The reliability of the constructs in the categories of information security policy, asset classification and control, system access control, systems development and maintenance, communications and operations management was above .8.These five categories are part of the ISO17799/27002 standard but each section has its own group of questions that are part of the individual information security practices (IISP) at work.

Assessing reliability of the construct self-efficacy in information security (SEIS), the authors Rhee, Kim and Ryu (2009) calculated Cronbach's alpha with a result value of .965 and the factor loadings for SEIS were greater than .8. The rest of the constructs' reliability of this research was above .7. According to Nunnally (1978), .7 is acceptable for Cronbach's Alpha. The factor loadings were greater than .7. The survey items that measured SEIS construct included questions developed by Rhee, Kim and Ryu (2009) for the protection of the information.

Outcome expectations have been considered by many researchers including Davis (1989) and Davis et al. (1989) who used the term "usefulness" to reflect beliefs (or expectations).The authors measured perceived usefulness in regards to using IBM-PC based graphic system (Chart Master). All of the items were taken and adapted to information security context. For example the question "Using Chart Master in my job would enable me to accomplish tasks more quickly" was changed to "Information Security systems enable me to accomplish tasks more quickly". The reliability of the construct "perceived usefulness" was .97.

Perceived mandatoriness in information security was taken from the study of Boss, Kirsch, Angermeier, Shingler, & Boss (2009). The reliability of this construct was above .8.

The effects of encouragement by others, was taken from the study of Compeau and Higgins (1995) who studied if the use of computers was encouraged by others. This construct was adapted in the context of information security to evaluate if the use of information security tools was encouraged by others. The study shows that the reliability of this construct was above .7.

Compeau and Higgins (1995) pointed out that the behavior of others with regard to the use of technology was the basis of information used to develop individual's self-efficacy and outcome expectation. They used a 5-point likert -type scale to evaluate the items. These items were taken as they are and applied to the information security context in order to evaluate information security practices by others. This construct's reliability was above .7

In this study, all the items were measured with a 7-point likert-type scale to become more reliable varying from "Strongly Disagree" to "Strongly Agree".

4.3 Structural Model Analysis

This research model was evaluated using a SEM (structural equation modeling) method to test the research hypotheses. SEM was performed in Smart PLS which is a predictive technique that can handle multiple independent, mediating and dependent variables even when predictors display multicollinearity like in the present research study. In addition, it simultaneously models the structural paths (i.e., theoretical relationships among latent variables) and measurement paths (i.e., relationships between a latent variable and its indicators) (Chin, Marcolin, & Newsted, 1996). SEM can concurrently test the convergent validity and discriminant validity of the scales used to measure theoretical constructs and the proposed related links between theoretical constructs like in the present research study (Lowry, & Gaskin, 2014).

5. PRESENTATION OF RESULTS

5.1 Hypothesis Testing Results

The results of t-values and path coefficients are shown in table 1 (t>1.65; *p<0.1, t >1.96;**p < .05, t>2.57;***p<0.01). Path coefficients values and the significance of the relationships are shown in figure 2.Those values describe how strong the effect of one variable is on another variable. Most of the paths coefficients are significant except the paths between ENCO->SEIS and ISPO->OEIS. When the size of the outcome t-value is above 1.96, it is assumed that the path coefficient is meaningfully different from 0 at a significance level of 5 percent. The critical t-values for significance levels of 1 percent and 10 percent probability of error are 2.57 and 1.65 respectively (Noppa, 2010). According to (Hair, Hult, Ringle and Sarstedt, 2013) the rule of thumb for sample sizes of up to about 1000 observations, the path coefficients with values above 0.20 are usually significant and those with values below 0.10 are usually not significant.

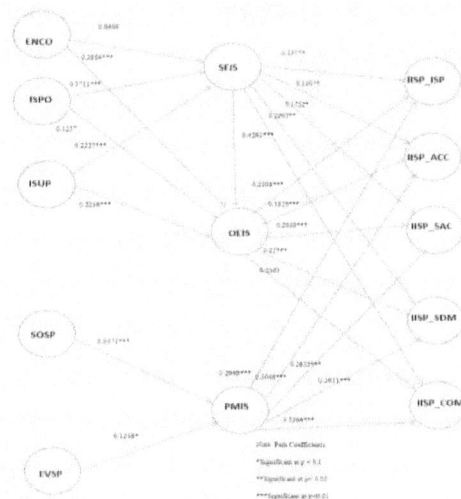

Figure 2 Path coefficients

Hypothesis 1, which predicts that Individual's self-efficacy in information security (SEIS) is positively associated with individual information security practices (IISP) at work, was supported. SEIS affected individual information security practices (IISP) at work in regards to IISP_ISP (1.679>1.65; *p<.10; significant), IISP_ACC (1.793 >1.65; p<.10; significant), IISP_SAC (1.947> 1.65; *p<.10, significant), IISP_SDM (2.360>1.96; **p< .05; significant) and IISP_COM (5.119> 2.57;***p< .01; significant). In addition, it affected positively individual's outcome expectations in information security (OEIS) (2.577>2.57; ***p<.01; significant). Hypotheses that had low effect size (coefficient less than .2) were the following SEIS-> IISP_ACC, SEIS->IISP_ISP, and SEIS->IISP_SAC. This means that self-efficacy had low effect size on individual information security practices (IISP) at work in regards to communications and operations management, information security policy and system access control.

Hypothesis 2, which predicts that Individual's outcome expectations in information security is positively associated with individual information security practices (IISP) at work was supported. OEIS predicted IISP at work in regards to IISP_ISP (3.028>2.57; ***p<.01; significant), IISP_ACC (2.981>2.57; ***<.01; significant), IISP_SAC (3.537>2.57;***p<.01; significant), IISP_SDM (2.416>1.96;**p<.05; significant), but it did not affect IISP_COM (0.538>1.96, not significant).

Hypothesis 3, which predicts individual's perceived mandatoriness of compliance with existing information security policies and procedures, is positively associated with individual information security practices (IISP) at work was supported. PMIS predicted IISP at work in regards to IISP_ISP (3.509>2.57;***p< .01; significant), IISP_ACC (3.899>2.57; ***p< .01; significant), IISP_SAC (3.266>2.57;***p< .01; significant), IISP_SDM (3.050>2.57;***p< .01; significant), IISP_COM (4.755>2.57;***p< .01; significant).

Hypothesis 4, which predicts high encouragements by others in the use of information security tools is positively associated with individual's outcome expectations in information security was supported except the relationship with SEIS.ENCO predicted OEIS (2.937>2.57; ***p<.01 significant) but did not affect SEIS (0.479>1.96;**p< .05; not significant).This result supports the work of Compeau and Higgins (1995) which pointed out that encouragement of use of computing technology from family, friends and subordinates did not represent an important source of persuasion.

Hypothesis 5, which predicts that Information Security Practices by others (ISPO) in one's reference group is positively associated with individual's Self-efficacy in information security (SEIS) was supported except the relationship with OEIS. ISPO predicted SEIS (4.131>2.57; ***p<.01; significant).

Hypothesis 6, which predicts that instrumental support (ISUP) to individuals for information security in the organization, is positively associated with individual's self-efficacy in information security (SEIS) was supported. In addition, the relationship with OEIS was supported. ISUP predicted SEIS (2.681> 2.57; ***p< .01; significant) and OEIS (2.732> 2.57; ***p< .01; significant).

Hypothesis 7, which predicts that the specification of security policy (SOSP), is positively associated with perceived mandatoriness in information security (PMIS) was supported. SOSP predicted PMIS (7.666>2.57; ***p< .01; significant).

Hypothesis 8, which predicts that individual's evaluation of security policy (EVSP) is positively associated with perceived mandatoriness of compliance with existing security policies and procedures was supported (1.689>1.65; *p<.10; significant) but had low effect size (coefficient less than .2).

Hypotheses	Relationship	Path Coefficient	T-statistic	Hypothesis Support

Table 1 Results Summary of tested hypotheses

6. DISCUSSION OF FINDINGS

The outcomes of this study provide support for all of the research questions regarding Social Cognitive Theory and Control Theory assessment on Individual Information Security Practices (IISP) at work using ISO17799/27002.The following research questions were examined.

RQ1. How do encouragement by others, information security practices by others, and instrumental support affect self-efficacy in information security and outcome expectations in information security?

Encouragement by others (ENCO) was shown to have a positive effect on outcome expectations in information security (OEIS) that is statistically significant. The result of the analysis showed that encouragement by others in the use of information security tools affected individual's outcome expectations in information security (OEIS). The result is consistent with the predictions of the original hypothesis. This supports the work of Albion (2001), Davis (1989) and Delcourt & Kinzie (1993) in which they point out that outcome expectations motivates individuals to keep up with behaviors over extended periods of time if they believe their actions generate desired results. Hence, information security tasks are accomplished quickly and job productivity is increase if individuals are encouraged to use information security tools by peers, family, friends, and managers.

Information security practices by others (ISPO) was shown to have a positive effect on SEIS that is statistically significant but not on individual's OEIS. This result was intuitive to the original hypothesis; however given observational learning nature of ISPO in its social cognitive theory context, the positive influence is explained. Individual's SEIS is high when Information Security Practices are being followed by peers, family, friends, and managers. Individuals feel confident in handling different information security threats such as viruses and spywares. They are more confident in using different programs and applying security patches to the servers in order to protect the information against intruders. In addition, they are confident in learning advanced skills and using user's guide when help is needed to protect the information. This supports the work of Bandura (1977) in which he states that self-efficacy assumes, that different modes of influence change individual behavior in a way of generating self-perceptions of efficacy.

Instrumental support (ISUP) was shown to have a positive effect on SEIS and OEIS that is statistically significant. This result was intuitive to the original hypothesis; however given the assistance nature of ISUP in its social cognitive theory context, the positive influence is explained. Individuals feel more confident in handling information security issues such as viruses, spywares and security patches, when individuals have guidance in the selection of information security tools. In addition, they have a specific person or a group available for assistance.

RQ2. How do cognitive factors such as self-efficacy in information security and outcome expectations in information security affect individual information security practices at work?

SEIS was shown to have a positive effect on IISP at work based on ISO17799/27002 that is statistically significant. This result was intuitive to the original hypothesis; however given the belief nature of SEIS in its social cognitive theory context, the positive influence is explained. SEIS directly affects Individual Information Security Practices (IISP) at work based on ISO17799/27002 in regards to information security policy, asset classification and control, system access control, system development and maintenance, and communications and operations management. Individuals are more effective in following information security policy, providing feedback to individuals responsible with the update and maintenance of the information security policy, and finally following management's intention to support information security programs. In addition, they are able to protect the information when they feel confident handling viruses, spywares, terms related to information security, web browsers to different security levels.

SEIS was shown to have a positive effect on OEIS and is statistically significant. This result was innate to the original hypothesis; however knowing the belief nature of SEIS in its social cognitive theory context, the positive influence is explained. Individuals are able to protect the information when they feel confident handling viruses, spywares, terms related to information security, web browsers to different security levels, and advanced skills.

OEIS was shown to have a positive effect on IISP at work based on ISO17799/27002 that is statistically significant. This result was innate to the original hypothesis; however knowing the motivation nature of OEIS in its social cognitive theory context, the positive influence is explained. OEIS directly affects Individual Information Security Practices (IISP) at work based on ISO17799/27002 in regards to information security policy, asset classification and control, system access control, system development and maintenance, but it does not affect communications and operations management. Individuals are more effective in following information security policies, providing feedback to individuals responsible with the update and maintenance of the information security policy, and following management's intention to support information security programs when information security systems support critical aspect of their job.

RQ3. How do individual perceptions about mandatoriness in information security influence individual information security practices at work?

Perceived mandatoriness in information security (PMIS) was shown to have a positive effect on IISP at work based on ISO17799/27002 that is statistically significant. This result was innate to the original hypothesis; however knowing the mandate nature of PMIS in its control theory context, the positive influence is explained. PMIS directly affects Individual Information

Security Practices (IISP) at work based on ISO17799/27002 in regards to information security policy, asset classification and control, system access control, system development and maintenance, and communications and operations management. Individuals are more effective in following information security policies, providing feedback to individuals responsible with the update and maintenance of the information security policies, and following management's intention to support information security programs, when they comply with organization's security policies and procedures.

RQ4. How do specification and evaluation influence perceived mandatoriness in information security?

Specification of security policy (SOSP) was shown to have a positive effect on PMIS that is statistically significant. This result was innate to the original hypothesis; however knowing the specify nature of SOSP in its control theory context, the positive influence is explained. Individuals understand and comply with organization's security policies and procedures when they are familiar with organization's IT security policies, procedures and guidelines. This study extends the work of Schneider et al. (2005) who found out that the action of specifying a desired behavior shows the way to perceptions of mandatoriness. In addition, this study extends the work of S. Boss, Kirsch, Angermeier, Shingler, & R. Boss, (2009) who found out that policies give a clear path to individuals with the objective of achieving desired behaviors.

6.1 Limitations of the study

This study had to rely on self-reported data about individual information security practices at work. We do not know their practices for sure at work so we have to rely on self-reporting data. This could be problematic and could lead to common method bias.

A major limitation of this study is that 71% of the sample is younger than 29 years old, 70% does not have a bachelor's degree and 76% has less than five years of experience working with Information Systems. Hence, the sample is skewed towards younger individuals, less educated, and less experienced.

The survey of Individual Information Security Practices (IISP) at work was based on ISO 17799/27002. Since Information Security is a developing area that changes constantly, the latest ISO 27002:2013 standard has some improvements to maintain an adequate information security management system (Disterer, 2013). These improvements should be included in future research of IISP at work.

7. CONCLUSION

This research study concluded that cognitive forces of the social cognitive theory such as self-efficacy and outcome expectations applied to information security played an important role on individual information security practices (IISP) at work based on ISO17799/27002. In addition, self-efficacy and outcome expectations in information security were found to be positively influenced by encouragement by others, information security practices by others or instrumental support. Other findings were that elements of control such as specification and evaluating behaviors of security policy affected positively on perceived mandatoriness in information security. In addition, perceived mandatoriness in information security was effective in motivating individuals to follow information security practices at work based on ISO17799/27002. .

8. REFERENCES

[1] Albion, P. R. (2001). Some factors in the development of self-efficacy beliefs for computer use among teacher education students. Journal of Technology and Teacher Education, 9(3), 321-347.

[2] Angel, I. (1993, October, 1993). Computer security in these uncertain times: the need for a new approach. Paper presented at the Proceedings of the 10th international conferences on computer security, audit and control (CompSec), London.

[3] Bandura, A. (1965). Influence of models' reinforcement contingencies on the acquisition of imitative responses. Journal of Personality and Social Psychology, 1(6), 589-595.

[4] Bandura, A. (1971). Influence of Models' Reinforcement Contingencies on the Acquisition of Imitative Responses. In A. Bandura (Ed.), Psychological Modeling: Conflicting Theories (pp. 112-127). Chicago, IL.

[5] Bandura, A. (1977). Self-efficacy: Toward a unifying theory of behavioral change. Psychological Review, 84, 191-215.

[6] Bandura, A. (1977). Social Learning Theory. Englewood Cliffs, New Jersey: Prentice Hall.

[7] Bandura, A. (1977). The self and mechanisms of agency. In J. Suls (Ed), Social psychological perspectives on the self. Hillsdale, N.J.: Erlbaum, in press.

[8] Bandura, A. (1978). Reflections on Self-Efficacy in Advances in Behavioral Research and therapy. Pergamon Press, 237-269.

[9] Bandura, A. (1982). Self-efficacy Meachism in Human Agency. American Psychologist, 37(2), 122-147.

[10] Bandura, A. (1986). Social foundations of thought and action: A social cognitive theory. NJ: Prentice Hall.

[11] Bandura, A. (1988). Self-Regulation of motivation and action through goal systems. Dordrecht, Netherlands: Kluwer Academic Publishers.

[12] Bandura, A. (1989). Human Agency in Social Cognitive Theory. American Psychological Association, 44(9), 1175-1184.

[13] Bandura, A. (1994). Self-efficacy. In Ramachaudran (Ed.), Encyclopedia of human behavior (Vol. 4, pp. 71-81). New York: Academic Press: Academic Press.

[14] Bandura, A. (1997). Self-efficacy: The exercise of control. New York: W.H. Freeman and Company.

[15] Bandura, A. (2002). Social Cognitive Theory in Cultural Context. Applied Psychology: An International Review, 51(2), 269-290.

[16] Bandura, A., Adams, N., & Beyer, J. (1977). Cognitive Processes Mediating Behavioral Change. Journal of Personality and Social Psychology, 35(3), 125-139.

[17] Bartol, K., & Srivastava, A. (2002). Encouraging knowledge sharing: the role of organizational reward systems. Journal of Leadership and Organizational Studies, 9(1).

[18] Bartoli, A., Hermel, P., & Ramis-Pujol, J. (2003). Innovation Assessment as a management information tool: a case study. Measuring Business Excellence, 7(2), 6-20.

[19] Boss, S., Kirsch, L., Angermeier, I., Shingler, R., & Boss, R. (2009). If someone is watching, I'll do what I'm asked: mandatoriness, control, and information security. European Journal of Information Systems, 18(2), 151.

[20] Brown, S.A., Massey, A.P., Montoya-Weiss, M.M., Burkman, J.R. (2002). Do I really have to? User acceptance of mandated technology. European Journal of Information Systems112002;, 283–295.

[21] Chae, B., & Poole, M. (2005). Mandates and technology acceptance: a tale of two enterprise technologies. Journal of Strategic Information Systems, 14(2), 147-166.

[22] Chin, W. W., Marcolin, B. L., & Newsted, P. R. (1996). A Partial Least Squares Latent Variable Modeling Approach For Measuring Interaction Effects: Results From A Monte Carlo Simulation Study And Voice Mail Emotion/Adoption Study. Proceedings of The Seventeenth International Conference On Information Systems.

[23] Collete, R., & Gentile, M. (2006). The security architect: bridging the gap between business, technology and security. The Information Systems Security Association Journal, 42-44.

[24] Compeau, D. R. and C. A. Higgins (1995a). "Application of social cognitive theory to training for computer skills." Information Systems Research 6(2): 118-143.

[25] Compeau, D. R., & Higgins, C. A. (1995b). Computer self-efficacy: Development of a measure and initial test. MIS Quarterly, 19(2), 189-210.

[26] Compeau, D., Higgins, C. A., & Huff, S. (1999). Social Cognitive Theory and Individual Reactions to Computing Technology: A longitudinal study. MIS Quarterly, 23(2), 145-158.

[27] D'Aquila, J. M. (2001). Financial accountants' perceptions of management's ethical standards. Journal of Business Ethics, 31(3), 233-244.

[28] Davis, F. D. (1989). Perceived Usefulness, Perceived Ease of Use, and User Acceptance of information Technology. MIS Quarterly, 13(3), 319-340.

[29] Davis, F. D., Bagozzi, R. P., & Warshaw, P. R. (1989). USER ACCEPTANCE OF COMPUTER TECHNOLOGY: A COMPARISON OF TWO THEORETICAL MODELS. Management Science, 35(8), 982-1003.

[30] Delcourt, M. A., & Kinzie, M. B. (1993). Computer technologies in teacher education:The measurement of attitudes and self-efficacy. Journal of Research and Development in Education, 27(1), 35-41.

[31] Dhillon, G., & Backhouse, J. (2000). Information system security management in the new millennium. Communications of the ACM, 43(7), 125-128.

[32] Disterer, G. (2013). ISO/IEC 27000, 27001 and 27002 for information security management. Journal of Information Security, 4(2), 92-100. Retrieved from http://search.proquest.com/docview/1349963585?accountid=28844

[33] Dreikurs, R. (1981). Social Equality: The Challenge of today. Chicago: Alfred Adler Institute.

[34] Eisenhardt, K. M. (1985). Control: organizational and economic approaches. Management Science, 31(2), 134-149.

[35] FFIEC. (2014). Architecture Considerations. Retrieved from http://ithandbook.ffiec.gov/it-booklets/information-security/information-security-strategy/architecture-considerations.aspx?prev=1

[36] Hair, J., Hult, T., Ringle, C., & Sarstedt, M. (2013). A Primer on partial least Squares Structural Equation Modeling (PLS-SEM): SAGE Publications, Inc.

[37] Hinson, G. (2003). "Human factors in information security." Innovative information security awareness programs: 5.

[38] ISO. (2013). Introduction To ISO 27002 (ISO27002). Retrieved from http://www.27000.org/iso-27002.htm

[39] ISO-17799. (2000). Information technology, code of practice for information security management. Geneva: International Standards, Organisation.

[40] Jaworski, B. (1988). Toward a theory of marketing control: environmental context, control types, and consequences. Theory of Marketing Control, 52, 23-39.

[41] Keyvani, A., & Mozafari, M. (2009). Encouragement, Punishment, Offering New Solutions. International Journal of Management Perspectives, 1(4), 74-85.Lucie Press.

[42] Kirsch, L. (1996). Contextual influences on self-control of IS professional engaged in systems development. Accounting, Management, & Information Technology, 6(3), 191-219.

[43] Kirsch, L. J. (2004). Deploying common solutions globally: The dynamics of control. Information Systems Research, 15(4), 374-395.

[44] Latham, G. P., & Saari, U. M. (1979). Application of Social-Learning Theory to Training Supervisors through Behavioral Modeling. Journal of Applied Psychology, 64(3), 247-246.

[45] Lent, R., Brown, S., & Hackett, G. (1994). Toward a unifying social cognitive theory of career and academic interest, choice, and performance. Journal of Vocational Behavior, 45, 79-121.

[46] Lorange, P., & Scott-Morton, M. (1974). A framework for management control systems. Sloan Management Review, 16(1), 47-56.

[47] Lowry, P., & Gaskin, J. (2014). Partial Least Squares (PLS) Structural Equation Modeling (SEM) for Building and Testing Behavioral Causal Theory: When to Choose It and How to Use It. IEEE TRANSACTIONS ON PROFESSIONAL COMMUNICATION, 57(2), 36.

[48] Ma, Q., & Pearson, J. M. (2005). ISO 17799: "Best Practices" in information security management? Communications of the Association of Information Systems, 15, 577-591.

[49] MacKenzie, K. (2006). Employees may be opening doors to criminals. Retrieved from http://www.ft.com/cms/s/458807fe-efec-11da-b80e-0000779e234

[50] Manz, C. C., & Sims, H. P. (1986). Leading self-managed groups: A conceptual analysis of a paradox. Economic and Industrial Democracy, 7(141-165).

[51] Markus, M. L. (1983). Power, politics, and mis implementation. Communications of the ACM, 26(6), 430-444.

[52] NCSA. (2005). Top Ten Cybersecurity Tips. National Cyber Security Alliance, Washington DC.

[53] NIST. (1998). Information technology training requirements: A role and performance-based model. Washington D.C.: U.S. Department of Commerce.

[54] Noppa. (2010). How to Run SmartPLS. Retrieved from https://noppa.lut.fi/noppa/opintojakso/ab40aj200/luennot/instructions.docx

[55] Nunnally, J. C. (1978). Psychometric theory (2nd ed.). New York: McGraw-Hill.

[56] Ouchi, W. (1979). A conceptual framework for the design of organizational control mechanisms. management Science, 25(9), 833-848.

[57] Peltier, T. (2000). How to build a comprehensive security awareness program. Computer Security Journal, 16(2), 23-32.

[58] Peter, S., Straub, D., & Rai, A. (2007). Specifying Formative Constructs in Information Systems Research. IS Research, 31(4), 623-656.

[59] Rhee, H., Kim, C., & Ryu, Y. (2009). Self-efficacy in information security: Its influence on end users' information security practice behavior. Computer & Security, 28(8), 816-826.

[60] Ryan, James Emory (2006) A comparison of information security trends between formal and informal environments. Ph.D. dissertation, Auburn University, United States -- Alabama. Retrieved October 22, 2007, from ProQuest Digital Dissertations database. (Publication No. AAT 3225287).

[61] Schneider, F., Gruman, J., & Coutts, L. (2005). Applied Social Psychology: Understanding and Addressing Social and Practical Problems. Thousand Oaks, CA: Sage Publications.

[62] Schunk, D. (1981). Modeling and Attributional Effects on Children's Achievement: A self-efficacy analysis. Journal of Educational Psychology, 73(1), 93-105.

[63] Siponen, M. (2000a). A conceptual foundation for organizational IS security awareness. Information Management & Computer Security, 8(1), 31-41.

[64] Siponen, M. (2000b). Critical analysis of different approaches to minimizing user-related faults in information system security: implications for research and practice. Information Management & Computer Security, 8(5), 197-209.

[65] Siponen, M. T. (2000). A conceptual foundation for organizational information security awareness. Information Management & Computer Security, 8(1), 31.

[66] Siponen, M., & Willison, R. (2009). Information security management standards: Problems and solutions. Information & Management, 46(5), 267-270.

[67] Siponen, M., Mahmood, A., & Pahnila, S. (2009). Are Employees Putting Your Company At Risk By Not Following Information Security Policies? Communications of the ACM, 52(12), 145-147.

[68] Straub, D. W. (1990). Effective IS Security: An Empirical Study. Information Systems Research, 1(3), 255-276.

[69] Theoharidou, M., Kokolakis, S., Karyda, M., & Kiountouzis, E. (2005). The insider threat to information systems and the effectiveness of ISO17799. Computers & Security, 24(6), 472-484.

[70] Venkatesh, V., & Davis, F. D. (2000). A theoretical extension of the Technology Acceptance Model: Four longitudinal field studies. Management Science, 46(2), 186-204.

[71] Warkentin, M., Shropshire, J., & Johnston, A. (2007). The IT security adoption conundrum: an initial step towards validation of applicable measures. Proceedings of the 13th Americas Conference on Information Systems.

[72] Whitman, M., & Mattord, H. (2008). Management of Information Security (2nd ed.). Boston, Ma: Thompson Course Technology.

Cracks in the Security Foundation: Employee Judgments about Information Sensitivity

Michelle L. Kaarst-Brown
Syracuse University
Syracuse, NY USA
1.315.443-1892
mlbrow03@syr.edu

E. Dale Thompson
Thompson & Associates
Dallas, Texas USA
eedeetee@sbcglobal.net

ABSTRACT[1]

Despite the increased focus on IT security, much of our reliance on 'information sensitivity classifications' is based on broadly specified technical 'access controls' or policies and procedures for the handling of organizational data – many of them developed incrementally over decades. One area ignored in research and practice is how human beings make "sensitivity judgments" or 'classify' information they may encounter in everyday activities. This has left what we view as a crack in the IT security foundation. This crack has created a tension between formal IT security classification schema, technical controls, and policy, and the sensitivity judgments that everyday workers must make about the non-coded information they deal with. As noted in government and private reports, a new look at information sensitivity classification is vital to the expanding reach and criticality of information security. Based on a grounded theory study that elicited 188 judgements of sensitive information, we found valuable lessons for IT security in how workers, both in IT and outside of IT, recognize, classify, and react to their human judgments of sensitive information.

Categories and Subject Descriptors

H.0 Information Systems – General; K.4.0 Computers in Society – General; K.

General Terms

IT Security, Information Sensitivity, Sensitive Information, Information Classification.

Keywords

Employee Judgments; IT Security; Classification; Information Sensitivity; Security Awareness; Security Judgments.

---

[1] Both authors contributed equally to this manuscript.

1. INTRODUCTION

This study was initially prompted by proposed solutions in the information technology (IT) field to deal with problems with security of electronic networks. A recommended first step was for organizations to decide which information needed protection. This required organizations to segregate information based on sensitivity [4], such as the identification of sensitive information in organizational communications [10].

Despite the increased focus on IT security, much of our reliance on 'information sensitivity classifications' is based on broadly specified technical 'access controls' or policies and procedures for the handling of organizational data, many of them developed incrementally over decades [18, 26]. More recently, the use of ICT's in virtual and cloud environments has increased vulnerability from insider threat activities and the magnitude of potential damage from release of sensitive information [13, 14]. Perhaps due to our reliance on technical security controls and formalized classification policies, an area ignored in research and practice is how human beings make judgments or 'classify' the sensitivity of information they may encounter in everyday activities [26, 23, 24].

Protection of sensitive information is further complicated, however, by the fact that not all security incidents are "attacks from without", nor are they all malicious in nature. Further, not all *insider* security breaches or information misuse cases are malicious. Many cases are the result of "well meaning" or unintentional use of broadly defined *sensitive information* [25]. Where deliberate malfeasance occurs, however, research on insider threats shows that perpetrators do not share a common profile or motivation, and that motivation to cause harm may not be a useful predictor [12, 16, 17, 25]. A gap exists between traditional IT security protocols and human judgments that warrants further exploration.

1.1 Cracks in the Foundation: Human Judgments vs IT Security Classifications

Human judgments about the sensitivity of information come from many sources. Outside authority imposes classification rules through laws and regulations, (for example, HIPAA, and classification guidelines for national security information). Similar prescriptions from within an organization also exist, (such as not releasing competitive information about research and development activities). While individuals may be deterred from inappropriate information use or violation of IT security rules [5], employees are exposed to an array of information that is non-codified (or defined) and left to their personal judgment of whether it qualifies as sensitive or not. Conflicts in interpretation of "information sensitivity" can lead to unintended, and unauthorized, disclosure of information damaging to the organization, or to specific individuals within or outside the organization. These tensions are heightened between IT personnel and others in the organization when the information becomes reified in electronic form on the network [11, 3]. These inconsistencies further support the need to understand human judgments about information sensitivity as a critical source of classification for effective information security.

Indeed, human thinking about the need for sensitive information is sometimes contradictory. On the one hand is the idea that sensitive information must be kept from "unauthorized" disclosure because of the damage that can come from such "leakage". On the other is the idea that we must err on the side of information transparency, again to protect us from damage that might occur without some type of external oversight. This tension between the need for secrecy and the need for transparency can have a serious impact on judgments about information and content management.

To complicate this, IT security workers are often not well schooled or involved in the day-to-day work of the organization and have an uneasy relationship with human judgments that fall outside the limits of technical controls. As custodians of the infrastructure that houses and transports the information vital to organization processes, IT personnel are not privy to the day-to-day uses that give life to security restrictions. IT folks do not get to drive classification, as they are generally empowered only to tweak settings. The IT function often lacks the attitude, knowledge, or skills to develop normative ideas of what is sensitive information or to revise classification schema in use. As a result, they are often limited in their ability to be fine-grained about security classification and so cannot go beyond an arms-length view. When it comes to information within their purview, such as network settings, security protocols, and account management, IT personnel are the masters. At the same time, however, they still have to lobby others about judgments that grow from employee experience and practice. Rather than view employees as users who need to be managed and controlled, we argue that the IT security discipline needs to shift the focus on the user to one of respected decisions makers and engage them in the development of new classification schema and cues. This is so much more than a technical issue.

Thus, we arrive at the need to understand these internal conflicts in the everyday handling of information by an ever-broadening IT workforce.

2. INFORMATION CLASSIFICATION AND IT SECURITY

Existing theory regarding sensitive information is fragmented, developed within the theoretic framework of many diverse research streams [22]. Consequently, there is no overarching theory about sensitive information. This study takes a small step in helping us understand how sensitive information is actually reified in organizational practice. Categorization of information in organizations is closely intertwined with the classification schemas that intersect in an organization. Kwasnik [8] outlined four typical ways of organizing information and the principles underlying each: hierarchies, trees, paradigms, and facets. Kwasnik makes the point that these systems of organizing information can also be useful in knowledge discovery as well, a point reinforced by Begthol [1]. In addition to these basic organizing principles, Bowker and Star [2] put forward the thesis that "all category systems are moral and political entities" (p.

324). This means that categories that "survive" the political process are imbued with the moral and professional ethos of the organization. Unfortunately, individual employees are more than the sum of their current organizational settings and formal rules.

Others have hinted that the process of organizing information consists of a complex mixture of formal and informal systems that co-exist within the organization [2, p.32]. A number of such systems, e.g., those which arise from rule-bearing dicta, attempt to force a formal structure, while others arise as workers attempt to make sense of their environment and to communicate with each other about that environment.

Categorization and classification are closely intertwined. Jacob [7] made a valiant effort at drawing a distinction between the two. It is apparent that, at best, we can say that once a category is formed in the mind, a classification schema is born at the same time. It is impossible to say if classification or categorization comes first. The very process of formulating the category entails a classificatory thought process deciding what is "in" and what is "out". It is useful, however, to conceive of a classificaation system as being a collection of categories linked together by relationships between the different categories.

2.1 Classification of Sensitive Information – Codified Judgements

There exist well-developed classification systems for national security information for most countries in the world. Classification systems for other types of sensitive information are not well documented. As more and more governmental information began to go online, the need for a classification system for sensitive information not related to defense or intelligence purposes became apparent. In 2000, a U.S. General Accountability Office (GAO) report addressed government-wide information security policy [27]. The report highlights the need for a set of data classifications that could be used by all federal agencies *to categorize the criticality* and *sensitivity* of the data they generate and maintain. The report offers a suggested range of categories that could be used from "non-critical, publicly available information" to the "highly-sensitive and critical."

This sentiment is reflected in the private sector by Peltier [15] who asserts that, "information classification drives the protection control requirements, which allows information to be protected to a level commensurate with its value to the organization" (p. 43). Thus, classification of sensitive information sits at the nexus of any system of protection.

More recently, there has emerged the realization that the problems of protecting information in electronic worlds are the same as those encountered with the protection of other content, such as movies and songs that come under the purview of intellectual property regimes. We saw two examples in 2014, with well-publicized hacking events related to the photos of celebrities stored in so-called "cloud" storage services, and the hacking exposure of a new movie about to be released by SONY Pictures. The classification schemas for this type of content have been elaborated in the intellectual property world (copyright, trademark, etc.).

2.2 Conceptualizing Sensitive Information and the IT Workforce

Drawing upon existing research, Thompson and Kaarst-Brown [23] proposed a multi-faceted model of four potential classifications of sensitive information: economic, legal, social, and psychological. They argued, for example, that sensitive information might be regarded as an asset or resource (Economic classification). Similarly, sensitive information could also be viewed much the same as property, protected by a regime of rights with elaborate rules specifying who has the right to control the information (Legal classification). Sensitive information might also be viewed as a type of social capital, protected by the same social inhibitions that mediate social relationships while also serving as the "glue" in the social fabric (Social classification). To the individual, sensitive information could be information about his/her own self and protected simply by not speaking of it or, if held electronically, ensuring that no one else sees it (Psychological classification).

These broad classifications of sensitive information are the foundation of many of our current privacy and security policies and standards, both manual and automated. Unfortunately, these simple categories are not sufficient to understand human judgments of information sensitivity when considering the complexity and contextual elements of the multiple forms of information that our workforce encounters.

As noted in government and private reports, a new look at information sensitivity classification is vital to the expanding reach and criticality of information security. In addition to paper or electronic files, organizations' critical information may be tacit, making sensitive information less concrete and more contextual [26]. This complicates IT security issues and frequently leaves the challenge of classification to individual workers who must determine if the chunk they are dealing with is "sensitive" in its whole or part and how to act in response. Ongoing discussions with senior risk and security managers support that this issue of human judgments about information sensitivity remains a challenge when attempting to automate security protocols or provide information-security awareness training [6, 27].

3. RESEARCH DESIGN

The main research question driving this study was how humans make judgments about sensitive information[2]. This question was broken down into three sub-parts: (1) *human conceptualizations of sensitive information*, (2) *how sensitive information differs* from other organizational information, and (3) *factors that influence judgments* about the *degree of sensitivity*. Since this study deals with human categorical thought, it was deemed essential to proceed using a grounded approach as suggested by Strauss and Corbin [22] and Star [21]. The study was conducted at the individual level of analysis, with "judgments" as the unit of analysis. Although conducted at the individual level, informants were questioned about their experiences at the organizational level. The judgments were individual, even when the information was organizational in nature.

The primary data collection method was face-to-face, semi-structured interviews using a broadly based interview guide to gather life history and biographical experiences (stories) involving security and sensitive information. *After* the formal interview, two card-sorting exercises were conducted. Written on cards were types of sensitive information mentioned by previous informants. The informants were asked to sort the cards in two ways; one according to how they were alike or different and another according to the degree of sensitivity.

Data was analyzed using content analysis of interview transcripts. This was supplemented by interview notes maintained to capture impressions and thoughts as the study progressed and to address validity. The following provides additional details about the methods.

3.1 Data Collection: Interviews and Card Sorts

Spradley [19] suggests three types of questions: (1) descriptive, (2) structural, and (3) contrast. Descriptive questions encouraged the informant to describe their everyday encounters with sensitive information in terms they normally use. Structural questions helped the researcher understand how the informants organized information in general, and sensitive information in particular. It aided in the analysis of domains (categories) and organizing structures in-use by informants on a daily basis. Contrast questions helped lead the informant to tell us (1) how sensitive information differed from non-sensitive information, (2) how one type of sensitive information differed from another, and (3) what type of organizing principles might be at work. Spradley suggested also that informants would proceed to answer unasked questions on their own. We observed this phenomenon also.

This elicitation strategy maintained focus on specific events that workers recalled from their experiences. These techniques also helped detect and deal with recalled events for which the informant had no firsthand knowledge, but which had become part of the organizational lore (myth). Some of these came out as secondhand stories, i.e., told to the informant by someone else. In addition, the card-sorting task exposed the interviewee to responses obtained from previous informants. This served to elicit comments and stories about similar events in his/her own organization, thus capturing similar phenomena in different organizational settings, providing a cross-organization perspective on sensitivity judgements. This aided the results by increasing the amount and the richness of the data for subsequent content analysis, as well as validating the consistency of responses across informants.

3.2 Informant Sampling

Our goal was to gain understanding of the basis for judgments about sensitive information from workers in various organizational settings. To accomplish this, we used both snowball and quota sampling methods. When the sampling was complete, stories were captured from workers in five different industries: Education, Healthcare, Law, Information Technology, and Facility Construction/Maintenance. There were at least two different types of organizations represented for each industry, increasing the insight into practices across each. In addition, interviews were obtained from workers at a variety of levels and specialties within each of the industries represented. Roles included Librarian, Salesman, CIO, Provost, Professor, Legislator, Bookkeeper, and IT Professional, to name only a few.

In our study, there were seven full-time IT personnel: two CIOs, four who currently work in IT positions, and a programmer. Other informants provided stories from IT jobs previously held.

Thirty informants were engaged to be a part of study. (Prior to the interview, one of the informants (#21) passed away. Thus, informant #21 is missing from the Table 2.) Of the twenty-nine

---

[2] A pilot study revealed that the phrase "sensitive information" had the highest probability of eliciting the responses about the phenomenon in question.

informants that participated, there were nine women and twenty men, all over the age of 21.

Table 1 shows the primary sampling techniques utilized, with the rationale and desired outcome.

Table 1. Sampling Methods, Rationale, and Outcome

Selection Technique	Rationale	Outcome
Referral or Snowball Sampling	Useful to obtain different perspectives of a single industry and level in the organization Locate individuals with a variety of perspectives	Increased number of categories Richer, thicker descriptions of judgments Increased data reliability and validity
Quota sampling	Inclusion of human differences such as age and socioeconomic status known to show variance in the results	Increased generalizability Increased validity

3.3 Data Analysis

From the 29 informants, *135 stories* were collected. These stories reflected *188 judgments about sensitive information*. The unit of analysis *is each single instance of a judgment about sensitive information* as related by the interviewees. The definition of a judgment was coded based upon the words of the informant. In many instances, an obvious punchline highlighted the point the informant making. In terms of narrative structure, this was the climax of the story in question. Each informant's judgments were compared to those that came before in a chronological fashion as the study progressed. This approach was used for two reasons: (1) to allow the informants the opportunity to comment upon each other's responses and (2) to allow the researcher to construct a generalized view of sensitive information and the factors involved.

A story was defined as a recounting of experience during which any four of the following were included: who, what, where, when, why, and how. A story consisted of a description of an incident, event, or a set of circumstances that were logically connected, or when an informant attempted to explain about the handling of sensitive information in their organization. (In many interviews, an individual unique story may have been broken up into several pieces throughout the interview transcript as the informant thought of more to say about that particular story. In such cases, this was counted as one story.)

A sensitivity judgment consisted of a statement or a string of statements that included words that identified some kind of organizational information accompanied by words that suggested that the informant was involved in making a decision or judgement to resolve a classification conflict. Several judgments could be included in each story. Some judgments were rendered without the benefit of any accompanying story. These short statements were captured throughout the interview process. Many of these came out during the card-sorting phase of the interview when the informants made comments about an example of sensitive information on the card. In a few instances, the information on the card prompted the informant to elaborate on his comment. In some cases, the informants provided a story of their own about either the information shown on the cards or some similar information in their experience that was stimulated by the information shown on the card.

Out of these stories and the subsequent card sorting exercises, there were 188 statements selected as "judgments" about sensitive information. There were 146 judgments that were unique and 42 judgments that were non-unique (duplicates). A unique judgment was one in which the sensitive information being discussed was different from that provided by the other informants. A non-unique judgment was the same as one told by a previous informant.

In addition to multiple coding for different types of jobs, the story coding was more complex. There was multiple coding in terms of the types of information handled by the informants. Table 2 illustrates that a single informant can, and did, provide stories about sensitivity judgments that cross several organizational levels and industries, independent of the actual job the informant currently held. The numbers in the cells indicate the code number of the informant.

An example of this multiple coding occurs with informant #6. He told a story relating to his work as a county legislator, and described another incident related to his work as a real estate developer. In addition, he provided stories from earlier in his career. Similarly, informant #1 shared stories that occurred during his legal work at the middle level of a law firm and during his work as a legal consultant. Consequently, this is not so much an informant matrix as it is an informant/job/story matrix.

We find an interesting example of how sensitive information held by a single employee crosses roles, organizational levels, and media in informant #26, an IT professional who worked as a system administrator in a law firm that handled health care information. The *information* handled was a combination of the three areas: IT, healthcare, and legal.

Table 2. Informant Job/Story Matrix

	Educ.	Health	Legal	IT	Construc. /Maint.
Upper	4	19	6 22	3 12	6 13
Middle	1 5	16	20 26	26 27	2 8 29
Lower	7 23 24	14 26	6 25	9 11 14 18	15 17
Consult.	1	30	20	10 28	8

With a goal of holistic understanding, the researchers did not attempt, save from focusing on the research questions, to proceed in a reductionist manner with the analysis in order to arrive at one best solution. All possibilities suggested by the data were treated equally, with emphasis on looking for connections and relationships. Categorical responses were analyzed for evidence of relationships between the categories. Analysis of metaphors and symbols helped to get at the underlying conceptualizations for which the individuals lacked either vocabulary or semantic tools to describe. Research suggests that this helps in simplifying the conceptualizations [9]. It also helped in condensing a large amount of data into a few simple concepts. Metaphorical associations helped in understanding informant interpretation, in understanding the organizing principles, and in helping to understand how the informants dimension the perceived degree of sensitivity.

4. FINDINGS & IMPLICATIONS

Our analysis of 135 stories and 188 judgments revealed four main findings.

4.1 Finding #1: Sensitive vs Non-Sensitive Information

Our first finding is that informants had no problem discussing examples of sensitive information when requested to do so, supporting that some formal (organizational) or informal (self-determined) cues exist upon which these judgments are made. They were also able to explain how sensitive information differed from other "non-sensitive" information. Informants were not confused about the idea of non-classified sensitive information in their organization, nor why they viewed it as sensitive despite this lack of classification. Their role or professional background (IT or non-IT) did not influence their ability to identify examples of sensitive information that could have detrimental consequences for themselves, other individuals, or the organization.

The significance of this finding is that workers can relate to the notion of the umbrella term "sensitive information", which is not a term that they usually use. They understand it, and they "know it when they see it," to quote a participant. This study was designed to bring out the sensitive information within each worker's immediate work environment. The extent to which they can identify, and agree upon, sensitive information outside their purview will require additional research. In addition, the study did not explore how the informants came about their understanding of the "sensitive". Did they come to their job with this understanding, or did they become aware of it through experience and/or training or cultural influences? That too remains for further research in local and global contexts.

An associated sub-finding is that, while people can identify and understand sensitive information, they *may not be empowered within the organization* to "speak" for the rationale behind the sensitivity. In a sense, the sensitivity is "owned" by various groups within the organization (e.g. professional elites such as doctors, lawyers, engineers, psychologists, and IT professionals).

One implication of this sub-finding is that workers may be aware of the sensitivity, but they have to defer to the "owner" of this information or content whenever conflicts or misunderstandings arise, especially when these conflicts involve the client, patient, or patron. This is particularly salient for IT workers who are "owners" of sensitive information in the IT domain, but they must defer to others for the "correct" judgment about sensitivity of other information. This provides an opening for considerable more thought and research, especially on the degree to which IT workers agree with other workers about sensitivity judgments.

4.2 Findings #2: No Formal Organizational Classification System so Look for "Chunks"

That said, however, our second finding centers on that which was absent in the data: very little mention of a formal classification system for sensitive information within their organizations, apart from the overall security or privacy classification system for all information. The usual system was one centered on persons or events (e.g., cases or projects). As far as the person-orientation is concerned, the information was oriented toward the clients, patrons, patients, etc. with which they dealt, (e.g. in education the student, in healthcare the patient, in legal the client, and in construction/building maintenance it is the customer). While informants in the IT field talked in terms of the clients, patrons, or patients of concern to the organizations in which they worked, it was clear that their overriding "classification" system was ruled by the tree structure associated with the network as a whole, and the file organization imposed by the operating system for the computers in use.

Apart from this general person-centered organization of the information, the denizens of organizations do not, as a rule, deal with information on a piecemeal basis. Rather, people work with information in "chunks", which may have in them this 'sensitive information'. As such, their main concern is to "protect the chunk". These chunks were referred to variously as files, folders, records, etc. Of interest is the notion that, while they talked about the chunk as if it were a unit, there may also be other "sub-chunks" stored in various places based on a special purpose. For example, informant #7, a secretary in a public school spoke about various other pieces held in the district office (electronic), in the counseling office, and in the vice principal's office (disciplinary actions). Note that parts of the overall "student record" were held in separate, more-secure offices under control of the "owner" of that information. This is comparable to the "compartmented" approach noted in environments entrusted with so-called national security information.

These chunks existed in both manual and electronic files. In the manual world, the information was "chunked" in file folders locked away in file cabinets. Even though the information in the IT world was "locked away" in electronic files separated into different servers, the environments for the information were analogous, and the tasks were roughly similar. There was no difference in the judgments made about information sensitivity based on storage media or source.

The significance of this finding for practice is that these chunks provide an excellent reference point for constructing security processes and procedures. The significance for research is that efforts to get at the cues or other stimuli that bring forth the "urge to protect" this sensitive information will have to deal with the "chunky" nature of the information.

4.3 Finding #3: Clusters and Cues

A third finding is that cues about sensitive information fall into one of five clusters of "sensitive information": Life and Love, Propriety and Correctness (Inappropriateness), Opinion of Others, Exchanger Information, and Keys. Space constraints limit our ability to provide rich examples of each; however, Table 3 provides a summary of the clusters and examples of specific cues for each.

The significance of the cues is that these provide the basis for a faceted classification system for sensitive information. Using these facets, anyone not involved with an organization can predict, prior to entering the organization, almost all of the sensitive information that is located within. This is a powerful notion. Thus, instead of conducting focus groups and other methods to create a list of sensitive information, one could build an *a priori* list from the clusters and cues mentioned here to elicit further examples. Theoretically, a researcher or practitioner could use the list to survey a random sample of workers using a "check the box" approach. This would allow organizations to skip quickly over the laborious, and costly, process of creating a classification system from scratch, and move on to questions about how the information is stored and handled within their setting. Additional research is needed to (1) verify that this approach would capture all, or most, of the sensitive information that would be encountered in the organization, and (2) figure out how to get past the "chunk" view of the world or, alternatively, how to take advantage of the "chunk" perspective to simplify, and possibly strengthen, the security classification system.

Table 3. Clusters of Cues for Judgments about Sensitive Information

Cluster	Cues	Examples
Love & Life	Information related to basic fundamental aspects of human biological existence	Information about pregnancy, birth, mating, marital relationships, family life, illness, and death
Propriety & Correctness	Information about personal sense of propriety and correctness	Violation of professional ethics Improper work practices Inappropriate dress Violation of workplace behavioral norms
Opinion of Others	Positive or negative information that reveals a person's feelings about, or candid opinions of others	Performance evaluations Promotion lists Results of worker surveys Opinion of supervisors or company strategy
Exchanger Information	Information provided to organization by someone who interacts with the organization and is generally referred to as being "outside" the organization; Often exchanged outside	Patient health records Student Records Client data Supplier transaction data Bids Bid processes
Keys	Information that serves as a key to gaining access to other information	Passwords Product formulas Trade secrets

4.4 Findings on Employee Judgments about Information Sensitivity as a Foundation for Strengthening IT Security Classifications

Two primary factors are identified that have relevance for security and information classification efforts of these chunks or clusters (1) the projected interpretation of the information by others and (2) the consequence that would result if another person were to receive the information. These first two factors resulted in a process of (3) human differentiation about the degree of sensitivity and decisions about (4) how they should handle that information.

Figure 1 summarizes this general process. Each of these stages is relevant not only to human judgments about information sensitivity, but is also very relevant to security protocol, training, and practices.

Figure 1: General Process of Sensitivity Judgments

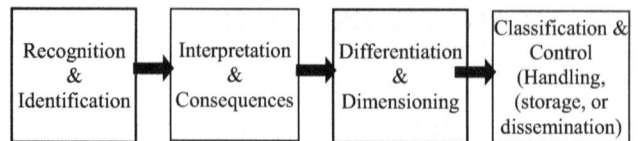

Recognition and identification refers to a process by which someone either does or does not comprehend the sensitivity of the information. Our data supports that degree of sensitivity was not always known by an employee, and required a judgment. Interpretation and assessment of consequences reflected a cognitive and affective evaluation based on known and implied implications of that chunk of sensitive information. Differentiation and dimensioning refers to the ways in which the individuals distinguished between different types of sensitive information. Sensitive information was differentiated based on the cues and influences with respect to the information considered. Classification and control simply refer to what the person did with the information after it was judged sensitive. New information and experiences can lead to interpretive changes about the sensitivity. This is where gaps – the cracks in the foundation – in formal and informal information-security policies and practices are most critical and can lead to the worst consequences.

As noted earlier, an interesting aspect of this study was that we found that most workers had many different roles within their respective organizations. In particular, many workers who would not ordinarily be considered IT workers were actually performing IT work and making judgments about sensitivity that became embedded in IT security protocols. One informant (#9) described herself as the bookkeeper for a small firm. The interview revealed that she performed many roles, including that of system administrator for their network. Another informant (#8), made several judgments about sensitive information relating to software, although he worked as a salesperson. Thus, individual judgments made in the IT realm were made by both IT and non-IT workers, some of whom were performing IT-related work in their organizations. Our IT security protocols, both local and global, frequently ignore the importance of human judgments by employees about sensitivity of information existing in digital, paper, and oral forms. This becomes even more complex when global cultural factors are added.

5. CLOSING COMMENTS

This study provides a foundation for further exploration of information sensitivity judgments. At the level of employee training, employees would benefit from discussion of formal and informal sensitivity cues and judgments. This is especially important given the opposing reality that not all sensitive information is written down/digitally stored, and yet electronic media enables easier disclosure of all types of sensitive information. IT and other security professionals should similarly review their current security classification schema and evaluate if these have become too routinized, or take too large or too small a view of information "chunks". Appropriately captured in a software program, the larger model could be used as the basis for a *machine learning approach* to the classification of sensitive information. As noted by this study, information sensitivity is a surprisingly green field for formal exploration, despite decades of security research. Our study is among the first of its type and we encourage others to build on our results to explore new questions.

6. ACKNOWLEDGMENTS

We wish to extend our sincere thanks to the participants who shared so generously of their time, experiences, and insights. Our thanks also to the anonymous reviewers who provide valuable feedback and encouragement to SIGMIS-CPR authors.

7. REFERENCES

[1] Beghtol, C. (1995) 'Facets' as Interdisciplinary Undiscovered Public Knowledge. Journal of Documentation, 51(3), 194-224.

[2] Bowker, G. C., Star, S. L. (1999). Sorting Things Out. Cambridge: MIT Press.

[3] Boyer, B. (2014) Managing sensitive information online. Daily Record (Sep 14). Retrieved from http://search.proquest.com/docview/1562412660?accountid=14214

[4] BSI British Standards Institute (2000). Information Technology – Code of Practice for Information Security Management (standard 0-580-36958-7). London

[5] D'Arcy, J., Hovav, A., & Galletta, D. (2009). User awareness of security countermeasures and its impact on information systems misuse: A deterrence approach. Information Systems Research, 20(1), 79-98.

[6] Giraldo, Grace (2014) "Motivating Information Security Awareness (ISA): An Action Research Study". Doctoral Dissertation. Syracuse University.

[7] Jacob, E. K. (2001). The everyday world of work: Two approaches to the investigation of classification in context. Journal of Documentation, 57(1), 76-99.

[8] Kwasnik, B. H. (1991). The Importance of Factors That Are Not Document Attributes in the Organization of Personal Documents. Journal of Documentation, 47(4), 389-398.

[9] Lackoff, G. & Johnson, M. (1980). Metaphors We Live By. Chicago: University of Chicago Press.

[10] Liddy, E. D. (2001). Information Security and Sharing. *Online*, 28-30.

[11] Moturu, S. T., & Liu, H. (2011). Quantifying the trustworthiness of social media content. Distributed and Parallel Databases, 29(3), 239-260. doi:10.1007/s10619-010-7077-0.

[12] Munshi, A., Dell, P., & Armstrong, H. (2012). Insider threat behavior factors: A comparison of theory with reported incidents. 2012 45th Hawaii International Conference on System Sciences (HICSS), IEEE. doi:10.1109/HICSS.2012.326.

[13] ODNI. (2014). Insider threat. Retrieved May 10, 2014, 2014, from http://www.ncix.gov/issues/ithreat/index.php.

[14] Patel, A., Taghavi, M., Bakytiyari, K., & Junior, J. C. (2013). An intrusion detection and prevention system in cloud computing: A systematic review. Journal of Network and Computer Applications, 36(1), 25-41.

[15] Peltier, T. R. (1998). Information Classification. *Information Systems Security*, 7(3), 31-43.

[16] Randazzo, M. R., Keeney, M., Kowalski, E., Cappelli, D., & Moore, A. (2005). Insider threat study: Illicit cyber activity in the banking and finance sector. In Service, U. S. S. (Ed.): National Threat Assessment Center & CERT Program.

[17] Roberts, J. A., & Wasieleski, D. M. (2012). Moral reasoning in computer-based task environment: Exploring the interplay between cognitive and technological factors on individuals' propensity to break rules. Journal of Business Ethics, 110(3), 355-376.

[18] Shils, E. A. (1956). The Torment of Secrecy, the Background and Consequences of American Security Policies. Glencoe, Ill.: Free Press.

[19] Spradley, J. P. (1979). The Ethnographic Interview. Holt, Rinehart, and Winston.

[20] Star, S. L. (1998) Grounded Classification: Grounded Theory and Faceted Classification. Library Trends, 47(2), 218-232.

[21] Strauss, A. L. & Corbin, J. M. (1997). Grounded Theory in Practice. Thousand Oaks: SAGE Publications.

[22] Thompson, E. Dale (2008) Sensitive Information: An Inquiry into the Interpretation of Information in the Workplace from an Individual's Perspective Using Qualitative Methods. Unpublished dissertation. Syracuse, NY.

[23] Thompson, E. Dale & Kaarst-Brown, M.L. (2005). Sensitive Information: A Review and Research Agenda. *Journal of the American Society for Information Science and Technology*, 56(3).

[24] Thompson, E. Dale & Kaarst-Brown, M.L. (2009). Love, Death, Sex… Are Judgments about Information Sensitivity Really That Simple? IFIP 8.2: OASIS Workshop 2009, Phoenix AZ, USA

[25] Wall, D. S. (2012). Enemies within: Redefining the insider threat in organizational security policy. Security Journal, 26(2), 107-124.

[26] U.S. CRS Congressional Research Service. (2003). "Sensitive but Unclassified" and Other Federal Security Controls on Scientific and Technical Information: History and Current Controversy." Washington, D.C.: Government Printing Office.

[27] U.S. GAO (2006). Managing Sensitive Information. Washington, DC: General Accountability Office.

Using Stakeholder Knowledge for Data Quality Assessment in IS Security Risk Management Processes

Christian Sillaber
University of Innsbruck
Technikerstrasse 21a
6020 Innsbruck
christian.sillaber@uibk.ac.at

Ruth Breu
University of Innsbruck
Technikerstrasse 21a
6020 Innsbruck
ruth.breu@uibk.ac.at

ABSTRACT

The availability of high quality documentation of the IS as well as knowledgeable stakeholders are an important prerequisite for successful IS security risk management processes. However, little is known about the relationship between stakeholders, their knowledge about the IS, security documentation and how quality aspects influence the security and risk properties of the IS under investigation. We developed a structured data quality assessment process to identify quality issues in the security documentation of an information system. For this, organizational stakeholders were interviewed about the IS under investigation and models were created from their description in the context of an ongoing security risk management process process. Then, the research model was evaluated in a case study. We found that contradictions between the models created from stakeholder interviews and those created from documentation were a good indicator for hidden security risks. The findings indicate that the proposed data quality assessment process provides valuable inputs for the ongoing security and risk management process. While current research considers users as the most important resource in security and risk management processes, little is known about the hidden value of various entities of documentation available at the organizational level. This study highlights the importance of utilizing existing IS security documentation in the security and risk management process and provides risk managers with a toolset for the prioritization of security documentation driven improvement activities.

Keywords

information systems security risk management; information system security documentation quality; data quality of information system security documentation; stakeholder knowledge driven process

1. INTRODUCTION

An increasing number of studies shows that the majority of incidents related to information system security can be traced back to internal stakeholders (e.g. [4, 23, 3]). Over the last years, IS security literature has been constantly moving from portraying users as

the weakest link in IS security (e.g. [27, 19]) to viewing them as the solution to multiple IS security issues (e.g. [21, 20, 1]).

Calls for more research in IS security and risk management processes to investigate stakeholders and artifacts created by them in more detail have been frequently made [20, 25, 2, 13, 18]. While many studies followed this call and examined the value provided by stakeholders in IS security and risk management processes, literature is scarce with empirical studies that examine more closely how available artifacts can be utilized in IS security risk management processes.

Based on the premise that, besides focusing on the participation of stakeholders as mere subjects of IS security policies, it is worthwhile to investigate already available artifacts, such as IS security documentation, the present paper's research question asks how, these artifacts can bring value during analysis phases of the IS security and risk management process.

User participation in IS development and its influence on implementational success has been extensively researched and it has been repeatedly argued that the information exchange and knowledge transfer resulting from such participation is the single most important effect [9]. Accordingly, the inclusion of multiple stakeholders in the risk management process has already been included in most established IS security risk management processes [14, 24].

The objective of this paper is to examine the utilization of existing IS security documentation in analysis phases of the IS security risk management processes and to examine how data quality of the documentation impacts the IS security and risk management process. In doing so, this paper answers calls for empirical research on user participation in IS security risk processes [10] and validates the findings in a case study at the organization under investigation. The research presented in this paper generalizes our research on stakeholders' business process awareness and its contribution to an ongoing IS security and risk management process [17].

The remainder of this paper is organized as follows. First, related work on user participation in IS security and risk management settings is presented and an overview on existing state-of the art research is presented. Next, the study's multi-method research design is outlined, followed by a qualitative exploratory study that examined data quality in IS security documentation and its contribution to the IS security and risk management process. A theoretical model informed by IS development theories and the qualitative study is then tested in a confirmatory quantitative study. Finally, the paper concludes with a discussion of the implications of the study, limitations, and suggestions for future research.

2. RELATED WORK

IS security risk management is the continuous process to identify and assess risk and to apply methods to reduce risks to an acceptable extent. Recent research has increasingly focused on human factors influencing the outcome of IS security and risk management processes. Previous research focuses on behavioral theories [1], describing the entire IS security and risk management process, security awareness [20, 11], behavior [6], communication [7] and the positive impact of audits [22] and standardization efforts [12].

Following a synthesis of theories explaining user participation in IS security contexts, Spears et al. [20] define *user participation in information systems security risk management* as the set of behaviors, activities, and assignments undertaken by business users during risk assessment and the design and implementation of IS security controls that is expected to add value to security risk management. By focusing on the *assessment* (i.e. analysis) phase, we re-conceptualize the success outcomes, actors, activities and hypothesized links between outcomes and activities to fit the concepts under investigation in the present paper, as suggested in [20]. Therefore, the present paper examines the link between static artifacts i.e. IS security documentation and activities and the value they add to the overall process.

3. MULTI-METHOD RESEARCH DESIGN

A combination of data collection and analysis methods were used on separate samples to examine data quality in the analysis phase of IS security and risk management processes. In a first step interviews were conducted. Then, in the next step, a qualitative analysis on a different sample of professionals who participated in an organizational IS security and risk management process was conducted.

This multi-method or mixed-method approach was chosen based on the premise that separate and dissimilar data sets would provide a richer picture and thus compensate for the fact that experimentations in IS security and risk management processes are difficult to conduct [8, 26]. A sequential design was used in that the qualitative exploratory study informed a subsequent confirmatory study.

Qualitative methods were appropriate as they provide a rich understanding of the activities, behaviors and assignments that define user participation in the context of this study [8]. Furthermore, they allow for the construction of a framework for analysis. As the theories were used as a framework of analysis, data collection for the qualitative study was not based on any *a-priori* theories and can therefore be considered as an exploratory study.

Quantitative methods were then employed to test the theoretical framework derived from the quantitative study based on the researchers' understanding. Hypotheses that were constructed from the qualitative study formed a model that examined the degree to which data quality of information system security documentation explained variation in pre-specified outcome variables. Thus, combining qualitative and quantitative methods provided both a rich context and testability to the study.

4. EXPLORATORY STUDY

An exploratory study was conducted in two phases to better understand the connection between data quality of information system security documentation and the quality of the IS security and risk management process and to investigate its outcomes.

The first phase of the exploratory study was conducted during an ongoing research project that investigated the efficient management of security requirements at an organization. The organization under investigation is one local branch (Company A; $\approx$ 1200 employees) of a multinational IT service provider, providing various cloud services.

The second phase of the exploratory study, where the findings from the first phase were refined and extended, was conducted during an ongoing action design research project [15] seeking to improve the IS security risk management process currently used by the organization. The organization under investigation is one local branch (Company B; $\approx$ 100 employees) of a multinational engineering company, focusing on the development of distributed information systems within a highly regulated domain.

The remainder of this section describes the data collection and analysis process as well as the findings of the exploratory study.

4.1 Data Collection

To conduct the exploratory study, informants currently involved in the management of security requirements (Company A), or the IS security and risk management process were identified within the organization.

At company A, six interviews were conducted with six informants including one chief security officer, two security managers, one internal auditor and two external auditors. The external auditors were not directly affiliated with company A but closely involved in the aforementioned research project and therefore included to obtain an external view. Each interview lasted between 10 and 90 minutes and the informants were granted anonymity.

At company B, five semi-structured interviews were conducted with five informants including three product managers, one deputy chief information security officer and one technological executive. This convenience sample included three employees with a degree in computer science and one with a specialization in IS security. Each interview lasted approximately 45 minutes and was recorded. The informants were granted anonymity. The interviews were conducted as part of an ongoing action design research project and informants were told the purpose of the study was to gain a better understanding of the fit between business needs and the IS security risk management process.

All informants were asked to recall information on the business security requirements, available documentation, and quality issues related to the system and business processes under investigation in the IS security and risk management process and to identify security requirements and risks accordingly. In parallel, information system security documentation, documentation on the business processes, as well as security guidelines and policy documents were obtained from internal knowledge bases documenting information system development and information system usage.

4.2 Analysis

An iterative process of three manual coding techniques was applied to interview transcriptions. First, selective coding was used to develop an initial code list that contained: attributes of data quality (e.g. *incomplete, not available, outdated*), references to information system security documentation (e.g. specific documents or tools), system components and their link to information system security documentation (e.g. *"Security requirements for component XY can be found in file Z"*) and risks. Next, open-ended coding was used to identify new codes as they emerged from interview transcripts and to identify differences between the two companies. Finally, relationships between information system security documentation data quality, security requirements, stakeholder participation in the IS security and risk management process and risks were identified.

As informants described the information system currently under risk analysis, they were asked which parts of the information system relate to which risks and to describe their knowledge on different aspects of the available information system security documentation.

Once the data had been collected, segments of interview transcripts were coded as related to information system security documentation data quality when informants recalled specific documents when eliciting risks or security requirements. These coded segments were subsequently grouped and assigned new codes that categorized the activities in which users participated. Relationships among codes were then analyzed. These findings are presented in the next section.

4.3 Results

Informants described their roles and activities in relationship to different parts of the IS under investigation during the IS security and risk management process. They described information system security documentation they were aware of, quality problems related to these documents and processes and workflows that use these documents. Then they described possible contributions of these documents to the IS security and risk management process in terms of identified risks, elicited security requirements and business needs from their perspective. Each of these aspects is described below, providing contextual detail of information system security documentation data quality and the derived benefit to the IS security risk management process.

All informants indicated that they had participated in the past in creating or maintain information system security documentation - at least at an informal level, thus confirming the observations made in [20]. The informants also confirmed, that the information system security documentation that is available at the organization is a main source of information for the IS security and risk management process. Furthermore, all informants (except for the external auditors at company A) stated they have already provided input to past IS security and risk management processes based on their respective domain knowledge.

As for the information system security documentation itself, we could elicit the following classification for data quality:

- **Missing**: the stakeholder could not identify a document related to the security of a specific system component.

- **Incomplete**: the stakeholder could only identify documents that were missing information (e.g. missing documentation of responsible roles). We differentiated between missing documentation and incomplete information system security documentation if a document had at least one reference to the system under investigation.

- **Wrong**: the documents identified by the stakeholder were either contradicting observations made in the system (e.g. outdated information) or were factually wrong (e.g. a non-existing stakeholder was referenced).

Regarding the participation of stakeholders during the risk management process and the information system security documentation used there, stakeholders reported their past involvement during (1) the analysis (2) the risk mitigation strategy creation (3) control design and (4) control implementation phase [20]. The informants reported on their utilization of information system security documentation during all phases.

All informants reported that they felt most confident when asked about areas of the information system where they had complete and correct information system security documentation available. If the available information system security documentation was incomplete or (partially) wrong, stakeholders a) complained about the bad quality, b) asked to consult external sources or c) started an internal change process to improve the documentation. Furthermore, stakeholders expressed the suspicion that the bad data quality might indicate problems with the information system that the documentation should cover. During the ongoing IS security and risk management process at company B, we asked stakeholders to recreate information system security documentation of one specific component as all available documentation was using an informal notation, unsuitable for the IS security and risk management process. During the recreation process (during an on-site workshop) we could observe that the new documents partially contradicted the previous documentation. We could trace back the contradiction to two stakeholders that were responsible for the components with the contradicting security requirement (Mutatis mutandis): Stakeholder 1 relied on stakeholder 2 to implement security controls and stakeholder 2 assumed that the security controls have been implemented by stakeholder 1.

We could observe, that components of the information system under investigation with severe data quality problems were often associated with higher risk levels and ill-defined security requirements during the IS security and risk management process. This observation is further examined in the confirmatory study by testing the hypothesis:

> **H1:** Data quality issues in information system security documentation are an indicator for security problems in corresponding areas of the information system under investigation in an IS security and risk management process.

Informant answers related to the data quality of the available information system security documentation varied largely on the context of use. We observed that stakeholders working in management roles had a different understanding of information system security documentation data quality than the rest of stakeholders. While managerial stakeholders were more concerned with availability and up-to-date information (e.g. in a central knowledge base), other stakeholder were more concerned with completeness of the information. Furthermore, we observed that no concise definition of data quality for information system security documentation existed at both companies. For instance, Anton (name changed for anonymity) a CISO said that: *"I do not know what [good data quality] means in this context, but I know what [bad data quality in information system security documentation] is if I see it.".* However, all stakeholders agreed that if existing information system security documentation contradicts the (newly created) information system security documentation during the IS security and risk management process, special attention should be given to the areas of the information system where contradictions exist.

The observation that, in absence of formal data quality models and structured information system security documentation, contradictions in information system security documentation are viable indicators for potential security problems, is further examined in the confirmatory study by testing the hypothesis:

> **H2:** Contradictions between pre-existing information system security documentation and information system security documentation created by stakeholders as part of an ongoing IS security and risk management are viable indicators for the data quality of information system security documentation and therefore potential security problems.

Finally, the risk manager should be able to select and prioritize areas of the information system for investigation in the information system security documentation process by some metric in case they need to prioritize due to limited time and budget. We therefore formulated the following hypothesis (cf. [17]):

> **H3:** Prioritization of information system components according to identified contradictions in the comparison of information system security documentation created by stakeholders with pre-existing information system security documentation is viable and improves the quality of early stages of the IS security and risk management process.

5. CONFIRMATORY STUDY

To validate the hypotheses and to further triangulate the results from the exploratory study, four case studies were conducted at the organization under investigation. Four components of the information system under investigation were selected for an in-depth analysis. Stakeholders from the organization (including the stakeholders from the exploratory study) were asked to participate in each of the assessments. Information on the expected results from IS security risk analysis were gathered in close collaboration with senior risk managers.

5.1 Measurement setting

We devised the measurement setting to validate the hypotheses in our confirmatory study. The five step process was executed for each component of the information system under investigation.

- **Step 1 - Collection of information system security documentation:** In this step, we collected any available information system security documentation at the organization under analysis. We worked together with process owners and information system stakeholders to identify any written artifacts.

- **Step 2 - Creation of reference models:** In this step, we "sanitized" any information system security documentation identified in the previous step by converting all documents in a common format and simplifying terminology. We created a information system security documentation reference model from the available documentation. This step required multiple rounds of feedback with stakeholders from the organization to clarify terminology and notations used.

- **Step 3 - Stakeholder interviews and model creation:** In this step, we asked stakeholders to elicit security requirements for the components of the information system under investigation. This required stakeholders to recreate information system security documentation to a large degree. We collected both verbal statements from stakeholders as well as models and artifacts created on paper / whiteboard during multiple workshops.

- **Step 4 - Creation of models for comparison:** In this step, we again "sanitized" the information system security documentation created by stakeholders in the previous step. We created information system security documentation models describing the security aspects of the information system under investigation from the artifacts produced by stakeholders.

- **Step 5 - Identification of contradictions:** In the last step, we compared the models created in step 2 against the models created in step 4 and identified contradictions between them.

For each contradiction identified, a survey was used. The survey items used to measure the research model variables were primarily derived from the qualitative study. All model constructs were measured with indicators are described next.

Contradictions in the asset model: Omitted assets (O_a): we analyzed which assets could be found in the reference models but not in the models created from stakeholder input. New assets (O_n): We analyzed which assets were found in the comparison models, but not in the reference models. And (O_c): we analyzed asset elements that were included in both models, but were described with different attributes.

Contradictions in the security requirements model: Following the taxonomy proposed in [16], we observed inner specification contradictions (S_i), outer specification contradictions (S_o), process contradictions (S_p) and source contradictions (S_s). Contradictions related to roles and risks could not be observed as those were out of scope of this research project. Table 3 includes examples for the previously defined measures.

5.2 Data Collection

Content validity We made an effort to ensure that the modeling tasks were clearly understood by the participants and that the informants responded to questions that we intended to ask. The survey was conducted verbally and clarifications were provided by the researchers. Participants could create models on a whiteboard or paper and were provided with access to any organizational knowledge source that is normally available to them. During the workshops, researchers modeled the artifacts described by stakeholder live in Archimate [5] for further clarification and to avoid inconsistencies due to different notations used by different stakeholders.

Survey study We conducted each workshop of the study at the premises of the organization under investigation and told stakeholders to view the researchers as risk managers conducting an IS security risk analysis. To perform steps 1 and 2, we contacted selected stakeholders from the organization responsible for the management of the internal knowledge base and documentation system to obtain access to relevant information system security documentation. The reference models (Step 2) were created by researchers. To perform steps 3 and 4 with all stakeholders, we went through all components of the information system while asking the survey questions and voice recording their answers. All stakeholders were promised anonymity and the organization was promised confidentiality regarding specific security risk related results and the architecture of the IS under investigation.

We interviewed the stakeholders for at least one hour per workshop. All participants were IS professionals and were product manager or senior developers. Despite the small sample size, we are confident that we provide a reasonably adequate representation of the target population, as we are not interested in perceived effects (requiring a broad sample size) but rather objectively measurable influence in IS security risk management, which would not be gatherable in a broad fashion. A discussion of further limitations and future evaluation in a broader study is presented in the next section.

As the exploratory study has shown, it was hard to define proper quality metrics to assess and evaluate the data quality of information system security documentation. Therefore, and to test hypothesis H2, we compared the number of security requirements for a specific components that were elicited a) without utilization of the identified contradictions and b) with utilization of the identified contradictions. For both settings, a workshop was held at the organization and the participating stakeholders were different (except for one CISO who attended both meetings).

5.3 Analysis

The descriptive statistics of the data are provided in Table 1 and Table 2. Each line contains the respective measurements for each IS Artifact under investigation that was in the scope of this study. The column "entire IS" aggregates the findings of all artifacts that are part of the overall IS. The number of security requirements elicited (SR_{wm}) is shown in the last row. The number of total elicited security requirements is smaller (marked with *) than the sum of each single security requirement, as some security requirements apply to multiple IS artifacts.

We found that outdated documentation (On) explained better than assets that were omitted by stakeholders (Oa) the contribution to the number of elicited security requirements, indicating that outdated information system security documentation is a major inhibitor to IS security and risk management processes. Stakeholders also agreed during the first exploratory study that outdated information system security documentation is an indicator for potential security issues. The more information system components were found that were not documented, the more security requirements were elicited Both observations seem to confirm H1.

The results of the two workshops that were held to validate hypothesis H2 (Are contradictions in information system security documentation a viable indicator for data quality and underlying security issues?) had shown that the number of security requirements that were elicited increased if stakeholders focused on the identified contradictions. We found that using our proposed contradictions method in information system security documentation vastly improved the number of elicited security requirements SR_{wm} as compared to the number of elicited security requirements SR_{wo} that were elicited without our method (9 vs 4 and 11 vs 3).

	IS Artifact 1	IS Artifact 2
O_a	2	3
O_n	3	5
O_c	2	1
S_i	1	8
S_o	3	0
S_P	0	2
S_S	0	0
SR_{wo}	4	3
SR_{wm}	9	6

Table 2: Results from eliciting security requirements for two information system artifacts with (SR_{wm}) and without (SR_{wo}) information system security documentation contradictions.

To analyze the resulting security requirements in terms of quantity and quality, we validated whether the elicited security requirements a) had an understandable description, b) were linked to at least one artifact of the IS, and c) were linked to at least one business source (e.g. customer contract, law) that establishes the business need for each security requirement. If all three conditions were met, we counted the security requirement as properly elicited. Then (depending on the context) those security requirements were matched to the set of already elicited security requirements from a previous IS security risk analysis (i.e. without our information system security documentation contradiction approach).

As a result, we could confirm the hypothesized relationship between existing contradictions in information system security documentation and their possible contribution to the IS security risk management process. Furthermore, we could confirm the hypothesized possibility to prioritize and select areas of the information system based identified contradictions in information system security documentation covering these areas in the IS security risk management process. The following section discusses the results in more detail and presents contributions to research and industry.

6. DISCUSSION

The present paper examined data quality of existing information system security documentation through contradictions identified in the comparison with information system security documentation created during an ongoing IS security and risk management process. In a multi-method research study we assessed the impact of identified contradictions on the IS security and risk management process. Utilization of contradictions to structure and prioritize areas of the IS for investigation was shown to improve the elicited security requirements in both number and accuracy. Thus, our proposed method of indirectly assessing data quality of information system security documentation through contradictions was found to add value to an organization's IS security and risk management process. We observed that outdated information system security documentation was the most important predictor for potential security issues.

6.1 Research Contribution

In extension to existing research on user participation and experimentation in IS security and risk management, the present study examined how data quality of information system security documentation impacts the IS security and risk management. Both the qualitative and quantitative studies found evidence that the data quality of information system security documentation, correlates with potential security risks and that contradictions of information system security documentation created by stakeholders and existing information system security documentation is a viable measure to support the IS security and risk management process. This study provides a first step towards the analysis of data quality of information system security documentation and its contribution to the IS security and risk management process. Secondly, the multi-method research design of the study contributed a first method of identifying data quality issues in information system security documentation within an ongoing IS security and risk management process.

6.2 Implications for Practice

The results of the present study at first and foremost add to the growing body of evidence that suggest that documentation of IS and its security are, together with stakeholder contribution the most important success factors of IS security and risk management. As our research has shown, it is highly desirable for organizations to not only document the security of their IS once, but to keep it continuously updated. Also, identified gaps in information system security documentation should not only be seen as an opportunity to update the information system security documentation but also to investigate potential security issues in the IS covered by that document.

A second implication of the study is the call for increased transparency of IS security documentation and the need for standardized information system security documentation formats. Study findings suggest that there is a benefit from making information system security documentation available to all stakeholders. In particular, it seems to be desirable to include a thorough analysis of existing information system security documentation in the ongoing IS security and risk management process to maximize results.

Finally, study findings suggest that the utilization of identified contradictions in the IS security and risk management process is highly desirable and that the proposed method can lead to a better fit of IS security risk analysis results to the business needs.

	IS Artifact 1	IS artifact 2	IS artifact 3	IS artifact 4	IS artifact 5	Entire IS
O_a	2	3	7	0	4	16
O_n	3	5	0	2	1	11
O_c	2	1	1	0	3	7
S_i	1	8	0	1	1	11
S_o	3	0	2	0	0	5
S_P	0	2	0	1	0	3
S_S	0	0	2	0	0	2
SR_{wm}	9	6	11	1	5	21^{*}

Table 1: Measurement results for the IS artifacts under investigation.

O_a	The stakeholders did not identify components that were documented. *Reference:* All existing components are A-Z *Comparison:* All existing components are A-F
O_n	The information system security documentation was outdated and did not include a component mentioned by the stakeholders. *Reference:* All existing components are A-F *Comparison:* All existing components are A-Z
O_c	Description of assets contained contradictions *Reference:* Components A and B run on VM01 on Cluster01 *Comparison:* Component A runs on VM01 and B runs on VM02 on Cluster01
S_i	The description of the security requirements differs in content. *Reference:* Security Requirement 001: "[...] All ports must be blocked for incoming traffic" *Comparison:* Security Requirement 001: "[...] No incoming traffic must be accepted."
S_o	The security requirement is linked to a different asset. *Reference:* Security Requirement 001 applies to components A,B,C *Comparison:* Security Requirement 001 applies to components A,B,F
S_p	A security related process was described differently *Reference:* Stakeholder A is responsible for the secure data removal process *Comparison:* Stakeholder B is responsible for the secure data removal process
S_s	A security requirements source was differently described *Reference:* Law XYZ applies to components A,B,C *Comparison:* Law XYZ applies to components A,C

Table 3: Observed instances of identified contradictions.

6.3 Study Limitations

Several limitations of this study need to be acknowledged. First, contradictions in the information system security documentation were selected for inclusion based on a simple yes/no scheme. This measurement might contain subjective errors and should therefore be used with caution.

A second limitation of the study is that it was conducted within the relatively low population of two organizations. This limitation is applicable to all surveys with an in-depth focus on a problem from industry, where objective experimentation or broad surveys are not possible. To limit the threat to generalizability of the findings, we tried to exclude industry-specific security requirements for measurement and made sure that the IS security and risk management analysis process did not require industry-specific knowledge.

A third limitation of the present study stems from the fact that contradictions were identified in models created by the researchers, based on the input documents received from the organizations. Due to organizational constraints at the organizations under investigation, it was not possible to conduct group modeling sessions with multiple rounds of feedback. In particular, step 2 was created without any feedback from the organization (apart from some clarifications) and thus might introduce subjective errors. We tried to mitigate these issues by including any organizational knowledge source available to gather information.

A fourth limitation results from the modeling process itself. As we used ArchiMate for modeling during the workshops and to create our reference models, errors might have been introduced as not all stakeholders were familiar with the tool and notation. We tried to mitigate this issue by explaining the notation and provided clarification if stakeholders had problems with it.

6.4 Suggestions for Future Research

The present study suggests two areas where future research would be valuable. First, a broad examination of information system security documentation and the value it provides to organizations is required. The present study examined information system security documentation from a rather abstract point of view. Specific aspects of the information system security documentation and associated processes might be worthwhile to investigate in future studies, including different workflows and tools currently used by industry and data management strategies.

Given, that information system security documentation data quality was found to be an important indicator for possible security issues, it seems worthwhile to investigate the alignment of business needs, IS security risks and documentation further. For example, how can data quality and improvements be valuated? Are existing processes to manage information system security documentation sufficient? Which automated tools can be utilized to continuously update and adapt information system security documentation?

7. CONCLUSIONS

The present study provides evidence that data quality of information system security documentation is a major contributor to information system security documentation processes and that an approach based on identified contradictions in information system security documentation is a viable measurement. Identified contradictions in information system security documentation contributed to identified security requirements and uncovered potential security issues.

IS security risk managers can utilize the method proposed in the present study to prioritize the analysis of different information system components in the IS security and risk management process using an objective process.

8. ACKNOWLEDGMENTS

This work was supported by the Austrian Federal Ministry of Economy (BMWFW), QE LaB - Living Models for Open Systems (FFG 822740) and the Tyrolean business development agency through the Stiftungsassistenz QE-Lab.

9. REFERENCES

[1] R. Alavi, S. Islam, and H. Mouratidis. A conceptual framework to analyze human factors of information security management system (isms) in organizations. In T. Tryfonas and I. Askoxylakis, editors, *Human Aspects of Information Security, Privacy, and Trust*, volume 8533 of *Lecture Notes in Computer Science*, pages 297–305. Springer International Publishing, 2014.

[2] I. Benbasat. An Empirical Study of Rationality-Based Beliefs in Information Systems Security. *MIS Quarterly*, 34(3):523–548, 2010.

[3] Computer Security Institute. CSI Computer Crime & Security Survey. Technical report, Computer Security Institute, 2008.

[4] Ernst and Young. Into the cloud, out of the fog; Global Information Security Survey. Technical Report November, Yourg, Ernst, 2011.

[5] T. O. Group. *{ArchiMate} 1.0 Specification*. Van Haren Series. Van Haren Publishing, 2009.

[6] K. H. Guo, Y. Yuan, N. P. Archer, and C. E. Connelly. Understanding nonmalicious security violations in the workplace: a composite behavior model. *Journal of Management Information Systems*, 28(2):203–236, 2011.

[7] R. L. Heath and H. D. O'Hair. *Handbook of risk and crisis communication*. Routledge, 2010.

[8] F. Kohlbacher. The use of qualitative content analysis in case study research. *Forum Qualitative Sozialforschung / Forum: Qualitative Social Research*, 7(1), 2006.

[9] E. A. Locke, M. Alavi, and J. A. Wagner III. Participation in decision making: An information exchange perspective. In *Research in personnel and human resources management, Vol. 15*, pages 293–331. Elsevier Science/JAI Press, US, 1997.

[10] M. L. Markus and J.-Y. Mao. Participation in development and implementation-updating an old, tired concept for today's IS contexts. *Journal of the Association for Information Systems*, 5(11):14, 2004.

[11] R. Mejias. An integrative model of information security awareness for assessing information systems security risk. In *System Science (HICSS), 2012 45th Hawaii International Conference on*, pages 3258–3267, Jan 2012.

[12] T. R. Peltier. *Information Security Policies, Procedures, and Standards: Guidelines for Effective Information Security Management*. Taylor & Francis Ltd, Hoboken, NJ, 2013.

[13] P. Puhakainen and M. Siponen. Improving employees' compliance through information systems security training: an action research study. *Mis Quarterly*, 34(4):757–778, 2010.

[14] J. J. Ryan, T. a. Mazzuchi, D. J. Ryan, J. Lopez de la Cruz, and R. Cooke. Quantifying information security risks using expert judgment elicitation. *Computers & Operations Research*, 39(4):774–784, Apr. 2012.

[15] M. K. Sein, O. Henfridsson, S. Purao, M. Rossi, and R. Lindgren. Action design research. *MIS Quarterly*, 35(1):37–56, Mar. 2011.

[16] C. Sillaber and R. Breu. Quality matters: Systematizing quality deficiencies in the documentation of business security requirements. In *Availability, Reliability and Security (ARES), 2014 Ninth International Conference on*, pages 251–258, September 2014.

[17] C. Sillaber and R. Breu. Using business process model awareness to improve stakeholder participation in information systems security risk management processes. In *Wirtschaftsinformatik Proceedings*, 2015. Paper 79.

[18] M. Siponen and H. Oinas-Kukkonen. A review of information security issues and respective research contributions. *ACM Sigmis Database*, 38(1):60–80, 2007.

[19] M. T. Siponen. Critical analysis of different approaches to minimizing user-related faults in information systems security: implications for research and practice. *Information Management & Computer Security*, 8(5):197–209, 2000.

[20] J. L. Spears and H. Barki. User participation in information systems security risk management. *MIS quarterly*, 34(3):503–522, 2010.

[21] J. Stanton, K. Stam, P. Mastrangelo, and J. Jolton. Behavioral Information Security. *Human-Computer Interaction and Management Information Systems: Foundations*, page 262, 2006.

[22] P. J. Steinbart, R. L. Raschke, G. Gal, and W. N. Dilla. The relationship between internal audit and information security: An exploratory investigation. *International Journal of Accounting Information Systems*, 13(3):228 – 243, 2012. 2011 Research Symposium on Information Integrity and Information Systems Assurance.

[23] S. Subashini and V. Kavitha. A survey on security issues in service delivery models of cloud computing. *Journal of Network and Computer Applications*, 34(1):1–11, Jan. 2011.

[24] H. Susanto, M. N. Almunawar, and Y. C. Tuan. Information security management system standards: A comparative study of the big five. *International Journal of Electrical & Computer Sciences*, 11(5):2011, 2011.

[25] A. Vance. Neutralizaiton: New Insights into the Problem of Employee Information Systems Security. *MIS Quarterly*, 34(3):487–502, 2010.

[26] V. Verendel. Quantified security is a weak hypothesis. *Proceedings of the 2009 workshop on New security paradigms workshop - NSPW '09*, page 37, 2009.

[27] J. Wade. The weak link in IT security. *Risk Management*, 51(7):32–37, 2004.

Maintaining Cyber Security: Implications, Cost and Returns

Nishtha Kesswani
Central University of Rajasthan
Bandarsindri
Ajmer
+91-1463-238755
Nishtha@curaj.ac.in

Sanjay Kumar
Central University of Rajasthan
Bandarsindri
Ajmer
+91-1463-238755
sanjaygarg@curaj.ac.in

ABSTRACT

Cyber security is one of the most critical issues that are faced globally by most of the countries and organizations. With the ever increasing use of computers and the internet, there has been tremendous growth of cyber-attacks. The attackers target not only high end companies but also banks and government agencies. As a result the companies and governments across the globe are sparing huge amount of money to create a cyber-secure niche.

In every organization, whenever an investment has to be made, everybody is concerned about the return which the organization will be getting from that investment. Every investment has to be justified from the point of view of return. Investments made in cyber security are never preferred by the organizations as they do not give any return. Return on Investments made in Cyber security is not measured in terms of profits and gains, but rather in terms of prevented losses.

This paper provides an insight in to various established approaches which can be used for measurement of return on cyber security investment. Cost-benefit analysis of cyber security investments can be useful to the organization to have insight into whether money is well spent or not.

Categories and Subject Descriptors
L0, L4, M4

General Terms
Cyber Security, Cyber-attacks, Investment, Return on Investment

Keywords
Annual Loss Expectancy Approach, Gordon & Loeb Approach, Net Present Value Approach, Cost Benefit Analysis.

1. INTRODUCTION
The potential cyber threats to any organization include, viruses attacking the entire system, altering, damaging or even deleting the files, a hacker attacking other computers using your system or stealing your personal information.

As a result not only corporations, but governments are taking stringent actions towards curbing the cyber-attacks. One of the steps that are taken in this direction is the increase in the cyber security workforce. The need of the day is a security that can monitor all the activities without affecting the performance of the system, which can predict, detect and prevent major threats and recover from attacks without having much effect on the valet. All the nations across the globe are affected by cyber-attacks. And the major target of the attackers are top notch industries for financial and other reasons. Various techniques are used by attackers to affect the companies in a narrow and the entire nation in broad perspective. Statistics reveal enough evidences that cyber security is the need of the hour not only for industry, organizations, governments, but for all.

2. INVESTMENTS IN CYBER SECURITY
In the recent years, there is severe increase in the cyber-attacks across the networks and organizations. So it has resulted in increase in cost involved with the maintenance of cyber security. There are two types of costs, direct cost and Indirect Cost which are related with occurrence of an incident or cyber-attack in an organization. The total cost of an incident or attack includes direct losses such as website downtime, replacement of hardware and software, data loss etc and indirect losses such as investigation time, loss of goodwill & reputation, impact on image, loss of business & productivity etc.

Cyber-attacks are still hard to detect. So organizations are still reluctant to put more money for investment for maintenance of cyber security. It is less appealing to the organizations as it is considered to be a cost saving not a revenue generating measure. In order to justify an increase in the investment made in cyber security, there should be sufficient number of cases of breaches in security. It is very difficult for the Cyber security personnel to demand more budgets for the department as when budgets are allocated, there is less number of cases of breaches of security. Thus, no further increase in the budget allocation is made by the senior management.

2.1 Return on Investments

An Investment is sacrificing something today in anticipation of gain on some future date

Return can be calculated by using the following formula

$$Return = \frac{(Regular\ Income\ from\ Investment + Capital\ Gain\ from\ Investment)}{Cost\ of\ Investment} \quad ...(1)$$

The simplest form of calculating return from an investment can be expressed as follows:-

$$ROI = \frac{(Current\ value\ of\ Investment - Cost\ of\ Investment)}{Cost\ of\ Investment} \quad ... (2)$$

$$ROI = \frac{Gain\ from\ Investment}{Cost\ of\ Investment} \quad ... (3)$$

Return on Investment made in real assets and financial assets are easy to calculate as the gains obtained from these investments are clearly measurable and quantifiable. But when some investments are made on security for the organization resources, whatever type of security it may be, the gains are not clearly measurable and quantifiable.

2.2 Return on Investment on Cyber Security

Security Investment is not a revenue generating Investment and so is the case with cyber Security. When we make investment in Security, the focus is on to prevent losses. Cyber security and IT professional are concerned that they do not get much attention and funding from the senior management. It is very difficult to calculate return on investment made in the security. They are not at the priority because there are no positive returns on the investment made in the cyber security. Their funding and allocation of resources are only meant to prevent bad things from happening. Calculation of return on security investment is not an easy task.

3. EXISTING VIEWS

There is very little literature available for measurement of return on investment made in cyber security. Some of them are as follows:-

Gordon & Loeb (2002) has clearly found out through their model that expenditure incurred on security does not increase proportional to the increase in the vulnerability of the organization and it never exceeds 37% of the potential loss.

Schneier (2008) in his paper "Security ROI: Facts or Fiction" was of the view that Return on Investment is not meant for security. According to him, amount spent on security should not be considered as an investment. It does not provides a return but it is an expense that pays for itself through loss prevention.

European Network and Information Security Agency (ENISA) (2012) has given Annual Loss Expectancy (ALE) approach for measurement of return on investment made in security. According to the approach, investment made in security does not generate any return, so its return on investment can be calculated on the basis of how much loss was prevented and how much we spend on to prevent it.

4.   APPROACHES TO RETURN ON INVESTMENT IN CYBER SECUIRTY

4.1 Existing Approaches

There are different approaches for calculation of return on investment made in security. These existing approaches can be used to measure the return on investment made in Cyber Security. Some of these approaches, which have been modified according to the calculation of return on investment made in cyber security are as follows:-

4.1.1. Annual Loss Expectancy (ALE) Approach:

This approach has been suggested by European Network and Information Security Agency (ENISA). If we want to quantify it, the comparison should be made between how much loss was prevented and how much amount was spent to prevent it.

This can be calculated by quantifying the risk components. As suggested by ENISA, Following can be the major risk components:-

Single Loss Expectancy (denoted by SLE)

= *the amount of loss which can incur due to one occurrence* ... (4)

Annual Rate of Occurrence (denoted by ARO)

= *the probability that the loss/risk will occur in a year*   ... (5)

Annual Loss expectancy (denoted by ALE)

= *Single Loss Expectancy * Annual Rate of Occurrence*

= *SLE * ARO*   ... (6)

Monetary Loss Reduction = ALE – Modified ALE   ... (7)

ALE is Annual Loss Expectancy prior to implementation of Solution

Modified ALE is Annual Loss Expectancy after implementation of Solution

By using these risk parameters we can calculate return on security investment

Return on Security Investment (denoted by ROSI)

= *(Monetary Loss Reduction - Cost of solution) / Cost of Solution*   ...(8)

For example a company suffers 8 viruses attracts every year and the each attack resulted in loss of data and productivity of 20000 USD. An anti-virus is purchased by the organization and it has resulted in reduction of occurrence of attack to 2. It license cost 80,000 USD per year.

Here SLE is $ 20,000, , ARO is 8

ALE is SLE * ARO= 20,000* 8= $ 160,000

Modified ALE is 20,000 * 2 = $ 40,000

Monetary Loss Reduction = 160,000- 40,000 = $ 120,000

ROSI = (120,000- 80,000) / 80,000 =50%

It can also be written like this

(ALE* Mitigation Ratio – Cost of Solution\) /
Cost of Solution ... (9)

The limitations of this approach are that most of the parameters are based on estimates which may not be true.

4.1.2. Gordon & Loeb Approach

Gordon & Loeb model is based on particular information set which is characterized by three parameters which are:-

- Amount of loss on occurrence of a security
- Probability of the threat occurring
- Vulnerability which is the probability that a threat once realized would be successful

According to the model, Expected Benefits of an Investment in Information Security (EBIS) are equal to the reduction in expected loss.

Expected Net Benefits from an Investment in Information Security (ENBIS)

= EBIS - Cost of the security ... (10)

By using this model with that data available, the authors determined that for two large security breach probability classes that represent a wide range of functions, the optimal investments in information security never exceeded 36.79% of the expected loss.

4.1.3. Net Present Value Approach

Net Present Value method is one of the old methods used for calculation of return on any investment. According to the method return on any investment can be calculated by the following formula:

Return on investment = Net Present Value
of Income/ inflows – Net Present Value of Costs /outflows... (11)

So in this case the return on security investment can be calculated as follows:-

NPV of Unmitigated Breach - NPV of
Mitigated Breach - NPV of Countermeasure ... (12)

4.2. Proposed Modifications to ALE Approaches

There are certain other new approaches which can be used to calculate return on cyber security investments. These approaches are proposed modifications to the annual loss expectancy approach. Some of these approaches which can be used for calculation of return on investment made in cyber security.

4.2.1. Annual Compliance Benefit Approach

This can be one of the potential approaches which are a variant of ALE approach. There are certain industries in which the organizations are required to comply with the cyber security norms otherwise they have to face with the heavy monetary fines and negative consequences. These fines are the potential losses which a firm can avoid by following the compliances. For example Federal Regulatory energy commission (FREC) has compliance norms for the energy sector So compliance benefits resulted by avoiding potential losses and fine can be factored in to ALE approach. So modified ALE can be calculated as follows:-

ACB Annual Loss expectancy (ACBALE)

= (SLE * ARO) – ACB ... (13)

Monetary Loss Reduction

= ALE – ACBALE ...(14)

In the previous example, if purchase of antivirus has resulted in avoidance of potential fine of $ 8,000

ACB Annual Loss expectancy is 20,000 * 2 – 8,000 = $ 32,000

Monetary Loss Reduction = 160,000- 32,000 = $ 128,000

ROSI = (128,000- 80,000) / 80,000 =60%

4.2.2. New Business Benefits Approach (NBB)

This can also be a potential approach and a variant to ALE approach. An organization which spends more on cyber security attracts more customers and business as they are safe to deal with. More potential businesses are generated by these organizations due to their spending on the cyber security. So a certain percentage of potential revenue generated by the organization from new businesses due to maintenance of cyber security can also be deducted at the time of calculation of annual loss expectancy.

NBB Annual Loss expectancy (NBBALE)

= (SLE * ARO) – NBB ... (15)

Where

New Business Benefits (NBB) = Revenue
from new business * Profit Margin ... (16)

Monetary Loss Reduction= ALE – NBBALE ... (17)

In the previous example , If the organization has generated additional business revenue of $ 200,000 due to maintenance of cyber security and a margin of 8 percent is earned on the revenue, Return of security investment as per this approach will be as follows :-

NBBALE is (20,000 * 2) – (200,000 *8%) = $ 24,000

Monetary Loss Reduction = 160,000- 24,000 = $ 136,000

ROSI = (136,000- 80,000) / 80,000 =70%

4.2.3. Goodwill Loss Expectancy Approach (GLE)

Any organization which faces cyber-attacks or security breach has loss of reputation and brand. Ultimately it resulted in to loss of goodwill. Keeping the image and reputation of the business clean is a major driver of cyber security. Goodwill is included in the balance sheet of an organization and protection to the loss of the goodwill can be included in the ALE equation.

GLE Annual Loss expectancy (GLEALE)

= (SLE * ARO) + (GLE *ARO) ... (18)

Monetary Loss Reduction

= ALE – GLEALE ...(19)

In the previous example, if the organization has goodwill loss of $ 5000 each time cyber-attack is made before the implementation of antivirus while it has goodwill loss of $ 2000 each time cyber-attack is made after the purchase of antivirus.

Here SLE is $ 20,000, ARO is 8

GLE is $ 5000, ARO is 8

ALE is = (SLE * ARO) + (GLE *ARO)

(20,000* 8) + (5000*8) = $ 200,000

GLEALE is (20,000 * 2) + (2,000 * 2) = $ 44,000

Monetary Loss Reduction = 200,000- 44,000 = $ 156,000

ROSI = (156,000- 80,000) / 80,000 =95 %

4.2.4. Shared Reduced Loss Approach (SRL)

When an organization spend more on cyber security, other organizations are comfortable with it in information and data sharing. This information sharing can result in reduction in cyber-attack and security breach. Organization may become more aware about the new ways of cyber-attacks and security when information is shared among the organizations with in the sector and industry. By improving the overall security, it may result in reduction in threats and vulnerability and thus may result in reduction in potential losses.

$$= (SLE * ARO) – SRL \qquad \dots (20)$$

Monetary Loss Reduction

$$= ALE – SRLALE \qquad \dots (21)$$

So in the previous example, if purchase of antivirus has resulted in Shared reduced loss of $ 4,000 due to sharing of information among the organizations.

Modified ALE is 20,000 * 2 – 4,000 = $ 36,000

Monetary Loss Reduction = 160,000- 36,000 = $ 124,000

ROSI = (124,000- 80,000) / 80,000 =55%

4.2.5. Combined ALE Approach

This approach takes in to consideration ALE approach with Annual Compliance Benefits, New Business Benefits, shared reduced loss, Goodwill loss expend for calculation of return on security investment.

Combined Annual Loss expectancy (CALE)

$$= (SLE * ARO) + (GLE *ARO) - ACB –NBB – SRL \quad \dots (22)$$

Monetary Loss Reduction

$$= ALE – CALE \qquad \dots (23)$$

Consider the previous example

ALE is = (SLE * ARO) + (GLE *ARO)

(20,000* 8) + (5000*8) = $ 200,000

Whereas Combined ALE is

= (SLE * ARO) + (GLE *ARO) - ACB – NBB - SRL

(20,000 * 2) + (2000*2) – 8000 -16000 - 4000 = $ 16,000

Monetary Loss Reduction = 200,000- 16,000 = $ 184,000

ROSI = (184,000- 80,000) / 80,000 =130 %

5. DISCUSSIONS AND OPEN CHALLENGES

The paper has discussed the financial implications of using cyber security and how the companies can save more and more by investing in cyber security rather than having financial losses and loss of repute due to the attacks. Several approaches to calculate return on investment in cyber security have been discussed in this paper. Combined Annual Loss Expectancy Approach can be considered to be the best among all the approaches for investment made in security especially cyber security as it factors in all the related variables of cyber security in to the consideration.

6. CONCLUSIONS

Calculation of return on investment is based on cost-benefit analyses that compare costs and returns in either financial or non-financial terms. Security investment is not given priority by the organizations as it does not generate any return. There are certain other areas of the business also which do not yield return but still business houses spend lots of money on those Although Investment in security does not generate any return, but it can be quantified in terms of prevention of losses. A well quantified, measured approach focusing on cost benefit analysis for calculation of return on security investment can make cyber security & IT professionals more convincing in asking for more attention and budgeting from the management.

7 REFERENCES

[1] Bruce Schneier, B. (2008). "Security ROI: Fact or Fiction." https://www.schneier.com/essays /archives/2008/09/security_roi_fact_or.html

[2] Campbell, T. (2004) "An Introduction to the CSIRT Set-Up and Operational Considerations." http://cyber-defense.sans. org/resources/papers/gsec/introduction-computer-security-incident-response-106281

[3] European Network and Information Security Agency – Introduction to the Return on Security Investment.(2012). https://www. enisa.europa.eu /activities/cert/other work/ introduction-to-return-on-security-investment

[4] Gordon, L. & Loeb, M. (2002). "The economics of Security Investment." ,http://ns1.geoip.clamav.net/~mfelegyhazi/courses/BMEVIH IAV15/readings/04_ GordonL02economics_security_ investment.pdf

Author Index